TERRORIST EVENTS WORLDWIDE 2021

EDWARD MICKOLUS, PHD

WW

WANDERING
WOODS
PUBLISHERS

Terrorist Events Worldwide 2021

By Edward Mickolus, PhD

ISBN: 978-1-949173-17-8

Published in the United States by
Wandering Woods Publishers
EdwardMickolus.com

Book Design, Cover and Typesetting by
Cynthia J. Kwitchoff (CJKCREATIVE.COM)

DISCLAIMER

All statements of fact, opinion, or analysis expressed are those of the author and do not reflect the official positions or views of the Central Intelligence Agency (CIA) or any other U.S. Government agency. Nothing in the contents should be construed as asserting or implying U.S. Government authentication of information or CIA endorsement of the author's views. This material has been reviewed by the CIA to prevent the disclosure of classified information. This does not constitute an official release of CIA information.

ABOUT THE AUTHOR

Edward Mickolus, PhD, is the President of Vinyard Software, Inc. He served a 33-year career with the Central Intelligence Agency, has written 48 books, and has taught intelligence tradecraft courses at numerous federal agencies. Vinyard Software's International Terrorism Data Center provides universities, research institutions, governments, the media, and others interested in international terrorism the best publicly-available data on terrorists and events around the world. His books include:

Terrorism Events Worldwide 2019-2020

Terrorism Worldwide, 2018

Terrorism Worldwide, 2017

Terrorism Worldwide, 2016

Terrorism 2013-2015: A Worldwide Chronology

Terrorism 2008-2012: A Worldwide Chronology

Terrorism, 2005-2007

with Susan L. Simmons Terrorism, 2002-2004: A Chronology, 3 volumes

with Susan L. Simmons Terrorism, 1996-2001: A Chronology of Events and a Selectively Annotated Bibliography, 2 volumes

with Susan L. Simmons Terrorism, 1992-1995: A Chronology of Events and a Selectively Annotated Bibliography

Terrorism, 1988-1991: A Chronology of Events and a Selectively Annotated Bibliography

with Todd Sandler and Jean Murdock International Terrorism in the 1980s: A Chronology, Volume 2: 1984-1987

with Todd Sandler and Jean Murdock International Terrorism in the 1980s: A Chronology, Volume 1: 1980-1983

with Peter Flemming Terrorism, 1980-1987: A Selectively Annotated Bibliography

International Terrorism: Attributes of Terrorist Events, 1968-1977, ITERATE 2 Data Codebook

with Susan L. Simmons The 50 Worst Terrorist Attacks

with Susan L. Simmons The Terrorist List: North America

with Susan L. Simmons The Terrorist List: South America

with Susan L. Simmons The Terrorist List: Eastern Europe

with Susan L. Simmons The Terrorist List: Western Europe

with Susan L. Simmons The Terrorist List: Asia, Pacific, and Sub-Saharan Africa

The Terrorist List: The Middle East, 2 volumes

The Literature of Terrorism: A Selectively Annotated Bibliography

Transnational Terrorism: A Chronology of Events, 1968-1979

Combatting International Terrorism: A Quantitative Analysis

Stories from Langley: A Glimpse Inside the CIA

More Stories From Langley: Another Glimpse Inside the CIA

Briefing for the Boardroom and the Situation Room

The Counterintelligence Chronology: Spying by and Against the United States from the 1700s through 2014

Spycraft for Thriller Writers: How to Write Spy Novels, TV Shows and Movies Accurately and Not Be Laughed at by Real-Life Spies

TABLE OF CONTENTS

Find the Author at:

Books: EdwardMickolus.com

Terrorism Data: VinyardSoftware.com

INTRODUCTION

This book uses the same **definition** of terrorism as found in its 19 predecessors, allowing comparability across decades. Terrorism is the use or threat of use of violence by any individual or group for political purposes. The perpetrators may be functioning for or in opposition to established governmental authority. A key component of international terrorism is that its ramifications transcend national boundaries, and, in so doing, create an extended atmosphere of fear and anxiety. The effects of terrorism reach national and worldwide cultures as well as the lives of the people directly hurt by the terrorist acts. Violence becomes terrorism when the intention is to influence the attitudes and behavior of a target group beyond the immediate victims. Violence becomes terrorism when its location, the victims, or the mechanics of its resolution result in consequences and implications beyond the act or threat itself.

The book is divided into three sections: a region-by-region (and within each, a country-by-country) look at terrorist incidents, a separate section updating events that occurred prior to 2021, and a bibliography.

The Incidents section is based solely on publicly available sources. This section is not intended to be analytical, but rather comprehensive in scope. As such, the section also includes descriptions of non-international attacks that provide the security and political context in which international attacks take place. In some cases, the international terrorists mimic the tactics of their stay-at-home cohorts. Often, these are the same terrorists working on their home soil against domestic, rather than foreign, targets. Domestic attacks often serve as proving grounds for techniques later adopted for international use. I have therefore included material on major technological, philosophical, or security advances, such as: the use of letter bombs; food tampering; major assassinations; attempts to develop, acquire, smuggle, or use precursors for an actual chemical, biological, radiological, or nuclear weapon; key domestic and international legislation and new security procedures; key arrests and trials of major figures; and incidents involving mass casualties. Non-international entries do not receive an eight-digit code.

The section also provides follow-up material to incidents first reported prior to January 1, 2021. For example, updates include information about the outcome of trials for terrorist acts occurring prior to 2021 and "where are they now" information about terrorists and their victims. The update is identified by the original incident date, and I have included enough prefatory material to give some context and to identify the original incident in the earlier volumes.

The international terrorist incidents and airline hijackings are identified by an eight-digit code. The first six digits identify the date on which the incident became known as a terrorist attack to someone other than the terrorists themselves (e.g., the date the letter bomb finally arrived at the recipient's office, even though terrorists had mailed it weeks earlier; or the date on which investigators determined that an anomalous situation was terrorist in nature). The final two digits ratchet the number of attacks that took place on that date. In instances in which either the day of the month or the month itself is unknown, "99" is used in that field.

The information cutoff date for this volume is December 31, 2021.

The Bibliography section includes references drawn from the same public sources that provide the incidents, literature searches, and contributions sent by readers of previous volumes. It does not purport to be comprehensive. The citations are grouped into topic areas that were chosen to make the bibliography more accessible, and includes print and web-based material. The Bibliography gives citations on key events and may be referenced for more detail on specific attacks described in the Incidents section.

ACTIVITIES OF KEY TERRORIST GROUPS

FATES OF KEY TERRORISTS

Of particular note was the apparent death by suicide bomb of Boko Haram leader Abubakar Shekau. While his death had been announced by various sources five earlier times, in this instance, his demise was cited by a rival terrorist group, ISWAP, which claimed it had been chasing him, hoping to talk him into joining their band. Shekau's group did not confirm his death, but no statements/videos/audios of Shekau denying his passing followed. Meanwhile, in August, the army announced that 335 Boko Haram terrorists, plus their families, surrendered to the armed forces.

Ahmed Jibril, 83, founder/leader of the Popular Front for the Liberation of Palestine-General Command (PFLP-GC), followed the pattern of other Palestinian terrorist leaders who had long lifetimes, and often died of natural causes. The pattern appears almost distinctive to Palestinian (and Palestinian-affiliated) terrorist leaders, who, if they do not die on the battlefield, waste away in prison on life sentences until their deaths (again by natural causes or sometimes suicides), or go on to more traditional political careers. Among them were:

- George Habash, founder of the Popular Front for the Liberation of Palestine (PFLP), died at age 81 from a heart attack while being treated for cancer

- Wadi Haddad, founder of the Popular Front for the Liberation of Palestine-Special Operations Command (PFLP-SOC), died at age 50 from leukemia

- Nayef Hawatmeh, founder of the Democratic Front for the Liberation of Palestine (DFLP), as of this writing, active in Jordanian politics at age 82

- Sabri al-Banna, alias Abu Nidal, founder of Fatah Revolutionary Council, died at age 65 either by his own hand or by Iraqi intelligence

Other terrorist leaders still leading long lives include:

- Ilich Ramirez Sanchez, alias Carlos the Jackal, operational leader for PFLP attacks, 71 as of this writing, in a French prison

- Leila Khaled, 77 as of this writing, PFLP operative who became the first woman to hijack a plane, has been active as a member of the Palestinian National Council

- Ayman al-Zawahiri, successor to Osama bin Laden as head of al-Qaeda, 70 and at large as of this writing

- Zohra Drif, 86 as of this writing, who in 1956 set off a bomb at the Milk Bar in Algeria, killing three, wounding dozens, and changing the character of the Algerian underground resistance

Manuel Rubén Abimael Guzmán Reynoso, founder of the Peruvian Shining Path, died in prison at age 86.

Saadi Yacef, 93, guerrilla leader of the National Liberation Front (FLN) that fought for and eventually obtained independence from France in 1962, died at age 93 while serving as a senator in the Algerian Council of the Nation.

Ali Atwa, believed to be in his 60s, died of cancer in 2021. He was one of the FBI's Ten Most Wanted Fugitives for his role in the 1985 TWA Flight 847 hijacking that included the murder of U.S. Navy diver Robert Stethem.

Senior Terrorists Killed in 2021

This list includes those killed by coalition and Russian forces, including by airstrikes, and by rival terrorist groups, plus those who died of natural causes.

Al-Qaeda

- Salim Abu Ahmad, based on Idlib, Syria, responsible for planning, funding, and approving trans-regional al-Qaeda attacks
- Abdul Hamid al-Matar, a senior leader in Syria

Al-Qaeda in the Islamic Maghreb (AQIM)

- Baye ag Bakabo, variant Bayes ag Bakabo, Malian jihadi leader believed to have helped in the kidnapping and killing of Ghislaine Dupont and Claude Verlon, French journalists working for *Radio France Internationale*, in November 2013

AQAP

- Saad Atef al-Awlaqi, deputy chief, who was killed in October 2020. The UN announced his death on February 4, 2021.

Boko Haram

- Abubakar Shekau (this was the fifth time since 2009 he was officially declared dead)

Daulah Islamiya of the Philippines

- Salahuddin Hassan, leader of the ISIS-linked group

East Indonesia Mujahideen (MIT)

- Ali Kalora, the group's leader and Indonesia's most wanted militant

ISIS

- Abu Yasar al-Issawi, deputy commander and IS chief in Iraq

Islamic State in the Greater Sahara

- Soumana Boura, leader of dozens of fighters in the west of Niger
- Adnan Abu Walid al-Sahrawi, the group's leader

Islamic State in West Africa Province (ISWAP)

- Abu Musab al-Barnawi, the group's leader
- Malam Bako, al-Barnawi's successor

Jaish e-Muhammad India

- Mohammad Ismail Alvi, alias Lamboo, alias Adnan, the group's commander

Lashkar-e-Islam (Army of Islam in Pakistan)

- Manghal Bagh, the group's commander

Lashkar-e-Taiba (in Indian Kashmir)

- Saqib Manzoor, deputy chief of the Resistance Front, an LeT front
- Abbas Sheikh, head of the Resistance Front, an LeT front

National Liberation Army (ELN) of Colombia

- Angel Padilla Romero, alias Fabian, head of the ELN's Western Front

New People's Army (of the Philippines)

- Jorge Madlos, 72, alias Ka Oris, a senior commander and spokesman for decades

Pakistani Taliban

- Niaz, alias Zeeshan, who was active with the Pakistani Taliban in Punjab Province's Hazro area of Attock district and in league with Lashkar-e-Jhangvi

Popular Front for the Liberation of Palestine-General Command

- Ahmed Jabril, founder, of natural causes

Shining Path of Peru

- Manuel Rubén Abimael Guzmán Reynoso, founder, 86, died of natural causes while serving life in prison in Peru

OTHER TERRORISTS KILLED IN 2021

Abu Sayyaf

- al-Al Sawadjaan, a bomb-maker, would-be suicide bomber, and younger brother of AS commander Mundi Sawadjaan, who belongs to a faction aligned with ISIS
- Injam Yadah, an AS commander involved in beheadings and kidnappings of Filipinos and foreigners

Ahlu Sunnah Wal Jama'a (ASWJ) jihadis in Mozambique

- Awadhi Ndanjile, a religious leader instrumental in recruiting and indoctrinating ASWJ members

Arm of the Arab Revolution Palestinian terrorists

- Anis Naccache, who participated in the barricade-and-hostage attack on OPEC oil ministers in 1975 in Vienna, Austria, died of COVID-19

East Indonesia Mujahideen (MIT)

- Jaka Ramadan, who died alongside MIT leader Ali Kalora in a clash with troops

Kashmiri rebels

- Mehraj-ud-din Halwai, a senior commander in India's northwestern Handwara area

Second Marquetalia Movement (of Colombia) FARC dissidents

- Seuxis Hernandez, alias Jesús Santrich, former chief negotiator for the Revolutionary Armed Forces of Colombia (FARC), who later broke from a peace deal to found SMM
- Hernán Darío Velásquez, alias El Paisa, a former FARC dissident leader believed killed in Venezuela

KEY TERRORISTS CAPTURED/SURRENDERED IN 2021

Boko Haram

- Yawi Modu, a senior member in Borno State

ISIS

- Basim, a close aide to erstwhile ISIS caliph al-Baghdadi
- Sami Jasim al-Jaburi, alias Haji Hamid, who had been a deputy of ISIS founder Abu Bakr al-Baghdadi and was ISIS's finance chief
- Mohammed Khalifa, Saudi-born Canadian citizen who was a leading figure in the English-language media unit of ISIS
- Ghazwan al-Zobai, alias Abu Obaida, the Iraqi mastermind behind a deadly July 3, 2016 suicide car bombing in a Baghdad shopping center in the central Karradah district, which killed 292 people and wounded 250

Jemaah Islamiyah

- Abu Rusdan, believed to be the group's leader

Lashkar-e-Taiba

- Zaikur Rehman Lakhvi, chief of operations

Lotta Continua

- Giorgio Petrostefani, 77, co-founder

Revolutionary Armed Forces of Colombia (FARC)

- Rodrigo Granda, the group's former chief diplomat

Regional Developments

Southern, north, east, west, and central **Africa** saw the expansion of ISIS affiliates, along with continuation of operations by a few die-hard al-Qaeda affiliates. Chad, which lost 30-year president Idriss Deby on the battlefield, Burkina Faso, Mali, Cameroon, Congo, Niger, Nigeria, Mozambique, Somalia, and Kenya were particularly hard-hit. Separatist and ethnic-based groups were also active in numerous countries, including Nigeria, Sudan, and the Central African Republic.

Boko Haram, an ISIS affiliate, ransom-seeking bandits, and others were all suspected in a rash of kidnappings of hundreds of Nigerian schoolchildren and teachers, a continuation of trends seen in earlier years. Hundreds of hostages escaped or were rescued, but hundreds remained missing.

The death of Boko Haram leader Shekau opened an opportunity for the local ISIS branch to attempt to assimilate many jihadis facing the BH leadership vacuum. But the death in October of ISWAP leader Abu Musab al-Barnawi and his successor, Malam Bako, diverted that ISIS affiliate's attention to a prolonged succession struggle.

Al-Shabaab terrorists continued to spill over from Somalia into Kenya.

In **Asia**, authorities in the Philippines, India, and Pakistan killed the leaders of second-tier rebel groups, but still faced ongoing insurgencies by more prominent violent Islamist and separatist organizations. Indonesia released Abu Bakar Baaysir, 82, spiritual leader of Jemaah Islamiyah; jihadis from several groups soon increased their operational tempo, particularly in attacking Christian targets. Kashmiri separatists in India and the Pakistani Taliban were also especially active.

In **Latin America and the Caribbean**, ongoing gang-related chaos in Haiti culminated in the early July assassination of President Jovenel Moïse. Haitian police quickly arrested 17 suspects, including 15 retired Colombian Army soldiers and two Haitian-Americans, who were believed assisted by Haitian residents. Succession became a stumbling block, as the Constitutionally-named successor, the supreme court chief judge, had succumbed to COVID-19 and the parliament had not met since 2020 and most parliamentary terms had expired. Not to be outdone, proliferating gangs kidnapped hundreds for ransom, including 17 American and Canadian missionaries, demanding $1 million/hostage.

Europe featured the start of a massive trial of the ISIS terrorists and facilitators responsible for the 2015 Paris attacks that killed 130 and wounded 300, as well as a separate trial in Germany for an individual who attacked a Jewish restaurant in 2018.

The **Middle East and South Asia** was focused on the transition from Afghanistan as a war zone involving an international coalition led by the U.S. for 20 years to a civil war pitting an overmatched government against a resurgent Taliban force that quickly turned the war into a rout. Even before the U.S. withdrew in August, the Taliban had negotiated in bad faith, executed surrendering soldiers, and fired RPGs on the presidential palace. Further complicating matters was the continuation of terrorist activities by ISIS-K, not a part of the peace process and which could serve as a spoiler for a new government, as it had when its killing of 13 Marines in a suicide bombing threw a monkey wrench into the airlift evacuation of more than 100,000 people. The Taliban's blitzkrieg in seizing provincial capitals surprised many, who wondered if they would match the Viet Cong's success in achieving a speedy takeover following a U.S. withdrawal. They did. Despite their claims of being willing to work with moderates and the international community, the interim government included many wanted terrorists and Gitmo alumni. The Taliban shrugged off a U.S. offer to cooperate in ridding the country of ISIS-K, which immediately began a campaign of mass casualty bombings of civilian targets, including mosques, mirroring early Taliban operations. The Taliban, bereft of foreign assistance and facing widespread poverty, damages from the decades-long war, COVID-19, and the daily difficulties facing any government, also had to deal with fighting on the other side of an insurgency and terrorist campaign. Skills developed in fighting a rural-based insurgency might not easily translate into providing security in urban areas.

In the **United States**, the year got off to an unpromising start on January 6, when President Donald Trump, clinging to dashed hopes of staying in office, called for attendees at a rally in Washington, D.C. to continue to fight for his being declared the winner of the November 2020 election. He called on his followers to march on the Capitol, where Vice President Mike Pence was chairing the ceremonial counting of the Electoral College ballots that certified President-elect Joe Biden's win. The march quickly turned into a riot by hundreds of individuals deemed by the media to be domestic terrorists, who broke through police barricades, smashed windows, and ran into the Capitol building, taking over the well of the Senate and occupying House Speaker Nancy Pelosi's office. A security officer shot to death a rioter as she broke into the building through a broken window. A police officer died of his injuries when the mob attacked him. Three other people died of medical emergencies. It was the largest assault on American democracy in its history. Apologists for the right-wingers soon claimed that the attack was the work of antifa instigators. Department of Justice prosecutors filed charges against nearly 500 rioters, including police, veterans, leaders of violent militias, and other agitators.

Spates of attacks by right-wingers, white supremacists, anti-Semites, anti-Asians, and other individuals were part of the secondary effects of the riot. The country also saw a dramatic rise in multi-casualty active shooter attacks throughout the country, as the reopening of the country despite the ongoing pandemic made it easier for would-be killers to more freely move about and convenient targets congregated in workplaces, shopping areas, and places of entertainment. Some of these attackers were linked to extremist right wing groups; other expressed similar sentiments on social media.

Right-wing terrorism by 2021 had replaced jihadi extremists as the key domestic threat within the United States. In 2017, the Government Accountability Office had noted that since 9/11 through December 2016, there had been 23 "violent extremist" attacks by jihadis, but 62 by far-right groups.

MARKING 20 YEARS AFTER 9/11

The Taliban's takeover of Afghanistan and the U.S. military's speedy evacuation, with American civilians and Afghan allies in tow, led jihadis to celebrate the end of the 20-year war in Afghanistan and the 9/11 attacks that started it all. While no spectacular attacks took place to rival those of 9/11, September 11, 2021 was a particularly active day for terrorists, including the following:

Middle East: Al-Qaeda leader Ayman al-Zawahiri appeared in an hour-long video entitled "Jerusalem Will Never be Judaized", marking the 20th anniversary of 9/11 as rumors of his death continued. He praised al-Qaeda attacks including one by Hurras al-Deen, a group aligned with al-Qaeda, that targeted Russian troops near Raqqa, Syria on January 1, 2021.

Middle East: The pro-al-Qaeda *Wolves of Manhattan* magazine, affiliated with the jihadist group Jaysh al-Malahim, called for more attacks with planes.

Syria: The Supporters of Abu Bakr al-Siddiq Company set off a roadside bomb that hit a convoy of Turkish troops following a search and screening operation in Idlib Province's de-escalation zone, killing two non-commissioned infantry officers and wounding three soldiers.

Iraq: Two drones carrying explosives targeted Irbil international airport, causing no casualties.

Yemen: Houthi rebels fired a ballistic missile and five explosive-laden drones at al-Makha port on the Red Sea, destroying humanitarian aid warehouses but causing no casualties.

Peru: Manuel Rubén Abimael Guzmán Reynoso, alias Presidente Gonzalo, 86, founder of Sendero Luminoso (the Maoist Shining Path), died of natural causes while serving life in prison.

Costa Rica: Gunmen shot Nicaraguan political activist Joao Maldonado, who opposes the government of President Daniel Ortega, critically injuring him.

Nigeria: Gunmen killed 12 Nigerian security forces at a military base in Mutumji in Zamfara State, stole weapons, and torched buildings.

Ukraine: Two Ukrainian soldiers were killed and 10 others wounded in clashes with Russian-backed separatists in Ukraine's eastern Donetsk.

ADDITIONAL RESEARCH SOURCES

For those who prefer to run textual searches for specific groups, individuals, or incidents, a computer version of the 1960-2021 ITERATE (International Terrorism: Attributes of Terrorist Events) textual chronology is available from Vinyard Software, Inc., 502 Wandering Woods Way, Ponte Vedra, Florida 32081-0621, or e-mail via vinyardsoftware@hotmail.com.

The data set comes in a WordPerfect and Microsoft Word textual version and looks remarkably like the volumes in this series of hardcopy chronologies. A numeric version offers circa 150 numeric variables describing the international attacks from 1968-2020 (and soon 2021). The data sets can be purchased by specific year of interest. See www.vinyardsoftware.com for further details.

Vinyard also offers the Data on Terrorist Suspects (DOTS) project, where you will find a detailed biographical index of every terrorist suspect named in the previous volumes of this chronology.

Comments about this volume's utility and suggestions for improvements for its likely successors are welcome and can be sent to me via vinyardsoftware@hotmail.com. Please send your terrorism publication citations to me at Vinyard to ensure inclusion in the next edition of the bibliography.

2021 CHRONOLOGY

AFRICA

BENIN

February 5, 2021: *AFP* reported that gunmen fired on the car of Benin presidential candidate Ganiou Soglo, a former minister and son of ex-president Nicephore Soglo, soon after he filed his papers to run in the April 11 presidential election. He was injured on the way to his farm in Zinvie, 22 miles from Cotonou. He was one of 20 candidates, including incumbent Patrice Talon.

BURKINA FASO

February 18, 2021: *Reuters* reported that gunmen killed nine people and wounded nine in a morning ambush on a road between Markoye and Tokabangou, where residents were on their way to a weekly market across the nearby border in Dolbel, Niger.

March 28, 2021: *AFP* reported that gunmen killed three people in Tanwalbougou, a village about 30 miles from Fada N'Gourma.

April 1, 2021: *AFP* reported that six militia volunteers were killed in an ambush in Dablo while searching for a missing colleague.

April 4, 2015: *AFP* reported that security forces repelled a jihadi ambush in Gourma Province.

April 5, 2021: *AFP* reported that several dozen gunmen on motorbikes killed three police and five members of the civilian anti-jihadist force Volunteers for the Defence of the Motherland (VDP) in Tanwalbougou in Gourma Province during the night. Another gendarme and a VDP member were hospitalized in Fada N'Gourma.

April 26, 2021: *UPI, Movistar Plus, AP,* and the *New York Times* reported that gunmen ambushed 40 people at the Arly National Park nature reserve in the east, injured six people, including two soldiers, and kidnapped two Spanish journalists from northern Spain and Rory Young, the Irish director of the Chengeta Wildlife Foundation. A Burkinabe soldier was reported missing. The three hostages were killed the next day. Christophe Deloire, secretary general of Reporters Without Borders, noted that the three journalists were investigating poaching in Burkina Faso. Spanish Prime Minister Pedro Sanchez tweeted that the Spanish nationals were David Beriain, 43, and Roberto Fraile, 47. Beriain had reported from Afghanistan, Congo, Iraq, and Libya and directed a documentary about the Fukushima, Japan nuclear disaster. Roberto Fraile, father of two children, covered multiple conflicts as a freelance cameraman and had been injured by shrapnel in the pelvis in the civil war in Aleppo, Syria in 2012. Beriain and Fraile were working with Young on a documentary about poachers in a national park bordering Benin. The three men were traveling with an anti-poaching patrol. The jihadi al-Qaeda-linked JNIM released an audio message saying, "We killed three white people.

We also got two vehicles with guns, and 12 motorcycles."

Yendifimba Jean-Claude Louari, the mayor of Fada N'Gourma, said that the country's special military wildlife unit was ambushed in the morning while traveling with the foreigners, 9 miles from their base at Natiaboni.

One soldier was shot in the leg and the other in his arm, which was amputated. 21042601

April 26, 2021: During the evening, gunmen killed 18 people and severely injured one in Yattakou village in the Sahel region's Seno area. Jihadis were suspected.

Earlier in April, jihadis killed 10 local defense fighters in Gorgadji in Seno Province.

May 3, 2021: *BBC, AP,* and *AFP* reported that in the morning, jihadi gunmen attacked Kodyel village in Foutouri district in Komandjari Province near the border with Niger, killing 30 people and setting fire to homes. Resident Mediempo Tandamba said some 100 jihadis arrived on motorcycles, tricycles, and pick-up trucks. Four of his brother's children were killed. Another 20 people were injured, some seriously. Some observers said the terrorists attacked the Gurma-majority community because residents had joined a self-defense militia.

May 18, 2021: *ABC News* reported that jihadis were suspected of attacking a baptism party near Tin-Akoff in the Sahel region, killing 15 people.

June 4, 2021: The *New York Times, Reuters, AFP, BBC,* and *AP* reported that at 2 a.m., gunmen raided a position of the Volunteers for the Defence of the Motherland (VDP), an anti-jihadist civilian defence force which backs the national army, in Solhan village in the Sahel's Yagha Province, killing 100 people and torching homes and the market. No one claimed credit. The government blamed jihadis. Rida Lyammouri, a senior fellow at the Morocco-based Policy Center for the New South, said that gunmen believed affiliated with the Islamic State in the Greater Sahara first attacked an artisanal gold mine, then went after civilians. *CNN* said the government announced that 132 civilians, including seven children, were killed and 40 wounded. *AFP* reported on June 7 that the death toll had reached 160, including 20 children, buried in three mass graves. The *Washington Post* reported on June 24 that the attack was perpetrated mostly by boys between the ages of 12 and 14 forced to become child soldiers.

In another evening attack by suspected jihadis, gunmen killed 14 people, including an armed volunteer in Tadaryat village in the same region.

The al-Qaeda-linked Group for the Support of Islam and Muslims (GSIM) and the Islamic State in the Greater Sahara (EIGS) had been battling for control of Yagha Province.

June 21, 2021: Gunmen ambushed police officers near Barsalogho in the center-north region, killing 11. Another four police were missing. Seven officers survived. Jihadis were suspected.

July 16, 2021: *AFP* reported that two bombs hit a military vehicle and a motorbike near Dablo as a joint force of army, police, and gendarmes was returning from an operation. Three soldiers died and five were wounded.

Security forces claimed to have killed "dozens of terrorists" and destroyed a base in the forests of Toulfe and Tougrebouli. One civilian militiaman was killed and eight soldiers were wounded. Soldiers recovered weapons, ammunition, and camping gear.

August 4, 2021: Aime Barthelemy Simpore, assistant to the minister of defense, announced that jihadis attacked several villages outside Markoye in Oudalan Province near the border with Niger, killing eleven civilians, 15 soldiers, and four volunteer defense fighters. The civilians died at midday; the others were ambushed at 4 p.m. after responding to the attack. Ten jihadis died.

August 8, 2021: *Al-Jazeera* and *AFP* reported that at 3 p.m., suspected rebels ambushed an army patrol near Doukoun village in the Toeni commune in the Boucle du Mouhoun region in Sourou Province near the border with Mali, killing 12 Burkinabe soldiers and injuring eight. Another seven soldiers who went missing were found at dawn on August 9. One had been wounded in the thigh. The attackers destroyed or captured several vehicles. Authorities believed the attackers were avenging the August 7 deaths of Sidibe Ousmane, alias Mouslim, and spiritual leader Bande Amadou, who were active in the Boucle du Mouhoun region. The duo were killed by a special army unit in a clash between Diamasso and Bouni, in Kossi Province.

August 18, 2021: Jihadis were suspected of ambushing a convoy, killing 30 civilians and 17 soldiers and volunteer defense fighters. No one claimed credit. *Reuters* reported on August 20 that the death toll had reached 80.

September 12, 2021: *Reuters* reported that gunmen killed six gendarmes and wounded seven others in a 1:30 p.m. attack on a convoy of empty fuel trucks returning from the Boungou gold mine, which is owned and operated by London and Toronto-listed Endeavor Mining, on a stretch of road between Sakoani and Matiacoali in the east. Gendarmes were protecting the convoy, which was hit by a land mine, followed by heavy gunfire.

October 4, 2021: At 5 a.m., heavily-armed extremists attacked the Yirgou military barracks near Barsalogho in Sanmatenga Province, killing 14 soldiers and injuring seven.

Menastream, a conflict monitoring consultancy, reported that six bombs went off within seven days, killing eight and wounding several others. Three of the explosions occurred in the west and southwest, including one in the Cascades region.

November 14, 2021: Jihadis in pick-up trucks and motorcycles attacked a gendarme post in Inata in Soum Province, near the border with Mali, at 5 a.m., killing 28 officers and four civilians. An attack on a detachment in neighboring Kelbo was repelled. *AFP* reported on November 17 that the death toll had reached 53, including 49 gendarmes and four civilians.

Since October, explosives were found outside the main town of Djibo.

November 21, 2021: Gunmen hiding behind a group of displaced people attacked a healthcare center in Foube in Center-North Region, killing 19 people, including nine security force members, injuring numerous others, including a staff member from the aid group Doctors Without

Borders, and burning down the center. The attackers also hit a gendarme post a few hundred meters away.

November 28, 2021: *AFP* reported that at 5 a.m., gunmen fired at an army unit in Solle in Loroum Province bordering Mali, killing four soldiers and wounding several others. A government spokesman said 10 terrorists were killed and a civilian was among the casualties.

December 9, 2021: *Al-Jazeera* reported that gunmen killed 14 members of the government-backed Homeland Defence Volunteers civilian militia in an ambush six miles from Titao. No one claimed credit.

December 10, 2021: The Burkinabe military announced that its joint operation with Niger's army killed 100 extremist rebels, arrested 20 suspects, and seized significant equipment from the rebels in the previous fortnight. Thirteen soldiers were killed and seven others were wounded.

December 13, 2021: Four Burkinabe soldiers were killed and nine others wounded when they hit an improvised explosive device in Komandjari Province.

December 14, 2021: *Reuters* reported that the army announced that the armed forces killed about 100 militants in the second phase of the joint Taanli operation with Niger between November 25 and December 9 in the border zone. The hundreds of troops arrested 20 suspects, seized guns and hundreds of motorcycles, and destroyed 15 improvised explosive devices.

December 23, 2021: *Al-Jazeera* and *Reuters* reported that 41 people, including members of a government-backed civilian self-defence force Volunteers for the Defence of the Motherland (VDP), were killed in an attack by gunmen on a convoy of traders escorted by VDP near Ouahigouya in Loroum Province, near the Mali border. The dead included VDP leader Ladji Yoro.

BURUNDI

September 18, 2021: *AFP* reported that rebel group RED-Tabara claimed on *Twitter* a series of mortar attacks launched overnight on Bujumbura's airport, a day before President Evariste Ndayishimiye was due to fly out to address the U.N. General Assembly in New York. The three mortar shells caused no injuries or damage. RED-Tabara has its rear base in South Kivu in the Democratic Republic of Congo. It began operations a decade earlier and became the most active of Burundian rebel groups. It had conducted ambushes since 2015 and in 2020, was behind attacks in which it said more than 40 people were killed among security forces and the youth league of the ruling CNDD-FDD party.

September 20, 2021: Grenade attacks at the main bus terminal and at a market in Bujumbura killed two people and injured 102. No one claimed credit. Prime Minister Alain Guillaume Bunyoni deemed them "terrorist acts" by people who seek to profit from insecurity.

CAMEROON

January 8, 2021: *Al-Jazeera* and *AFP* reported that Boko Haram was blamed when a female suicide bomber killed 12 civilians, including eight children, and seriously injured two others in a northern village. Mahamat Chetima Abba, Mozogo village chief, said that the attackers arrived at 1 a.m. brandishing machetes. The girl set off her explosives while the villagers ran into the nearby forest.

July 24, 2021: *Reuters* and state broadcaster *CRTV* reported that at 4 a.m., jihadis raided an army outpost in Sagme, killing six Cameroonian soldiers and wounding four. Lazare Ndongo Ndongo, administrative head of the district in the Far North Region, said "There were six to seven vehicles and motorcycles and some were on foot."

August 19, 2021: *Reuters* reported that battles between Choa Arab herders and Mousgoum fishermen and farmers in the Far North killed 32 people and left 19 villages torched.

August 29, 2021: *AFP* reported that Anglophone separatists kidnapped a Catholic priest, Monsignor Julius Agbortoko of Mamfe diocese,

releasing him on September 2. The kidnappers had demanded a ransom of more than 20 million CFA francs ($36,000, €31,000).

October 5, 2021: *Reuters* and *Ghanaian Times* reported that distant machine gun fire from nearby mountains interrupted a speech by Prime Minister Dion Ngute during a visit to Bamenda, capital of the restive North West region, that Anglophone separatists had vowed to disrupt.

CENTRAL AFRICAN REPUBLIC

January 9, 2021: *AFP* reported that rebels attacked government troops and U.N. peacekeepers in Bouar following the controversial re-election of President Faustin Archange Touadera. 21010901

January 13, 2021: Security forces halted a rebel attempt to seize the capital in the morning at the entrance to Bangui, near its PK11 and PK12 areas and in the Bimbo neighborhood. Two Rwandan U.N. MINUSCA peacekeepers, including at least one Rwandan, were killed. Prime Minister Firmin Ngrebada said 30 rebels were killed. 21011302

January 15, 2021: Two Bangladeshi U.N. peacekeepers were injured in a rebel ambush near Grimari. 21011503

A Burundian U.N. peacekeeper was killed in a second rebel ambush near Grimari. 21011504

January 19, 2021: *UPI* quoted the U.N. as saying that gunmen killed two peacekeepers from Gabon and Morocco in an ambush blamed on the militant group UPC and anti-Balaka members near Bangassou. 21011901

January 21, 2021: *Deutsche Welle* reported that presidential spokesman Albert Yaloke Mokpeme announced a 15-day state of emergency after rebels attempted to blockade Bangui in an attempt to overturn the December 27 election of President Faustin Archange Touadera.

January 25, 2021: *Al-Jazeera* reported that the International Criminal Court (ICC) took into custody Mahamat Said Abdel Kani, 50, a leader of the Seleka faction, suspected of war crimes and crimes against humanity. The ICC had issued an arrest warrant, under seal, against him on January 7, 2019, regarding alleged crimes committed in Bangui in 2013. Seleka ("alliance" in the Sango language) refers to a coalition of mostly northern and predominantly Muslim rebels, whose brutal rule gave rise to the opposing Anti-balaka Christian militias. He was suspected of imprisonment, torture, persecution, enforced disappearance, and other inhumane acts; and the war crimes of torture and cruel treatment. The ICC also held Anti-balaka leaders Alfred Yekatom, accused of crimes against humanity, and CAR football chief Patrice-Edouard Ngaissona.

January 26, 2021: Prime Minister Firmin Ngrebada said on his *Facebook* page that soldiers in Boyali killed 44 rebels in an offensive against fighters that had attacked the government of the newly re-elected President Faustin-Archange Touadera.

May 10, 2021: Attorney General Eric Didier Tambo announced that police arrested French national Juan Remy Quignolot, 55, for supporting rebels after discovering a cache of weapons, ammunition, military fatigues, and bank notes in multiple currencies at his residence. Photos on social media showed Quignolot alongside Ali Darassa, the leader of the Union for Peace in Central African Republic (UPC) rebel group. Quignolot, a former soldier and paratrooper in the French army, claimed he was a trainer for a private security company in Bangui. The company denied any affiliation with him. UPC members had been part of the mostly Muslim rebel coalition known as Seleka that overthrew the president in 2013.

June 26, 2021: *Al-Jazeera* reported that two gunmen on a motorcycle attacked a Doctors Without Borders (Medecins Sans Frontieres (MSF)) team, killing a woman who was accompanying a patient being transported by MSF staff near Batangafo. A motorbike rider and two patients—a woman and her baby—were hospitalized in stable condition. MSF said the motorbike riders were MSF staff.

July 31, 2021: *AFP* reported that the U.N.'s MINUSCA peacekeeping mission said that at dawn, Return, Reclamation, Rehabilitation (3R) rebels killed six civilians and wounded several in an attack on Mann village in the northeast. 3R includes members from the Fulani ethnic group.

October 5, 2021: *U.S. News and World Report* and *Reuters* reported that rebel gunmen ambushed and set alight a convoy of three semi-trucks filled with passengers travelling to Alindao from Bambari, seat of Ouaka Prefecture, killing 20 and wounding six. The government blamed the Coalition of Patriots for Change (CPC), an alliance of rebel groups formed ahead of the December 2020 presidential election to oppose President Faustin-Archange Touadera. CPC is supported by former president Francois Bozize.

November 28, 2021: *AFP* reported that rebels simultaneously attacked Kaita and Bayengou, near the border with Cameroon and 300 miles from Bangui, killing 30 civilians and two soldiers. The government blamed 3R (Return, Reclamation, Rehabilitation) rebels, composed of fighters from the Fulani ethnic group.

December 9, 2021: *Al-Jazeera* reported that the Hague-based International Criminal Court announced that it would try alleged Seleka leader Mahamat Said Abdel Kani, 51, on charges of war crimes and crimes against humanity. Charges referred to alleged torture, imprisonment, and cruel treatment in Bangui between April and August 2013 against detained people suspected to be supporters of the ousted President Francois Bozize. The court rejected similar accusations against him over alleged crimes committed elsewhere in Bangui between September and November 2013.

December 30, 2021: *AFP* reported that three MINUSCA Tanzanian peacekeepers were wounded in a mine explosion in the west. 21123001

December 31, 2021: *AFP* reported that three Bangladeshi MINUSCA peacekeepers were injured when their vehicle hit a mine in Bohong in Ouham-Pende Province. 21123101

CHAD

April 19, 2021: *AFP* and *AP* reported that the army claimed it had killed more than 300 rebels and captured 150, including three senior rebels, while five soldiers had died and 36 were wounded. The rebel offensive in the provinces of Tibesti and Kanem had begun on April 11, presidential election day. The results extended the 30-year rule of President Idriss Deby Itno, 68. However, the next day, the government announced that Deby had died of injuries while visiting the battlefield. The raid was attributed to the Libya-based Front for Change and Concord in Chad (FACT), based in Libya. The US Embassy in N'Djamena had ordered non-essential personnel to leave the country.

April 29, 2021: Anti-government National Front for Change and Concord in Chad rebels claimed to have shot down a military helicopter and that they controlled Nokou, 186 miles north of the capital, N'Djamena.

CONGO

January 15, 2021: *AFP* reported that the Allied Democratic Forces (ADF) attacked Abembi Village in the local chiefdom of Walese Vonkutu in Ituri Province, killing 46 Pygmies and wounding two others.

February 14, 2021: *AFP* reported that in the morning, separatist gunmen attacked the Kimbembe and Kibati military camps in Lubumbashi, killing 11 people. Lubumbashi Mayor Ghislain Robert Lubaba Buluma said four members of the security forces, one civilian, and six insurgents died. Civil society leader Fortune Mbaya said the attackers claimed they were members of the separatist Bakata-Katanga militia.

February 22, 2021: *NPR, Reuters, CNN, ABC News,* the *Washington Post,* and *AFP* reported that at 10:15 a.m., six gunmen attacked a two-vehicle UN convoy near Kanyamahoro in Nyiaragongo Territory en route to a World Food Program (WFP) school feeding program in Kiwanja in the area of Rutshuru near Goma, killing Italian

Ambassador Luca Attanasio, 43, and Vittorio Iacovacci, 30, an Italian Carabinieri soldier who was riding in Attanasio's car. The WFP said one of its Congolese drivers, Mustapha Milambo, 56, was killed. Others were injured. Attanasio had served in Kinshasa since 2017 and became Ambassador in 2019. He joined the Ministry of Foreign Affairs and International Cooperation in 2003, and had earlier served in Switzerland, Morocco, and Nigeria. He sustained gunshot wounds to the abdomen. He left behind a wife and three young daughters. The convoy belonged to MONUSCO, the U.N. peacekeeping mission in Congo. The Rwandan Hutu Democratic Forces for the Liberation of Rwanda (FDLR) militia and the Congolese Revolutionary Army, alias M23, operate in the area.

The *Washington Post* and *Reuters* said the attack was a kidnapping attempt. The gunmen stopped the convoy by firing warning shots, killed the driver, then led the Italians into a forest next to the road. Virunga Park rangers fired on the kidnappers. The Ambassador and police officer were killed in the exchange of gunfire.

AFP reported on February 25 that Italy held a state funeral for the two Italians. Attendees included Prime Minister Mario Draghi, the presidents of the Senate and the Chamber of Deputies, several government ministers, and Cardinal Angelo De Donatis.

Congolese authorities accused the FDLR, which denied any involvement and blamed the Rwandan and Congolese armies. 21022201

February 28, 2021: *AFP* reported that the ADF was suspected when gunmen killed ten civilians in two overnight attacks in the east. Army spokesman Lieutenant Jules Ngongo said the ADF decapitated eight villagers in Boyo in Ituri Province, and shot dead two civilians in Kainama in North Kivu Province on the border with Uganda. Houses were burned.

March 10, 2021: *Reuters* reported that the United States designated the ADF as a foreign terrorist organization, accusing it of links to ISIS. *Upstream* reported that the Department also placed ISIS-Democratic Republic of Congo (Islamic State Central Africa Province (ISCAP)) and its leader, Seka Musa Baluku, on its terrorist list.

March 14, 2021: *Reuters* reported that civil rights groups blamed the ADF for an overnight attack on Bulongo village that killed 12 people. The terrorists were armed with knives, pickaxes, machetes, and other weapons.

March 19, 2021: *Al-Jazeera* reported that a UN-HCR study indicated that more than 200 people had been killed and 40,000 displaced since January in attacks in Beni Territory in North Kivu Province and nearby villages in Ituri Province attributed to ADF terrorists and other groups affiliated with ISIS. UNHCR spokesman Babar Baloch added that "In less than three months, the ADF has allegedly raided 25 villages, set fire to dozens of houses, and kidnapped over 70 people."

May 1, 2021: Several days of rebel attacks killed 19 people. Gunmen shot to death Sheikh Ali Amin Uthman, the representative of the Islamic community of Beni, during evening prayers in the town's central mosque. The ADF had threatened him for more than a year.

May 9, 2021: *AFP* reported that Congolese army killed 10 ADF rebels in North Kivu and Ituri Provinces. An army spokesman said 10 died in Halungupa in the Rwenzori area.

May 18, 2021: *AFP* reported that the army claimed that it had killed 22 ADF rebels since the beginning of its offensive against the militia on May 6. Regional army spokesman Antony Mualushayi said the army arrested 60 ADF collaborators, including a dozen foreigners, mostly Ugandans, and seized eight AK-47 machine guns.

May 25, 2021: *AFP* reported that the ADF was suspected in an overnight attack in the mountainous Rwenzori area of greater Beni that killed 26 people.

May 27-28, 2021: *AFP* reported that the ADF was suspected in two overnight attacks that killed seven people along the road linking Beni and Kasindi in Kivu. Two other people were missing. Some 33 people had been killed in four days. Territorial administrator Donat Kibuana said that "the targets were firstly a truck that was carrying cocoa cargo towards Kasindi. The driver was shot dead and two other people were burned inside the vehicle… Then the same ADF (fighters) burned five people in their home."

May 30-31, 2021: *AFP* reported that the ADF was blamed for two overnight attacks in the east that killed 50 people. The Kivu Security Tracker (KST) group said 28 people were killed in Boga and 22 in Tchabi. The gunmen attacked a camp for displaced people in Boga; local officials said they had found 36 bodies. The KST reported that the wife of a traditional leader in Benyali-Tchabi had been killed in the attack on Tchabi. *Al-Jazeera* added on June 4 that the U.N. High Commissioner for Refugees reported that the ADF terrorists using guns and machetes had killed 57 civilians, including seven children, in displacement camps in the attacks. Several others were wounded, 25 were abducted, and more than 70 shelters and stores were torched. Some 31 people were killed in Boga.

June 8, 2021: *AFP* reported that Virunga National Park director Emmanuel De Merode announced that wardens in suburban Butembo had arrested suspected Mai-Mai Jackson militia chief Jackson Muhukambuto, believed to have led a three-year killing spree that had left 19 wildlife rangers, along with civilians and members of the armed forces, dead. Muhukambuto was a former army commander with good connections among tradespeople in the Nande ethnic group. He earlier helped the army's fight against a Rwandan Hutu group, the Democratic Forces for the Liberation of Rwanda (FDLR).

June 27, 2021: The government banned public gatherings for two days after two bombs went off in Beni. Congolese army spokesman Lt. Anthony Mwalushay said a Ugandan suicide bomber belonging to the ADF hit a busy intersection in Beni, while another bomb hit a Catholic church in Beni's Butsili district, seriously injuring two people. Mwalushay said two suspects were arrested. *AP* reported on June 29 that the Islamic State's Central Africa Province claimed credit for both attacks, including for its first suicide bombing in the country. The group said the suicide bomber was targeting Christians at a local bar. 21062701

July 1, 2021: ADF rebels were suspected when gunmen killed nine civilians, including women, in Beni's Rwangoma neighborhood. Beni's police chief, Col. Narcisse Muteba, said, "These rebels used the kidnapped civilians (as shields) to escape the Congolese army." Lt. Anthony Mwulushayi said that some victims were killed in their homes; others were taken to the center of the neighborhood, then shot and beaten with machetes or pieces of concrete. He added, "Alongside the human toll, businesses were looted before being set on fire, and residences were also set on fire."

July 22, 2021: *Al-Jazeera* and *AFP* reported that in the evening, gunmen ambushed and killed 16 civilians on a highway between the towns of Maimoya and Chani-chani as they were returning from a weekly market 25 miles from Beni in North Kivu Province. Jerome Munyambethe, head of the hospital in Oicha, said that six women and a child were shot. The ADF was suspected. Lewis Saliboko, a representative of grassroots groups in Oicha, said "They also fired a rocket."

July 24-26, 2021: *AFP* reported that during three days of clashes, the armed forces attacked positions held by the ADF in Tchabi in Ituri Province, freeing 150 hostages who had been used as human shields. Seven soldiers and 15 ADF gunmen died.

July 27, 2021: *AFP* reported that ADF gunmen conducted two attacks in North Kivu, killing eight people. Lewis Thembo said fighters raided the Bulongo commune in Beni overnight, killing four women and two men. Thembo, president of the local civil service organization, added that "They abandoned a baby on its mother's body. Meanwhile, the army said that gunmen attacked a public bus in South Kivu Province, killing a civilian businessman and an unarmed soldier before kidnapping the driver and stealing the businessman's "briefcase containing money".

August 2, 2021: *Al-Jazeera* reported that the ADF was suspected in an attack that killed 16 people. The victims, including two women, had been taken hostage weeks earlier by the ADF. Local official Dieudonne Malangai said this time they were knifed to death along a main highway near Idohu in Ituri Province.

August 27, 2021: *AFP* reported that ADF gunmen killed 19 civilians, burning and hacking them to death in an attack on Kasanzi village in the Beni territory of North Kivu Province. Red Cross workers found 14 bodies in a nearby forest on August 28.

September 1, 2021: *Reuters* reported that 80 people were feared missing in Ituri Province after suspected ADF rebels ambushed a convoy under escort by U.N. peacekeepers in the MONUSCO force and the Congolese army and torched 14 cars and two minibuses. *AFP* reported that suspected jihadists killed four people near the town of Ofai. Captain (or Lieutenant—reports differed regarding his rank) Jules Ngongo, spokesman of military operations in Ituri, said "We have managed to find more than 60 people who fled (the attack) into the bush." *AP* claimed five people were killed and 20 remained missing hours after the initial attack, which occurred when the convoy stopped to repair a disabled vehicle.

September 4, 2021: *AFP* reported that the Allied Democratic Forces (ADF) were suspected when rebels shot or hacked to death 30 people in Ituri Province. Augustin Muhindo Musavuli, a village elder, said that some had their throats slit, others were disemboweled.

October 20, 2021: *U.S. News and World Report* and *Reuters* reported that the Islamic State claimed credit on *Telegram* for an attack on Kalembo, 25 miles east of Beni, that killed 16 people and burned houses. A local human rights group blamed the ADF.

October 21, 2021: Army spokesman Capt. Anthony Mwalushayi said that at 6 p.m., ADF rebels killed 16 people and kidnapped several others from a farm 15 miles from Beni. The ADF burned three civilian houses.

October 29, 2021: *AFP* and the *Kivu Security Tracker* reported that at 4 a.m., the Cooperative for the Development of the Congo (CODECO-UDPC) and the Alliance for the Liberation of the Congo (ALC) attacked Gina village, which is mainly inhabited by Lendu, in Ituri Province, sparking a seven-hour raid that killed 14 civilians. They later attacked Nizi in the same area, killing four civilians, including two trying to flee. A vehicle of Doctors Without Borders was attacked in the same area. 21102901

November 3, 2021: *AFP* reported that gunmen attacked Bukavu in South Kivu Province at 1 a.m. Six rebels, two policemen, and a soldier died. Governor Theo Ngwabidje Kasi said that "The FARDC (armed forces of Democratic Republic of Congo) and police... killed six assailants, wounded four others, took 36 captives and recovered 14 weapons... We also sadly lost three members of our security force." A military source said the gunmen were from the previously-unknown CPC64. Regional military commander Bob Kilubi Ngoy said the attackers wanted to free members whom police had arrested several days earlier. Authorities detained several attackers and confiscated 14 weapons.

November 7, 2021: *Reuters* reported that gunmen seized Tshanzu and Runyoni villages simultaneously at 11 p.m. near the border with Uganda and Rwanda. *The Globe and Mail* added that Lieutenant-Colonel Muhindo Luanzo, assistant to the administrator of Rutshuru territory, blamed fighters from the M23 rebel group.

November 11, 2021: *AFP* reported that during the night, the ADF attacked a health center in Beni in North Kivu Province, stealing medical supplies before torching the hospital, killing five civilians, including a hospital guard, a guard who was ill, and a patient, and taking two male nurses and other people as hostages. *AFP* reported on November 15 that the death toll had risen to 38. A Red Cross official said bodies were found tied up, with their throats slit by machetes. The army killed eight ADF members in Kisunga.

November 14, 2021: *AFP* reported that regional army spokesman Major Dieudonne Kasereka said that overnight, vigilantes of the Ngumino Twigwaneho coalition from the Banyamulenge community (Congolese Tutsi with distant origins in Rwanda in South Kivu Province) killed six people and torched a dozen homes. Twigwaneho means "self-defence"; Ngumino means "We are staying here."

November 15, 2021: *AFP* reported that Patriotic and Integrationist Force of Congo (FPIC)

gunmen killed 17 civilians in Chabusiku in Ituri Province, leaving some victims to be burnt alive in their homes. The FPIC militia claims to defend the Bira ethnic group, and the attack targeted the rival Hema community.

November 20, 2021: The Congolese Institute for Nature Conservation said that in an evening attack, 100 gunmen believed to be former M23 rebels attacked a patrol post near Bukima in North Kivu Province, killing Chief Brigadier Etienne Mutazimiza Kanyaruchinya, 48, a conservation park ranger in Virunga National Park. Other rangers escaped unharmed. Kanyaruchinya left behind a wife and four children.

November 21, 2021: *CNN* reported that during the night, gunmen killed a policeman and kidnapped five Chinese nationals near a mine near Mukera in South Kivu Province. 21112101

November 22, 2021: *Reuters* reported that militiamen killed 20 people during an attack on displaced civilians in the northeast. *Al-Jazeera* added that at least a dozen people were killed in Ituri Province. Jules Ngongo, a spokesperson for Ituri's military government, told *Reuters* that the Cooperative for the Development of the Congo (CODECO) raided Drodro on during the night, killing six children, four men and two women.

November 27, 2021: *Al-Jazeera* and *AFP* reported that civil society leader Isaac Nyakuklinda said that two overnight attacks in Ituri Province killed nine civilians.

November 28, 2021: *Al-Jazeera* and *Reuters* reported that the second attack within a week on the Ivo camp for internally displaced people in Ituri Province killed 22 civilians. Red Cross coordinator Mambo Bapu Mance accused gunmen from CODECO of the attack.

November 30, 2021: Uganda People's Defense Forces spokeswoman Brig. Gen. Flavia Byekwaso tweeted that the Congo's military and Uganda's army launched joint air and artillery strikes against ADF camps in eastern Congo.

December 25, 2021: *AFP* and *Reuters* reported that a suicide bomber killed five people and himself at the In Box restaurant in the city center of Beni. More than 30 people were celebrating Christmas at the café. Local radio announcer Nicolas Ekila told *AFP*, "There was a motorbike parked there. Suddenly the motorbike took off, then there was a deafening noise."

EQUATORIAL GUINEA

March 7, 2021: The *Washington Post, TVGE, AP, CNN, ABC News, AFP,* and *Reuters* reported that four explosions of unknown origin went off during the afternoon at the Nkoa Ntoma military camp in the Mondong Nkuantoma neighborhood of the port city of Bata, killing 107, hospitalizing 615, and destroying dozens of buildings. The civil protection corps and firefighters rescued 60 people from the rubble. *Reuters* reported that President Teodoro Obiang Nguema, 78, who had ruled the country for nearly 42 years, blamed negligence in handling dynamite. Vice President Teodoro Nguema Obiang Mangue, the president's son, said the fire may have begun when a farmer set fire to his plot to prepare it for food production and a breeze spread the flames to the nearby barracks where ammunition was stored. *AFP* added that Human Rights Watch claimed there were "far more" deaths than the official total. *AFP* reported on March 26 that numerous people were rendered homeless, many sheltering with relatives.

   AFP reported on June 13, 2021 that prosecutors charged two soldiers with homicide and negligence. Military prosecutor Alejandro Mitogo told state channel *TVGW* that the head of the camp, Lieutenant-Colonel Valentin Nzang Ega, and Corporal Jose Antonio Obama Nsue would appear before a military court for "homicide, damage, fire, and negligence". He requested 70 years in prison for Nsue and 30 years for Ega.

ETHIOPIA

February 4, 2021: *Reuters* and the *Ethiopian Press Agency (EPA)* reported that authorities had arrested 15 people plotting at the direction of foreigners to attack the United Arab Emirates embassy in Addis Ababa. Authorities seized arms, explosives, and documents. *EPA* said, "The group took the mission from a foreign terrorist group and was preparing to inflict significant damage on properties and human lives." *EPA* added that a second group planned to attack the UAE's diplomatic mission in Sudan. *EPA* noted that one of the masterminds of the plot was arrested in Sweden.

May 29, 2021: Ethiopian citizen Negasi Kidane, from the Tigrayan city of Adigrat, and working for an Italian charity, was hit by a stray bullet during a fire fight in the Tigray region and was killed. He had worked for the International Committee for the Development of Peoples (CISP) since 2016.

June 25, 2021: Three members of Doctors Without Borders were murdered in the Tigray region. The aid group said two Ethiopian colleagues and one from Spain were found dead that morning. The previous day, colleagues lost contact with them while they were traveling. Their bodies were found a few meters from their empty vehicle. 21062502

July 18, 2021: *AFP* reported that a ten-vehicle World Food Program convoy was attacked 70 miles from Semera, capital of the Afar region, "while attempting to move essential humanitarian cargo into Tigray region". Tigray People's Liberation Front (TPLF) spokesman Getachew Reda denied involvement. 21071801

July 24, 2021: *Reuters* reported that the government of Ethiopia's Somali region accused militia from the Afar region of killing hundreds of civilians in an attack in an area known as both Gedamaytu and Gabraiisa.

August 5, 2021: *AFP* reported on August 10 that an attack on civilians in Galicoma in the Afar region killed 12 people and injured nearly 50; some 75 percent had bullet wounds. Survivors blamed the TPLF. Ayish Yasin, head of Afar's bureau for women and children, and Golbe Sila, chief of staff for Afar's regional president, said more than 200 died. Ayish said many of the victims were killed by artillery fire while seeking shelter at an area where food aid was being stored. She added, "Out of the 200 bodies recovered, 107 are children—48 girls and 59 boys."

August 18-19, 2021: On August 26, the Ethiopian Human Rights Commission announced receipt of reports from residents that an attacks on August 18 by the Oromo Liberation Army in East Wollega in the Oromia region killed 150 people, including 135 Amhara. A retaliatory attack the next day killed another 60. Oromo Liberation Army spokesman Odaa Tarbii posted that the allegations were "a gross distortion of facts on the ground".

October 31, 2021: *Reuters* reported that the government claimed that TPLF rebels summarily executed more than 100 youths in Kombolcha.

IVORY COAST

March 29, 2021: *Al-Jazeera* and *AFP* reported gunmen attacked a military camp around 1 a.m. at Kafolo, near the Burkina Faso border, killing two soldiers and injuring one. *Reuters* reported that two attackers died. An Ivorian army source claimed the attackers were from Burkina Faso. 21032901

June 7, 2021: *AFP* reported that during the night, gunmen attacked the village of Tougbo in Bouna district near the border with Burkina Faso, killing a soldier.

KENYA

February 10, 2021: *AFP* reported that 126 schools in Mandera County remained closed due to an exodus of teachers because of armed attacks and roadside bombs by al-Shabaab. The governor noted several attacks on "non-local" teachers in recent years.

March 5, 2021: *AP* reported on March 12, 2021 that George Kinoti, the head of criminal investigations, said that police believed that a man who grabbed a gun from a police officer and shot randomly at people in Kisumu the previous week, killing two and seriously wounding six, was likely a jihadi. A mob killed the attacker when he ran out of bullets. Police were unable to trace his background, and no one claimed the body. Kinoti said detectives "have reasons to believe that the assailant was not just the ordinary criminal, but prior to the attack received training in tactical maneuvers and weapon handling". Three ID cards found on the man belonged to three different people who do not know the killer. Police said the man, wearing gloves and a hood, overpowered a police officer, grabbed his gun, and shot him. No group claimed credit.

March 24, 2021: A bus ran over an improvised explosive device on a main road in Mandera County, killing four passengers and wounding dozens. Al-Shabaab was suspected. 21032401

May 3, 2021: A vehicle hit an explosive device believed planted by al-Shabaab in Lamu County near the Somali border, killing two people delivering supplies to a construction site where Kenya is building a fence and trenches along the Somali border to prevent extremists, bandits, and illegal immigrants from entering Kenya. The driver of the water bowser, his assistant, and a passenger worked for a private contractor building a wall at the Kenya-Somalia border wall construction site. The passenger survived with slight injuries. 21050302

May 12, 2021: At 2 a.m., al-Shabaab attacked a cell phone tower in Mandera County and killed two police reservists. A few hours later, they killed another police reservist while firing a rocket-propelled grenade at a cell phone tower in Wajir County. Two other police reservists were wounded.

May 18, 2021: Al-Shabaab attacked soldiers on a routine morning patrol in the Baure area of Lamu County, killing seven troops whose vehicle ran over an explosive device along the Bodhei-Kiunga road. Another soldier went missing. 21051802

July 15, 2021: Gunmen killed conservationist Joannah Stutchbury at her home in Kiambu County. She had worked to conserve the Kiambu Forest.

MADAGASCAR

July 20, 2021: *Newsweek, France24,* and *Reuters* reported that authorities, following a months-long investigation, arrested six people, including foreigners and local citizens, for allegedly plotting to assassinate President Andry Rajoelina, 47. Attorney General Berthine Razafiarivony said, "these individuals had devised a plan for the elimination and neutralization of a number of people including the head of state". Public security minister Rodellys Fanomezantsoa Randrianarison said one detainee is a foreign national, two are dual nationals, and three are Madagascar citizens. *France24* reported that two detainees were retired French military officers. Rajoelina came to power in a March 2009 coup against President Marc Ravalomanana. *France24* added that the gendarmerie announced on June 26 they foiled an assassination attempt on General Richard Ravalomanana.

Mali

January 2, 2021: *AFP* reported that French soldiers Sergeant Yvonne Huynh, 33, and Brigadier Loic Risser, 24, were killed when their vehicle hit an improvised explosive device in the Menaka region. Huynh was the first female soldier sent to the Sahel region since the French Barkhane operation began. Both were members of an intelligence regiment. A third soldier was injured. 21010201

January 13, 2021: A U.N. peacekeepers' vehicle hit a land mine, killing four Ivory Coast peacekeepers and wounding five others during a security operation along the Douentza and Timbuktu axis in the Timbuktu region north of Bamabara-Maoude. Gunmen fired at the survivors. 2111301

January 15, 2021: An Egyptian U.N. peacekeeper was killed in Kidal region and another was seriously injured when their vehicle hit a land mine during a logistics convoy. 21011501
U.N. forces found and disabled a bomb in Tessalit. 21011502

January 21, 2021: *AFP* reported that a bomb killed three Malian soldiers in the Mondoro area.

January 23-24, 2021: *AFP* reported that two 3 a.m. jihadi raids on army positions at Boulkes-

sy and Mondoro, near the border with Burkina Faso, killed three soldiers and five attackers and wounded seven soldiers and several jihadis, who abandoned 25 motorcycles while fleeing. Attacks in September 2019 by the Support Group for Islam and Muslims on the same facility killed 50 soldiers.

January 27, 2021: The army announced that it and French forces killed at least 100 Islamic extremists in 2021. In a joint operation carried out from January 2 to 20, authorities seized 20 motorcycles, weapons, and other materials. The armed forces pushed out extremists from Serma, Foulssaret, Doni, and Boulikessi.

February 10, 2021: In the morning, gunmen attacked a temporary U.N. base in Kerena, near Douentza, injuring 20 peacekeepers. No group claimed credit. 21021001

March 16, 2021: *Reuters* and *AP* reported that in the afternoon, 100 jihadis ambushed a Malian army convoy near Tessalit in the Gao region, killing 33 soldiers and injuring 14. The U.N. MINUSMA peacekeeping mission helped evacuate the wounded soldiers. *Al-Jazeera* reported that the Islamic State claimed the attack.

April 2, 2021: *AP* and *AFP* reported that at dawn, 100 jihadis on motorbikes and vehicles attacked a U.N. MINUSMA peacekeeping force's camp in Aguelhok in the Kidal region, killing four Chadian peacekeepers and injuring 34 peacekeepers. The U.N. mission said that the attackers abandoned 23 of their dead. *AFP* reported on April 5 that MINUSMA chief Mahamat Saleh Annadif said a search of the battlefield determined that more than 40 jihadis, including senior commander Abdallaye Ag Albaka, a right-hand man to Iyad Ag Ghaly, leader of the al-Qaeda-affiliated Group to Support Islam and Muslims (GSIM) in the Sahel, were killed in a three-hour counter-attack. Ag Albaka was a former mayor of Tessalit. A U.N. security source said he had risen to number 3 in the GSIM. Authorities captured four jihadis. 21040201

April 8, 2021: The *Washington Post, AFP, AP, Reuters,* and *al-Jazeera* reported on May 5, 2021 that Christophe Deloire, the chief of Reporters

Without Borders, announced that Group to Support Islam and Muslims (JNIM) jihadis kidnapped French journalist Olivier Dubois, 46, on April 8 while he was working in Gao. Dubois did not return to his hotel after lunch. He works for *Liberation* and *Le Point Afrique*. JNIM released a 21-second video on May 5 in which Dubois said, "I'm Olivier Dubois. I'm French. I'm a journalist. I was kidnapped in Gao on April 8 by the JNIM (an al-Qaeda-linked group). I'm speaking to my family, my friends, and the French authorities for them to do everything in their power to free me." *Reuters* and *RTL* radio reported on May 23 that French Foreign Affairs Minister Jean-Yves Le Drian confirmed that Dubois had probably been taken hostage by jihadis. 21040801

April 13, 2021: *Al-Jazeera* and *AFP* reported that in the morning, two gunmen killed former northern rebel leader Sidi Brahim Ould Sidati, in his 60s, outside a mosque close to his home in Bamako. He died hours after the attack at the Golden Life American Hospital. He had signed a 2015 peace accord. He was the rotating president of the Coordination of Azawad Movements (CMA), a mostly ethnic Tuareg alliance that battled the central government in 2012. He also had been mayor of Ber near Timbuktu, and was one of the major figures of the Arab Movement of Azawad (MAA), part of the CMA that he helped found. No one claimed credit.

April 25, 2021: *Al-Jazeera* reported that a rocket attack on a base in Tessalit that houses Malian soldiers, U.N. peacekeepers, and French troops gravely wounded three MINUSMA peacekeepers. 21042501

June 21, 2021: *Reuters* reported that a suicide car bomb went off near a French military armored vehicle on a reconnaissance mission near Gossi, wounding six soldiers and four residents. No group claimed responsibility. 21062101

June 24, 2021: *Reuters* reported that jihadis were suspected when gunmen killed 19 villagers in and around Danga Zawne in the Tillaberi region near the border with Mali.

June 25, 2021: A vehicle bomb exploded at a temporary MINUSMA operational base near Ichagara village in the Gao region, injuring 15 U.N. peacekeepers, including a dozen German soldiers, three seriously. 21062501

July 17, 2021: *AFP* and *al-Akhbar* reported that gunmen on motorbikes kidnapped three Chinese nationals and two Mauritanians and stole five pick-up trucks from a road construction site 34 miles from Kwala. The gunmen torched fuel tanks and destroyed a crane and dump trucks belonging to the Chinese COVEC construction firm and the Mauritanian ATTM road-building company. Jihadis were suspected.

Reuters reported on November 1, 2021 that the office of the presidency announced that security forces rescued three Chinese nationals from the COVEC construction company who were abducted from a construction site on July 17. The gunmen had also kidnapped two Mauritanians with the road-building company ATTM, 34 miles from Kwala. *AFP* added that the Mauritanians were freed 10 days after being kidnapped. *Al-Jazeera* and *AFP* reported that the Malian army said that the Chinese captives escaped and were found by ground and air forces the following day, aided by "anonymous people of good will". 21071701

July 20, 2021: *AP, AFP, CNN,* and *Reuters* reported that a man tried to stab transitional President Col. Assimi Goita, 38, at Bamako's Grand Mosque during Eid al-Adha celebrations. The attack occurred following holiday prayers and a sermon as the imam went to slaughter a sheep in a ritual animal sacrifice. A man with a knife and another man with a gun were involved. Goita, a special forces colonel, was not hurt. One person was injured. Mosque director Latus Toure said an attacker had lunged at the president but wounded someone else. Jihadis were suspected. Two people were in custody. *Reuters* reported on July 25 that the man accused of the stabbing attempt died in a hospital while in the custody of the security services.

July 22, 2021: *Reuters* reported that French armed forces minister Florence Parly said that during an overnight operation, the French army killed two members of the EIGS, which has links to ISIS, in the Menaka region.

July 25, 2021: The U.N. peacekeeping mission's camp in Aguelhok in the Kidal region came under indirect fire, causing no injuries or damage. 21072501

July 26, 2021: A bomb hospitalized five U.N. peacekeepers in Aguelhok in the Kidal region. 21072601

August 8, 2021: *AP* and *Reuters* reported that at 6 p.m., self-identified jihadis attacked the villages of Ouatagouna, Karou, and Deouteguef along the borders of Mali, Niger, and Burkina Faso, killing 51 people, injuring several others, ransacking and burning homes, and stealing herds of livestock in apparent retribution for the recent arrest of several jihadi leaders who had been denounced by residents of the villages. No group took credit.

August 17, 2021: *AP, Reuters,* and *CNN* reported on September 15, 2021, that French President Emmanuel Macron tweeted that French forces had killed Adnan Abu Walid al-Sahrawi, variant Adnan Abou Walid al-Sahraoui, leader of the Islamic State in the Greater Sahara (ISIS-GS), in a drone strike in the Dangalous Forest on August 17. The drone hit a motorbike carrying two people during a French-led air and ground operation between August 17 and 22, according to French Minister for the Armed Forces Florence Parly. French authorities said the operation had backup from U.S., European Union, Malian, and Nigerien military forces. A French military team verified that 10 terrorists were killed.

Al-Sahrawi had claimed responsibility for the October 4, 2017 attack in Niger that killed four U.S. military personnel and four Nigerien soldiers. The group also had abducted foreigners in the Sahel and was believed to be holding American Jeffrey Woodke, who was kidnapped from his home in Niger in 2016, and a German hostage.

Al-Sahrawi was born in the Western Sahara and later joined the Polisario Front. After spending time in Algeria, he moved to northern Mali and became an important figure in the Malian al-Murabitun, a regional al-Qaeda affiliate, that controlled the major northern town of Gao in 2012. In 2015, he released an audio pledging al-

legiance to ISIS. The U.S. Department of State designated ISIS-GS a Foreign Terrorist Organization in 2018, and in 2019 offered $5 million for his capture. The French government accused him of "cowardly and particularly deadly" attacks targeting civilians and security forces in Niger, Mali, and Burkina Faso, and in August 2020 had "personally ordered" the killing of six French humanitarian workers and their driver and guide.

August 19, 2021: Gunmen ambushed a Malian army convoy heading from Douentza to Boni, killing 15 soldiers. Jihadis were suspected.

September 12, 2021: Morocco's *MAP* news agency and *Reuters* reported that masked gunmen wearing bulletproof vests killed two Moroccan truck drivers and injured a third 300 kilometers from Bamako. The attackers fled without stealing anything. 2091203

September 24, 2021: *Reuters* reported that a sniper killed French soldier Maxime Blasco in an early morning clash with gunmen in a forested area near the border with Burkina Faso. His French military unit's mission was to track down a suspected militant group that had earlier been spotted by a drone. The unit was supported by two attack helicopters and a surveillance drone. French forces killed the sniper. 21092401

October 2, 2021: A roadside bomb hit a U.N. convoy near Tessalit in Kidal region, killing an Egyptian peacekeeper and injuring four others. 21100201

October 6, 2021: Gunmen ambushed Malian army troops in the Mopti region between Koro and Bandiagara, destroying three army vehicles that hit roadside bombs, killing nine soldiers, and wounding 11 others. No group claimed credit.

October 30, 2021: *AFP* reported that a military pick-up truck hit a roadside bomb near Segou, killing five soldiers on patrol. Authorities arrested two suspects.

Earlier that day, two soldiers died and three were wounded in an attack near Mourdiah.

November 3, 2021: *AFP, Newsweek, AP,* and the *Washington Post* reported that French aid worker Sophie Petronin, 76, who was kidnapped by gunmen in December 2016 in Gao and held hostage along with leading Mali opposition figure Soumaila Cisse until October 2020, days after the Mali government freed hundreds of militants, had reentered Mali on her own initiative. She apparently had been in Mali since March 2021, entering illegally after her visa request was turned down. French radio said she could not adapt to life in a Swiss village following her release. French government spokesman Gabriel Attal called her action "a form of irresponsibility", compromising her security and that of French troops. He added, "When our citizens are taken hostage abroad, our soldiers go to save them, risking their lives... Some of our soldiers have died in operations to save hostages who were taken in foreign countries", and called for "respect for our soldiers". Petronin has an adopted daughter in Mali. Local authorities were searching for her in Sikasso.

November 22, 2021: *AFP* reported that on December 6, a MINUSMA soldier died from injuries inflicted by a roadside bomb near Tessalet on November 22. He had been rushed for treatment to Dakar, Senegal with two other injured troops. 21112201

November 25, 2021: International Criminal Court appeals judges reduced by two years the sentence of Ansar Eddine radical Ahmad al-Faqi al-Mahdi, a former teacher who pleaded guilty to overseeing the destruction of historic mausoleums in Timbuktu, Mali. He was sentenced to nine years in 2016 for the war crime of intentionally attacking buildings of a religious and historical character. He pleaded guilty for the destruction of nine mausoleums and a mosque door by pickax-wielding rebels in June-July 2012.

December 3, 2021: *Reuters* reported that gunmen fired on a U.N. peacekeeping mission's convoy traveling from Kidal to Gao near Bourem, killing a civilian worker and wounding another. The nationality of the victims was not disclosed. 21120301

    Reuters, CNN, and *AP* reported that gunmen fired on a truck ferrying 50 civilians from Songho to a market in Bandiagara, six miles away in the Mopti region, killing 31 and injuring many more. Most people were burned. Two people were missing.

December 8, 2021: *AP* and *AFP* reported that U.N. spokesman Stephane Dujarric said seven U.N. peacekeepers from Togo were killed and three critically injured when their vehicle hit an improvised explosive device in the Bandiagara area in the Mopti region. The peacekeepers were part of a U.N. logistics convoy traveling from Douentza to Sevare. 21120801

MAURITANIA

March 25, 2021: Authorities arrested a man who boarded an empty Mauritania Airlines plane sitting on the tarmac at Nouakchott's international airport and threatened to set it on fire. There were no passengers on board. The man was believed to be a foreigner residing in Mauritania. The government news agency said he had identified himself in English as an American who "had problems with Mauritania". 21032501

MOZAMBIQUE

January 1, 2021: *Bloomberg* reported that security forces fought off an attack by IS-affiliated jihadis on the village of Quitunda, within the area of Total SE's $20 billion liquefied natural gas concession area, known by its Portuguese acronym Duat.

March 11, 2021: *Upstream* reported that the U.S. Department of State designated the Mozambique-based al-Shabaab (no relation to the Somali al-Shabaab) as a terrorist group and placed its leader, Abu Yasir Hassan, a Tanzanian, on its terrorist watch list. The Department also placed ISIS-Democratic Republic of Congo (Islamic State Central Africa Province (ISCAP)) and its leader, Seka Musa Baluku, on its terrorist list. Listing freezes property and interests in the U.S. and prohibits Americans from engaging in transactions with listees.

    The State Department said ISIS-Mozambique uses the names Ansar al-Sunna, al-Shabaab, Ahl al-Sunna Wa al-Jamma, and Ansaar Kalimmat Allah. Hassan, alias Abu Qim, was thought to be aged between 38 and 40. He is based in both Cabo Delgado, Mozambique and the Pwani region on the coast of central Tanzania.

March 16, 2021: *AFP, Reuters,* and *AP* reported that the UK-based charity Save the Children said children as young as 11 had been beheaded by al-Shabaab jihadi insurgents in Cabo Delgado Province.

March 24, 2021: *AFP* and the *New York Times* reported that late in the afternoon, suspected al-Shabaab jihadis attacked a police checkpoint and residential neighborhoods in Palma, the hub of the $20 billion liquified natural gas (LNG) exploration project in Cabo Delgado Province. The *New York Times* reported on March 28 that 300 gunmen were involved in the attack, which killed several people and injured dozens. The terrorists surrounded four hotels known to house foreigners. A plane about to land in Afungi turned back due to a "heavy weapons attack". Human Rights Watch said gunmen indiscriminately shot civilians in their homes and on the streets. Seven international businesses, including French oil giant Total, Italy's Eni, and the American firm Exxon-Mobil, are involved in the project. *Mozambique News Reports and Clippings* reported that the defense ministry said the terrorists attacked from three directions.

AFP reported on March 26 that 180 people, including expatriate gas workers trapped for three days in the Amarula Palma Hotel, were evacuated during the night to Afungi peninsula. *Bloomberg* and *UPI* added that some died in a subsequent ambush of 17 military trucks taking 80 hotel residents to safety. Only seven vehicles reached the relative safety of the beach.

A South African government official said that one South African national had been killed.

AP reported on March 27 that the siege was continuing, with hundreds hiding in Quitunda, a village near the LNG project. *AFP* and *AP* reported on March 28 that more than 100 people, including numerous foreigners—South Africans, Britons, French, and American—were still missing as fighting continued. Some of the dead were beheaded. Total said none of its staff at the Afungi site were victims.

The *New York Times* added that in the initial attack, 100 terrorists split into two groups and walked into the Palma area. Once they had taken over the town, another 100 gunmen attacked villages en route, cutting off roads. The terrorists torched several government buildings and set off bombs at three banks and the town's health clinic. 21032402

April 7, 2021: *AFP* reported that President Filipe Nyusi announced that the government had retaken Palma from Islamic State-linked al-Shabaab terrorists, which had attacked the town since March 24. State television *TVM* said the terrorists had vandalized a hospital and torched banks and a prosecutor's office.

April 26, 2021: *AFP* reported that French energy firm Total confirmed that it had suspended work on the $20 billion gas project in the Afungi peninsula in the Cabo Delgado Province following the March 24 al-Shabaab assault on Palma that killed dozens.

June 9, 2021: *Al-Jazeera* reported that Save the Children had determined that terrorists had kidnapped 51 children, most of them girls, in 2020 in Cabo Delgado Province, citing reported cases collected by the Armed Conflict Location and Event Data Project. Victims were often subjected to sexual violence, early marriage, and becoming child soldiers.

August 9, 2021: Mozambican and Rwandan troops retook Mocimboa da Praia, a strategic port, from al-Shabaab jihadis who held the town in northern Mozambique for a year. Some 1,000 Rwandan troops deployed to Mozambique in July 2021.

September 25, 2021: Regional southern African forces killed 19 jihadis, including Awadhi Ndanjile, a religious leader instrumental in recruiting and indoctrinating members of the Ahlu Sunnah Wal Jama'a (ASWJ), during a raid on a terrorist base in the Nangade district of Cabo Delgado. *Reuters* and *Today Online* reported on October 4, 2021 that Mozambique President Filipe Nyusi, to mark Peace and National Reconciliation Day, called on jihadis in the north to surrender after allied Rwandan, Mozambican, and southern African forces pushed them out of territory, including the town of Mocimboa da Praia in Cabo Delgado, they had been occupying.

December 9, 2021: *AFP* reported that during the previous week, insurgents torched dozens of homes, beheaded one person, and shot to death two others in Cabo Delgado's Macomia district, according to residents. Resident Abudo Sitaupe that the terrorists shot to death an elderly woman, then threw her corpse into a burning building.

NIGER

January 2, 2021: *AFP* reported that at 11 a.m., terrorists on roughly 100 motorcycles killed more than 100 people in attacks on the Tchoma Bangou and Zaroumadareye villages in the western Tillaberi region, according to Almou Hassane, the mayor of the Tondikiwindi commune that administers both villages. "There were up to 70 dead in Tchoma Bangou and 30 dead in Zaroumadareye...There have also been 75 wounded, some of whom have been evacuated to Niamey and to Ouallam for treatment." Residents had killed two rebel fighters before being attacked. The Islamic State in the Greater Sahara was suspected.

February 21, 2021: Seven National Electoral Commission members died and three were severely injured when their car hit a roadside bomb in Gotheye in the Tillaberi region.

March 15, 2021: *AFP* and *al-Jazeera* reported that gunmen attacked a bus travelling to Chinedogar and nearby villages in the Banibangou area in the Tillaberi region near the border with Mali, killing 66 people. A local resident said 20 people were killed in the bus raid. A second resident said the victims had been shopping at Banibangou, a major market town. A security source added that gunmen then attacked villages at 6 p.m., killing more than 30 people. *Al-Jazeera* added that the terrorists then raided the village of Darey-Daye, killing inhabitants and torching grain stores.

March 21, 2021: *AP, AFP, Deutsche Welle, al-Jazeera,* and *Reuters* reported that gunmen on motorbikes killed 137 Tuaregs in the villages of Intazayene, Bakorat, and Wistane in the Tahoua region near the Malian border. A security source blamed the Islamic State affiliate. No one immediately claimed credit.

March 24, 2021: *AFP* reported that gunmen on motorbikes attacked three villages in Tillaberi, near the Malian border, at 5 a.m., killing 11 people. They killed three people at Zibane-Koira Zeno, one at Zibane Koira-Tegui, and seven in Gadabo. One person was wounded. They also stole animals, torched school classrooms, and looted a health center.

April 17, 2021: Gunmen on motorcycles fired on people praying at a mosque in Gaigorou village in the Tillaberi region during the evening, killing 19 people and wounding several others.

April 30, 2021: Soldiers intercepted suspected extremists who were preparing to attack Baibangou during the night. The Defense Ministry announced, "While in police custody, before being transported to Niamey, the suspected terrorists tried to escape around 4 a.m. and 24 of them were shot dead by the army."

May 1, 2021: In the evening, gunmen on motorcycles ambushed a military patrol near Niger's border with Mali, killing 16 Niger soldiers and wounding six. Another soldier was missing. The patrol was returning from a security mission in Tillia in the Tahoua area.

June 11-12, 2021: *Al-Jazeera* reported that during the night, two gunmen on a motorbike fired machine guns at the home of Seini Oumarou, 70, president of Niger's National Assembly, killing a guard and seriously wounding a second. Oumarou's National Movement for the Society of Development was in power between 1999 and 2010. Niger's interior ministry said that the two attackers failed to steal a 4×4 vehicle parked in front of the building. Oumarou placed third in the first round of the December 2020 presidential election, then supported eventual winner Mohamed Bazoum. In February 2021, protesters attacked Oumarou's home, shooting dead one of his bodyguards.

July 31, 2021: Jihadis attacked a military supply mission in the Torodi area of the Tillaberi region, killing 15 soldiers and injuring seven others who were transporting supplies to Boni. Six soldiers were missing.

August 11, 2021: *AFP* reported that Human Rights Watch said that more than 420 civilians were killed in jihadist attacks in western Niger in 2021.

August 14, 2015: *Al-Jazeera* reported that gunmen killed 37 civilians, including 14 children, in the Tillaberi region.

August 20, 2021: *Al-Jazeera* reported gunmen attacked the village of Theim in the Tillaberi region during Friday prayers, killing 16 people.

September 28, 2021: Gunmen attacked the Gatawa community.

October 17, 2021: *AFP* reported that during the night, jihadis on motorbikes attacked a border checkpoint at Petelkole in the Tillaberi region near the borders with Mali and Burkina Faso, killing three policemen, wounding seven others, burning two vehicles, and stealing weapons. The terrorists had tried to attack in the afternoon, but were repelled. In May 2017, gunmen killed two policemen and a civilian at the same post.

October 21, 2021: Gunmen on motorcycles fired rifles and rockets at a convoy 11 miles from Bankilare in Tillaberi region, killing six members of the national guard and destroying two military vehicles. The prefect of Bankilare and his bodyguard were not injured.

November 2, 2021: The *Washington Post* and *CNN* reported that suspected jihadis ambushed a self-defense brigade near Banibangou, killing 69 people, including the mayor, and wounding 15 members of the village defense group near the border with Mali. No group claimed credit.

November 4, 2021: *Al-Jazeera* reported that in the afternoon, gunmen in several vehicles and dozens of motorcycles ambushed a convoy of cars and motorbikes at Adab-Dab outside Dagne, clashed with soldiers on the village's outskirts, and killed 11 soldiers and injured one. Another nine soldiers went missing. No group claimed credit.

November 16, 2021: *AFP* and *AP* reported that jihadis were suspected of killing 25 civilians in a clash against a self-defense force in Bakorat in the Tahoua desert area near the border with

Mali. *Air Info* newspaper put the death toll at around 20 "young civilians", noting that a survivor claimed "The assailants arrived... aboard six 4x4s preceded by several motorbikes." No group claimed credit.

December 5, 2021: Extremist gunmen riding 100 motorcycles attacked the Fonion military camp near Tera in the Gorouel area near Niger's southeastern border with Burkina Faso, killing 12 soldiers. The Interior Ministry said dozens of terrorists were killed.

December 20, 2021: The French military announced that it had killed Soumana Boura, leader of dozens of fighters in the west of Niger, who was hiding north of the town of Tillabéri. He was believed to have been involved in the murder of six French humanitarian workers, their local driver, and a local guide in a wildlife reserve for endangered animals Niger in August 2020, which he filmed. The Islamic State in the Greater Sahara was suspected. He was also suspected of a separate attack that killed four U.S. soldiers in 2017.

NIGERIA

January 23, 2021: *AP* and *CNN* reported that gunmen kidnapped eight children and two adults, including a male staff member and a matron carrying a months-old baby at the Rachel's Orphanage Home in Abuja. Numerous gunmen broke into the home and grabbed the girls and boys, aged 10 and 13, according to Rachel Alajeshe, founder of the home. Board member Alaje Odewu said that the kidnappers threatened to "waste" the children if they did not receive a ransom of 10 million naira ($26,230). The kidnappers released the matron, baby, and another girl.

February 4, 2021: *AFP* reported that Nigerian troops backed by jets overran Islamic State West Africa Province (ISWAP) camps, including the Dole camp, in Yobe and Borno states in the northeast after a month-long military operation. Two senior commanders, Modu Sulum and Ameer Modu Borzogo, fled, possibly to the Lake Chad area, after several senior terrorists were killed. Troops rescued several hostages and seized dozens of vehicles.

In a second front, troops took over five camps from the jihadists in Kidari, Argude, Takwala, Chowalta, and Galdekore villages.

February 6-7, 2021: *AFP* reported that 19 people were killed when gunmen raided Birnin Gwari and Kajuru districts in Kaduna State.

February 9, 2021: *AFP* reported that Auwalun Daudawa, 43, a Nigerian criminal gang leader behind the kidnapping by dozens of gunmen of hundreds of schoolchildren from school hostels in Kankara in Katsina State in December, surrendered to authorities in an amnesty agreement. Six of his gang surrendered with him, turning over 20 Kalashnikov rifles and other weapons. Some 340 children were released within days. Boko Haram leader Abubakar Shekau claimed responsibility in a video showing some of the children in a bush. Jihadis had infiltrated some of Nigeria's criminal gangs. Security sources claimed Daudawa, at Shekau's behest, kidnapped the children by working with two bandits with a strong following. Daudawa had been fencing stolen government guns for Boko Haram.

Meanwhile, *CNN* reported that gunmen killed more than 23 people in simultaneous raids on Birnin Gwari, Giwa, Chikun, Igabi, and Kauru districts in Kaduna State.

February 14, 2021: Gunmen kidnapped 21 passengers from a Niger State Transport Authority bus and demanded a $1.3 million ransom. On February 16, Commissioner of Information in the State Mohammed Idris said the kidnappers had freed ten people. No ransom was paid.

February 17, 2021: In a 1:30 a.m. raid, gunmen attacked student hostels of the Government Science College, variant Secondary School, in Kagara in Niger State, killed one student by shooting him in the head, and abducted scores of students and teachers. The number of people taken increased as new reports filtered in during the day. The *Washington Post* initially reported that 20 students were taken; *AP* said it was 26 students and 16 staff and family members; *CNN* said 27 students were abducted; *AFP* and *CBS News* said hundreds of the 650 students at the

school were taken, citing a government source. Teacher Aliyu Isah said the gunmen, wearing military camouflage, tied up the students in pairs. Niger State governor Abubakar Sani Bello closed the state's schools, saying three teachers and 12 family members were also kidnapped. Bandits and Boko Haram were suspected. *AP* reported on February 27 that the chief press secretary for the Niger state governor, Mary Noel-Berje, announced that 42 people, including the 27 students, three teachers, and nine family members, had been freed.

February 22, 2021: *Al-Jazeera* reported that kidnappers freed 53 people, including 20 women and nine children, who had been taken from a state-owned bus in Kundu village in Niger State the previous week. State representatives had refused to pay a ransom. It was unknown if a ransom was paid. Gunmen the previous week killed 10 people and abducted 23 others in two other attacks in Niger State. Bandits were suspected.

February 23, 2021: *AP* reported that at 5:45 p.m., jihadis attacked two locations in the area of Maiduguri, killing 10 people (which soon escalated to 16) and injuring 60. *AFP* reported that Boko Haram claimed credit for firing rocket-propelled grenades that killed 16, including nine boys who were playing soccer, and injured dozens. BH leader Abubakar Shekau issued a six-minute video in which he said, "We heard that our brothers carried out an attack on Tuesday in Maiduguri... We are happy. News has reached me our boys carried out the attack."

February 24, 2021: *CNN* reported that gunmen killed 36 people in two attacks. The terrorists hit Kaduna and Katsina States, killing 18 people in each location, injuring several others, and burning down homes.

February 26, 2021: The *Washington Post, UPI, CNN,* and *Reuters* reported that gunmen driving pickup trucks and 20 motorcycles attacked the Government Girls Science Secondary School in Jangebe in Zamfara State at 1:45 a.m., kidnapping 317 schoolgirls from their hostels and killing a police officer. The terrorists left with their hostages around 3 a.m., forcing them to walk into the forest. No one claimed credit, although ransom-seeking bandits and Boko Haram's factions were suspected. A resident said the gunmen also attacked a nearby military camp and checkpoint four miles away, preventing soldiers from responding. *CNN* reported that 500 students are normally at the boarding school.

NBC News, CNN, AFP, UPI, Reuters, and *AP* reported on March 2, 2021 that Zamfara state governor Bello Matawalle tweeted that all 279 girls dressed in light blue hijabs and barefoot had been freed. *Reuters* said some victims, including Umma Abubakar, told how their abductors had beaten and threatened to shoot them. She recalled, "Most of us got injured on our feet and we could not continue trekking, so they said they will shoot anybody who did not continue to walk." Farida Lawali, 15, said, "They carried the sick ones that cannot move. We were walking in the stones and thorns... They started hitting us with guns so that we could move. While they were beating them with guns, some of them were crying and moving at the same time."

Matawalle said "repentant bandits" working with the government under an amnesty program had helped secure the girls' release. Matawalle's special media adviser, Zailani Bappa, said Zamfara authorities had paid no ransom. Zamfara government spokesman Sulaiman Tanau Anka said the total was 279, not 317, because some of the girls had fled into the bush. Authorities sent a dozen freed girls to the hospital.

Lawal Abdullahi, father of seven kidnapped daughters, said "It's a ploy to deny our girls ... from getting the Western education in which we are far behind... We should not succumb to blackmail. My advice to government is that they should take immediate precautions to stop further abductions."

CNN reported on April 26, 2021 that Habiba Iliyasu, 15, was one of the 279 schoolgirls who were kidnapped from their Government Girls' Secondary School dormitory beds in Jangebe in Zamfara State by gunmen on motorbikes. The gunmen forced them to walk into the forest to their camp, where Habiba found that her farmer father, Iliyasu Magaji, 65, and her mother Rukkaya Iliyasu, 58, had been taken. She later also found her sister, Raliya Gusaram, 33, and Raliya's two children Isah, 4, and Rabiatu, 2. The kid-

nappers demanded a ransom of 10 million naira (about $26,000). The gunmen freed Habiba and her schoolmates after three days.

The Nigeria Security Tracker (NST) reported that as of April 26, there had been more than 200 kidnappings, many of them nonpolitical, involving 2,043 victims, compared to 437 kidnappings involving 2,879 victims in 2020.

March 1, 2021: Late in the night, Islamic State of West Africa Province jihadis arrived in trucks and motorcycles to attack the northeastern town of Dikwa and humanitarian posts there. The member representing Dikwa at the Borno State House of Assembly, Zakariya Dikwa, said they burned down the police station and the primary health center, attacked humanitarian offices, and stole their vehicles. He claimed, "The attack was massive because the Boko Haram fighters went there with over 13 gun trucks — all of which had their bodies pasted with mud." *AFP* reported on March 4 that the Nigeria INGO Forum said that six civilians died and six were injured in the attack which "directly targeted" aid facilities. The Forum said the terrorists torched the hospital.

March 11-12, 2021: *CNN, UPI, Reuters, NBC News,* and *AP* reported that gunmen attacked the Federal College of Forestry Mechanization, Mando, Kaduna (also identified as the Federal College of Forestry Mechanization, Afaka, in the Igabi local government area of Kaduna State) between 11:30 p.m. and 3 a.m., opened fire, and kidnapped 39 students. Jamilu Abdullahi, a student at the college, said the armed men ran to the female hostel, even though the male dormitory is nearer the fence where they came in. Samuel Aruwan, Commissioner for Kaduna State Ministry of Internal Security and Home Affairs, said 23 females and 16 males were kidnapped; an indeterminate number of staff were also kidnapped. Aruwan said the military fought the attackers and brought 180 staff and students to safety. Several students were injured.

Reuters reported on March 14 that on March 13, the gunmen released a video of the kidnapped students being beaten with sticks while begging for help in English and Hausa. One said the captors demanded a 500 million naira ($1.31 million) ransom. He added, "If anybody comes to rescue them without the money they are going to kill us." Gloria Paul recognized her daughter, Joy Kurmi Paul, 20, in the video. Ibrahim Shamaki, a father of one of the kidnapped students, died of shock.

AFP reported on April 5 that Nigerian soldiers found five of the kidnapped students.

Reuters, AFP, and *al-Jazeera* reported on May 5, 2021 that the kidnappers released the remaining 29 college students. One female student could not walk unaided and was carried into the building; another was taken to a hospital. Abdullahi Usman, chairman of the parents' association, said a ransom was paid.

March 13, 2021: *Reuters* reported that during the night, would-be kidnappers attacked another school and senior staff quarters in Ifira village in the Igabi local government area of a local government office near Kaduna airport in Kaduna State. All 307 students at the Government Science Secondary School in Ikara were accounted for.

March 15, 2021: *Reuters* reported that gunmen kidnapped primary school pupils and teachers in the Birnin Gwari local government area in Kaduna State. Local resident Sarkin Mota said his son and three of his teachers were kidnapped. *Deutsche Welle* reported the next day that Kaduna State Security Commissioner Samuel Aruwan said "three teachers, Rabiu Salisu, Umar Hassan, and Bala Adamu have been kidnapped". Aruwan said that two pupils originally feared kidnapped "took to their heels in the course of the commotion, as the bandits invaded the premises on motorcycles… No single pupil was kidnapped from the school. Other than the three teachers previously mentioned, no staff or pupil of the school is missing following the attack."

March 31, 2021: Boko Haram released a seven-minute video saying that it shot down a Nigerian Air Force fighter jet on a mission to support ground troops in Borno State. A Hausa-speaking Boko Haram fighter said that the video showed the remains of the alleged pilot. The Nigerian Air Force NAF 475 inscription on the plane matched the registration number of the Alpha-Jet which the Air Force said went missing during combat. Air Force spokesman Air Commodore Edward Gabkwet said the plane lost contact with radar in Borno State "while on interdiction mission in support of ground troops". The Air Force said the plane had two crew members—Flight Lieutenants John Abolarinwa and Ebiakpo Chapele. *CNN* determined on April 3 that the video was a hoax, noting that a smoke trail and the shape and color of the explosion's fireball were identical to a mid-air explosion of a helicopter over Ma'arrat al-Nu'man, Syria, near Idlib, in 2012. The video was not rebroadcast by official ISIS outlets. *CNN* added that BH does not have ground-to-air missiles that could down a fast-flying jet at altitude.

April 5, 2021: *AFP, AP,* and *CBS News* reported that at 2 a.m., gunmen armed with machine guns and rocket-propelled grenades attacked Owerri in Imo State in southeastern Nigeria, freeing 1,844 inmates at the local prison in a two-hour gun battle. Gunmen also assaulted police and military buildings. Nigeria prison spokesman Francis Enobore said that 35 inmates stayed behind during the prison break. Police said they repelled a raid on the armory at police headquarters. There was no immediate claim of credit. Indigenous People of Biafra (IPOB) separatist movement spokesman Emmanuel Powerful denied involvement. President Muhammadu Buhari blamed "anarchists" for an "act of terrorism". The inspector general of police blamed a paramilitary wing of the Eastern Security Network secessionist movement, which claims it is fighting for the protection of the Igbo people from foreign armed invaders.

April 10, 2021: IS-affiliated jihadis were suspected of attacking and torching the offices of several international aid groups in Damasak during the night. The Norwegian Refugee Council said its five staffers were unharmed, but the group destroyed relief supplies, vehicles, and the guest house. The gunmen stole an ambulance and drugs from a hospital. 21041001

April 14, 2021: *AFP* reported that the Islamic State West Africa Province (ISWAP) attacked Damasak in Borno State, killing eight people and wounding 12. Another 8,000 fled across the border into Chetimari and Gagamari in neighboring Niger. UNHCR's Protection Desk reported that the gunmen burned down several buildings, including a police station, a clinic, and residences of local dignitaries. *AP* reported that UNHCR spokesman Babar Baloch in Geneva added that "Assailants looted and burned down private homes, warehouses of humanitarian agencies, a police station, a clinic, and also a UNHCR facility." Terrorists in several trucks fitted with machine guns fired on troops outside the military base in an attempt to overrun it. *AP* reported that by April 16, nearly 65,000 refugees had fled their homes, including 80% of the population of Damasak. 21041403

It was the fourth assault on the town since April 10. The terrorists had also attacked the town on April 11 and 13, destroying humanitarian facilities and killing four people, including a soldier. On April 13, they burned a divisional police station after a failed attempt to raid the base.

April 20, 2021: *AFP* and *Reuters* reported that gunmen attacked the private Greenfield University in Kaduna State, killing a staff member and kidnapping some students at 8:15 p.m. Twenty students and three staff members were reported missing; some may have fled. A university staffer said 17 male students were kidnapped. *AFP* noted on April 23 that Samuel Aruwan, Kaduna State's internal security and home affairs commissioner, announced that the captors shot to death three of their kidnapped students. *CNN* reported on April 27 that the kidnappers killed two more students.

AP and *Reuters* reported on May 29 that kidnappers released 14 students and staff. One person was killed during the kidnapping. Commissioner Aruwan announced that the 14 were found released along the Kaduna-Abuja road at 2 p.m. The gunmen had demanded hundreds of thousands of dollars in ransom and had executed five other students. Aruwan did not say whether any ransom was paid. Local newspapers said that parents were negotiating a ransom.

April 21, 2021: *AFP* reported that Nigerian President Muhammadu Buhari condemned the killing of "tens" of villagers in Magami district in northwestern Zamfara State. Local residents said

60 people could have been killed in the attacks on 13 villages by motorcycle-riding gunmen, but only nine bodies had been recovered. Another 51 people were missing and feared dead. The gunmen also looted food supplies and burned homes in Kangon Farimana, Ruwan Dawa, Madaba, Arzikin Da, Mairvairai, Gidan Maza, Unguwa Malam, and Katohin.

April 27, 2021: *CNN* reported that Niger State Governor Abubakar Bello said that Boko Haram raised its flag in Geidam in Yobe State, and in a remote district around Kaure in Shiroro Local Government Area in Niger State, in Nigeria's Middle Belt region, and kidnapped the wives of fleeing residents "and forcefully attached to Boko Haram members".

April 29, 2021: *AFP* reported that Nigerian bandit chief Awwalun Daudawa, 43, who orchestrated the December 2020 abduction of more than 500 students from Government Science Secondary School in northwestern Kankara State, had reneged on an amnesty deal with the government and returned to crime. He had surrendered to authorities in February 2020. Boko Haram had claimed credit for the attack. Security sources said Daudawa acted on Boko Haram leader Shekau's orders in collaboration with local bandits Idi Minorti and Dankarami. *AFP* added that on April 30, he and four of his commanders died in an afternoon clash while trying to steal the herd of a rival gang in Dumburum forest on the border with Katsina State.

May 6, 2021: Authorities blamed the banned separatist Indigenous People of Biafra (IPOB) when gunmen killed two police officers during an attack on a police station in Anambra State.

May 7, 2021: Gunmen driving a Toyota Hilux van attacked a checkpoint at Choba Bridge in the oil-rich Rivers State at 8:30 p.m., then drove to two police stations, killing seven officers and burning patrol cars. Police killed two attackers. The gunmen killed two officers at the checkpoint, then killed two more officers and set fire to a patrol car at Rumuji police station. Police shot two attackers. The remaining gunmen then killed three more officers at the Elimgbu police station.

May 10, 2021: *AFP* reported that at 1 a.m., gunmen kidnapped 10 worshippers from a mosque in Jibya in Katsina State near Nigeria's northwestern border with Niger. Security forces rescued 37 others during an overnight vigil during Ramadan. State police spokesman Gambo Isa said that the kidnappers were believed to have come from Dumburum forest in neighboring Zamfara State where they maintain camps.

May 19, 2021: *AFP* reported that Boko Haram (Jama'tu Ahlis Sunna Lidda'awati wal-Jihad) leader Abubakar Shekau was seriously wounded after attempting suicide to avoid surrendering to ISIS-affiliated Islamic State in West Africa Province (ISWAP) terrorists during clashes in Borno State's Sambisa forest. He reportedly shot himself in the chest; the bullet pierced his shoulder. Another source said he set off explosives in his safehouse.

On June 6, *Reuters* reported that ISWAP leader Abu Musab al-Barnawi said on an audio recording that Shekau died around May 18 after detonating an explosive device when he was pursued by ISWAP fighters. "Shekau preferred to be humiliated in the afterlife than getting humiliated on earth, and he killed himself instantly by detonating an explosive."

May 30, 2021: *AP, Reuters, BBC, This Day,* and the independent *Channels TV* reported that gunmen on motorcycles kidnapped some 200 students, some only five years old, at the Salihu Tanko Islamic School in Tegina in the local government area of Rafi in Niger State. One person was killed and one injured by gunfire. People traveling in a car were also abducted.

On July 25, *Reuters* reported that bandits took hostage a male negotiator, 60, who had been sent to pay ransom money to secure the release of 136 students kidnapped on May 30. The kidnappers had demanded a 30 million naira ($72,993) ransom. The school contributed to the ransom and some parents sold property to raise cash. The kidnappers said the ransom he brought was short. Among the parents was Ibrahim Salihu, father of two of the children.

AP reported on August 26 that head teacher Abubakar Garba Alhassan announced that gunmen had released dozens of hostages, who were on their way to Minna, the state capital. The *Washington Post* reported on August 27 that 90 children were reunited with their parents. One of the children died during the ordeal and four others were given medical treatment. Authorities initially said 136 students were kidnapped but lowered it to 91.

Abubakar Alhassan said a ransom of more than 30 million naira (about $73,000) was paid to secure the children's release. Families came up with most of the money, and the school raised some cash by selling a plot of land where they had planned to expand the campus.

June 3, 2021: *AFP* reported that dozens of cattle thieves on motorcycles attacked the seven villages of Koro, Kimpi, Gaya, Dimi, Zutu, Rafin Gora, and Iguenge in Danko-Wasagu district in Kebbi State, killing 88 people. Many people fled and remained missing. The attackers were believed to have camps in neighboring Zamfara and Niger States.

June 8, 2021: *AFP, Al-Jazeera, BBC, Reuters,* and *AP* reported on July 21 that kidnappers released 100 hostages, including nursing mothers and children, they had abducted from Manawa village in Zamfara State on June 8. Four people died during the capture. Police spokesman Mohammed Shehu said the government "successfully secured the unconditional release of the victims…without giving any financial or material gain" to the bandits. The hostages were kept in a forest hideout. Negotiators had assured the kidnappers that no action would be taken against them.

June 10, 2021: *AP* and *AFP* reported that Kaduna State Commissioner for Internal Security and Home Affairs Samuel Aruwan said gunmen kidnapped eight students and two lecturers during the night at the government-owned Nuhu Bamalli Polytechnic in Zaria in Kaduna State. One student was fatally shot and another was wounded. The gunmen also kidnapped the wife and two children of one of the staff members, but released them soon after. *Reuters* reported that in the evening of July 8, six students and two officials were released after relatives paid a ransom.

June 10-11, 2021: *Al-Jazeera* and *AFP* reported that motorcycle-riding gunmen killed 53 people in overnight raids on the villages of Kadawa, Kwata, Maduba, Ganda Samu, Saulawa, and Askawa in the Zurmi district of Zamfara State.

June 18, 2021: *Reuters* reported that gunmen killed a police officer, shot a student, and kidnapped 94 students, most of them girls, and eight staff, including five teachers, from a federal government college in Birnin Yauri in Kebbi State. Security forces were searching a nearby forest. One kidnapped female student was later found dead. Authorities rescued five students and two teachers. Troops also recovered 800 stolen cattle. By June 20, two girls and a boy were found dead, two with gunshot wounds in their legs. Nine abductees had escaped or been rescued. The kidnappers used the students' phones to demand a 60 million naira ($146,341) ransom from the parents. *ABC News* and *AP* reported on October 22, 2021 that 30 more Federal Government College students had been released, but dozens remained hostage in Kebbi State.

July 4, 2021: *Reuters* reported that in the early morning, gunmen kidnapped eight people from the National Tuberculosis and Leprosy Centre hospital's staff residential quarters in Zaria in Kaduna State, while terrorists were attacking a nearby divisional police station. Hostages included two nurses, one with her one-year-old child, a laboratory technician, a security guard, and one other staff member. Police at the station injured some of the attackers and recovered dozens of shell casings from rifles and machine guns.

July 5, 2021: *CBS News*, the *Washington Post*, *BBC*, and *AFP* reported that around 2 a.m., gunmen scaled a fence, killed two security guards, and kidnapped 121 students from the Bethel Baptist High School, a co-education boarding college established in 1991 at Maramara village in Chikun district outside Kaduna. Another 28 students and one female teacher escaped. Meanwhile, gunmen attacked a nearby divisional police station. Authorities repelled the attackers and collected spent shell casings. *AFP* added on July 7 that the kidnappers demanded food—rice, beans, oil, and seasoning—for their captives. *AP*

reported on July 7 that the kidnappers had contacted the Reverend Ishaya Jangado, head of the Kaduna Baptist Conference that manages the school. He talked with some hostages. *Reuters* reported on July 25 that Reverend Ite Joseph Hayab, who was involved in negotiations for the hostages, announced that the kidnappers released 28 children. Another 81, including the daughter of Radika Bivan, remained in captivity. *Reuters* reported on August 3 that the kidnappers were demanding a one million naira ($1 = 411.00 naira) ransom for each child. Hayab said three students escaped before the 28 were released in July but they were kidnapped again by an unidentified person in the forest who demanded a ransom and was paid over one million naira by parents. *Reuters* reported on August 22, 2021 that the bandits had released another 15 students after parents paid a ransom. *AP* reported on September 23, 2021 that Nigerian police arrested three "key suspects". All but 21 hostages had been released as of the report, including 10 freed the previous week. Police spokesperson Frank Mba said that one assault rifle was recovered from each of the suspects. *AP* reported on September 26 that gunmen freed another 10 students that afternoon after collecting a ransom. Eleven remained hostage. *Reuters* reported on October 9, 2021 that five students, among the 150 who were kidnapped from the Bethel Baptist High School, were released after ransoms were paid.

July 7, 2021: *Reuters* reported that jihadis were suspected when gunmen on motorcycles killed 18 people and injured others in a 5 a.m. raid in Dabna near the administrative area of Hong in Adamawa State. The terrorists torched two churches and a house.

AFP reported that bandits killed 18 people in Tsauwa in Katsina State.

July 8, 2021: *Reuters* reported that jihadis were suspected when gunmen on more than 100 motorbikes killed 45 people in Faru in northwest Nigeria around noon. Another 11 people were hospitalized.

AFP said motorcycle-riding attackers killed 35 people in Gidan Adamu, Tsauni, Gidan Baushi, Gidan Maidawa, and Wari villages in Maradun district in Zamfara State. Local residents said the death toll was 43 with seven injured in the late night attacks.

July 11, 2021: *AFP* reported that gunmen raided the palace of Alhassan Adamu, 83, emir of Kajuru, outside Kaduna, kidnapping him and 13 other family members, including women and children. The "bandits" soon released him but demanded a ransom for the family.

July 17, 2021: *Thomson-Reuters Foundation* reported that during the night gunmen on 70 motorbikes kidnapped 60 people in five villages in the Shinkafi area of Zamfara State in northwestern Nigeria. The bandits fired a rocket that hit the house of the senior district head of the local council. Each motorbike carried three gunmen, according to Junaidu Badarawa, one of five hostages who were freed.

July 19, 2021: *AFP* reported that "heavily-armed criminals" shot down an Air Force Alpha light attack fighter jet in Zamfara State. The pilot safely ejected and evaded capture, eventually getting to a military base. The plane was made by a Franco-German consortium in the 1970s and 1980s.

Meanwhile, gunmen ambushed and killed 13 policemen as they deployed to protect a village in Zamfara State from imminent attack.

August 7, 2021: *AP* and *Reuters* reported that Ogun State police spokesman Abimbola Oyeyemi said gunmen kidnapped a Swiss man and his Nigerian driver. Police shot to death two kidnappers. 21080701

August 9, 2021: *Reuters* reported that during the night, gunmen kidnapped Mohammed Sani Idris, a member of the state government in northern Niger State, from his home in Baban Tunga.

August 9, 2021: Military spokesperson Onyema Nwachukwu announced that 335 Boko Haram terrorists, including two top commanders—the group's chief bomb expert and his deputy—had laid down their arms and withdrawn from the sect. He displayed photos of the men holding placards asking for forgiveness. Hundreds of women and children from the terrorists' families also surrendered.

August 14, 2021: *Reuters* reported that gunmen ambushed people riding buses returning from a Muslim festival in Bauchi State, killing 23 on Rukuba road in Jos North in Plateau State. Authorities arrested 20 suspects.

Bombs left on a bridge killed three children, critically injured three children, and mildly injured another two in Borno State.

August 15, 2021: *Reuters* reported that during the night, gunmen fired on guards, killing a police officer and two guards, then abducted 15 students and four staff members from the College of Agriculture and Animal Science in Bakura in Zamfara State. Authorities rescued three staff members. Local media reported on August 18 that the kidnappers demanded a ransom of more than $850,000. On August 27, police spokesperson Mohammed Shehu said that 15 students had been handed over to officials.

August 16, 2021: *Reuters* reported that gunmen attacked a project site of the Lee Engineering oil and gas services company in Assa in Imo State, killing six employees and a police officer.

August 19, 2021: Police spokesman Isah Gambo said that earlier in the week, gunmen on motorcycles abducted nine students on their way home from an Islamic school in Katsina State.

August 24, 2021: *ABC News, AFP,* and *AP* reported that gunmen attacked the Nigerian Defense Academy, the country's main officer training school, in Kaduna State in the morning, killing a lieutenant commander and a lieutenant, wounding another officer, and abducting a major. No one claimed credit.

CNN reported that during the night, terrorists attacked a village near Jos in Plateau State, killing 36 people and destroying buildings. Plateau State Governor Simon Lalong said security forces had arrested 10 suspects and were pursuing others. A local resident said the attackers were Fulanis from a nearby area involved in a feud with the Yelwa Zangam community.

August 27, 2021: Authorities in northern Nigeria announced three separate groups of kidnapped students were freed within a 24-hour period.

September 1, 2021: *Reuters* reported that numerous children were believed kidnapped from the Government Day Secondary School in the Maradun Local Government District in Kaya in Zamfara State. A staffer said 500 students were enrolled at the school. *AP* and *UPI* put the number of kidnapped students at 73. A former local council member told *Punch* that four of his daughters were taken. *CNN* reported Zamfara's Information Commissioner, Ibrahim Dosara, announced that primary and secondary schools in Zamfara State were ordered closed. *AP* and *Reuters* reported on September 2 that authorities had rescued five female students. *Reuters* reported that UNICEF claimed that 100 students aged between 14 and 19 and a teacher were kidnapped, of whom 23 had escaped and returned home. Two of the escapees had been shot. *Reuters* and *AP* reported on September 13 that 75 children were released after their abductors came under pressure from a military crackdown. No ransom was paid. The government said some repentant kidnappers assisted with the rescue.

September 2, 2021: Army spokesman Bernard Onyeuko announced that nearly 6,000 jihadis had surrendered in the country's northeast in recent weeks.

September 9, 2021: Army spokesman Onyema Nwachukwu announced the arrest of senior Boko Haram member Yawi Modu along the Damboa-Wajiroko road in northern Borno State. In two raids in the area, authorities seized homemade bombs and 251 bags of Urea fertilizer used to make bombs. The sites were believed to have been used by Boko Haram and the Islamic State in West Africa Province (ISWAP).

September 11, 2021: *AFP* reported gunmen killed 12 Nigerian security forces at a military base in Mutumji in Zamfara State, stole weapons, and torched buildings.

September 12-13, 2021: *Newsweek, CNN,* and *Vanguard* reported that at 11:45 p.m. on September 12 and extending into the next morning, tens of gunmen fired on soldiers and freed 240 inmates from a medium-security federal correction center on the Lokoja highway in Kabba in Kogi State. A soldier and a policeman were killed while guarding the perimeter. The gunmen used explosives to destroy three sides of the perimeter fence. Local media outlets claimed that 100 of the escapees were recaptured.

September 16, 2021: *AFP* reported that ISWAP terrorists ambushed a patrol on a highway in Borno State, killing 16 Nigerian soldiers and two anti-jihadist Civilian JTF militia, wounding 11 troops, and destroying several military vehicles. The terrorists set off seven roadside bombs, fired rocket-propelled grenades and heavy weapons on the convoy traveling between Maiduguri and Monguno, a garrison town, then took two soldiers hostage. ISWAP claimed it had killed 25 troops.

September 26, 2021: *AP, al-Jazeera,* and *AFP* reported that terrorists armed with guns and machetes killed between 34 and 37 people in the evening in Madamai village in the Kaura council area in Kaduna State as part of an ongoing religious crisis between northern Hausa-Fulani residents and southern Christians. Authorities questioned two suspects.

September 27, 2021: *Reuters* and *Premium Times NG* reported that Nigerian troops in Operation Hadarin Daji killed scores of ISWAP terrorists and bandits in Sokoto State and suffered casualties in clashes. The terrorists had attacked the Forward Operation Base (FOB) at Burkusuma, a remote border settlement with the Niger Republic in the Sabon Birni Local Government Area of Sokoto State.

September 27-28, 2021: *AFP* reported that Boko Haram gunmen in speed boats attacked an ISWAP hideout on the Nigerian side of Lake Chad, leaving more than 100 dead and seizing the strategic Kirta Wulgo island after a nine-hour gun battle. Boko Haram drew its fighters from camps in Gegime and Kwatar Mota on the Niger side of the lake and Kaiga-Kindjiria on the Chadian side. After mustering at Tumbun Ali island on the Nigerian side of the lake, they overran six ISWAP checkpoints before hitting Kirta Wulgo.

Bakoura Buduma had led Boko Haram since the death of Abubakar Shekau. The group fled Shekau and regrouped in Niger's Gegime-Bosso axis of Lake Chad. ISWAP still had strongholds in Sabon Tumbu (where ISWAP leader Abu Musab al-Barnawi has his base), Jibillaram, and Kwalleram. Al-Barnawi's deputy lives in Jibillaram. Other senior ISWAP commanders reside in Sigir and Kusuma islands close to Kirta Wulgo.

September 28, 2021: At 2 a.m., gunmen attacked Kachiwe in the Muya local government area in Niger State, killing 14 people and abducting seven women.

The gunmen then attacked two other nearby communities, killing two on the way and 16 people in the villages.

Gunmen abducted 17 people from their homes in the Sabon Birni local government area in Sokoto State.

October 2, 2021: *Reuters* and the *African Mirror* reported that gunmen fired on a public transport vehicle, killing passenger Mohammad Hassan, 37, a nurse employed by Doctors Without Borders in Shinkafi in Zamfara State. Medecins Sans Frontieres run a 33-bed therapeutic feeding center and in-patient pediatric department at the local general hospital in Shinkafi.

October 5, 2021: *Reuters* reported that at 9 p.m., dozens of gunmen on motorbikes killed 18 people and torched cars and shops in Kuryan Madaro in Zamfara State.

October 7, 2021: Zamfara police spokesperson Mohammed Shehu announced that Nigerian security forces had rescued 187 hostages, including babies, from a forest in Zamfara State, where they had been held for several weeks. No ransom was paid.

October 9, 2021: *Reuters* reported that gunmen on motorcycles attacked a market and torched nine cars in Sokoto State, killing 20 people.

October 11, 2021: During the night, gunmen kidnapped five student priests from the Catholic Christ The King Major Seminary in the St. Albert Institute For Higher Education in Kaduna State. Rev. Joseph Hayab, chairman of the Kaduna State chapter of the Christian Association of Nigeria, said the gunmen opened fire at the cafeteria where five of the students were sitting after dinner. The gunmen soon released two of the seminarians. Six seminarians were injured. The three hostages were in their fourth and final year of classes before becoming priests.

October 12, 2021: Six women and nine children who had been kidnapped in two separate incidents in October 2020 and May 2021 by Boko Haram in Borno and Adamawa States escaped by walking six days through the Buni Yadi forest to freedom in Borno State.

October 14, 2021: Gen. Lucky Irabor, Nigeria's chief of defense staff, claimed that Abu Musab al-Barnawi, the leader of ISWAP, had died. Al-Barnawi's father, Mohammad Yusuf, had founded Boko Haram.

October 17, 2021: *Reuters, AFP,* and *AP* reported that in a nighttime attack, gunmen killed 40 people at a market in the Goronyo community in Sokoto State.

October 22, 2021—Nigeria—*AP* and *al-Jazeera* reported that Nigerian national security adviser Babagana Monguno announced that earlier in the week, Nigerian security forces killed Malam Bako, who recently succeeded Abu Musab al-Barnawi as leader of ISWAP.

In a nighttime attack, gunmen freed 575 inmates from Oyo correction center in Oyo State.

October 25, 2021: Gunmen believed to be Fulani nomadic herders attacked a mosque in Mazakuka village in the Mashegu local government area of Niger State, killing 18 and wounding four worshippers during early morning prayers. The gunmen escaped.

November 2, 2021: In the morning, gunmen kidnapped four staffers and two of their children from the University of Abuja. Geoffrey Nwaka, a soil science professor who lives close to campus, observed, "The gunshots lasted from after midnight until 2 a.m… It's not secure at all. Our security guards don't have enough weapons to defend the area. Nobody is safe." One captive is a prominent economics professor.

November 8, 2021: Gunmen ambushed police officers on patrol in a vehicle along the Magami road in Zamfara State, killing seven officers.

November 9, 2021: Gunmen invaded the Katoge and Yanturaku quarters of Batsari local government area in Katsina State during the night, firing AK-47s and killing 11 people.

November 10, 2021: Some 40 gunmen on motorcycles invaded two villages in the Karim Lamido local government area of Taraba State in the morning and fired at residents in an apparent reprisal after two herdsmen were allegedly killed. The Abuja-based *Daily Trust* newspaper reported 15 killed.

November 13, 2021: *Reuters* reported that Army spokesman Brigadier General Onyema Nwachukwu said that in the morning, ISWAP in 12 gun trucks attacked armed forces in Borno State's Askira Uba local government area, killing army Brigadier General Dzarma Zirkusu and three soldiers, burning houses, shops, and a school and forcing residents to flee.

ISWAP also attacked troops near Maiduguri.

November 14-15, 2021: Overnight, gunmen attacked communities in Sokoto State, killing 15 people. Thirteen died in Illela, a town near the border with Niger. Two died in Goronyo.

November 25, 2021: The office of Nigeria's attorney-general, Abubakar Malami, announced the a court designated armed groups blamed for hundreds of abductions and killings in northern areas as terrorist organizations. Authorities can now charge suspected members of the groups with terrorism-related offences.

December 7, 2021: *Reuters* reported that gunmen torched a bus in Sokoto State, on a road linking the Sabon Birni local government area and the village of Gidan Bawa in Borno State, burning to death 30 passengers, including women and children. Sanusi Abubakar, spokesman for the Borno state police, said the bus was carrying 24 passengers and that seven people had escaped with injuries. Local residents at the scene said the overloaded bus carried more people.

December 9, 2021: Local government chairman Alhassan Isah Mazakuka said dozens of gunmen on motorcycles conducted an hours-long attack on Ba'are village in the Mashegu area of Niger State, killing 16 worshippers at a mosque and kidnapping others.

December 17, 2021: Gunmen killed nine people in three villages in Kaduna State. No one claimed credit.

December 19, 2021: Gunmen killed 38 people and burned houses, trucks, cars, and agricultural produce at some farms in Kaduna State. No one claimed credit.

December 23, 2021: *Reuters* and *India News Republic* reported that five people were killed and 15 were injured after several explosions near an air force base in Maiduguri, capital of Borno State. Four people died in the Gomalia Yafe district of Maiduguri, hundreds of meters from the air force base. Three houses were severely damaged. Residents suspected Islamic extremists.

December 30, 2021: *Reuters* reported that earlier in the month, Islamic State West Africa Province (ISWAP) gunmen killed six Multinational Joint Task Force (MTJF) troops, including two officers, from Nigeria and Niger, and wounded 16 during an operation in Borno State near the Lake Chad basin. The Nigerian military said 22 terrorists were killed, 17 others were captured, and gun trucks and other weapons and ammunition were destroyed. The gunmen fired mortars and set off bombs. 21129901

SOMALIA

January 7, 2021: *UPI* reported that a joint U.S.-Somali air strike in the area of Saaxa Weyne killed five suspected al-Shabaab members, including one leader. U.S. Africa Command said that no civilians were harmed. U.S. Air Force Maj. Gen. Dagvin Anderson, Joint Task Force - Quartz commander said, "This strike targeted known al-Shabaab leaders who facilitated finance, weapons, fighters, and explosives. One is suspected of being involved in a previous attack against U.S. and Somali forces."

During the previous week, two airstrikes killed three al-Shabaab members and destroyed six buildings in their compound.

January 31, 2021: *AFP, AP,* and *Reuters* reported that a car bomb hit the entrance gate of the Afrik Hotel near Mogadishu's K-4 junction during the afternoon. Al-Shabaab terrorists then ran in, shooting at staff and patrons. Five civilians were killed and 15 people were hospitalized. Well-known retired Army General Mohamed Nur Galal, 80, was killed; al-Shabaab said he was the main target, observing "Galal was trained and committed for so long in the fight against sharia law, while using his knowledge and military intelligence experience to fight mujahidin." Police rescued more than 100 people, including the hotel's owner and another army general. Al-Shabaab's radio *al-Andalus* said, "A martyrdom operation by the mujahideen goes on at Hotel Afrik, which is a cover-up for officials from the apostate government." Fighting ended around midnight after eight hours. The four terrorists died; one set off a suicide bomb, the others were shot after using hand grenades and rocket-propelled grenades.

Galal commanded Somalia's armed forces during the 1977 Ogaden War between Somalia and Ethiopia. He was also a government minister and intelligence chief. He also led the popular uprising against Mohamed Siad Barre that led to his ouster in 1991. Al-Shabaab claimed that Galal was responsible for the death of former al-Shabaab chief Adan Hashi Ayro, who died in a U.S. airstrike in 2008.

A mortar shell exploded in Golweyn, 25 miles north of Merca, killing eight children and injuring 11. Osman Nur, chairman of Shalambood town, said the children were aged between four and 12.

February 13, 2021: *AP, CNN,* and *AFP* reported that a suicide car bomb exploded at 9:10 a.m. near a checkpoint at the Sayidka Junction outside the presidential palace in Mogadishu, killing the driver and three civilians and wounding eight civilians. The driver refused to stop and police fired on him. More than a dozen vehicles were destroyed. Al-Shabaab claimed the attack on its *Shahada News Agency.*

March 5, 2021: *Reuters* reported that a suicide car bomb went off outside the Luul Yemeni restaurant near Mogadishu's port in the evening. Dr. Abdulkadir Aden, founder of AAMIN Ambulance services, said, "So far we have carried 20 dead people and 30 injured from the blast scene." No one claimed credit; al-Shabaab was suspected.

April 3, 2021: Al-Shabaab claimed credit when suicide car bombs went off in and around Somali Army bases in the Bariirre and Awdhegleh villages of Lower Shabelle region. General Mohamed Tahlil Bihi, commander of the infantry forces of the government, said that "we lost nine of our soldiers and 11 others got wounded from our side." He added, "from the Shabaab, we killed 60 of their militias on one spot and 17 others near the other base". General Odawa Yusuf Ragheh, commander of the Somali National Army, cited "heavy losses" among the attackers, who "even left some of the bodies of their slain commanders". Al-Shabaab spokesman Sheikh Abdulaziz al-Musab claimed on *Radio Andalus* that the group had killed 47 government fighters.

Police spokesman Sadiq Ali Adan said that in the evening, a suicide bomber hit a tea shop in Mogadishu, killing six people and wounding four. No one claimed credit.

April 10, 2021: *AP* and *SONNA* reported that a suicide bomber detonated a bomb outside a cafe in Baidoa, killing four people and wounding more than six others. He was targeting Bay region governor Ali Wardhere, who was outside the Suez Cafeteria. Wardhere escaped unharmed. Two of his bodyguards, who also serve as policemen, were wounded. Al-Shabaab claimed credit on its *Radio Andalus.*

A bomb exploded in Mogadishu's Huriwa district, killing a government soldier and wounding a bystander. No one claimed credit.

May 9, 2021: During the night, al-Shabaab claimed credit when a suicide bomb hit the Waberi district police station in Mogadishu, killing six people and wounding six.

June 15, 2021: *AP* and *Reuters* reported that police spokesman Sadiq Ali Aden said that a suicide bomber set off his explosives vest at a Somali National Army's General Degaban military training center in Mogadishu's Madina district, killing 15 and wounding more than 20. Fourteen were seriously wounded. Army recruit Ahmed Ali was struck in the head by shrapnel. The terrorist had impersonated a trainee. Al-Shabaab claimed credit.

June 27, 2021: *Reuters* reported that al-Shabaab used two car bombs in an attack on a military base in Wisil in the semi-autonomous Galmudug State, sparking an hour-long firefight with troops and armed locals that killed 17 soldiers and 13 civilians. A witness said 30 people were injured. The Somalia state news agency *SONNA* reported that the government said 41 al-Shabaab terrorists died. Al-Shabaab claimed responsibility for the attack on its *Radio al-Andalus.*

July 2, 2021: *Al-Jazeera* and *AFP* reported that at 5:30 p.m., an al-Shabaab suicide bomber hit a crowded tea shop near the Juba Hotel and heavily guarded government institutions, including the headquarters of the Somali intelligence service, in Mogadishu, killing 10 people and wounding dozens.

July 10, 2021: *AP, Reuters,* and *AFP* reported that an al-Shabaab suicide car bomber at an intersection in Mogadishu killed nine people and injured eight others. Somali police spokesman Sadiiq Dudishe said the target, Benadir regional police commissioner Col. Farhan Mohamud Qaroleh, was unhurt. His vehicle was destroyed. Mogadishu is part of Qaroleh's jurisdiction.

July 20, 2021: *UPI,* the *New York Times,* and *Military.com* reported that Pentagon spokeswoman Cindi King announced the Biden administration's first drone strike against al-Shabaab targets near Galkayo after gunmen attacked the Danab, a U.S.-trained Somali commando force.

July 30, 2021: *Reuters* reported that a bomb exploded on a bus carrying soccer players in Kismayo, killing five players.

August 24, 2021: *The Hill* and *Reuters* reported that al-Shabaab stormed a Somali military base in Amara in the morning. A suicide bomber was involved. The terrorists captured 11 armored vehicles, then burned seven of them. Somali state TV said the country's army and Darawish forces launched airstrikes in response, killing several fighters.

September 24, 2021: *BBC* and *Voice of America* reported that a military court sentenced British man Darren Anthony Byrnes and Malaysian citizen Ahmad Mustakim bin Abdul Hamid to 15 years for belonging to and recruiting foreigners for al-Shabaab via the Internet. They had 30 days to appeal. The prosecution said that Byrnes converted to Islam in 2006, then travelled to Mombasa, Kenya, where he married a Somali woman. He entered Somalia in 2010. The prosecution argued that the duo tried to recruit cells to carry out an attack in Paris, France. They were captured in 2019 while trying to board a boat to Yemen.

September 25, 2021: *AP* and *Reuters* reported police spokesman Abdifatah Adam Hassan said that an al-Shabaab suicide vehicle bomber rammed cars and trucks at a checkpoint leading to the entrance of the Presidential Palace in Mogadishu, killing eight people and wounding nine.

November 25, 2021: Al-Shabaab claimed credit for setting off a bomb in the morning outside a school near the K4 junction in Mogadishu, killing eight people, including students, and wounding 17. Al-Shabaab said on *Andalus* radio that it targeted Western officials being escorted by the African Union peacekeeping convoy. Witness Hassan Ali said that a private security company was escorting the officials and said he saw four of the security personnel wounded. Abdikadir Abdirahman, director of Aamin Ambulance services, told *Reuters* that five were killed and 23 injured. The bomb collapsed the walls of the nearby Mucassar primary and secondary school.

December 30, 2021: *AFP* reported that al-Shabaab gunmen armed with machine guns and RPGs raided Balcad, killing four people, including two members of the security forces, and wounding eight others.

SOUTH AFRICA

February 21, 2021: Two gunmen shot to death exiled Rwandan opposition politician Seif Bamporiki in Nyanga township near Cape Town. He was the Rwanda National Congress party's coordinator in South Africa. Owner of a bed business, he and another male, 50, were delivering a bed when he was attacked. Western Cape Province Police announced that, "The deceased was pulled from his vehicle and shot, while the 50-year-old male who accompanied him managed to escape unharmed. The suspects, who are yet to be arrested, fled with the deceased's vehicle," wallet, and cell phone. Rwandan exiles had earlier blamed Rwandan intelligence for similar attacks. 21022101

SUDAN

January 14, 2021: *CNN* reported that the government claimed that five women were killed in border attacks by Ethiopian government-supported militias.

January 19, 2021: During the night, gunmen tried to storm the Genena residence of West Darfur Governor Mohammed Abdalla al-Douma, but were driven off by guards after an hour-long clash. There was no immediate claim of responsibility for the attack in the Gamarek neighborhood. The previous day, battles in South Darfur Province between the Rizeigat and non-Arab Falata tribe killed around 70 people following the killing of a shepherd in al-Twaiyel village.

April 3-6, 2021: Tribal clashes between the Arab Rizeigat and the Masalit tribes in Genena, capital of West Darfur Province, killed 56 and wounded 132.

The U.N. humanitarian affairs agency said armed men on April 3 shot dead two Masalit people and wounded two others.

The Sudanese doctors' committee in West Darfur said armed men shot at an ambulance during the evening of April 4, wounding three health care workers.

A shell hit a camp for displaced people in Genena on April 5, causing a fire that burned several houses.

June 6, 2021: The state-run *SUNA* news agency reported that tribal clashes between Arab Taaisha and non-Arab Falata in the area of Um Dafuk in South Darfur Province killed 36 people.

August 5, 2021: *Reuters* and state news agency *SUNA* reported that the non-government General Coordinating Committee for Refugee and Internally Displaced Camps accused 200 Janjaweed gunmen of an attack on Habouba village in South Darfur that killed seven people and wounded 16.

September 28, 2021: The General Intelligence Agency said suspected Islamic State foreign terrorists fired on GIA forces raiding their hideout in Khartoum's southern Gabra neighborhood, killing five intelligence officers and wounding an officer. GIA arrested 11 suspects; another four fled.

October 3, 2021: The General Intelligence Agency raided a hideout in Omdurman, arresting eight suspected foreign militants.

October 4, 2021: Security forces killed four suspected Islamic State terrorists in raids on their hideouts in Khartoum's southern Gabra neighborhood. One military officer died and three people were wounded, including two from the General Intelligence Agency and one policeman. GIA detained four other suspected militants in two hideouts. The gunmen fired on authorities with Kalashnikov rifles, RPGs, and grenades.

December 8, 2021: Clashes between Arabs and non-Arabs in Jebel Moon and the adjacent Tanjeki village in West Darfur Province killed 33 people and wounded ten. A battle earlier in the week in Kreinik in West Darfur killed 88.

TANZANIA

June 15, 2021: After eight years of detention, Farid Hadi and Msellem Ali Msellem, leaders of the Association for Islamic Mobilization and Propagation (UAMSHO), which advocated for independence for the semiautonomous region of Zanzibar, were freed and terrorism-related charges against them were dropped. They were represented by attorney Juma Abdullah Juma.

The director of public prosecution, Sylvester Mwakitalu, announced the release.

August 25, 2021: Five people, including three police officers and a member of the auxiliary police, were shot dead in a confrontation with a foreign man, possibly a Somali, near the entrance of the French Embassy in Dar es Salaam. The gunman also died. Six people were injured. Local media aired video of a man in a checked shirt and white Islamic cap armed with an assault rifle. Inspector General of Police Simon Sirro added that the attack could be linked to the jihadi insurgency in Mozambique. On September 2, *AFP* reported that police director of criminal investigations Camillus Wambura announced that gunman Hamza Mohamed was "a terrorist" who became radicalized through the Internet, observing, "He spent much of his time to learn about the kinds of terrorism incidents such as those conducted by al-Shabaab and ISIS through the Internet, like many terrorists do." Neighbors said Mohamed lived with his mother in a flat two kilometers from the incident. 21082501

UGANDA

February 4, 2021: *AP* and *The World* reported that Presiding Judge Bertram Schmitt announced that the International Criminal Court (ICC) in The Hague convicted former child soldier Dominic Ongwen, 45, who rose to leadership of the Ugandan rebel group the Lord's Resistance Army, of dozens of war crimes and crimes against humanity, ranging from multiple murders to forced marriages. The group had kidnapped him at age nine. He faced life in prison after being convicted of 61 offenses, mostly attacks on camps for displaced civilians in northern Uganda in the early 2000s, and his abuse of women who were forced to be his "wives". He was convicted of crimes against women, including rape, forced pregnancy, and sexual slavery.

On April 15, 2021, *Reuters* reported that Ongwen told ICC judges that he was not responsible for any atrocities and felt powerless to stop them. He told judges, "I cannot ask everyone in northern Uganda for forgiveness when there were other people in northern Uganda who were corrupt, who were encouraging this (war)…I did

not have any capacity to stop the things that were happening… Every time I have hallucinations, I hear gun shots, I hear people talking. I see dead bodies, people I killed, people I slaughtered." Ongwen was arrested in 2015, and convicted in February 2021 of dozens of crimes, including rape, sexual enslavement, child abductions, torture, and murder. Prosecutors sought a prison sentence of at least 20 years. His defense counsel requested no more than ten years.

On May 6, 2021, *Deutsche Welle, AFP, AP,* and *Reuters* reported that a three-judge ICC panel sentenced Ongwen, alias White Ant, 45, to 25 years in prison after being convicted in February 2021 for 61 of 70 war crimes and crimes against humanity including murder, rape, forced marriage, forced pregnancy, sexual enslavement, torture, child abduction, and using child soldiers in the early 2000s. Presiding Judge Bertram Schmitt said that his kidnapping as a 9-year-old schoolboy and being forced to become a child soldier saved him from a life sentence. Defense attorneys planned to appeal his conviction.

Ongwen had claimed that the LRA's initiation ceremony included forcing him to eat beans soaked with the blood of the first people he was forced to kill.

AFP noted that the United Nations indicated that since its 1987 founding, the LRA killed more than 100,000 people, kidnapped 60,000 children, and caused the displacement of 2.5 million people.

June 1, 2021: *AFP, NBS,* and *AP* reported that in the morning, four masked gunmen on two motorcycles fired scores of bullets at the vehicle of Minister of Works and Transportation General Edward Katumba Wamala, injuring him in the arm and killing his daughter and driver. The bodyguard fired back, saving Wamala by shielding him. Wamala was chief of the defense forces between 2013 and 2017 and chief of police. The attack occurred near Wamala's home in Kiasasi, a Kampala suburb. *Reuters* reported on June 28, 2021 that suspects Sserubula Hussein Ismael and Nyanzi Yusuf Siraji were charged with murder and attempted murder.

October 23, 2021: *AP, Reuters,* and *NTV* reported that an explosion went off at 9 p.m. in the

Digida Pork Joint restaurant in Komamboga, a Kampala suburb, killing a waitress, 20, and injuring seven, two critically. Detectives sought to "determine whether the explosion arose from an intentional act or not". Uganda Police chief political commissar Asan Kasingye said later that day that two people were killed. *CNN, AP,* and *Reuters* reported that Ugandan President Yoweri Museveni tweeted that it appeared to be an act of terrorism, offering, "The information I have is that 3 people came and left a package in *kaveera* [plastic bag] which later on exploded." The trio left a plastic polythene bag under a table; its contents later exploded. The bag was packed with nails and shrapnel. ISIS claimed credit on *Telegram* for bombing a public place "frequented by elements and spies of the Crusader Ugandan government were gathering". Security officials blamed the Allied Democratic Forces.

October 25, 2021: *AP* reported that a bomb exploded at 5 p.m. on a Swift Safaris bus traveling in Lungala from Kampala, killing one person. The Red Cross said a senior police officer was injured in the leg. *Al-Jazeera* added that several people were wounded. By November 1, no group had claimed credit. Security officials blamed the Allied Democratic Forces.

Reuters reported on November 1, 2021 that Uganda's police announced that they had arrested 48 suspects in the bombings on October 23 and 25 linked to IS.

November 16, 2021: *BBC, UPI, NPR, Reuters,* and *AP* reported that police spokesman Fred Enanga announced that three suicide bombers set off explosives within three minutes of each other just after 10 a.m. in downtown Kampala, killing four and wounding 33, five critically. Two suicide bombers were on a motorbike, the other walked up to his target. One went off outside the Central Police Station; the other near the parliament building. ISIS claimed credit, saying Ugandans were responsible. Officials blamed a "domestic terror group" linked to the Allied Democratic Forces (ADF), an armed group now based in the Congo. Authorities found two more bombs elsewhere in Kampala. *UPI* reported that police said they foiled a third explosion and disarmed the bomber.

AP and *BBC* reported that on November 18, 2021, Ugandan authorities killed five people, including Muslim cleric Sheikh Muhammad Abas Kirevu, accused of having ties to the extremist group responsible for the November 16 suicide bombings in Kampala. Four men were killed in a shootout in a frontier town near the western border with Congo as they tried to sneak into Uganda. Kirevu was killed in "a violent confrontation" when security forces raided his home outside Kampala. A second cleric, Sheikh Suleiman Nsubuga, was the subject of a manhunt. The government said the two clerics radicalized young Muslim men and encouraged them to join underground cells to conduct violent attacks. Police spokesman Enanga said 21 suspects believed linked to the perpetrators were in custody.

December 23, 2021: *Reuters* reported that Uganda charged 15 people with offences including terrorism and aiding terrorism related to their alleged role in bombings in Kampala and elsewhere in October and November 15 that killed nine people. On November 16, a suicide bomber hit a police station in Kampala; three minutes later, two other suicide bombers set off their explosives along a road that leads to the parliament. Those attacks killed seven people, including the bombers, and injured dozens. October bombings at a restaurant and on a bus killed two people. The Islamic State claimed credit for the November 16 attack and the restaurant bombing. The charge sheet said the 15 "intentionally and unlawfully, manufactured, delivered, placed and detonated an improvised explosive device ... with intent to cause death or serious bodily injuries" for the purposes of influencing the government or intimidating the public. The next court hearing was scheduled for January 13, 2022.

WESTERN SAHARA

January 23, 2021: *AFP* and *SPS* reported that during the night, the Polisario Front fired four rockets at the Guerguerat buffer zone under Moroccan control in the far south of the desert territory near the Mauritanian border. The Rabat administration dubbed the attack part of a "propaganda war".

ASIA

BANGLADESH

September 29, 2021: *AP, AFP,* and *Reuters* reported that during the night, gunmen shot to death prominent Rohingya Muslim leader Mohib Ullah, 46, a renowned advocate for Myanmar's persecuted Rohingya minority who rose to prominence as a community leader among his fellow refugees in Bangladesh, while chatting with other refugee leaders outside his office at a refugee camp near Cox's Bazar. Ullah visited President Donald Trump at the White House in 2019 as part of a delegation of victims of religious conflicts around the world. The former teacher had received numerous death threats while heading the Arakan Rohingya Society for Peace and Human Rights. His brother blamed militants, saying Mohib had received death threats from the Arakan Rohingya Salvation Army in recent months and at least eight men from the group took part in the attack. Police have said at least four unidentified assailants were involved in the shooting.

October 22, 2021: Two groups of Rohingya refugees clashed in a camp in Cox's Bazar district after one side opened fire, killing four people at the scene; another two died at a hospital. Fighting wounded ten others. Authorities detained one armed Rohingya man.

CHINA

March 22, 2021: *Deutsche Welle* and the *Guangzhou Ribao* newspaper reported that an explosion at a government office hospitalized several people in Guangzhou. The state-run *Global Times* reported that the Guangzhou Panyu Public Security Bureau announced that "a criminal act has taken place in Mingjing Village, Hualong Town, Panyu, Guangzhou, resulting in casualties... The Panyu police quickly dispatched personnel to the scene and coordinated with local government authorities to deploy emergency fire and rescue services." *DW* reported that local social media users claimed there is an ongoing dispute in the village between residents and officials over an alleged land grabbing scheme.

April 28, 2021: *ABC News, NDTV, Xinhua,* and *Reuters* reported that at 2 p.m., a knife-wielding man with the last name of Zeng, 24 or 28, broke into the private Jianle kindergarten in Xinfeng, in Beiliu City in Guangxi Province and slashed students and teachers during nap time, injuring 18 people, including two teachers and 16 children, two seriously. Police detained the attacker. Hong Kong news outlets, including *Oriental Daily* and *Apple Daily,* reported that he was going through a divorce and his wife worked at the school. He also claimed he had been bullied at the school as a child. *BBC* later reported that two children died.

BBC, Times Now Digital, and *Weibo* reported that China's Guangxi Beibu Gulf Airlines canceled flight GX8814 from Weifang to Haikou, in the provinces of Shandong and Hainan, after a male passenger with the last name of Wang threw six coins into the engine of a plane for good luck. Police arrested Wang. Airport staffers spotted the coins on the floor under the engine during a pre-takeoff inspection. He had wrapped the coins in red paper for good luck. The circa 150 passengers were escorted off the flight, which resumed the next day.

June 5, 2021: In the afternoon, a man with a knife stabbed pedestrians on the street in Anqing in Anhui Province, killing five and hospitalizing 15. Police arrested the attacker.

June 7, 2021: Professor Jiang, 39, stabbed to death Wang Yongzhen, 49, the Communist Party secretary at the school of mathematics at Fudan University, during the afternoon. Police said that Jiang bore a grudge against Wang and confessed.

June 22-23, 2021: *CNN* reported that police shot to death a suspected thief, 36, at his rented apartment in Guan'an in Sichuan Province after he repeatedly threatened to detonate four explosive devices during a 16-hour siege. He claimed there were dozens of kilograms of extra explosives in the apartment. Police later found seven homemade bombs in the apartment.

HONG KONG

July 1, 2021: *Al-Jazeera* reported that in the evening, a man, 50, stabbed a male Hong Kong police officer, 28, in the shopping district of Causeway Bay before killing himself by stabbing himself in the chest. The victim underwent surgery for a punctured lung. The city's security chief, Chris Tang, said the "lone wolf" had been politically "radicalized", citing materials found on the attacker's computer. *RTHK* reported that the attacker was unmarried and lived with his parents.

CNN and AFP added on July 10 that civilians left white flowers to honor the murderer, whom they saw as fighting an unelected regime that stifles dissent. The student union of Hong Kong University passed a motion to say they "appreciated his sacrifice". His employer, beverage company Vitasoy, saw its stock drop 14.6% after it offered condolences to the attacker's family in a leaked internal memo.

A user on the *Reddit*-like *LIHKG* forum claimed to be planning a similar attack against a police officer.

July 6, 2021: *AP, BBC,* and *UPI* reported that police arrested nine people, including six secondary school students, on suspicion of engaging in terrorist activity for plotting to set off homemade triacetone triperoxide (TATP) bombs in courts, the Cross-Harbor Tunnel, railways, and trash cans "to maximize damage caused to the society". Police found a bombmaking laboratory in a hostel, along with a "trace amount" of TATP, operating manuals, and 80,000 Hong Kong dollars ($10,300) in cash. Police froze another 600,000 Hong Kong dollars ($77,200) in assets possibly linked to the plot. Senior Superintendent Li Kwai-wah of the Hong Kong Police National Security Department said that the detainees were between 15 and 39 years old. The *Hong Kong Free Press* reported that Police National Security Senior Lt. Steve Li said five males and four females were involved in the plot by the political group Returning Valiant.

Hong Kong chief executive Carrie Lam said that an envelope of "white powder" had been sent to her office.

INDIA

January 29, 2021: *Reuters* and *UPI* reported that a small bomb containing ball bearings wrapped in plastic went off on a sidewalk near the Israeli embassy in New Delhi, causing no injuries but damaging the windshields of 4-5 cars. 21012901

March 2021: A roadside bomb, believed planted by Naxalite Maoist rebels, killed five Indian policemen and wounded 14 traveling on a bus in the Narayanpur district of Chhattisgarh State as they were returning from an anti-Maoist operation.

March 27, 2021: *AFP* reported that bombs were thrown at a polling station, seriously injuring a police officer, as West Bengal held elections.

April 1-2, 2021: Indian troops killed three suspected militants in Kashmir's Pulwama district, sparking an overnight gun battle pitting government forces and Kakpora villagers. Inspector General Vijay Kumar said two of the three slain militants were involved in fatally shooting a policeman guarding the home of a local politician from India's ruling party in the region's main city on April 1. Troops recovered two rifles and a pistol from the site of the April 2 clash; the militants had taken one of those weapons from the slain policeman. Residents said troops used explosives to blast a civilian house during the fighting.

April 3-4, 2021: *AP, Reuters,* and *CNN* reported that hundreds of Indian police and paramilitary soldiers, including the Central Reserve Police Force's elite CoBRA unit, the District Reserve Guard, and the Special Task Force, acting on intelligence, raided a Maoist rebel hideout in Bastar Division in Bijapur district in the forests of Chhattisgarh State. During the ensuing four-hour overnight gun battle during which the Naxalite rebels used automatic weapons and grenades, 22 paramilitary troops and one rebel died and 31 security personnel were injured, seven critically. Authorities recovered the body of a female rebel. State-run *All India Radio* tweeted that 20 security personnel were missing. Paramilitary officer Hemant Kumar Sahu said 400 rebels had gathered in the area.

April 8-9, 2021: Separatist gunmen hid inside a mosque as government authorities sealed off a neighborhood in Shopian. When the gunmen refused to surrender, a clash began, ending the next day. Indian army spokesman Lt. Col. Emron Musavi said five militants were killed and three soldiers and an army officer were wounded. Shopian residents marched in solidarity with the rebels.

April 9, 2021: In the Tral area of Kashmir, government forces killed two rebels and seized seven rifles and two pistols.

April 10, 2021: Gunmen fired at voters at a polling station in the Cooch Behar district of West Bengal State, killing one person.

Troops killed five suspected rebels, including a teenager, in gunfights in Indian-controlled Kashmir. Troops had cordoned off two villages in southern Kashmir's Shopian and Bijbehara areas after receiving intelligence that anti-India militants were hiding there. Inspector General Vijay Kumar said that three terrorists, including a teen boy, were killed and two soldiers wounded in Shopian, where troops recovered a rifle and a pistol. The teen had joined the terrorists a few days earlier. Government forces killed two more gunmen in Bijbehara.

June 2, 2021: During the night, gunmen shot to death Rakesh Pandita, a member of Prime Minister Narendra Modi's Bharatiya Janata Party, in Tral, Kashmir, where he was an elected municipal official. Tral was visiting a friend. Police blamed anti-India rebels. No group claimed credit.

June 3, 2021: Police killed detainee Mohammed Amin Malik, 38, a laborer who they said snatched an officer's automatic rifle and fired at officials during his interrogation inside a counterinsurgency police camp in Tral, Kashmir, calling him a "terror operative". One officer was critically wounded. Police brought Malik's mother, Mughli, to the camp but he ignored her calls to surrender and fired at police throughout the night. Police had arrested Malik on May 30 and seized a hunting rifle without a license and explosives. The former militant was arrested in 2003 and was released a few years later. His younger brother died in a clash with Indian troops in 2019.

June 12, 2021: Two police and two civilians died when gunmen fired on police who were enforcing coronavirus restrictions in the main market of Sopore in disputed Kashmir. Two officers and a civilian were injured.

June 27, 2021: Gunmen killed special police officer Fayaz Ahmad, his wife, and their daughter, 23, after breaking into their home in the Tral area in Indian-controlled Kashmir during the night. Special police officers are lower-ranked police recruited mainly for intelligence gathering and counterinsurgency operations. Ahmad's son works in the Indian military's counterinsurgency unit.

July 1-2, 2021: In a gunfight involving scores of counterinsurgency police and soldiers, an army soldier and five suspected rebels died in a village in southern Pulwama district in Indian-controlled Kashmir.

July 7, 2021: The army said its soldiers killed a suspected militant who was infiltrating into the Indian-administered side of Kashmir.

Indian troops apprehended senior rebel Mehraj-ud-din Halwai in the northwestern Handwara area. Following his interrogation he led them to a hideout where he was killed in a firefight. Police said he "picked up his hidden AK-47 rifle and started firing indiscriminately upon the joint search party which led to an encounter." Halwai was wanted for several killings of police and village officials.

July 8, 2021: Two soldiers and two insurgents were killed in a gun battle along the Line of Control, the de facto frontier that divides Kashmir between Pakistan and India, after soldiers intercepted a group of militants who crossed into the Indian-controlled portion of Kashmir from Pakistan. The Indian military said two foreign terrorists from Pakistan were killed.

In the morning, Indian troops killed four suspected militants in two clashes in southern Kashmir's Pulwama and Kulgam districts. Soldiers recovered two rifles and two pistols.

July 11, 2021: *AFP* reported that Anti-Terrorism Squad (ATS) police arrested two men with alleged ties to Ansar Ghazwat-ul-Hind, a Kashmir offshoot of al-Qaeda, in Lucknow in Uttar Pradesh State. The duo were planning attacks on crowded market places in Lucknow before August 15, India's Independence Day. Kumar said they had collected arms, explosives, and a pressure cooker. The group was founded by Zakir Musa, who said he was fighting to establish an Islamic caliphate in Kashmir. Government forces killed him in Kashmir in 2019.

July 14, 2021: Soldiers killed three suspected militants in an eight-hour shootout in Indian-controlled Kashmir after gunmen fired at soldiers and police as counterinsurgency troops surrounded a neighborhood in Pulwama on a tip that militants were hiding there. Authorities recovered two rifles and a pistol. Troops set fire to one house and set off explosives at another.

August 23-24, 2021: Soldiers killed two senior rebel commanders and three other militants in two separate counterinsurgency operations in Kashmir.

Police and soldiers raided a village in the Sopore area on August 23, killing three militants hiding in a house. Troops recovered a rifle and two pistols on August 24.

Ten counterinsurgency police wearing civilian clothes fatally shot the chief of The Resistance Front rebel group and his deputy in Srinagar, Kashmir. Inspector-General Vijay Kumar said Abbas Sheikh and Saqib Manzoor fired at the police but were killed in a shootout. Police say the group is a front for Lashkar-e-Taiba. Abbas Sheikh was a senior rebel commander who had been arrested twice by government forces but rejoined militants fighting against Indian rule in the region. He helped revive militancy in Srinagar and recruited at least seven men to his group. Police said the duo were involved in the killings of several pro-India political activists, police officials, and civilians and attacked government forces.

October 5, 2021: *AP* and the *New York Times* reported that gunmen killed three men in separate attacks in Srinagar that police blamed on militants. Victims included:

- Makhan Lal Bindroo, a prominent Kashmiri Hindu minority pharmacist

- a street food vendor from Bihar
- a taxi driver

The Resistance Front anti-India rebel group was suspected. Police rounded up 500 suspects.

October 7, 2021: *AP* and the *New York Times* reported that gunmen crashed into a school, demanding to know the religious affiliation of its teachers, then shot at close range two non-Muslim schoolteachers in the outskirts of Srinagar in Indian-controlled Kashmir, killing both. The terrorists fired at Supinder Kaur, a female Sikh school principal and teacher, and her male Hindu colleague, Deepak Chand, inside a government school, then fled. The Resistance Front claimed credit, saying it "carried out the attack on two non-locals who had harassed the parents of the students to salute the occupier's flag on August 15", India's Independence Day.

October 11, 2021: *AP* and *al-Jazeera* reported that soldiers and police clashed with militants in a forest in Surankote area in Kashmir. An army junior commissioned officer and four Indian soldiers died. No group claimed credit.

October 11-12, 2021: In two gun battles, government forces killed five suspected militants in Indian-controlled Kashmir's Shopian district. In the first clash in late October 11, soldiers and counterinsurgency police raided the Imamsahab area. Three terrorists died in the ensuing gun battle. In the second, two suspected terrorists were killed inside an apple orchard in Feeripora. One of the gunmen was involved in the killing of a street food vendor on October 5.

November 7, 2021: *Al-Jazeera* reported that around 7:45 p.m., police officer Tauseef Ahmad, 29, was shot dead outside his home in the Batamaloo neighborhood in the heart of Srinagar, Kashmir. He was survived by his wife and two children, aged four and five.

November 8, 2021: *Al-Jazeera* reported that in the evening, rebel gunmen were suspected of critically wounding Muhammad Ibrahim Khan, a resident of Astengo in the Bandipora district of Srinagar, Kashmir, near a grocery shop in the Bohri Kadal area. He worked at the shop owned by a Kashmiri Hindu. Khan died of his injuries at a nearby hospital. Police called the attack a "terror incident".

November 13, 2021: Five Indian soldiers and two civilians were killed in a suspected rebel ambush of a convoy of India's paramilitary soldiers in Manipur State on the border with Myanmar. The convoy was en route to inspect a remote village in Churachandpur district. The dead included a colonel of the Assam Rifles, a paramilitary force of the Indian army, his wife, and his son. Police suspected the Manipur-based rebel People's Liberation Army. No group claimed responsibility.

November 17, 2021: *Reuters* reported that the armed forces announced that during the week, Indian troops killed seven suspected militants in Kashmir, including a district commander, and two others suspected of helping the militants. Kashmir Police Chief Vijay Kumar said five militants from The Resistance Front (TRF), were killed in two gun battles south of Srinagar; the others died in a shootout in Srinagar.

December 13, 2021: *Al-Jazeera, Indian Express, New York Times, AFP, AP,* and *UPI* reported that hours after authorities killed two militants in a brief shootout, gunmen fired on a bus carrying police in the suburbs of Srinagar in Indian-controlled Kashmir, killing two police and wounding 12. No group claimed credit; police blamed Jaish-e-Mohammad. Constable Rameez Ahmad Baba died of his injuries the next day, bringing the death toll to three.

December 14, 2021: *Al-Jazeera* reported that in the early morning, Indian troops killed a suspected rebel during a gun battle in the Surankote area of Jammu region's Poonch district in Indian-administered Kashmir.

December 23, 2021: *UPI* reported that one person was killed when an explosive was set off inside a restroom at a court building in Ludhiana, northwest of New Delhi. Other news services said two people died. People speculated that the dead person could have been the bomber.

INDONESIA

January 4, 2021: *Reuters* reported that Rika Aprianti, spokeswoman of the corrections directorate general at the law and human rights ministry, announced it would release radical Muslim cleric Abu Bakar Baasyir, 82, believed to be the spiritual leader of Jemaah Islamiyah (JI) and alleged mastermind of the 2002 Bali bombings that killed more than 200 people, from prison on January 8 upon completion of his jail term. A court jailed him in 2011 for his links to militant training camps in Aceh Province. Baaysir denied any involvement in the Bali bombings. *AP* and *NBC News* confirmed on January 8 that Baaysir, an Indonesian of Yemeni descent, had walked free at dawn from Gunung Sindur prison in West Java's Bogor town.

January 6, 2021: An anti-terrorism police squad shot and killed Muhammad Rizaldy, 46, and his son-in-law, Sanjai Ajis, 23, suspected militants believed connected to the January 27, 2019 suicide bombing at Our Lady of Mount Carmel Roman Catholic Cathedral in Jolo in Sulu Province that killed 23 people and wounded nearly 100, and arrested 18 others. One of the 18 was hospitalized with gunshot wounds after resisting arrest. National Police spokesperson Ahmad Ramadhan said the duo had resisted arrest by wielding a machete and an air rifle during a raid at a house in Makassar, the capital of South Sulawesi Province. The duo were linked to a banned militant organization responsible for a series of attacks in Indonesia, Jemaah Anshorut Daulah, which pledged allegiance to ISIS leader Abu Bakr al-Baghdadi in 2015.

Authorities in Indonesia and the Philippines believe the attack was carried out by Indonesian couple Rullie Rian Zeke and Ulfah Handayani Saleh. Ramadhan said Rizaldy and Ajis "were involved in sending funds to the suicide bombers for the attack". The duo were also accused of harboring Andi Baso, a suspected militant who was involved in a 2016 church attack in Samarinda on Indonesia's Borneo island that killed a 3-year-old girl and wounded several other children. Indonesian authorities believe that Baso fled to the southern Philippines and joined with a militant group there.

February 2, 2021: *Al-Jazeera* and *AFP* reported that Indonesia detained British-born Muslim convert Tazneen Miriam Sailar, 47, who was on a list of 400 global terror suspects, and planned to deport her for visa violations. Her late husband, who was killed in Syria in 2015, was also on the list. She and her Indonesia-born son, 10, were held in Jakarta after being arrested in 2020 on allegations she did not have the required documents to remain in Indonesia. The couple was married in 2010 by radical Indonesian cleric Abu Bakar Baaysir, spiritual head of Jemaah Islamiyah. She was represented by attorney Farid Ghozali. She ran a charity named after her late husband, which sent aid to women and children in Syria. She arrived in Indonesia in 2005 as a medical volunteer for a Christian humanitarian foundation that assisted victims of natural disasters. She was born in Manchester, UK on February 20, 1973, and retained a British passport. The Indonesian list reported that she used two aliases.

March 2, 2021: A joint police and military team killed two East Indonesia Mujahideen members in a shootout in Andole village in the mountainous Poso district in Central Sulawesi Province. A soldier died. Central Sulawesi Police chief Abdul Rakhman Baso said the group had been attacking residents who refused to help them. One of the terrorists killed was the son of the group's former leader, Abu Wardah Santoso, who was killed in a shootout with security forces in 2016.

March 18, 2021: *AP* reported that Indonesian authorities said that 22 suspects arrested in recent weeks were connected to the banned Jemaah Islamiyah, including a convicted leader who was recruiting and training new members. Indonesia's elite counterterrorism squad flew the detainees from Surabaya in East Java Province to a police detention center in Jakarta. Twelve were picked up in different cities in East Java Province in late February; counterterrorism police arrested the other 10 in early March. National Police spokesperson Rusdi Hartono said that police also seized a pistol, knives, long swords, machetes, and jihadist books. Hartono added that the suspects conducted military-style training in East Java's Malang district and plotted to

attack on-duty police. The suspects built a bunker for weapons and bombmaking and prepared an escape route after carrying out their planned attacks.

Among the suspects was Usman bin Sef, alias Fahim, a convicted JI leader who fought in Afghanistan. Aswin Siregar, operation chief of police counterterrorism squad Densus 88, explained that Fahim was sentenced to three and half years in jail in 2005 for harboring Malaysian terror fugitive Noordin Top and for a plot to attack police. He added, "In the current operation, Fahim had established a training ground with a program to create a jihadist group to fight in Medina for next year."

March 28, 2021: *Reuters, CNN,* and *AP* reported that at 10:30 a.m., two jihadi suicide bombers killed themselves and wounded 20 people, including four guards and several worshippers, outside the Sacred Heart of Jesus Cathedral in Makassar on Sulawesi island during a Palm Sunday Mass. Police chief Listyo Sigit Prabowo said that one of the bombers, identified only as Lukwan, was involved in a 2019 suicide attack that killed 23 people at Our Lady of Mount Carmel Cathedral in the Philippine province of Sulu. The attackers were affiliated with Jemaah Anshorut Daulah, a group pledged to the IS. Guards prevented the male college student, L., and his wife, YSF, alias Dewi, from entering the Catholic church after they became suspicious of the couple on a motorcycle. The couple were linked to suspected terrorists arrested in Makassar on January 6, when a police counterterrorism squad shot and killed two suspects and arrested 19 others. There was no immediate claim of responsibility. *AP* added that the terrorists were married six months earlier.

Police arrested four suspects believed to have links with the attackers in a raid in Bima on Sumbawa island in East Nusa Tenggara Province.

Reuters reported on March 29 that police discovered explosives and arrested more suspected jihadis after a series of raids. National police chief Listyo Sigit Prabowo said 13 people in Greater Jakarta, West Nusa Tenggara and Makassar were arrested. Prabowo added that police found 5.5 kilograms (12.13 pounds) of explosives and triacetone triperoxide (TATP). The male terrorist wrote a letter to his family expressing his intentions to die for his beliefs. *AP* added that the couple used pressure cooker bombs. Neighbors said Lukman and Dewi were between 23 and 26 years old. Makassar city police chief Witnu Urip Laksana said the bombs contained nails to increase casualties.

On March 31, South Sulawesi police spokesperson E. Zulpan announced the arrests of eight suspected militants in addition to the nine earlier arrested in the case.

Reuters reported that Muhammad Lukman married his wife in a 10 p.m. ceremony at the home of Rizaldi, the head of their Islamic prayer group, on Sulawesi, in August 2020. Counter-terrorism forces shot Rizaldi to death in January 2021. The couple suicide-bombed a church in Makassar, Indonesia on Palm Sunday 2021. Lukman left behind a confessor letter to his mother, saying he wanted to die for Islam.

Rizaldi's sister, Ulfa Handayani Saleh, and her husband Rullie Rian Zeke, both Indonesians, bombed a cathedral in Jolo, in the southern Philippines, killing 23 and injuring more than 100 on January 27, 2019.

March 31, 2021: Police shot to death a woman who had pointed a gun at several officers inside the Indonesian National Police Headquarters in Jakarta. She was wearing a long black robe and a blue veil.

May 12, 2021: *ABC News* reported that police and military forces killed two Papuan independence fighters, including a rebel commander, after rebels set fire to several schools and killed two teachers in Beoga village in Puncak district in the east. Authorities attributed the attacks to the West Papua Liberation Army, the military wing of the Free Papua Organization. Iqbal Alqudussy, spokesperson for the joint operation, said it was conducted against dozens of rebels armed with military-grade weapons, axes, and arrows in Wuloni village. Security forces confiscated a military helmet, separatist flags, documents, and scores of axes, machetes, and arrows. One of the dead was rebel commander Lesmin Waker, who killed a member of the joint security forces in a gunfight two weeks earlier. The rebels earlier am-

bushed and killed Brig. Gen. Gusti Putu Danny Nugraha, chief of Papua's intelligence agency, while on a patrol after the guerrillas set fire to an elementary school and houses in a village.

May 31, 2021: Police announced the arrest of 11 suspected ISIS-affiliated Jemaah Anshorut Daulah jihadis accused of plotting attacks at several Christian churches in Papua Province. Merauke police chief Untung Sangaji said the elite counterterrorism squad arrested 10 suspects in several raids in Papua's Merauke district on May 28 after receiving information about planned attacks in the predominantly Christian province. Police detained another suspect on May 30, seizing chemicals for explosives, modified air guns able to fire real bullets, jihadist books, and documents on planned attacks. Some suspects were believed linked to a suicide attack outside a Roman Catholic cathedral during Palm Sunday Mass in March 2021 in Makassar, capital of South Sulawesi, that injured 20 people.

July 11, 2021: Maj. Gen. Richard Tampubolon announced that security forces shot and killed Rukli and Ahmad Gazali, suspected of ties with ISIS and believed to be connected to the killing of Christian farmers on Sulawesi island, during a pre-dawn raid by a five-man team of military and police in the densely forested village of Tanah Lanto in Central Sulawesi Province's mountainous Parigi Moutong district. Authorities had spotted the terrorists' camp on July 7. Three gunmen escaped.

Security operations in Central Sulawesi aimed at capturing members of the East Indonesia Mujahideen network, particularly targeting Ali Kalora, the group's leader and Indonesia's most wanted militant. The network pledged allegiance to ISIS in 2014. Seven members of the group were at large. In May, the group killed four Christians in Kalemago in Poso district, beheading one victim. Authorities believed the attack was in revenge for the killing in March of two militants, including the son of the group's former leader Abu Wardah Santoso. Security forces killed Kalora's predecessor in July 2016.

August 19, 2021: Police announced the arrests in 11 provinces in the previous fortnight of 53 suspected militants believed linked to banned extremist groups, including the ISIS affiliate Jemaah Anshorut Daulah, in a nationwide crackdown on a new cell of Jemaah Islamiyah.

August 23, 2021: *AP* reported that police on September 1 arrested four suspected members of the separatist Liberation Army group and accused them of involvement in the killings of two construction workers in Yahukimo district. Two bodies were found burned at a bridge project on August 23. Four other workers were killed days earlier in the same district.

September 2, 2021: The West Papua Liberation Army was suspected when 50 terrorists armed with arrows, machetes, and axes killed four soldiers and wounded two others in a morning attack on a military post in Kisor in Maybrat district. *AFP* reported that authorities arrested two suspects within hours. Papua rebels claimed credit.

September 10, 2021: Police spokesman Ahmad Ramadhan said Indonesia's elite counterterrorism squad, Densus 88, arrested in Bekasi four members of Jemaah Islamiyah, including radical cleric Abu Rusdan, 61, a convicted militant and suspected leader of an al-Qaeda-linked group blamed for several bombings, including the 2002 bombings in Bali that killed 202 people, mostly foreign tourists. Rusdan was born in Central Java. He was jailed in 2003 for sheltering Ali Ghufron, who was later convicted and executed for conducting the Bali bombings. He was released from prison in 2006.

September 18, 2021: Central Sulawesi's regional military chief Brig. Gen. Farid Makruf announced that in a nighttime raid on militants in Astina village in the remote Central Sulawesi Province's mountainous Parigi Moutong district, a joint team of military and police officers killed Ali Kalora—Indonesia's most wanted militant and head of the East Indonesia Mujahideen network (MIT) with ties to ISIS—and suspected extremist Jaka Ramadan, alias Ikrima. MIT pledged allegiance to ISIS in 2014. Four MIT members escaped. Police recovered the bodies of Kalora and Ramadan the next day. MIT had claimed credit for killing several police officers

and minority Christians. Kalora succeeded Abu Wardah Santoso, who was killed by security forces in July 2016. Central Sulawesi Police Chief Rudy Sufahriadi said that security forces seized two ready-to-use bombs from their backpacks, which also contained food and camping tools.

JAPAN

August 6, 2021: *AP, Kyodo News,* and *NHK* reported that a man in his 20s with a knife stabbed ten passengers on an Odakyu Electric Railway Co. commuter train in Tokyo's Soshigaya Okura Station, variant Seijogakuen. One passenger was seriously injured. Nine were hospitalized; the tenth was able to walk away. Police arrested the attacker after he left behind his knife and fled. He walked into a convenience store and said he was tired of running away. The store manager called police after seeing blood stains on the man's shirt. *NPR* reported on August 7 that the 36-year-old suspect told police that he wanted to kill women who appeared happy.

August 24, 2021: *AFP* reported that two people suffered burns in a nighttime acid attack at Tokyo's Shirokane Takanawa subway station. The middle-aged attacker fled. A businessman, 22, was burned on the face when someone sprayed liquid at him on an escalator. *NHK* said the man was severely injured by sulfuric acid. A woman, 34, fell and sustained minor leg burns.

October 31, 2021: *Reuters, NHK,* and *AP* reported that Kyota Hattori, 24, a man dressed in a Batman's Joker costume (green shirt, blue suit, purple coat) stabbed several passengers inside the Keio commuter train near the Kokuryo station in Tokyo with a knife before setting a fire during the evening. Seventeen people were injured, three seriously, one critically. The attacker was arrested on suspicion of attempted murder. *Reuters* added that acid was also involved. *Nippon Television* reported that he told police that "I wanted to kill lots of people" and get a death penalty. *Reuters* added on November 2 that police said the drifter planned his moves over months, buying a knife via the Internet. He quit his job in Fukuoka in June. A man in his 70s was in serious condition with stab wounds to his torso. Video showed

Hattori calmly smoking a cigarette on a seat in the train carriage. He was carrying four liters of lighter fluid in plastic bottles.

November 8, 2021: The *Washington Post* reported that a rider on a Japanese super-express train started a fire on the floor in the morning. He sprinkled liquid on the floor, lit a piece of paper with his lighter, and dropped it on the aisle floor next to his seat. Fellow passengers on the Kyushu Shinkansen "bullet" train quickly doused it. No injuries were reported. He allegedly wanted to mimic an attack on Tokyo commuter train on October 31 that caused several injuries. Kumamoto prefectural police official Tsuneo Kitada said the train was en route from the Kumamoto station to the Shin-Yatsushiro station in southern Japan. Police arrested Kiyoshi Miyake, 69, from Fukuoka, for attempted arson.

Malaysia

May 8, 2021: Authorities captured eight suspected Abu Sayyaf terrorists in Sabah state on Borneo island who were believed planning ransom kidnappings in Malaysia. Philippine military officials provided information that helped lead to the arrests. Philippine marine brigade commander Col. Hernanie Songano said that the AS terrorists had fled in March due to military assaults on their jungle bases in Sulu Province. Philippine military officials said the suspects were led by AS commanders Sansibar Bensio and Mabar Binda, who were involved in earlier gun battles with the Philippine military, including 2011 fighting in Sulu where a marine officer was beheaded. Bensio and Binda were believed involved in the kidnappings of Swiss citizen Lorenzo Vinciguerra and Dutch national Ewold Horn in Tawi Tawi Province in 2012.

August 13, 2021: *AP* and *Bernama* reported that a Malaysian air force officer shot to death three colleagues before putting the gun on his chin, killing himself, at a security post on an air force base in eastern Sarawak State on Borneo island. Sarawak deputy police commissioner Mancha Anak Ata said the gunman had stolen firearms from the security post. He shot in the stomach a victim who tried to calm him. The gunman then entered the post and killed two officers. The individual was under a COVID-19 quarantine.

Maldives

January 26, 2021: The Maldives Police Service uncovered a planned attack on a school involving eight suspected members of an Islamic State-affiliated group arrested in November 2020. The suspects attempted to build a bomb on a boat at sea, conducted training on uninhabited islands, and tried to recruit children. In a raid on the boat, police found bombmaking materials and gun cartridges. MPS credits tipoffs by foreign intelligence agencies. Seized cellphones contained evidence of a plan to attack a school during exams. Religious extremists in the country discourage people from giving their children anything other than a strictly Islamic education.

May 6, 2021: *AP, BBC, Reuters,* and *Business Insider* reported that the country's first democratically elected president and current Parliament Speaker Mohamed Nasheed, 53, was hospitalized with shrapnel wounds following an explosion of a bomb packed with ball bearings and fastened to a motorcycle near his home in Malé as he was walking to his car. The *Indian Express* reported that he suffered a deep cut to his arm and superficial wounds. State TV channel *PSM* and *Reuters* reported that two bodyguards and two bystanders, including a British tourist, were also injured. There was no immediate claim of responsibility.

Nasheed served as president from 2008 until 2012 when he resigned amid public protests. He was defeated in the following presidential election and was ineligible to run in 2018 due to a prison sentence. He was elected Speaker of the People's Majlis in 2019. As leader of the Maldivian Democratic Party, he had railed against global warming and religious extremism. The Sunni Muslim nation bans preaching and practicing other faiths.

AP reported on May 8 that a senior official said jihadis were responsible. *AFP* reported that police arrested two of four suspects, identified as Mujaz Ahmed, 21, and Thahmeen Ahmed,

32. Nasheed was in intensive care following 16 hours of surgeries to his head, chest, abdomen, and limbs. Shrapnel damaged his intestines and liver. A piece of shrapnel broke his rib and was a centimeter from his heart. He was moved to a German hospital.

AP and *AFP* reported on May 9 that at dawn, police arrested prime suspect Adhuham Ahmed Rasheed, 25, from the islet of Thinadoo in the Vaavu atoll and now held three of four suspects in custody. Police suggested he remotely detonated the bomb. The trio had criminal records.

AFP reported on May 20 that police had arrested a key suspect who was believed to have parked the bomb-laden motorcycle. 21050601

MYANMAR

March 27, 2021: *Newsweek* reported that the U.S. Embassy tweeted that shots were fired at the American Center at the corner of Inya Road and University Avenue in Yangon, causing no injuries. 21032701

April 7, 2021: *Reuters* reported that seven small explosions were heard at government buildings, a military hospital, and a shopping mall in Yangon, causing no casualties. The U.S. Embassy in Yangon received reports of "handmade 'sound bombs,' or fireworks meant to create noise and cause minimal damage". No one claimed credit. The Chinese-owned factory JOC Galaxy (Myanmar) Apparel Co. in Hlaing Thar Yar township, Yangon, was set on fire. There were no reports of casualties. In March, Yangon experienced 32 arson attacks on Chinese-invested factories. 21040701 21039901-32

May 1-26, 2021: *Reuters* reported that on June 2, the junta said that between May 1-26, there were 115 bombings or bombing attempts and 18 arson attacks at educational establishments.

May 3, 2021: *CNN, AP,* and *Reuters* reported that Kachin Independence Army (KIA) spokesman Colonel Naw Bu claimed that KIA shot down a military helicopter near Moemauk in Kachin State.

Myanmar Now, Reuters, and *Khit Thit* reported that around 5 p.m., a parcel bomb exploded in a village in Western Bago in south central Myanmar, killing five, including an ousted lawmaker, a resident, and three police officers who had joined a civil disobedience movement. Three explosions went off when a parcel bomb exploded at a house in the village, killing a regional lawmaker from deposed Aung San Suu Kyi's National League of Democracy (NLD) party. Another police officer involved in the civil disobedience movement was also severely wounded after his arms were blown off by the explosion.

The junta's head of the ward administration office in Yangon's Tharketa district was stabbed to death.

May 5, 2021: The military's *Myawaddy TV* reported that Phoe Thaw, 36, a mixed martial arts fighter who joined anti-coup protests, was wounded by a homemade bomb he was testing at a Yangon gym. He was arrested in a hospital while being treated for leg wounds. A former colleague told *Reuters* that a policeman posing as a civilian left the bomb at the gym's parking lot.

MRTV reported that bombs exploded at a bus station in Mandalay and a bank and a military-owned telecoms company in Naypyitaw.

May 7, 2021: KNLA Major General Ner Dah Mya said Karen National Liberation Army soldiers burned down the U Thu Hta government military outpost near the Salween River border with Thailand after capturing it without a fight when its defenders fled.

May 23, 2021: *Reuters* reported that dozens of anti-junta People's Defense Forces gunmen seized a police station in Mobye and claimed to have killed at least 13 members of the security forces and captured four police officers. *AFP* added that rebels claimed to have killed dozens of security forces.

May 31, 2021: *Reuters* reported on June 14, 2021 that the junta-controlled *Global New Light of Myanmar* newspaper and army-controlled *Myawaddy Television* accused the Karen National Defence Organisation (KNDO), an ethnic armed group, of killing 25 construction staff working on the Uhu Creek Bridge in the Myawaddy District, near the border with Thailand, after kidnapping 47 people, including 10 children and six women, on May 31.

June 12, 2021: *Reuters* reported that junta spokesman Zaw Min Tun said three of the country's two dozen Ethnic Armed Organisations (EAOs)—the Kachin Independence Army (KIA), the Karen National Union (KNU), and the Karenni National Progressive Party (KNPP), which has an armed wing—had provided training to "terrorists" to carry out a wave of daily bombings that it said had targeted public buildings, including schools.

Pakistan

January 2, 2021: *AP* and *Reuters* reported that Shakil Ahmed, an official with the counterterrorism police, announced the arrest of Zaikur Rehman Lakhvi, an alleged leader of Lashkar-e-Taiba, for running a Lahore medical dispensary that financed terrorist activities. He was detained after the November 2008 attacks in Mumbai, India that killed 166 people, but Pakistani courts released him on bail in 2015. Lakhvi was a prominent figure in Hafiz Saeed's charity Jamaat-ud-Dawa, which is believed to be a front for Lashkar-e-Taiba. Saeed is designated a terrorist by the U.S. A U.N. Security Council sanctions committee reported that Lakhvi is LeT's chief of operations who was involved in terrorist activities in Chechnya, Bosnia, Iraq, and Afghanistan. He was represented by attorney Imran Gill. *Al-Jazeera* and *Reuters* reported on January 8 that a Pakistan court sentenced Lakhvi to five years concurrently on three counts of "terrorism financing", with a fine of 100,000 rupees ($622) on each count.

January 3, 2021: *Reuters* and *AP* reported that in the morning, Islamic State gunmen kidnapped minority Shi'ite Hazara coal miners from a shared residential room near the Machh coal field in Bolan district, 30 miles east of Quetta in Baluchistan Province, took them to nearby mountains, bound their hands behind their backs, blindfolded them, then fired on them, killing 11. A security official said the throats of all 11 were slit. IS claimed credit via *Telegram*.

January 7, 2021: The Punjab Counter-Terrorism Department and the ISI intelligence agency raided three hideouts of the outlawed Shi'ite

Sipah-e-Mohammad militant group in Sargodha, Khusab, and Sahiwal in Punjab Province during a 24-hour period, arresting seven suspects who allegedly wanted to attack leaders of rival Sunni groups. Officers seized bomb-making material and guns. Officials said the suspects were directed by Mehmood Iqbal, who was hiding in an unnamed neighboring country. Officials have previously blamed Iran for backing Shi'ite militants.

January 14, 2021: *Al-Jazeera* reported that three Pakistani soldiers were killed in a clash during a raid on rebel hideouts in North Waziristan district of Khyber Pakhtunkhwa Province near the Afghan border. The Army said two terrorists, including a bombing expert, were also killed.

January 20, 2021: A roadside bomb exploded near a Frontier Corps paramilitary vehicle on patrol in Sibi district in Baluchistan Province, wounding 11 troops, four critically. Separatists were suspected.

January 24, 2021: *Al-Jazeera* reported that Pakistan's military killed five members of the Tehreek-e-Taliban Pakistan (TTP, or Pakistani Taliban), including two senior members of different factions of the armed group, in two separate security operations in the Mir Ali and Kaisoor areas of the northwestern North Waziristan district, which was once the headquarters of the Pakistan Taliban. The military said they had killed terrorist commanders Syed Raheem, alias Abid, of TTP (AKK Group) and Saifullah Noor of TTP (Gohar Group). The armed forces said Raheem had been involved in 17 attacks against Pakistani security forces since 2007, including recent targeted killings in the district. The military blamed him for the killing of four tribal elders in the Mir Ali area, three engineers, and numerous bombings. The army claimed he ran two suicide bomber training centers in Mir Ali and the Wana region of neighboring South Waziristan district. The military charged that Noor was "directly involved in different IED attacks on Security Forces in Khaisoor".

February 17, 2021: Pakistani Taliban militant Ehsanullah Ehsan, who in 2012 allegedly shot and badly wounded Nobel Laureate Malala

Yousafzai in the Swat Valley, tweeted a second threat on her life, saying in Urdu, "come back home because we have a score to settle with you and your father… {This time} there would be no mistake". *Twitter* permanently suspended his accounts. She tweeted in reply, asking the Pakistan military and Prime Minister Imran Khan to explain how her alleged shooter had escaped from government custody. Authorities had arrested Ehsan in 2017, but he escaped in January 2020 from a safe house where he was being held by Pakistan's intelligence agency. Ehsan was believed behind the 2014 attack on a Pakistani army's public school that killed 134, mostly children, some five years old. He traveled to Turkey, where he was believed to be living as of February 2021.

February 22, 2021: *NBC News* and *AP* reported that gunmen on two motorcycles ambushed a vehicle and shot to death four women who ran empowerment workshops for the Bravo College of Technology, a private vocational school in Peshawar in an area of North Waziristan that was once a base for the Pakistani Taliban. The women's driver, Abdul Khaliq, was wounded. The women were passing through the deserted Epi village near Mir Ali in North Waziristan. No group claimed credit.

March 18, 2021: A gunman shot to death Ajay Lalwani, 31, a reporter for the local *Royal News* television station and an Urdu language newspaper, who was having his hair cut at a barber shop in the Saleh Pat area of Sukkur in Sindh Province. Lalwani died in a hospital that night.

March 24, 2021: *Reuters* reported that the Pakistani Taliban claimed credit when a remotely controlled bomb planted in a motorbike exploded in Chaman, one of two major crossing points between Afghanistan and Pakistan, killing three people, including a shopkeeper, a passer-by, and a child, and wounding 13 people, including two security personnel. Deputy Commissioner of the district Tariq Javed Mengal said that the bomb targeted a vehicle carrying a senior police officer, who was not injured.

April 4, 2021: Police official Shoaib Khan said gunmen assassinated anti-terrorism court Judge

Aftab Ahmed Afridi, his wife, and two children, including their two-year-old son, and seriously injured two bodyguards as they travelled from the Swat Valley to Islamabad. No one claimed credit.

April 10-11, 2021: Counterterrorism police killed wanted Pakistani Taliban terrorist Niaz, alias Zeeshan, in Rawalpindi overnight. Officer Kashif Hussain said three accomplices escaped, leaving behind two pistols, an assault rifle, and ammunition. Niaz worked with Tahreek-e-Taliban in Punjab Province's Hazro area in Attock district and with Lashkar-e-Jhangvi. He was wanted for attacks in the region that killed more than two dozen citizens and security officials. Niaz planned a 2015 suicide attack that killed then-home minister of Punjab Province Shuja Khanzada, a high ranking police officer, and others. Authorities offered a $40,000 bounty. The counterterrorism department acted on intelligence that four terrorists on two motorcycles planned to attack secret service officers; police set up checkpoints on the road linking Attock with Rawalpindi. During the night, authorities spotted the terrorists approaching the Kheri Murat checkpoint. After they were asked to stop, the motorcyclists opened fire in an attempt to escape.

April 12-13, 2021: Police in Lahore arrested Saad Rizvi, the head of Tehreek-e-Labiak Pakistan, for threatening protests if the government did not expel France's ambassador over depictions of Islam's Prophet Muhammad. In anti-government demonstrations protesting the arrest, two demonstrators and a policeman were killed. A policeman was killed in overnight clashes while ten policemen were wounded in Shahadra near Lahore. Two Islamists were killed in Punjab Province. Protestors had blocked a main highway and roads, stranding thousands of people in their vehicles.

April 20, 2021: *Reuters* reported that a gunman shot and wounded in the ribs prominent journalist Absar Alam, in his 50s, in a park close to his Islamabad home. Alam is head of the state media regulator and has criticized the military and its alleged meddling in politics. He led the Pakistan Electronic Media Regulatory Authority (PEMRA) for two years under former Prime Minister Nawaz Sharif.

April 21, 2021: *Reuters, AFP, Time,* and *CNN* reported that a car bomb went off at 10:30 p.m. in the parking lot of the luxury 5-star Serena Hotel in Quetta where the Chinese ambassador, Nong Rong, had checked in, killing five, including security officials and hotel staff, and wounding 12, including a police constable. Rong was not in the building when the bomb went off. Foreigners frequent the hotel. Pakistani Taliban (Tehreek e Taliban Pakistan (TTP)) spokesman Muhammad Khurassani e-mailed *CNN* to claim credit. TTP said Pakistan security officials were targeted. 21042101

May 5, 2021: Gunmen in Afghanistan fired across the border at troops in Zhob in Baluchistan Province, killing four soldiers overseeing fencing installations, then fled. Another six soldiers were hospitalized in Quetta. No one claimed credit. The Pakistani Foreign Ministry said 20 terrorists were involved. 21050501

Three other troops and two insurgents died in a shootout with gunmen in North Waziristan district in Khyber Pakhtunkhwa Province.

May 9, 2021: *AP* and *CBS News* reported that gunmen conducted two nighttime ambushes against vehicles carrying paramilitary troops in the southwest, killing three soldiers and wounding five others before fleeing. In Quetta, capital of Baluchistan Province, gunmen killed three soldiers and wounded another. Four soldiers were injured by gunmen who "targeted soldiers patrolling" in Turbat district along the border with Iran. No one claimed credit.

May 21, 2021: A roadside bomb exploded near a vehicle carrying Abdul Qadir, a local leader of a faction of the Jamiat Ulema-e-Islam party, who was on his way to a rally in support of the Palestinian people. Seven people were killed and several others were wounded in Chaman in Baluchistan Province.

May 22, 2021: Gunmen in Afghanistan fired across the Durand Line border at a military post in North Waziristan district in Khyber Pakhtunkhwa Province in northwestern Pakistan during the night, killing a young soldier. No one claimed credit.

May 27, 2021: Security forces shot and killed four Pakistani Taliban members in a shootout on the outskirts of Quetta. Officers seized explosives and weapons. Authorities said that the four were involved in multiple attacks on security forces and civilians and were planning an attack on an important installation.

May 31, 2021: The military announced that suspected militants attacked a Pakistani security post in Quetta, killing four soldiers and wounding six troops. Authorities returned fire, killing four insurgents and wounding eight others.

Hours later, militants set off a roadside bomb under a security vehicle carrying troops in Turbat district in Baluchistan Province, wounding two soldiers.

No one claimed credit.

June 2021: *AP* reported on August 8 that during the night, counterterrorism police in Pishin killed five people involved in the late June ransom abduction in the Kuchlak area of Quetta and subsequent death of Malik Ubaidullah Kasi, leader of the secular Awami National Party. His body was found on August 5 near an Afghan refugee camp in Pishin district. Police arrested a suspect, who soon led investigators to the hideout in Pishin. Police seized machine guns, hand grenades, and hand guns.

June 3, 2021: During the night, Pakistani Taliban gunmen killed two policemen patrolling a residential area in Islamabad's Shamas Colony neighborhood. Hours later, Tehrik-e-Taliban Pakistan spokesman Mohammad Khurasani claimed credit.

Three children died and two were injured when a hand grenade they were playing with exploded in Quetta's Akhrot Abad residential area.

June 7, 2021: A gas cylinder exploded at a small roadside market in Mashkel, a remote town in Baluchistan Province bordering Iran, killing eight people and injuring two others. Local police official Hasil Khan said mud-brick shops collapsed. The dead included Afghan refugees. 21060701

June 9, 2021: Gunmen on a motorcycle in Mardan district in Khyber Pakhtunkhwa Province shot and killed two police officers assigned to protect polio vaccination workers in northwest Pakistan, then fled. Adnan Azam, a senior police officer, said that the officers were returning to a police station after providing security for the polio team. No one claimed credit.

Police in Lakki Marwat district in Khyber Pakhtunkhwa Province arrested Mufti Sardar Ali Haqqani after he posted a video threatening 2014 Nobel Laureate Malala Yousafzai, 23, with a suicide attack for her recent comments about marriage to *British Vogue* magazine. She had lived in the UK since 2012. She told *Vogue*, "I still don't understand why people have to get married. If you want to have a person in your life, why do you have to sign marriage papers, why can't it just be a partnership?"

June 14, 2021: A bomb exploded at a coal mine at Marget Mines 45 miles east of Quetta, killing four soldiers. No one claimed credit.

June 17, 2021: Gunmen fired on troops at a security post near an airport in the Turbat district of Baluchistan Province, killing soldier Aqeel Abbas and escaping. No one claimed credit.

June 20, 2021: In an overnight clash in the Spinwam area of North Wazirstan, two Pakistani Taliban gunmen and a soldier died.

June 23, 2021: *AP, al-Jazeera,* and *Reuters* reported that a car bomb exploded near the Johar Town residence in Lahore of jailed anti-India Lashkar-e-Taiba founder Hafiz Muhammad Saeed, killing four, including a child, 4, and wounding 25 others, six critically. Some police officers manning a checkpoint were injured. Saeed was serving 15 years for financing terrorism. He was unharmed. No one claimed credit. Reports differ as to whether Saeed was in jail or home confinement, and whether his sentence was 10 or 15 years. *AP* reported on June 24 that Pakistani security forces arrested a suspect, Pakistani David Peter, who was trying to leave the country via Lahore airport, and later picked up another man from Lahore. *AP* reported on June 26 that Pakistan's counterterrorism police made more arrests, including a man from the Mandi Bahauddin district of Punjab Province who sold the car used in the bombing. Two other men were

detained in Khyber Pakhtunkhwa Province for rigging the explosives in the car. Investigating officer Ahmed Wakeel said authorities found evidence of involvement of the Indian secret service.

June 25, 2021: Gunmen attacked security forces patrolling a remote district in Baluchistan Province's Sibi district, killing five of them, then escaping. No one claimed credit.

June 30, 2021: Gunmen in Afghanistan fired across the border at a Pakistani army post in North Waziristan district in Khyber Pakhtunkhwa Province, killing two soldiers. The Pakistani Taliban was suspected. 21063001

July 2, 2021: *Reuters* reported that police spokesman Ahmed Nawaz announced the arrest of a police constable, 21, for hacking to death in Sadiqabad district Muhammad Waqas, who in 2020 was acquitted of committing blasphemy in a 2016 capital case in which he was accused of sharing online content that insulted the Prophet Mohammad. The Lahore High Court overturned the conviction in 2020. The constable had joined the police months earlier.

July 5, 2021: Counterterrorism forces shot and killed five suspected militants during a raid on their hideout near Quetta. Officers seized weapons.

July 14, 2021: *CNN* reported that at 7 a.m., ten people, including six Chinese citizens, were killed and 31 Chinese citizens were injured in an explosion on a bus carrying Chinese engineers in the Upper Kohistan region of Khyber Pakhtunkhwa Province in northern Pakistan. The bus fell into a ditch. Arif Khan, deputy commissioner of police for the Upper Kohistan region, said the cause was unclear, suggesting a bomb or engine failure was responsible. The Chinese engineers, surveyors, and mechanical staff were heading to the Dasu Dam, a large hydroelectric gravity dam being built on the Indus River. *Reuters* and *al-Jazeera* put the death total at eight, including four Chinese and two male paramilitary security guards. *AFP* said 13 died, including nine Chinese. Islamabad said a "gas leak" was involved. Chinese Foreign Ministry spokesman Zhao Lijian blamed a bombing; the Chinese embassy in Islamabad said its nationals had come under "attack". Media later reported that investigators concluded that the bus driver had lost control after a suicide car bomber set off his explosives prematurely nearby. *Reuters* added on August 12 that Pakistan Foreign Minister Shah Mehmood Qureshi attributed the explosion that killed nine Chinese workers to a suicide bombing, blaming a "nexus of Indian RAW and Afghan NDS" intelligence services. 21071401

July 15, 2021: A roadside bomb exploded overnight in Pasni district in Baluchistan Province, killing two soldiers. The military blamed hostile intelligence forces. No one claimed credit.

July 16, 2021: *AP, Reuters,* and *al-Jazeera* reported that during the afternoon, gunmen attacked and kidnapped Silsila Alikhil, 26, daughter of Afghanistan Ambassador Najib Alikhil, as she was on her way home, in the middle of Islamabad, holding her for five hours. The Afghan Foreign Ministry said she was "severely tortured". A hospital medical report indicated that she suffered blows to her head, had rope marks on her wrists and legs, and was badly beaten. Doctors suspected that she had several broken bones and ordered X-rays. The Pakistani Foreign Ministry said the Afghan Embassy had indicated that she was riding in a rented vehicle. *AP, Reuters,* and *The Hill* reported that on July 18, the Afghan Foreign Ministry tweeted that Ambassador Alikhil and other senior diplomats had been called back to Kabul. 21071601

July 28, 2021: Gunmen on a motorcycle shot into a car carrying two Chinese factory workers in Karachi, wounding one before fleeing. 21072801

July 30, 2021: A hand grenade thrown at a police van in Peshawar killed a policeman and wounded two others while a government administrator was visiting market areas to ensure people were adhering to anti-COVID-19 social distancing rules. The attackers fled. No one immediately claimed responsibility.

August 1, 2021: Gunmen on a motorcycle killed a police officer returning home after security duty with polio vaccination workers in Peshawar in Khyber Pakhtunkhwa Province.

A roadside bomb exploded as a police van passed by while escorting a polio vaccination team in the Ladha area of South Waziristan district, injuring a police officer.

No vaccination team members were hurt. No one claimed credit.

August 2, 2021: Gunmen shot and killed police officer Dilawar Khan, who was assigned to protect a polio vaccination team in Kolachi in the Dera Ismail Khan district. He was riding his motorcycle en route to escort polio workers taking part in a nationwide anti-polio campaign. The gunmen escaped.

August 8, 2021: Counterterrorism police in Punjab Province killed three Tehreek-e-Taliban Pakistan terrorists during a raid on their hideout in a rented house in Ferozwala, a suburb of Lahore. Police said they were planning attacks on security forces and Shi'ite mourning processions. Police confiscated an explosives-filled vest, two assault rifles, three hand grenades, and two pistols. Authorities said the terrorists were Afghan nationals. 21080801

Al-Jazeera reported that a bomb planted on a motorcycle went off near a police mobile van at Tanzeem Square near the upscale Serena Hotel in Quetta, killing two policemen and injuring 21 people, including 12 policemen and four passersby. The separatist Baluch Liberation Army claimed credit.

August 9, 2021: Separatists were suspected when a hand grenade was thrown during the night at a store selling Pakistani national flags in Quetta, killing one man and wounding four people. No one claimed responsibility. The separatist Baluch Liberation Army was suspected, having earlier warned people not to celebrate Pakistan's Independence Day on August 14, marking the date in 1947 when Pakistan got independence from British colonial rule when India was divided.

August 10, 2021: Security forces shot and killed five suspected separatists in an operation in suburban Quetta.

August 14, 2021: Gunmen attacked a security vehicle near Shahrig in the Loralai district of Baluchistan Province, killing a soldier and wounding two. Security forces killed three attackers. No one claimed credit.

In the evening, gunmen attacked targeted a truck in Karachi, killing 12 people—seven women and five children—and wounding nine others, three of whom later died, who were returning from a wedding ceremony. Senior police officer Javed Akbar Riaz said more than 20 people, including women and children, in an extended family were riding in the truck. Investigators believed the attackers followed the truck and then lobbed hand grenades or bombs at one side of the truck. No one claimed responsibility, although Karachi police chief Imran Yaqub Minhas denounced the attack as an "act of terrorism" during Independence Day. Counterterrorism officer Raja Umar Khitab said pieces of a Russian-made hand grenade were at the scene near Mawach Goth.

August 19, 2021: A roadside bomb went off in a Shi'ite procession in the congested Muhajir Colony neighborhood of Bahawalnagar in Punjab Province, killing three and wounding more than 50 people.

August 20, 2021: A suicide bomber attacked three vehicles carrying Chinese workers that were being escorted by security forces in Baluchistan Province, killing two Pakistani children playing by the roadside and injuring a Chinese citizen and two Pakistanis. The bomber set off his explosives when officers tried to intercept him. Hours later, the separatist Baluch Liberation Army claimed responsibility in the port town of Gwadar. 21082001

August 28, 2021: *Al-Jazeera* reported on August 30 that shots across the Afghan border killed two Pakistani soldiers in Pakistan's Bajaur district. Pakistan said it retaliated, killing two or three attackers and injuring three or four others.

August 31, 2021: Before dawn, counter-terrorism units raided an Islamic State hideout in Mastung district in Baluchistan Province, killing 11 terrorists. Police seized suicide belts, hand grenades, and assault rifles.

September 4, 2021: *AP* and *CNN* reported that senior police officer Azhar Akram said that in

the morning a Pakistani Taliban suicide bomber on foot detonated his explosives near a Frontier Corps security checkpoint on Quetta-Mastung Road, 15 miles south of Quetta in Baluchistan Province, killing three paramilitary troops and wounding 15, some critically.

September 14-15: Overnight, the military raided a Pakistani Taliban hideout in the district of South Waziristan in Khyber Pakhtunkhwa Province bordering Afghanistan. In a shootout, seven soldiers and five insurgents died. The Pakistani Taliban said it had ambushed the troops.

September 19, 2021: Senior officer Khalid Suhail said gunmen on a motorcycle killed a police constable guarding polio vaccination workers in the village of Dhal Behzadi in Khoat district in rural northwest Pakistan, 47 miles south of Peshawar. The vaccination team was unhurt. No one claimed credit.

September 20, 2021: *Al-Jazeera* reported on September 29 that terrorists in Iran fired on a Pakistani Frontier Corps border post in Chukab, Balochistan, killing Sepoy Maqbool Shah and injuring a second soldier. No group claimed credit. 21092001

September 22, 2021: *Reuters* reported that Pakistan's Minister of Information Fawad Chaudhry claimed that a threat to New Zealand's cricket team that prompted them to call off a tour of Pakistan came in an email that "was generated from India through a VPN showing the location of Singapore". Chaudhry added that the West Indies team, due to arrive in December, had also received a threat.

September 24, 2021: During an overnight raid, counterterrorism police arrested three Baluchistan Liberation Army members in the Turbat area. Authorities said the trio had facilitated attacks on security forces and civilians, including the August suicide attack in the port city of Gwadar that killed four children playing alongside the road. The terrorists targeted a security forces convoy escorting Chinese nationals; one Chinese citizen was wounded. The trio were also involved in an attack on a luxury hotel in Gwadar in 2019.

Counterterrorism police in Punjab Province announced the arrests of eight members of banned militant and sectarian groups involved in spreading hate and jihadist literature. Police confiscated arms and ammunition. The suspects were collecting funds for banned groups.

September 25, 2021: Security forces, acting on intelligence, killed six members of the separatist Baluchistan Liberation Army, including two commanders, during an overnight raid on their hideout in Kharan district in the mountains of Baluchistan Province. The BLA members had fired on Frontier Corps troops. Authorities seized a large cache of arms and ammunition.

September 28, 2021: The military announced that security forces killed ten militants, including four insurgent commanders, in a shootout in South Waziristan district in Khyber Pakhtunkhwa Province on the border with Afghanistan. Soldiers seized a weapons cache. The terrorists were linked to past attacks on civilians and security forces and were planning more attacks.

September 30, 2021: Gunmen killed Satnam Singh, 45, a member of Pakistan's minority Sikh community, in his small clinic in Peshawar where he sold herbal medicine. The gunmen fled. No one claimed credit.

October 10, 2021: During the night, a roadside bomb went off near the car of a local Pakistani journalist in Hub in Baluchistan Province, killing Shahid Zehri, 35, who worked for the regional *Metro 1 News TV* news channel. The separatist Baluch Liberation Army claimed credit.

October 20, 2021: A roadside bomb struck a vehicle carrying security forces in Bajur district in Khyber Pakhtunkhwa Province on the border with Afghanistan, killing two police officers and two soldiers. A few years earlier, the Pakistani Taliban used the area as a base. No one immediately claimed credit.

October 21, 2021: Counter-terrorism forces killed three Afghan members of ISIS-K in a dawn raid on a hideout in Peshawar in Khyber Pakhtunkhwa Province. Two other terrorists fled. 21102101

October 22, 2021: *Reuters* reported that three police were killed in clashes with demonstrators from a banned Islamist group who demanded the release of their leader and the expulsion of the French ambassador over cartoons depicting the Prophet Mohammed.

October 23, 2021: In a raid in the Mastung area of Baluchistan Province, counterterrorism police killed nine terrorists who had fired on them. Authorities seized nine Kalashnikov assault rifles, explosives, and rocket-propelled grenades. No one claimed credit.

Two soldiers and a militant were killed in a separate overnight raid in Miran Shah in the North Waziristan tribal district bordering Afghanistan. The military seized weapons and ammunition.

In an evening raid, security forces killed six separatists in the Harnai district of Baluchistan Province.

Earlier in the week, the Pakistani Taliban claimed credit for a bomb that killed a police officer and wounded 19 in the Mastung area.

October 26-27, 2021: In an overnight attack, gunmen killed four members of a police patrol in Lakki Marwat in Khyber Pakhtunkhwa Province, then fled. No one claimed credit.

November 2, 2021: Local police official Din Mohammad Hassani announced that a roadside bomb exploded near a vehicle carrying security forces in a bazaar in the Kharan district of Baluchistan Province, injuring 13 people, mostly civilians. No one claimed credit.

November 10, 2021: *Dawn* reported that the Supreme Court summoned Prime Minister Imran Khan for questioning regarding his peace talks with the Tehrik-e-Taliban Pakistan, believed behind a 2014 assault on an army-run school that killed 147 people, including 132 schoolchildren. He had agreed to a month-long ceasefire with the TTP, facilitated by the Afghan Taliban.

November 11, 2021: The government removed Islamist leader Saad Rizvi from its terrorism watchlist, a first step to his release from detention under a deal to end weeks of deadly protests by his followers over an alleged blasphemy.

November 13, 2021: Abdus Samad Khan, Bajur District police chief, said a roadside bomb was remotely detonated at 10 a.m. in a tribal district that borders Afghanistan, killing two constables on security duty near the Raghan Dam in northwestern Khyber Pakhtunkhwa Province. No group claimed credit.

Reuters reported injuries to six people, including a young girl, a policeman, and three women, when a bomb on a motorcycle went off near a police patrol in the Quetta suburbs in Balochistan Province. Tehreek-e-Taliban Pakistan denied involvement, saying it would abide by the one-month ceasefire.

Reuters reported that IS claimed on *Telegram* that it set off an explosive device inside the barracks of the Pakistani police in the district of Bajaur, killing a police officer and a policeman.

November 21, 2021: In an early morning attack, gunmen killed three workers at a coal mine in the Sharag area in Harnai district in Baluchistan Province. No one immediately claimed credit. Baluch separatist groups were suspected.

November 26, 2021: In the night, gunmen attacked a Pakistani military post in the Datta Khel area of the district of North Waziristan in Khyber Pakhtunkhwa Province's northwestern tribal belt near the Afghan border, killing two soldiers. No one claimed credit.

December 11, 2021: Two Tehrik-e-Taliban Pakistan gunmen riding a motorcycle attacked two police providing guarding polio vaccination workers in the Chaddarah area in Tank district in Khyber Pakhtunkhwa Province, killing one constable and critically wounding a Frontier Constabulary officer. Members of the vaccination team were unhurt.

December 31, 2021: Security forces raided two militant hideouts in a former Taliban stronghold near Afghanistan. Subsequent clashes killed four soldiers and two insurgents. The first raid, in Tank, killed two terrorists. The second strike occurred in the North Waziristan district. Four soldiers died in the fighting; other troops captured one terrorist and seized a cache of weapons.

PHILIPPINES

March 8, 2021: Police and soldiers killed nine people in weekend raids against suspected communist insurgents. Authorities claimed the suspects shot first. Police served at least 24 search warrants, mostly for illegal firearms and explosives, in Cavite, Laguna, Batangas, and Rizal provinces. Police said six suspects were arrested and nine escaped. Rights groups complained of extrajudicial killings of activists.

April 16, 2021: Philippine soldiers killed suspected Egyptian would-be suicide bomber Yusop and two local Abu Sayyaf terrorists during a 10-minute nighttime firefight near a village off Patikul town in Sulu Province. Army brigade commander Col. Benjamin Batara, Jr., said troops recovered three assault rifles and bandoliers of ammunition. Yusop was the son of Egyptian terrorist Reda Mohammad Mahmud, alias Siti Aisyah, who was killed when she detonated a bomb and was shot by troops in 2019 at the gate of an army detachment in Sulu Province's Indanan town. His Egyptian stepfather was killed in a gun battle with troops at a military checkpoint in Indanan in 2019. Troops also killed suspected AS bomb maker Abu Khattab Jundullah and another still-unidentified terrorist. The trio belonged to an AS faction led by Mudzrimar Sawadjaan, suspected of a series of suicide attacks, including the January 2019 bombings by an Indonesian terrorist couple of a Roman Catholic cathedral in Jolo town in Sulu that killed 20 people and wounded more than 100 others. 21041602

The military's Western Mindanao Command said intelligence suggested that there could be four remaining foreign terrorists, including an Egyptian and two Indonesians, with the AS group in Sulu.

May 8, 2021: Dozens of Bangsamoro Islamic Freedom Fighters jihadis occupied a public market in the farming town of Datu Paglas in the southern Philippines overnight. They fled following a clash with government forces. No injuries were reported. Soldiers found four homemade bombs placed by the rebels along the highway. Datu Paglas Vice Mayor Mohammad

Paglas said that the mostly young Muslim rebels arrived via five trucks in the town center on May 7 to rest and mark the holy fasting month of Ramadan.

June 13, 2021: Shortly after midnight, Philippine soldiers killed four Abu Sayyaf members, including a commander blamed for beheadings and a suspected would-be suicide bomber, in a gun battle in Alat village in Jolo town in Sulu Province. The Army was backing police serving an arrest warrant for Injam Yadah when he and his men shot at them. The Army had accused Yadah of involvement in the kidnappings for ransom of Filipinos and foreigners, including eight Indonesian fishermen who were abducted at sea off Malaysia in early 2020 and brought to the southern Philippines. Three of the Indonesians were freed, one was shot to death while attempting to escape, and Filipino troops rescued four in March 2021. Yadah was also linked to the 2015 kidnappings of four people, including two Canadian tourists who were separately beheaded by their Abu Sayyaf captors, including Mujir Yadah, a brother of Injam. Also killed in the gun battle was al-Sawadjaan, a bomb-maker and would-be suicide bomber. Soldiers confiscated a rifle, a pistol, bomb parts, and 15 cellphones and detained Yadah's wife and three children. Sawadjaan was a younger brother of Abu Sayyaf commander Mundi Sawadjaan, who belongs to a faction aligned with ISIS.

October 29, 2021: In a 30-minute gun battle during a predawn raid, police and army forces killed Salahuddin Hassan, leader of the ISIS-linked Daulah Islamiya militant group, and his wife in a remote area of Talayan in Maguindanao Province. The military blamed them for bombings aimed at extorting money from businesses and transport companies, killings, and extortion in the south for more than a decade. Regional military commander Maj. Gen. Juvymax Uy added that more than two dozen gunmen escaped. Troops seized assault rifles, ammunition, and rebel documents.

Hassan and his group were allegedly involved in the 2016 bombing of a night market that left 15 people dead and scores wounded in Davao city; the 2014 bombing of a bus in the south that killed 11 people and wounded 15 others; and the June 2021 burning of a bus in M'lang town in southern Cotabato Province that killed four people and injured several others.

Hassan founded al-Khobar, which was blamed for bombings, extortion, and other attacks from 2007 to 2015. He was trained by rebel commander/bomb-maker Basit Usman and Malaysian militant Zulkifli bin Hir, alias Marwan. Hassan allegedly trained the Abu Sayyaf in bombmaking.

October 30, 2021: Defense Secretary Delfin Lorenzana said on November 1 that government forces killed New People's Army communist rebel commander Jorge Madlos, 72, alias Ka Oris, during a raid in Bukidnon Province on October 30. For several decades he was a leader and spokesman for the NPA in the southern mountains. Villagers alerted the military that 30 rebels were holding discussions with residents in a remote village near Impasug-ong. Fighter planes fired rockets at the rebel position; troops then launched a ground assault which lasted less than an hour after clearing land mines. Troops found the bodies of Madlos and his medical aide, their assault rifles, and ammunition.

November 30, 2021: Troops killed a fighter of the Daulah Islamiya in a clash in Shariff Saydona Mustapha in Maguindano.

December 2, 2021: Regional military commander Maj. Gen. Juvymax Uy announced that Army troops shot to death jihadi rebel leader and alleged bomb maker Asim Karinda, alias Abu Azim, and four others in an hour-long clash in a rural village near Mamasapano town a month after Karinda took over leadership of the ISIS-linked Daulah Islamiya after its leader, Salahuddin Hassan, died in an army offensive on October 29 in Maguindanao's Talayan town.

December 22, 2021: *Newsweek* reported that at 8:45 p.m., snipers wounded former Oroquieta Mayor Jason Almonte and the mayor of the town Lopez Jaena, Michael Gutierrez, at a Christmas party at a gas station owned by the Oaminals in Sitio Pulao, Barangay VII, in Tangub City in Misamis Occidental Province in the southern Philippines. The *Manila Bulletin* added that Congressman and gubernatorial candidate Rep. Henry Oaminal was also wounded and suffered minor bruises. *Rappler* reported that Almonte was hit by a splinter on the neck and a bullet passed through Gutierrez's temple and neck; he sustained severe brain injuries.

SINGAPORE

January 27, 2021: *AFP* reported that authorities announced the December 2020 arrest of a 16-year-old male student who made "detailed plans and preparations" to attack with a machete two mosques on the March 15 anniversary of a shooting rampage against Muslim worshippers in Christchurch, New Zealand, by Australian white supremacist Brenton Tarrant. Authorities said the Protestant student had prepared statements to be released before the attacks, one of which "borrowed heavily from Tarrant's manifesto". One called Tarrant a "saint" and that the Christchurch attacks were "justifiable". He intended to livestream the assaults and drive between the attack sites. The student was unable to purchase a gun online. He had also considered making a bomb and planned to torch the mosques.

SRI LANKA

January 13, 2021: A court in Batticaloa acquitted Sivanesathurai Chandarakanthan, who won a seat while in detention during the August 2020 parliamentary election, of charges that he was involved in the killing of ethnic Tamil legislator Joseph Pararajasingham during the midnight Christmas service at a church in Batticaloa in 2005, at the height of the island's long civil war. Four others were also freed. Chandrakanthan was a former child soldier in the Tamil Tiger rebel group. He later joined a renegade faction in 2004 that functioned as a paramilitary group supporting government forces. He soon became the government-backed chief minister of Eastern Province.

June 24, 2021: *Al-Jazeera* and *AFP* reported that President Gotabaya Rajapaksa pardoned 16 suspected Tamil Tiger rebels, all males, who

had been convicted under the Prevention of Terrorism Act (PTA), on the Buddhist festival of Poson. The men had been imprisoned for at least a decade.

THAILAND

June 24, 2021: *Reuters* reported that a former soldier, 23, fired gunshots in a coronavirus field hospital in Pathum Thani near Bangkok, killing a patient, 54, after hours earlier shooting dead a convenience store employee in a dispute. Regional police chief Amphol Buarabporn said that the shooter, who wore a combat uniform and red beret, believed that the patients in the hospital were drug addicts, whom he hated. The hospital was earlier a drug rehab center but now treated COVID-19 patients. Authorities arrested the suspect.

October 4, 2021: The *Defense Post* and *AFP* reported that soldiers and rebels exchanged gunfire since September 28 in a raid at a hideout in a swampy forest in Bachao district. Six people died, including a military unit's first officer and four suspected rebels.

AUSTRALIA/NEW ZEALAND

AUSTRALIA

February 10, 2021: *AP, al-Jazeera,* and the *Australian Broadcasting Corporation* reported that the High Court upheld a law that can keep extremists in prison after they have served their sentences. Five of the seven High Court judges dismissed a constitutional challenge by convicted terrorist Abdul Nacer Benbrika, 60, an Algerian-born Muslim cleric who remains in a Victoria state prison despite his 15-year sentence expiring in November 2020. High Court Justices Stephen Gageler and Michelle Gordon dissented. He was arrested in November 2005. He was the first to be incarcerated by a continuing detention order based on a 2017 anti-terror law regarding "high-risk terrorist offenders" who would "pose an unacceptable risk of committing serious... offences if released into the community". He was convicted in 2009 of being the Melbourne leader and member of a terrorist cell; charges included directing a terrorist group, being a member of a terrorist group, and possessing material associated with the planning of a terrorist act. He was one of a dozen men in Melbourne and Sydney convicted of planning attacks against various targets including the then-prime minister and a Melbourne Australian Rules Football match. The law permits additional post-sentence detention for three years if a judge grants a federal government application for a detention order. The order can be renewed after three years. Victoria Supreme Court Justice Andrew Tinney deemed it "highly unlikely" someone with his narcissistic personality traits, sense of infallibility and of religious and intellectual superiority would have changed his extremist views. In November 2020, Benbrika became the first person to be stripped of Australian citizenship while still in Australia; the government said he also had Fijian citizenship, but Fiji denied that claim.

March 22, 2021: *Reuters* reported that the government deemed the right-wing UK-based Sonnenkrieg Division (SKD) extremist group a terrorist organization, giving Canberra the power to imprison members of the neo-Nazi group. Peter Dutton, Australia's Minister for Home Affairs, posted, "SKD adheres to an abhorrent, violent ideology that encourages lone-wolf terrorist actors who would seek to cause significant harm to our way of life and our country." Mike Burgess, director of the ASIO intelligence agency, added that SKD and other right-wing groups accounted for 40% of terror-related investigations carried out in 2020.

April 7, 2021: *Business Insider* reported South Australian police arrested two men as part of an investigation into violent extremism. Police detained a man, 32, from Munno Para for possession of an improvised explosive device and instructions for manufacturing explosive, prohibited, and dangerous weapons, and detained a man, 28, from Surrey Downs for possessing extremist material. Tom Sewell, leader of the Australian neo-Nazi group National Socialist Network, added that one of the group's members was arrested during a search of 15 members' homes.

The new NSN was formed by a merger of the Lads Society and Antipodean Resistance. Sewell, a former Australian Defence Force member, was charged with assault after allegedly attacking a *Channel Nine* security guard in March 2021.

June 18, 2021: *Reuters* reported that following a seven-month investigation, the Australian Federal Police and the New South Wales police announced the arrest for membership in ISIS of a Sydney man, 24, who posted extremist rhetoric and possessed recipes for explosives. He faced ten years in prison.

November 24, 2021: The government announced it would add to its list of outlawed terrorist groups Lebanese Hizballah and The Base, a neo-Nazi white supremacist group formed in the United States in 2018.

November 27, 2021: *BBC* reported that a woman, 31, was charged with arson after allegedly lighting a fire under a bed in a room in the 11-storey Pacific Hotel she had been sharing with two children in the morning. The fire destroyed part of a COVID-19 quarantine hotel in Cairns, Queensland. More than 160 people were evacuated; no one was injured. Unvaccinated travelers must quarantine for 14 days in hotels in Australia.

December 2, 2021: *AP* and the *Australian Broadcasting Corporation* reported that Premier Mark McGowan blamed white supremacists in the United States for spreading online misinformation about COVID vaccines among First Nations people in his state. A senior Aboriginal affairs official in Western Australia, Wanita Bartholomeusz, said some misinformation came from *Facebook* groups, including one sporting a cover image of former U.S. president Donald Trump.

NEW ZEALAND

March 4, 2021: *Al-Jazeera*, *AP*, and *Reuters* reported that police arrested and charged a New Zealand man, 27, with threatening to kill after posting on *4chan* threats against two Christchurch mosques—the Linwood Islamic Centre and Al Noor mosque in Christchurch—that were the sites of the March 15, 2019 white supremacist terrorist attack that left 51 people dead and dozens others injured. He faced a seven-year prison sentence. Police had arrested two men and searched two Christchurch addresses. One of the men was later released without charges.

July 26, 2021: New Zealand agreed to repatriate suspected ISIS member Suhayra Aden, 27, who grew up in Australia and was detained by Turkish authorities in February as she attempted to cross the border from Syria illegally with her two young children. She had traveled from Australia to allegedly join ISIS and marry a fighter as a "jihadi bride" nearly seven years earlier. Her family moved to Australia from New Zealand when she was 6. She became a dual citizen. She left for Syria in 2014 on an Australian passport. Australia revoked her citizenship and canceled her passport. She was represented by attorney Deborah Manning. *Australian ABC* reported that Aden married and had three children with two Swedish men in Syria, who both died.

September 3, 2021: The *Washington Post, UPI, CNN, Stuff,* and *NPR* reported that at 2:40 p.m., Ahamed Aathil Mohamed Samsudeen, 32, a Sri Lankan Tamil Muslim lone wolf terrorist, stabbed and wounded seven people, three critically, at an Auckland Countdown grocery store in Lynn Mall before police shot him dead after he charged them with a knife. The victims included a woman, 29, and man, 77. Authorities said Samsudeen was inspired by ISIS. Prime Minister Jacinda Ardern said she had been briefed about him in May after he had been caught with a hunting knife and extremist videos. He was a known security threat and under "constant" police surveillance for 53 days, involving 30 officers. Two tactical police officers had followed the man to the supermarket and were trailing him, but hung back, as he was surveillance-conscious, often asking people if they were tailing him. He grabbed a knife from the shelves and attacked customers. Police killed him within 60 seconds of the start of the attack. Witnesses saw an elderly man stabbed in the abdomen and a woman with a shoulder wound. Bystanders said they heard 10 shots fired. The attacker had visited the store earlier.

Authorities said Samsudeen arrived in New Zealand in October 2011 on a student visa seeking refugee status, which he was given in 2013. He was placed on a terrorist watch list in October 2016 after he posted support for terror attacks and violent extremism on *Facebook*. Police arrested him in 2017 at Auckland Airport; he was planning on going to Syria. He was released on bail. He bought another knife in 2018; police found two more ISIS videos. He was jailed for three years after pleading guilty to various crimes and for breaching bail. He was also held for assaulting a corrections officer, according to the *New York Times.* In May 2021, a jury found him guilty on two counts of possessing objectionable videos, both of which had ISIS imagery, including the group's flag and a man in a black balaclava holding a semi-automatic weapon. The videos did not show ISIS murders and were not considered to be the worst kind of illicit material. A court report warned Samsudeen held extreme attitudes, lived an isolated lifestyle, and had a sense of entitlement. High Court Judge Sally Fitzgerald said that the videos showed religious hymns sung in Arabic. She said the videos described obtaining martyrdom on the battlefield by being killed for God's cause. She ordered him released and sentenced him to a year's supervision at an Auckland mosque. She banned Samsudeen from owning any devices that could access the Internet, unless approved in writing by a probation officer. Two months later, he took a train from a mosque in the Auckland suburb of Glen Eden, where he was living, to the Countdown supermarket in New Lynn. After ten minutes, he yelled "Allahu akbar" and began stabbing shoppers.

Samsudeen's brother Aroos said Ahamed had been suffering from mental health problems. His mother, Mohamedismail Fareetha, said he was radicalized in Sri Lanka and in Iraq by people who helped him recover from injuries after he fell several stories while attending a university in 2016.

AP, Reuters, and the *New York Times* reported on September 5 that Prime Minister Ardern vowed to fix loopholes that prevented the government from deporting or detaining him. The *New York Times* reported that Ardern would not use Samsudeen's name in public, observing, "No terrorist, whether alive or deceased, deserves their name to be shared for the infamy they were seeking."

The *New York Times* reported that Countdown and three other New Zealand supermarket chains suspended the sale of sharp knives; Countdown also stopped selling scissors.

AP reported on September 7 that while he was incarcerated in New Zealand, Samsudeen was moved from the Mt. Eden Corrections Facility to the maximum security Auckland Prison after punching two officers and another staff member and repeatedly throwing feces and urine at them. 21090301

EUROPE

ALBANIA

April 19, 2021: *Reuters* reported that a man, 34, stabbed five people in front of the Dine Hoxha mosque in Tirana following 2:30 p.m. prayers. Police arrested the attacker, whom the local media reported suffered from depression and was wanted for a stabbing incident in March.

AUSTRIA

January 2021: Austrian rapper Mr Bond was arrested and charged with "producing and broadcasting Nazi ideas and incitement to hatred". One of his neo-Nazi songs was used by a man who live streamed a deadly attack on a synagogue in Germany in 2019.

July 2021: Police confiscated automatic weapons and hand grenades in raids on a biker gang whose leader planned to establish a "militia of the respectable" to "overturn the system".

October 2021: *CNN* reported on November 17, 2021 that in October, police raided a house in Baden belonging to a man, 53, "suspected of national socialist Nazi activities", seizing 50 weapons, including submachine guns and pump-action rifles, 1,200 kilograms of ammunition, Nazi paraphernalia, and a large amount of gunpowder. He had shared numerous files on Internet fora. *Newsweek* reported on November 21, 2021 that Austria's State Office for the Protection of the Constitution and Fight Against Terrorism in Lower Austria, in Baden anti-terrorism police found the cache and arrested the man and his wife, also 53. *Newsweek* added that the cache included heavy machine guns, machine guns, at least two Israeli-made Uzi submachine guns, what appeared to be a Russian AK-47, WWII-era machine guns, handguns, a hand grenade, pipe bombs and other explosive materials, a sniper rifle with a scope, pump-action shotguns, firearms with silencers, and over 1,200 kilograms (2,646 pounds) of ammunition, brass knuckles, knives, pepper spray, and electric shock devices. Authorities also found a bust of German General Erwin Rommel, alias the "Desert Fox"; a steel helmet with a swastika; other Nazi devotional objects (flyers, medals, coins) and "various relevant literature".

BELARUS

September 29, 2021: An opposition figure fired on state security service (KGB) authorities who had arrived at his apartment to arrest him during the night. A security officer and the activist died in the shootout when police were looking for "individuals involved in terrorist activities". *AP* reported on October 1 that the Viasna human rights center said 100 people had been detained in Minsk and seven other cities. A U.S.-based IT company founded by Belarusians, EPAM Systems, said the dead civilian was its employee Andrei Zeltser.

BELGIUM

May 19, 2021: *AP, Belga, Reuters*, and *BBC* reported that Justice Minister Vincent Van Quickenborne announced that the government was searching for heavily armed rightwing extremist Jurgen Conings, 46, who was on a Belgian terror watch list and who had threatened several people, including Marc Van Ranst, a prominent virologist working on containing the COVID-19 pandemic, other celebrities, and Belgian institutions. Authorities said he was a military shooting instructor and could be hiding in Limburg Province's Dilserbos forest near the Dutch border, armed with a rocket launcher and guns. *BBC* noted that he left letters indicating he was prepared for a deadly battle with police and "could no longer live in a society where politicians and virologists have taken everything away from us". He had threatened Van Ranst on the website of the Viruswaanzin (Virus Insanity) group, which has protested COVID-19 curbs. Authorities found his SUV abandoned with four stolen LAW anti-tank rocket launchers inside close to Hoge Kempen National Park. *AFP* reported on May 25 that Belgian Defense Minister Ludivine Dedonder expressed concern over social media support, especially from military personnel, for Conings. *Facebook* shut down a pro-Conings page that obtained 45,000 members. The media called him the Belgian Rambo.

AP and *CNN* reported on June 20, 2021 that people walking in the woods near Silden-Stockem in Limburg Province found what authorities said was the body of Jurgen Conings, missing since May 17. Authorities believed he killed himself with a firearm.

BOSNIA-HERZEGOVINA

May 11, 2021: Bosnian police arrested Sena Hamzabegovic, 61, upon her arrival at the airport in Tuzla on suspicion of financially supporting her husband and other Bosnians who joined Islamic fighters in Syria and Iraq. She holds Bosnian and Swiss passports. She allegedly sent money and other support in 2013 to her husband.

CYPRUS

November 5, 2021: *AFP* reported that six people were scheduled to stand trial on December 6 on charges of conspiracy to murder, participation in a criminal organization, terrorism, illegal possession of firearms, and circulating false documents for allegedly plotting to attack Israeli businesspeople. An alleged Azeri hitman was arrested

in Nicosia on September 27, 2021 when police found a pistol and noise suppressor in his car while crossing from the Turkish-occupied north of Cyprus through a checkpoint on the Republic of Cyprus side. Israel accused Iran of plotting terrorist attacks. Four suspects were believed to be food delivery drivers from Pakistan. Another was a Cypriot of Lebanese origin.

AP added on November 9 that Cypriot police formally charged an Azeri man, 38, with eight charges, including conspiracy to commit murder, belonging to a criminal enterprise, terrorism, and illegal possession of firearms and ammunition on suspicion that he planned to carry out the contract killings of Israelis living in Cyprus. Police were tipped off by a "foreign agency". Two pistols seized by police were linked to the Azeri; one of the weapons was handed over to police by the Lebanese suspect.

December 2, 2021: Education Minister Prodromos Prodromou pledged to protect the country's teachers and schools from "bullying" after a bomb exploded in the early morning, shattering window panes at a primary school and a neighboring church. No one was hurt. People opposing compulsory mask-wearing for all schoolchildren aged 6 and above were suspected. A second explosive device at the school's main entrance did not go off.

December 6, 2021: An attempted arson at the Grand Mosque in Larnaca caused no injuries. No one was hurt. A Syrian man, 27, was detained on charges of attempted arson. A Cypriot official said the suspect was protesting having his request to stay overnight at the mosque rejected by the imam. A witness told police the suspect used Greek-language newspapers to light the fire. Turkey's pro-government *Daily Sabah* newspaper reported that Turkish President Recep Tayyip Erdogan said that attacks on Muslim houses of worship on Cyprus would "not go unanswered".

DENMARK

February 11-12, 2021: German and police authorities arrested 14 people suspected of preparing one or several attacks in the two countries. Police found an ISIS flag, suggesting the suspects "have a connection or sympathy with the terror organization". Danish police officers searched addresses in Apotekerhaven in Holbaek. Flemming Drejer, operative head of Denmark's Security and Intelligence Service, said the first seven individuals who were arrested in Denmark had acquired weapons and "we found things that can be used to make a bomb." Police found the ISIS flag, shotguns, and a rifle with a scope. Thirteen arrests occurred in Denmark. Three suspects are Syrian nationals, aged 33, 36, and 40. Authorities announced eight arrests on February 11; another six people were detained February 12. The first seven people arrested in Denmark were suspected "of having acquired ingredients and components for the manufacture of explosives, as well as weapons, or having participated in this... having planned one or more terrorist attacks or participated in attempted terrorism". German authorities had alleged the first three arrested suspects—two in Denmark and one in Germany—had purchased several kilograms of chemicals in January that could be used to manufacture explosives. German police found 10 kilograms (22 pounds) of black powder and fuses in a residence in Dessau-Rosslau, between Naumburg and Berlin. Police seized more chemicals in Denmark.

October 5, 2021: Copenhagen chief prosecutor Lise-Lotte Nilas charged three people with attempting to carry out acts of terrorism by acquiring bomb-making chemicals and equipment that were to be used for an attack "in an unknown place either in Denmark or abroad". In December 2019, police arrested two men, aged 22 and 23, then nabbed a woman, 39. One man is Danish; the other man and the woman have dual citizenships. They faced life in prison, which in Denmark averages 16 years. The woman was also charged with financing terrorist activities by acting through an intermediary to transfer money to people associated with ISIS, promoting terrorist activities by allegedly helping several people affiliated with ISIS to create social media profiles and communicate on the Internet, and by having spread ISIS propaganda online. The trial was scheduled to begin in November in Copenhagen.

October 6, 2021: *Bloomberg* reported that Denmark charged three Danish women with supporting terrorism and illegal traveling in conflict zones immediately after evacuating them from Syria's al-Roj refugee camp. They were airlifted with their 14 children.

FRANCE

April 3-4, 2021: Over night, police in Beziers in the Herault region arrested four women and a girl suspected of plotting a terrorist attack. The DGSI domestic intelligence service and national anti-terrorist prosecutor's office were handling the investigation, which centered on an 18-year-old woman living in a housing project in Beziers who was suspected of plotting an attack targeting nearby Montpellier. Mayor Robert Menard said that police arrested her mother and three sisters, one who is a minor. The 18-year-old had "boasted" to neighbors about watching ISIS videos.

April 13, 2021: *AP* reported on June 3, 2021 that Malaysian police in the northern resort island of Langkawi detained on May 30, 2021 French conspiracy theorist Rémy Daillet-Wiedemann, 54, who was wanted in France on charges of organizing the April 13 kidnapping of Mia Montemaggi, a girl, 8, in eastern France. She was found in Switzerland a few days later with her mother in an abandoned factory. The mother had lost a custody battle. Several right-wingers were indicted in the case. Acting police criminal investigation chief Dev Kumar said Daillet-Wiedemann was nabbed along with his pregnant wife and three children aged 18, 9, and 2, for possessing expired travel visas. The family was believed to have lived in Langkawi since 2015, but their visas expired on May 21. Daillet-Wiedemann was a former regional leader of France's centrist Democratic Movement party before he was expelled in 2010. He ran a website calling for the overthrow of the French government and supported such conspiracy theories as calls for a halt to the "undue placement of children" and the use of face masks and 5G technology. *BBC* reported on June 13 that Malaysian authorities deported him for overstaying his visa; French authorities arrested him on arrival.

On October 22, 2021, French prosecutors charged Daillet-Wiedemann with terrorist conspiracy in connection with an extreme-right Operation Azul plot by 12 individuals to attack vaccination centers, a masonic lodge, and other targets. He was earlier accused of orchestrating the international QAnon-style kidnapping of a girl on behalf of the child's mother, who had lost custody. He was jailed in eastern France in that case. The girl was found safe in Switzerland. Daillet-Wiedemann was in self-imposed exile in Malaysia at the time. His attorney, Jean-Christophe Basson-Larbi, described his client as a political prisoner who called for the peaceful end to the political system. He said he would run for president in France's upcoming elections.

On October 28, 2021, *BBC* and *BFM-TV* reported that he was charged with terrorism over an alleged plot to overthrow the French government, including recruiting soldiers for an attempt by Honour and Nation to seize the presidential palace in Paris. *France Info* reported that he used encrypted messaging to build a network of conspiracy theorists and an underground group of several dozen members sympathetic to anti-vaccine messages and neo-Nazism in eastern France. He also issued a manifesto arguing that face masks and 5G are harmful.

April 23, 2021: *AP, BBC, BFM Television, Insider, Reuters,* and *CNN* reported that Jamel G., 36, fatally stabbed in the neck an unarmed French police officer, Stephanie Monferme, 48 or 49, inside her police station 750 yards from the Rambouillet chateau southwest of Paris. The victim, who was returning from extending time on her parking space, served as an administrative employee at the station. Officers shot to death the Tunisian suspect, 36 or 37, at the scene of the 2:20 p.m. attack. The attacker arrived illegally in France in 2009, but in late 2019 obtained residency papers. Anti-terrorism prosecutor Jean-Francois Ricard explained that his office took over the probe because the attacker had staked out the station, because of statements he made during the attack, and because he targeted a police official. The attacker had no criminal record or record of radicalization. A French judicial official said that witnesses heard the Tunisia-born attacker say "Allahu akbar." The attacker came to France

several years earlier. *Newsweek* reported that officials believed the attacker had staked out the station in advance before stabbing the mother of two. *AFP* reported that 30 police raided the attacker's Rambouillet area home and detained Jamel's father and two other people for questioning. Police in the Paris region searched the home of the person who had sheltered Jamel G. when he first arrived in France. *AP* added on April 25 that French investigators detained five individuals, including Jamel G.'s father and two cousins, for questioning. One cousin provided Jamel with an address for mail. *Reuters* added on April 25 that anti-terrorism prosecutor Jean-Francois Ricard noted that Jamel G. had watched religious videos glorifying acts of jihad.

Investigator Ricard noted that the suspect went to psychiatric consultations in Rambouillet on February 19 and 23 but did not require hospitalization or treatment. Jamel visited Tunisia between February 25 and March 13.

At a memorial ceremony on April 30, French Prime Minister Jean Castex posthumously awarded Monferme France's highest medal, the Chevalier de La Legion d'Honneur. 21042301

April 28, 2021: *Reuters, AFP,* and *BBC* reported that French authorities arrested seven former members of leftist terrorist groups, including the Italian Red Brigades. The seven, and three others who remained at large, were convicted of terrorism charges in Italy in the 1970s and 1980s during the so-called Years of Lead. Former French President François Mitterrand offered the terrorists refuge in the 1980s under the "Mitterrand Doctrine", on the condition that they renounced violence and had not been convicted of murder.

Irène Terrel, attorney for five of the detainees, said the arrests constituted an "unspeakable betrayal on France's part… Since the 1980s, these people have been under the protection of France. They've remade their lives here for 30 years in the full view and knowledge of everyone, with their children and their grandchildren… and then in the early morning, they come looking for them, 40 years after the facts."

Also arrested was a co-founder of the far-left Lotta Continua (Struggle Continues), Giorgio Petrostefani, 77, who was convicted of the 1972 slaying of Milan Police Chief Luigi Calabresi and sentenced to 22 years in prison.

The seventh detainee was a member of the Armed Cells Against Territorial Power, which Italian police described as a subversive group, convicted of the 1979 killing of a Carabinieri police officer.

AP reported on May 5, 2021 that the nine detained leftist Italian terrorists were expected to appear for an extradition hearing in a Paris court, the first step in a possible 2-3-year process. The detainees included five erstwhile Red Brigades members; Giorgio Petrostefani; and a member of the Armed Cells Against Territorial Power, who was convicted of the 1979 (reports differed on the date) killing of a Carabinieri police officer.

On September 29, 2021, a Paris court asked Italy for more information before deciding whether nine Italian terrorists, now aged 63 to 77, can be extradited to serve prison terms for their roles in the extreme-left terrorism "years of lead" in Italy in the 1970s and 1980s. The Italians were convicted in Italy of terrorism, murder, or attempted kidnapping, and sentenced to terms ranging from 14 years to life. The Paris court scheduled its next hearing for January 12, 2022. One of the accused was represented by attorney Jean-Louis Chalanset.

Defendant Giorgio Petrostefani did not appear in a June 2021 hearing because of grave medical problems. During that hearing, Marina Petrella said she was so shocked that she could not answer questions. She and four other defendants were members of the Red Brigades.

April 29, 2021: Convicted Italian leftist Prima Linea terrorist Luigi Bergamin, 72, one of the three at-large Italian leftists, turned himself in to authorities at the Paris courthouse. He was earlier convicted of membership in an armed band, instigating attacks aimed at undermining the state, illegally holding and carrying arms, aggravated robbery, aggravated theft, criminal association, and aggravated murder. He was sentenced to 16 years, 11 months, and one day in the murders of Andrea Campagna of the anti-terrorism Digos agency, killed in Milan in April 1979, and Antonio Santoro, the head of prison police, murdered in Udine, northeastern Italy, in June 1978.

Italian media called him a co-founder in the late 1970s of the Armed Proletarians for Communism (PAC). *Corriere della Sera* added that he was arrested several times in Paris but always released, in 1985 and 1990.

May 4, 2021: *AP, Le Monde,* and *BFMTV* reported on May 7 that on May 4 police arrested two men, aged 29 and 56, and a woman, 53, alleged neo-Nazis, believed involved in a plan to attack at least one Masonic lodge in the eastern Moselle region. Police had arrested six people, including the trio, in the Bas-Rhin and Doubs regions. Three were released.

May 28, 2021: *AP, AFP, Deutsche Welle, DPA, Ouest France, BFM TV,* and *Reuters* reported that a man stabbed and critically wounded a police officer in her leg and hand at her station in the Nantes Suburb of La Chapelle-sur-Erdre, stole her gun, fled in a car that he crashed, then shot two other gendarmes trying to arrest him before police killed him in a shootout. Some 200 officers had joined the hunt for the attacker. The suspect had been released from jail in March following a conviction for violence. Prison staff said he had been radicalized in jail. An investigator told *AFP* that he was "suffering from a very serious psychiatric illness". *AP* reported that he had severe schizophrenia and had been on a jihadi watch list. He was a France-born Frenchman in his 40s who did not have any previous convictions for terrorist crimes. He had entered the police station claiming to have a car problem. He lived in La Chapelle-sur-Erdre.

June 10, 2021: *CNN* reported that President Emmanuel Macron announced that France would end Operation Barkhane, an anti-terror mission targeting Islamists in the Sahel region of West Africa since August 2014. The French Ministry of Defense reported that 5,100 French troops of Operation Barkhane operate in Chad, Mali, Niger, Mauritania, and Burkina Faso.

July 15, 2021: *Newsweek* and *France Info* reported that authorities evacuated a section of the Palais des Festivals after a bomb threat was received in the afternoon against the Cannes Film Festival.

July 26, 2021: *The Hill, Reuters, AFP, Fox News,* and *AP* reported that Cuban Foreign Minister Bruno Rodriguez blamed the U.S. for a "terrorist attack" when two individuals threw three Molotov cocktails at the Cuban Embassy in 15th arrondissement of Paris at 11:45 p.m. Two hit the embassy's façade and one entered the building, setting a fire. No injuries were reported. 21072601

August 9, 2021: Police arrested a Rwandan man, 40, who had been facing criminal charges for torching the 15th-century Cathedral of St. Peter and St. Paul, in the heart of Nantes, in July 2020, and for killing Catholic Father Olivier Maire, head of the Montfortain Missionary Order in Saint-Laurent-sur-Sèvre. The undocumented immigrant had faced expulsion from the country. The Rwandan had been living with Maire's order while he awaited trial after confessing to setting the fire that burned through a cherished Gothic cathedral in Nantes. He had been transferred to a psychiatric hospital until the end of July. He turned himself in to police on the morning of August 9.

September 22, 2021: *AFP* reported that jailed Venezuelan PFLP terrorist Ilich Ramirez Sanchez, 71, alias Carlos the Jackal, appeared in a Paris court on September 22, 2021 petitioning to have one of his three life sentences reduced. The case referred to a 1974 grenade attack at the Publicis Drugstore at Saint-Germain-des-Pres, in the heart of Paris's Left Bank that killed two and injured dozens. He was serving separate life sentences for the 1975 murders of two French policemen and a police informer, and for bombings in Paris and Marseille in 1982 and 1983 that killed 11 people and injured dozens.

November 1, 2021: *Newsweek, CNews,* the *New York Daily News,* and *BFM TV* reported that just before midnight, a man wielding a knife threatened security officers between tracks 20 and 21 at the St. Saint-Lazare metro station in Paris after he was stopped for refusing to wear a mask and not complying with officers. He was waiting to board a train to Pontoise. He yelled "Allahu Akbar" and rushed four officers on patrol, who shot him twice in the chest. He was in life-threaten-

ing condition in a French hospital. He was not known to intelligence services. Paris prosecutors told *Reuters* they had opened an investigation for attempted murder and promoting terrorism.

November 8, 2021: *Reuters* and *Fox News* reported that an Algerian with an Italian residency permit opened the door of a police car parked in front of a police station and tried to stab a policeman at the wheel in Cannes. The policeman's bulletproof vest deflected the knife. The attacker tried to attack another policeman in the car. The attacker sustained life-threatening injuries after a third officer shot him. The Algerian was in France legally and was not watchlisted. *BFM TV* and *Nice Matin* newspaper reported that he said he acted "in the name of the Prophet". *Fox* reported that he yelled "Allahu Akbar". The attack coincided with the ongoing trial of Salah Abdeslam for the November 2015 attacks in Paris that killed 130 people. *Reuters* reported on November 9 that French police arrested three persons linked to the suspect.

December 28, 2021: *BBC* reported that the prefect of Oise closed a mosque in Beauvais for six months because an imam's sermons "defended jihad", called jihadis "heroes", and incited hatred and violence. *AFP* and *Courrier Picard* reported that the imam was a recent convert.

GERMANY

January 22, 2021: *Deutsche Welle* and *DPA* reported that the trial began of a soldier, 45, from the Special Commando Forces (KSK) on charges of violating laws on war weapons, firearms, and explosives possession. In May 2020, weapons including an assault rifle with several thousand pieces of ammunition, two kilograms of explosives, a crossbow, a smoke grenade, a noise suppressor, and other arms parts, and neo-Nazi materials (including a songbook of the former Nazi SS militia, extreme right magazines, and stickers) were found at his property in Collm near Leipzig. He confessed to using the equipment for training, saying the materiel consisted of older items from the Bundeswehr inventory which he assumed were no longer suitable for Bundeswehr operations.

February 25, 2021: *DPA* and *AP* reported that in the morning, 800 German police officers, including SWAT teams, raided several locations in Berlin, including the Maerkische Viertel neighborhood, and the surrounding state of Brandenburg in the investigation of an organization banned over allegations of Islamic extremism.

February 26, 2021: Emil A., 33, an Italian man residing in Berlin, was convicted of attempted extortion for threatening to blow up a British National Health Service hospital unless he was paid 10 million pounds ($13.2 million) in Bitcoin. He was sentenced to three years in prison. The threat was made via e-mail in April 2020 from his home to the NHS, during the early months of the coronavirus pandemic. He sent another 17 threatening e-mails until he was arrested by police SWAT teams and federal agents on June 15, 2020. He had studied computer science and used an email address under the pseudonym "Combat 18", a neo-Nazi organization. He later threatened a Black Lives Matter protest and a U.K. lawmaker. He was convicted of a similar threat against a Dutch company in 2013 and sentenced to ten months probation.

March 9, 2021: *AP* reported on March 22, 2021 that the Karlsruhe-based Federal Court of Justice on March 9, 2021 upheld the conviction of German-Tunisian woman Omaima Abdi for membership in a terrorist organization, failing to properly care for her children, weapons offenses, and aiding in the enslavement of a 13-year-old Yazidi girl. She was the wife of German-born rapper Denis Cuspert, alias Deso Dogg, who joined ISIS in Syria and likely died in an airstrike in 2018. The FCJ found no legal errors by the Hamburg state court in its October 2020 conviction of the Hamburg-born woman of Tunisian heritage, who was 36 at the time. She was sentenced to 42 months in prison. On July 22, 2021, *Deutsche Welle* and *DPA* reported that a court in Hamburg imposed additional jail time to her, extending her earlier sentence to four years.

April 13, 2021: *AP* and *BBC* reported that the trial before the regional court in Stuttgart began of a dozen Germans accused of being part of or supporting the far-right Gruppe S that plotted

to carry out deadly attacks on Muslims with the aim of stoking civil unrest and overthrowing the government. Group members had stockpiled firearms, axes and swords for the planned attacks. The suspects, aged between 32 and 61, were arrested in February 2020. Prosecutors accused 11 suspects of seeking to "rock and ultimately overturn the state and social order of the Federal Republic of Germany". Targets included Muslims, political enemies, and parliament. Eight men were accused of founding a "terrorist organization" in September 2019, led by Werner S. and Tony E. Three others were accused of membership in the terrorist organization. They communicated by phone, messaging apps, and in person. An at-large defendant was tried in absentia.

The twelfth defendant, former police officer Thorsten W., who worked for the police in the state of North Rhine-Westphalia, was charged with supporting the group by offering €5,000 ($6,000; £4,300) to buy weapons for the attacks. *ZDF* and the *Stuttgarter Nachrichten* newspaper reported that Werner S. planned to acquire a Kalashnikov assault rifle with 2,000 rounds of ammunition, an Uzi submachine gun, and hand grenades. The group earlier amassed 27 unlicensed weapons, mostly pistols. Ralf Michelfelder, chief criminal investigator for Baden-Württemberg State, said "If the accused had been able to carry out their planned acts of terror, we would have had a totally brutal and massive killing machine running here."

An informant tipped off authorities in autumn 2019.

In February 2020 police arrested 13 men from five German states; one died in pre-trial detention.

German broadcaster *ARD* reported that most Gruppe S members belonged to other far-right groups, including the Bruderschaft Deutschland (German Brotherhood).

May 3, 2021: Berlin police arrested a German man, 53, on suspicion of sending threatening letters to dozens of politicians, lawyers, and journalists. They were signed by NSU 2.0, the acronym of the neo-Nazi National Socialist Underground. Police seized a hard drive. Frankfurt prosecutors said the man was earlier convicted for "numerous crimes, including ones that were motivated by right-wing ideology". Police believed he sent nearly 100 letters across Germany and Austria since 2018. *DPA* reported that he may have obtained personal data from official records or Darknet fora.

May 5, 2021: *AP* and *Reuters* reported that the government banned Ansaar International, a Muslim organization that it accused of supporting "terrorism globally with its donations". More than 1,000 police officers raided buildings and office spaces in 10 German states, confiscating €150,000 ($180,000). The Interior Ministry claimed that the money the organization collected ostensibly went into welfare projects as a ruse to help finance groups such as the Syrian al-Qaeda affiliate Nusra Front, the Palestinian group Hamas, and al-Shabaab in Somalia. Interior Minister Horst Seehofer said that Ansaar "spreads a Salafist view of the world and is financing terror around the globe under the disguise of humanitarian help". Ansaar is headquartered in Duesseldorf. Its website says it provides humanitarian aid to people affected by war and crises by building or financing the construction of hospitals, orphanages, and schools.

May 19, 2021: *Deutsche Welle* reported that the Interior Ministry banned three groups—German Lebanese Family, People for Peace, and Give Peace—for collecting money for the families of Lebanese Hizballah "martyrs". The bans had been announced in mid-April, and came into effect on May 19.

Police conducted early morning raids across seven German states, including Hamburg, North Rhine-Westphalia, Hesse, and Rhineland Palatinate.

May 20, 2021: *AP, AFP,* and *DPA* reported that the trial in Frankfurt's regional court began of German Army 1st Lt. Franco Albrecht, 32, who posed as "David Benjamin", a Christian fruit seller from Damascus, Syria who became an asylum-seeker, on charges of plotting to kill prominent politicians and blame the attack on refugees. Federal prosecutors said he was a far-right extremist. He was represented by attorney Moritz Schmitt-Fricke. Albrecht was arrested in February 2017 while retrieving a Nazi-era pistol he had hidden in a Vienna airport restroom. Prosecutors said he planned to attack then-Justice Minister Heiko Maas, deputy speaker of parliament Claudia Roth, and the Jewish leader of an anti-racism organization. He stockpiled four firearms, including an assault rifle, more than 1,000 rounds of ammunition, and more than 50 bombs, some stolen from military stores. He was charged with plotting "a serious act of violence that endangers the state", fraud, and illegal possession of weapons and explosives. He faced 10 years in prison. He was the son of a German mother and an estranged Italian immigrant father. A 2019 court document indicated that he viewed immigration as a form of genocide. The non-Arabic speaker obtained a space in a shelter and monthly benefits of €409 ($485). He eventually went back to his barracks in Illkirch on the French border. He had earlier been interviewed by the *New York Times* and *Le Figaro*.

May 28, 2021: Prosecutors charged four far-left activists for membership in a group involved in a series of attacks on neo-Nazis and other right-wing extremists over a period of two years. Lina E. was accused of deciding in 2018 to target far-right individuals based on a "militant extreme-left ideology" and helping to plan the attacks. Males Lennart A., Jannis R., and Jonathan M. allegedly joined her no later than the end of 2019. Prosecutors said they were based in Leipzig, and most of the attacks came in Leipzig and Wurzen. Some were believed involved in a 2020 attack with about 15 or 20 others on a group of six people in the Wurzen train station upon their arrival from a ceremony marking the 75th anniversary of the firebombing of Dresden. Several victims sustained serious injuries after being punched, kicked and hit with batons. Lina E., Jannis R., and Jonathan M. were accused of an attack in 2019 in Eisenach, where police say they and about ten to 15 others attacked a restaurant thought to be a meeting place of the far-right, beating five visitors and the owner with batons and causing serious injuries. The four were charged with causing serious bodily harm and other offenses. Lina E. had been in custody since her November 5, 2020 arrest. The others remained free.

May 28, 2021: *Deutsche Welle* and *DPA* reported that a man yelled "Allahu Akbar" at drivers in Hamburg before police used pepper spray and a taser. They later shot and killed the knife-wielding man after he damaged cars, threatened motorists, and came at police with the knife.

June 5, 2021: A man poured a bottle of liquid onto a synagogue wall in Ulm in an attempt to set it on fire, then fled. Firefighters extinguished the blaze, which caused no structural damage. The arsonist was 6 feet tall and wore a black hoodie and a white protective mask.

June 10, 2021: Peter Beuth, interior minister for Hesse State, announced the disbanding of a Frankfurt police commando unit over suspected far-right links to 19 active officers, with the majority suspected of sending messages in far-right chat groups, including Nazi symbols and "inciting content". Three supervising officers were accused of failing to stop or report the exchanges. Twenty officers were under investigation. The chat groups were found after examining the phone of an officer suspected of possessing and distributing child pornography. The public prosecutor announced that one officer was suspended, while the others were "banned from conducting official business".

June 16, 2021: The state court in Duesseldorf convicted German-Algerian woman Sarah O., 23, of membership in ISIS and of holding Yazidi women as slaves in Syria after she traveled there as a teenager. She was sentenced to 6 1/2 years in prison. She went to Syria in November 2013 (when she was a minor), joined ISIS, and married an ISIS member. She temporarily housed new members and tried to recruit others to come to Syria to join ISIS. The court said the couple held five Yazidi women and two girls as slaves. Judges found that the husband raped two of the women, with his wife's approval. She was convicted under juvenile law of offenses including membership in a foreign terrorist organization, committing crimes against humanity, being an accessory to rape, and unlawful detention. Her parents-in-law, Perihan S. and Ahmet S., were convicted of offenses including supporting a terrorist organization, and sentenced to 4 1/2 years

and 3 years, respectively. The court held that they knew their sons had joined ISIS in Syria and helped them between 2013 and 2015 acquire military equipment.

June 25, 2021: German state police and officers from a tactical response unit in the French town of Kehl arrested a 21-year-old German at the French border on suspicion of trying to buy a firearm in preparation for a jihadi attack. Prosecutors in Baden-Wuerttemberg State said the man tried to enter Germany from France, where he lives. German authorities said he had obtained several manuals for making bombs and incendiary devices, and shared them with others. Prosecutors said he was en route to Germany to buy an assault rifle. A judge in Karlsruhe ordered him jailed.

June 25, 2021: *AP, RTL, Deutsche Welle*, and *Reuters* reported that at 5 p.m., a Somali man, 24, armed with a long knife stabbed several people in Barbarossa Square in Wüerzburg, killing three people and injuring five, some seriously. A police officer shot the attacker in the thigh and arrested the perpetrator, who had lived in the city since 2015. Bavaria's top security official Joachim Herrmann said a young boy was injured; his father was probably dead. *Main Post* reported that a young boy and his father were killed. The Somali immigrant had been in psychiatric treatment before the attack and was known to police. Witness Julia Runze said, "many people tried to throw chairs or umbrellas or cellphones at him and stop him."

June 28, 2021: *AP* and *Reuters* reported that around 6 a.m., a German-speaking blond man stabbed two passersby, aged 45 and 68, in Erfurt before fleeing. Witnesses said he was about 20 to 30 years old with a scarred face. *AP* reported that police arrested the suspect at his apartment several hours later. He was hospitalized with self-inflicted injuries. The suspect and victims did not know each other; police said there was no reason to suspect a political motivation. Authorities said the man, 32, had a record of violent and other offenses and earlier suffered from mental health issues.

July 14, 2021: *Deutsche Welle, DPA,* and *AP* reported that police executed ten warrants in raids on numerous premises in Hesse State "on suspicion of terrorist financing and the preparation of a serious, state-endangering act of violence". The suspected ISIS supporters included eight men and two women aged between 20 and 51. The accused held German, Afghan, Kosovar, and Turkish citizenship, and were accused of having financed ISIS in Syria through donations. Police recovered cash and data carriers.

July 28, 2021: The Federal Prosecutor's Office in Karlsruhe charged Syrian doctor Alla Mousa with crimes against humanity, murder, severe bodily harm, attempted bodily harm, and dangerous bodily harm for allegedly torturing people in military hospitals in Syria and killing one of them. Mousa arrived in Germany in 2015 and practiced medicine before his 2020 arrest. He was accused of 18 counts of torturing people in military hospitals in the Syrian cities of Homs and Damascus. Prosecutors alleged that Mousa tried to make people infertile. Prosecutors said he poured alcohol over the genitals of a teenage boy and another man and setting fire to them with a cigarette lighter at military hospital No. 608 in Homs, Syria. He was also accused of torturing nine others in the same hospital in 2011 by kicking and beating them, and kicking and beating a jailed man who was suffering an epileptic seizure. Other charges included hanging people from the ceiling and beating them with a plastic baton; pouring flammable liquids over the hand of one of them and burning it; kicking another patient's open, infected wound, pouring disinfectant into it, and setting it on fire.

August 2021: On December 10, 2021, *AP* and *Der Spiegel* reported that police in Hamburg arrested a German Moroccan citizen, 20, after the suspected jihadi tried to buy a weapon and a hand grenade online to carry out an attack. Police found chemicals in his possession that could be used to make explosives.

August 2, 2021: A construction worker, a passerby, and an employee of the city's public transportation corporation were slightly injured in the morning when they were hit by darts several centimeters long likely fired from a blowgun in downtown Cologne's Barbarossaplatz square.

August 4, 2021: *Reuters* reported that police in Berlin detained Mouafak al-D., a Syrian man suspected of firing an anti-tank grenade into a crowd of Palestinian civilians waiting for food aid at the Yarmouk refugee camp near Damascus in 2014, killing seven and severely wounding three, including a child, 6. Prosecutors accused him of war crimes in Syria, fighting for the Free Palestine Movement militia on behalf of President Bashar al-Assad's forces.

August 19, 2021: The Federal Court of Justice rejected the appeals of three people who were convicted in high-profile murder trials involving a far-right group and confirmed the life sentence given to Beate Zschaepe, the only known survivor of the National Socialist Underground. In 2018, a Munich regional court found her guilty of 10 counts of murder for her role in the killing of nine men—eight of Turkish origin and one of Greek—and a police officer between 2000 and 2007, plus membership in a terrorist organization, participating in two bomb attacks and more than a dozen bank robberies, and of attempted murder for setting fire to the group's hideout after its existence came to light. Her two accomplices, Uwe Mundlos and Uwe Boehnhardt, were found dead in an apparent murder-suicide in 2011 after a failed robbery. The federal court upheld the convictions of two men who had helped the group: Ralf Wohlleben, found guilty of accessory to murder for helping supply the trio with a handgun and silencer he knew they planned to use for the killings; and Holger Gerlach, convicted of supporting a terrorist organization for providing the NSU group with a firearm and forged identity papers while its members were at large.

August 23, 2021: *AP, AFP,* the *Guardian, Business Insider,* and *BBC* reported that German police opened an attempted murder investigation after seven people were hospitalized with symptoms of suspected poisoning at the tea area of a kitchen in building L2-01 of the Institute for Material Sciences in Darmstadt Technical University's Lichtwiese campus south of Frankfurt in Hesse State. Police said that milk cartons and water containers in one of the university's buildings appeared to have been contaminated between August 20-23 with a harmful liquid with a powerful smell. Several students said they were nauseated and their arms and legs turned blue. One student, 30, was briefly in critical condition.

August 30, 2021: *Deutsche Welle* reported that federal prosecutors in Geretsried, near Munich, arrested Denise S. on suspicion of organizing money transfers to an ISIS woman who had been detained in a Kurdish refugee camp. Denise S. faced possible charges of supporting a foreign terrorist organization. Police believed she supported Aymen A.-J., an Iraqi man arrested earlier in 2021 as he tried to leave Germany to allegedly fight with IS in Syria or Africa. Prosecutors said he had "a central role in collecting money for IS in Germany" and had transferred several sums to the group in Syria and Lebanon between June and September 2020. He was accused of sending at least €10,170 ($12,000) to ISIS fighters in Syria.

September 4, 2021: Police announced that an Afghan man, 29, stabbed and severely injured a female landscape gardener, 58, who was working in a park in Berlin's Wilmersdorf district during the afternoon, apparently objecting to a woman working. He also severely injured a passerby, 66, who tried to rescue her. Police arrested the attacker for attempted murder and aggravated assault. Police said he might suffer from a mental illness. Prosecutors and criminal police were investigating him on suspicion that his attack may have been motivated by Islamist ideology.

September 16, 2021: *AP* reported that prosecutors said that in August, they had indicted four men on suspicion of supporting the Islamic extremist group Jabhat al-Nusra, which was formed as al-Qaeda's Syrian branch but later broke away. Prosecutors alleged that German citizen Marius A. traveled to Syria in October 2013 to join al-Nusra and remained a member until March 2014. He was detained in Senegal in September 2020 and extradited to Germany in May 2021. Prosecutors claimed that he received firearms training and took part in fighting at least once, and received funds for the group in Turkey. Ger-

man-American citizen Maher M., German-Algerian citizen Mohamed S., and Avid E.G.M., who holds German, Spanish, and Moroccan citizenship, were accused of collecting funds for al-Nusra at Marius A.'s request and transferring him the money in late 2013 or early 2014.

September 16, 2021: *Reuters, Der Spiegel,* and *AP* reported that police thwarted a possible jihadi attack on a synagogue in Hagen during Yom Kippur, arresting four people,

September 18, 2021: A German man, 49, was arrested for the fatal shooting of a young gas station clerk in Idar-Oberstein who asked a customer to wear a face mask. Authorities warned against the radicalization of Querdenken movement members who oppose pandemic restrictions such as masks and vaccines, conspiracy theorists, and some far-right extremists. Police said the suspect returned to the gas station 30 minutes later wearing a mask and fatally shot the clerk in the head. The suspect fled but surrendered to police on September 19. *DPA* reported that the man was not known to police and was not legally entitled to possess a firearm found at his house.

October 20, 2021: Police searched 14 premises in Berlin and three other states in connection with 15 suspects belonging to the Berserker Clan far-right extremist group whose members had discussed preparing for an armed revolt. Police confiscated firearms, ammunition and other weapons, electronic storage devices, drugs, and doping substances. The 15 were accused of forming or being members in a criminal organization.

CNN, Spiegel, and *BBC* reported that police arrested two former German Bundeswehr soldiers, Arend-Adolf G. and Achim A., at their respective homes in the Breisgau-Hochschwarzwald district on suspicion of attempting to create a mercenary paramilitary terrorist unit and recruit 150 other former soldiers and police officers to fight in Yemen's civil war. Police also searched their apartments in Bavaria and Baden-Württemberg. The group aimed at "pacifying" the region and forcing Houthi rebels and the Yemeni government to negotiate. Each member would receive monthly pay of €40,000

(£33,700; $46,560). Prosecutors said Achim A. tried to contact Saudi government representatives to secure funding for the group, but he was ignored. Arend-Adolf G. had contacted seven potential recruits.

October 25, 2021: *Sueddeutsche Zeitung, al-Jazeera, AP, AFP, BBC,* and *DPA* reported that Judge Joachim Baier of the Higher Regional Court in Munich convicted German Jennifer Wenisch, 30, from Lohne in Lower Saxony, of membership of a terrorist organization abroad, aiding and abetting attempted murder, attempted war crimes, and crimes against humanity and sentenced her to 10 years in prison. As an ISIS member in Iraq, she allowed a 5-year-old Yazidi girl she and her husband bought as a slave to die of thirst, chained in a courtyard, in the hot sun. Wenisch grew up as a Protestant but converted to Islam in 2013. She came to Iraq via Turkey and Syria in 2014 to join ISIS. In 2015, as a member of the ISIS *hisbah* "morality police anti-vice squad", she patrolled parks in Fallujah and Mosul, armed with an AK-47 assault rifle, a pistol, and an explosive vest, searching for women who did not conform to its strict codes of behavior and dress. In 2016, she was taken into custody while trying to renew her identity papers at the German embassy in Ankara. She was deported to Germany. The child's mother, Nora, also enslaved, testified about the couple's cruelty. Amal Clooney was part of the team that represented Nora. Prosecutors requested a life sentence; the defense suggested two years. Wenisch's Iraqi jihadi husband Taha al-Jumailly was on trial in Frankfurt.

November 2, 2021: Federal prosecutors charged Stephanie A., a German woman, with membership in two foreign terrorist groups, Jund al-Aqsa and ISIS, violating weapons law, and committing her son as a fighter to a foreign terrorist group. Prosecutors said she and her son, 13 at the time, left Germany in 2016 to live with her husband in ISIS-controlled Syrian territory. Upon arriving in Raqqa in 2017, she joined ISIS, initially living with her husband. Their son, at age 15, completed military training and died in a bomb attack in March 2018. She had a suicide belt and carried a rifle. The couple surrendered to Kurdish troops in

February 2019. She was arrested upon her arrival in Germany in March 2021.

November 6, 2021: At 9 a.m., a Syrian man, 27, stabbed four people with an 8-centimeter folding knife, apparently at random, on the high-speed Intercity Express train 928 traveling from Regensburg/Passau on the Austrian border to Nuremberg and Hamburg. He first attacked a 26-year-old man, wounding him in the head, then a 60-year-old man, who was wounded on his head and torso, and another 60-year-old man. He moved to another train car and stabbed a 39-year-old man on his upper body. Authorities said he showed signs of mental illness. His motives were unclear. He was immediately arrested when the train stopped at Seubersdorf, a station between the Bavarian cities of Regensburg and Nuremberg, and taken to a psychiatric clinic. The four victims were local German men. The attacker came to Germany in 2014 and was granted asylum in 2016. He had lived in Passau and reportedly lost his job on November 5. *AP* and *DPA* added on November 16 that German prosecutors were reconsidering an Islamic extremist motive. Police found ISIS propaganda videos on the suspect; *Facebook* postings had a similar bent.

DPA, Bayerischer Rundfunk, and *AP* reported that in the evening, a man, 57, stabbed a boy, 10, in the neck and shoulder with a kitchen knife in a TK Maxx department store in Munich. The boy was hospitalized with severe injuries. The attacker apparently did not know the child. The attacker was arrested on suspicion of attempted homicide.

November 16, 2021: A Berlin court charged Abdullah H., a Syrian man who allegedly supported ISIS ideology, with preparing a serious act of violence and terror financing in Germany. He was arrested in November 2019 in another case. Federal prosecutors said he decided by June 2019 to conduct an attack in Germany that would be on a similar scale to previous ISIS attacks in Europe, aiming to kill or wound as many people as possible. He acquired material to build improvised explosive devices, including acetone, hydrogen peroxide, and sulfuric acid. He explored using fertilizer as an explosive, acquired various metal parts and tools, and began to build a submachine gun.

November 30, 2021: *AP, AFP, DPA,* and *BBC* reported that the Frankfurt regional court sentenced former ISIS member Taha al-Jumailly, 29, an Iraqi, to life in prison, convicting him of genocide, crimes against humanity, human trafficking, aiding and abetting war crimes, bodily harm resulting in death, and committing a war crime over the death of Reda, a 5-year-old Yazidi girl he had purchased with her mother, Nora, as slaves at an ISIS base in Syria (or Mosul, Iraq—reports differed) in May-June 2015. The two were taken as prisoners from Kocho, Iraq, in August 2014 and sold and resold as slaves. Al-Jumailly then chained up Reda in Fallujah in the hot sun to die. The court ordered him to pay the girl's mother 50,000 euros ($57,000). Presiding judge Christoph Koller noted that this was the first genocide conviction in the world for a person's role in the systematic persecution by ISIS of the Yazidi religious minority. Al-Jumailly's German wife, Jennifer Wenisch, 30, was sentenced on October 25, 2021 to 10 years in prison for the girl's death. Al-Jumailly was arrested in Greece and extradited to Germany in 2019. He was prosecuted under the international legal principle of universal jurisdiction.

Prosecutors in Naumburg charged German woman Leonora M. with aiding and abetting crimes against humanity after she and her ISIS husband enslaved a Yazidi woman in Syria in 2015.

December 2, 2021: Authorities in Dresden arrested Ahmed B., 29, on suspicion of being part of the extremist Libya Revolutionaries Operations Room (LROR) since 2016 and extorting money through kidnappings. A judge ordered him held in custody the next day. He was accused of having commanded a military unit and of illegally obtaining money for the group. He allegedly passed information on Libyans in Germany to LROR. The information was apparently used to kidnap relatives of Libyans living in Germany and demand ransoms for their release.

December 15, 2021: *CNN, Reuters, AFP, BBC,* and *AP* reported that German police, including the special Soko Rex anti-extremist unit, searched five properties in Dresden and one in Heidenau in an investigation into a plot by Dresden Offlinevernetzung anti-vaccination activists to murder the state's prime minister, Michael Kretschmer, among others. The group discussed the plot on *Telegram.* Saxony police tweeted that the discussions suggested that the plotters might have sharp weapons and crossbows. The Frontal program had reported that its journalists had infiltrated the 103 Dresden Online Networking members communicating via *Telegram.* ZDF added that they met in parks. *UPI* added on December 15 that German Foreign Minister Annalene Baerbock announced that Germany expelled two Russian diplomats and summoned Russian Ambassador Sergej Netschajew.

AP reported that the Federal Court of Justice upheld neo-Nazi Andre Eminger's 2018 conviction and 2½-year sentence for supporting the National Socialist Underground terrorist organization. The court denied appeals from the defendant and from prosecutors, who had objected to his acquittal on other charges including accessory to attempted murder.

December 30, 2021: *Newsweek* and *Deutsche Welle* reported that authorities in Munich arrested a man claiming to be a Bundeswehr soldier around the rank of staff sergeant who posted a video making vague threats against government COVID restrictions. He opposed vaccine mandates for service members and health care workers. He said "this is a warning." Text said "soldiers are prepared for dialogue until 16:00 tomorrow."

GREECE

March 9, 2021: *Reuters* and *Athens News Agency* reported that Greece's top administrative court rejected a request by convicted far-left November 17 assassin Dimitris Koufodinas, alias Poison Hand, 63, against his transfer to a jail in central Greece, two months after he started a hunger strike on January 8. He suffered kidney failure in early March and was treated in intensive care at a hospital near the high-security prison of Domokos. He was serving multiple life terms for crimes including 13 murders, among them the brother-in-law of Prime Minister Kyriakos Mitsotakis. Koufodinas wanted to return to Korydallos prison in Athens, where other convicted members of November 17 are held. *Reuters* reported on March 14 that Koufodinas's lawyer, Ioanna Kourtovik, announced that he was ending his 66-day hunger strike.

April 27, 2021: *BBC* reported that Belgian police arrested Ioannis Lagos, 48, who faced jail in Greece for crimes linked to the neo-Nazi Gold Dawn party. The European Parliament voted 658-25 to lift his immunity. In October 2020, an Athens court convicted him, and 17 other members of the party leadership, of running a criminal organization. The court ordered him to serve more than 13 years in prison, but he was given immunity because he was an elected European Parliament member. *AP* reported on April 28 that Lagos refused extradition to Greece. The Brussels court was to decide within 15 days on the extradition request.

On May 15, 2021, *Reuters* reported that Belgium extradited Ioannis Lagos to Athens, where he is to serve a prison sentence alongside other party members for running a criminal gang linked to hate crimes during the country's economic crisis. Six former lawmakers, including Lagos and Golden Dawn leader Nikos Mihaloliakos, were given 13-year jail terms.

July 1, 2021: The police's anti-terrorism division captured and jailed Christos Pappas, 59, former lawmaker and fugitive deputy leader of Greece's extreme right-wing Golden Dawn party. Pappas had been at large for nearly nine months, disappearing before a court sentenced him in October 2020 to 13 years in prison for participation in a criminal organization. He was detained on a ground floor apartment in an Athens suburb with a woman, 52, who faced charges of aiding and abetting a fugitive. He was represented by attorney Pericles Stavrianakis.

July 7, 2021: A Greek man stabbed four people with a large knife outside a grocery store in the Zografou area of Athens. He called police, who arrested him in his basement apartment.

July 27, 2021: Anti-terrorism police arrested a Moroccan man, 28, suspected of ISIS membership since 2014. He appeared in a court in Thessaloniki the next day. He was held on an international arrest warrant issued in 2017 by Morocco, which requested extradition.

ICELAND

November 30, 2021: Authorities found a homemade bomb in a dumpster near an apartment building that houses the U.S. Ambassador's residence in Reykjavik. Police arrested three male suspects, two of whom were on probation and sent back to prison. The third was released.

IRELAND

May 30, 2021: Authorities diverted to Berlin a Ryanair flight en route from Dublin to Krakow, Poland after the crew were warned of a "potential security threat" on the plane.

ITALY

June 7, 2021: Interior Minister Luciana Lamorgese said Italian postal police and Carabinieri paramilitary police dismantled an online group dedicated to antisemitic and racist propaganda that incited young people to carry out extreme actions. Police took down the website of the group that claims 17,000 members, including people abroad. Members ranged in age from 26 to 62. *LaPresse* reported that 12 persons were ordered to regularly sign in with police. *LaPresse* said a "NATO structure" was among the targets of a planned bombing. The twelve were alleged to be associated with propaganda and instigating ethnic and religious discrimination. Ruth Dureghello, president of Rome's Jewish Community, tweeted that the group was planning attacks against Jews and non-European Union foreigners.

June 16, 2021: *Newsweek* and *Il Messaggero* reported that police found a bomb in a car in Rome's Prati area near Stadio Olimpico prior to the UEFA Euro 2020 Championship Group soccer match between Italy and Switzerland. *Il Messaggero* called it a "machine with some suspicious threads" coming from the top of it. *IM* said the cylinder filled with gunpowder and electrical wire was on the bodywork of Italian municipal executive Marco Doria's parked car. Police defused the device. Marco Doria is the president for the redevelopment of parks and historic villas in Rome.

Express reported that the Italian Metropolitan Police announced it had stopped four late-stage terror plots since the pandemic began.

July 5, 2021: *Reuters* reported that police arrested four unemployed men accused of wiring €30,000 from a money transfer agency in Andria to 42 collectors of funds for ISIS, in countries including Serbia, Germany, Turkey, Jordan, Thailand, and Russia. Luca Cioffi, a colonel in the Italian tax police, added that the 42 collectors had received €1 million in suspicious transfers from other sources. The payments included €5,000 sent to two Russians days before an attack on a church in southern Russia that killed five women.

August 9, 2021: *Reuters* reported that during the night workers in a mail sorting facility in Peschiera Borromeo near Milan seized an envelope addressed to Pope Francis containing three pistol bullets. The envelope, sent from France, was addressed to "The Pope, Vatican City, St Peter's Square".

September 9, 2021: *AP* and *Reuters* reported that anti-terrorism police raided the homes of eight people in Rome, Bergamo, Milan, Venice, and two other northern cities who allegedly advocated violence, particularly against journalists, in upcoming protests in Rome and elsewhere against the government's COVID-19 vaccine requirements. The eight had formed The Warriors on *Telegram*. Police said the eight planned to use home-made explosive devices at rallies, particularly one that weekend in Rome by opponents of the "Green Pass" certification, which is required to dine indoors, access gyms, and attend crowded venues, such as concerts. As of September, the requirements included domestic travel on planes, trains, buses, and ferries; local transport was exempt. The eight called for "blowing up trucks" operated by TV networks. Police seized brass knuckles during the raids.

September 12, 2021: *AP* and *RAI* reported that a Somali asylum-seeker, 26, slashed two female ticket controllers aboard a bus in Rimini, then wounded three other people, including a boy, 6, who was sitting with his mother in a local outdoor market, as he fled. The boy was in critical condition following surgery. Italian police opened an attempted murder investigation. They ruled out terrorism as a motive and suggested that he was on drugs. Police arrested the man on a side street flanking a hotel. *Corriere della Sera* reported that he apparently had been denied asylum in Denmark, Sweden, Germany, and the Netherlands, since arriving in Europe in 2015. *State TV* said he had applied for asylum in Italy and was living in a migrant residence run by a Catholic charity in Rimini.

Kosovo

October 27, 2021: Kosovo sanctioned seven local businessmen and the AID Properties company for links with Lebanese Hizballah, freezing their assets. The individuals may not leave the country nor receive money from other individuals or companies from Kosovo. Lebanon and the Palestinian Authority do not recognize Kosovo's 2008 independence.

November 24, 2021: Prosecutors charged S.Q., a local man who had allegedly joined ISIS in Raqqa, Syria, after entering through Turkey. S.Q. allegedly received training in Syria and took part in fighting. He was handed over to Kurdish forces and repatriated in July 2021. He faced 10 years in prison.

November 26, 2021: Fadil Gashi, police spokesman in Peja, said that at 6 pm., a masked gunman fired a Kalashnikov at a bus carrying eight teenagers in Gllogjan, killing the driver and two teens and injuring another.

December 3, 2021: Prosecutors charged an ethnic Albanian man from Kosovo, N.L., with terrorism for allegedly joining Jabhat al-Nusra with his son in Syria, where he had brought his family. Authorities claimed he trained as a fighter and participated in attacks in Syria. He allegedly returned to Kosovo in April 2013 to bring his wife, two daughters, and a daughter-in-law to Syria, then rejoined his son and the al-Nusra group. He was handed over to Syrian forces and repatriated to Kosovo. He faced 10 years in prison.

MEDITERRANEAN SEA

March 10, 2021: *Reuters* reported that Iranian state-run shipping company IRISL told semi-official *Nournews* that the Iranian container ship *Shahre Kord* was damaged by an explosive object which caused a small fire in a "terrorist" attack in the Mediterranean. No one was injured, but the ship was damaged.

NETHERLANDS

March 2021: Early in the month, a "homemade device" smashed windows at a coronavirus testing center in a small Dutch town but caused no injuries.

March 18, 2021: *AP* reported on April 8, 2021 that on March 18, police arrested a man, 37, on suspicion of plotting a crime with "terrorist intent" for allegedly planning to set off what they described as a "firework bomb" at a coronavirus vaccination center at the former town hall in the northern port of Den Helder, 55 miles north of Amsterdam. Prosecutors said the terrorist act "aimed to instill serious fear among the population and to disrupt the economic and social structures of the country… [He] sought to sabotage a crucial government process, the nationally coordinated vaccination program, in an extremely violent manner… This also affects public health: The fewer people can be vaccinated, the more victims the virus will claim."

June 15, 2021: *BBC* and *NOS* reported that Syrian refugee Ahmad al-Khedr, 49, went on trial for war crimes and terrorist offenses for a killing carried out during the Syrian conflict. He was arrested in 2019 after he was spotted in a 2012 video showing the murder of an unarmed Syrian Air Force lieutenant colonel. He admitted being present at the time, but denied he was part of the killing using the alias Abu Khuder, allegedly a local leader of the al-Nusra Front. His lawyer claimed that he wanted to exchange the captive for his brothers, who were being held in government prisons.

Al-Khedr told the court that he had fled to Turkey in 2013, then arrived in the Netherlands via Greece in April 2014. His wife and seven children eventually joined him. He volunteered at a local football club in Kapelle until his arrest.

On July 16, 2021, *Reuters* reported that a Dutch court sentenced Ahmad al-Khedr, alias Abu Khuder, 49, to 20 years in prison for war crimes over his role in the execution of a Syrian government soldier. He was a member of the al-Qaeda-affiliated Nusra Front in Syria. The court established that his voice could be heard in a video of the execution of a captured Syrian soldier who was shot on the banks of the Euphrates River. Al-Khedr was granted temporary asylum when he arrived in the Netherlands in 2014.

June 29, 2021: The Hague District Court convicted a woman, 32, and sentenced her to six years in prison for involvement in war crimes committed by ISIS in Syria and Iraq by spreading ISIS propaganda from her home near Amsterdam. The Court held that ISIS is a criminal organization with the aim of committing war crimes. Prosecutors had requested a three-year sentence; the judges replied that was "far too low" even though she had a "psychological impulse disorder". She had distributed ISIS propaganda on *Telegram* in 2019. She posted two videos of POWs being killed and provided her own "humiliating" commentary for one of the executions. She also incited others to commit terrorist crimes and war crimes, trained herself and others to make bomb vests, and sent money to people involved in terrorist activities. The court ordered her to undergo compulsory psychological treatment.

September 20, 2021: A Dutch court convicted two Syrian brothers of holding senior roles in Jabhat al-Nusra in Syria between 2011 and 2014, the first time Dutch judges convicted a suspect of leadership in a Syrian extremist organization. One brother was sentenced to 15 years and nine months, the other to 11 years and nine months. The brothers had been given asylum in the Netherlands.

September 26, 2021: *CNN* reported that the Public Prosecutor's Office announced that the Royal and Diplomatic Security Service in The Hague arrested Arnoud van Doorn, Dutch film producer and former far-right Dutch Freedom

Party (PVV) politician, after Prime Minister Mark Rutte's security detail suspected him of behaving suspiciously. Van Doorn had served as a senior political adviser for populist Freedom Party leader Geert Wilders. He was released the next day but the Public Prosecutor's Office stressed that he "remains a suspect" in connection with "trying to provide information to others to prepare a serious crime". *De Telegraaf* and *Reuters* reported that Rutte's security had been increased following fears he could be the target of an attack or kidnapping by a criminal gang.

September 30, 2021: Capping an 18-month cross-border investigation, Europol announced that police in the Netherlands and Germany arrested nine suspected members of a gang who robbed ATMs in Germany and believed to have set up a training center in Utrecht for blowing up cash machines. Police in Osnabrueck became suspicious when a Dutch man, 29, ordered several ATMs, saying they were for an art project in the Netherlands. The man and an accomplice video'd themselves blowing up the ATMs in a warehouse to get cash inside. The 29-year-old died in September 2020 while testing an explosive device at the training center. An accomplice was injured and arrested. Dutch police arrested three suspects on September 28 and raided seven properties, where they found equipment used for blowing up ATMs. The gang was accused of blowing up at least 15 ATMs across Germany, causing millions of euros in damage. Some 414 ATMs were blown up across Germany in 2020.

October 13, 2021: *UPI* reported that Yuvuz O., 22, faced charges in court the next week of making threats, incitement with a terrorist objective, and preparing to attack one or more politicians by plotting to assassinate Prime Minister Mark Rutte. He posted messages on *Telegram* asking where to obtain weapons and gunmen. *NL Times* reported he posted "Would you have what it takes to shoot them all? From a car. Open the window. Gun out. And shoot." Officials said he discussed the plot with people online and in person, suggesting "storming" the Dutch Parliament and shooting Rutte as he tried to escape.

October 27, 2021: Rotterdam District Court convicted an Iranian refugee, 42, who was linked to the separatist Arab Struggle Movement for the Liberation of Ahwaz, for preparing and financing terror attacks in his homeland targeting the Iranian government and its supporters, sentencing him to four years in prison. He was from Ahwaz. He had lived in the Netherlands since being granted residency as a refugee. The court said he discussed possible targets, offered financial support, and urged separatists to make video recordings of attacks.

NORTH MACEDONIA

July 17, 2021: Police spokesperson Toni Angelovski announced that four suspected former ISIS fighters and their 19 family members, including five women and 14 children, were repatriated to North Macedonia from Syria and Iraq. The four men were put in custody pending trial. The women and children were put into two-week health quarantine for COVID-19 medical exams and "possible participation in incriminating acts".

NORTHERN IRELAND

March 3, 2021: *Reuters* reported that Loyalist Communities Council chairman David Campbell informed UK Prime Minister Boris Johnson that Northern Irish loyalist paramilitary groups including the Ulster Volunteer Force, Ulster Defence Association, and Red Hand Commando temporarily withdrew support for the 1998 peace agreement due to concerns over the Brexit deal.

April 3-8, 2021: *CNN* reported that 3-day weekend clashes involved 30 petrol bombs in Belfast and Derry/Londonderry. Riots began in both cities on April 3 when the government decided not to prosecute leaders of the Irish nationalist party Sinn Fein for allegedly breaking coronavirus restrictions by attending the funeral of a former leading IRA figure during lockdown in 2020. The decision was being reviewed. Loyalists hijacked and burned a car at the Cloughfern roundabout in Newtownabbey, Belfast, on April 3. Masked men threw petrol bombs and hijacked cars in the Loyalist area North of Belfast. The Police Service of Northern Ireland (PSNI) noted that the clashes involved children aged 12. During the night of April 3, rioters threw 30 petrol bombs at police in Newtownabbey, Belfast and three vehicles were hijacked and set alight. Pro-British Unionists objected to the Northern Ireland Protocol of the Brexit withdrawal agreement which aims to eliminate the need for border controls between Northern Ireland and the Republic of Ireland, an EU member. The rioting continued into the next week. A city bus was hijacked and torched in Belfast on April 8. PSNI Assistant Chief Constable Jonathan Roberts said that 55 police had been injured.

April 7, 2021: *Reuters* reported that youths in a pro-British area of Belfast torched a hijacked bus.

April 19, 2021: *Reuters* reported that the PSNI said a bomb was found near the family home of a female part-time police officer in Dungiven, near Londonderry. Brandon Lewis, British cabinet minister for Northern Ireland, tweeted: "The attempted murder of this police officer is absolutely abhorrent. I completely condemn the actions of those involved." No one claimed credit.

November 1, 2021: *UPI* and *BBC Northern Ireland* reported that around dawn, masked gunmen hijacked and torched a bus, raising fears of the start of Brexit-related violence. The gunmen forced the driver to get off; there were no passengers. The gunmen mentioned the 1998 Northern Ireland Protocol, which prevents border checks, which was upheld when the UK was part of the European Union.

NORWAY

June 30, 2021: The Oslo District Court sentenced a Syrian teen to five years in prison for planning an act of terror in Norway by using poison or explosives, and for supporting ISIS. He was 16 years and two months old when Norway's domestic security agency arrested him in Oslo. The court suspended three years because of his youth. Judge Ingvild Boe Hornburg wrote that "The court has no doubt that the defendant had, despite his young age, made a conscious decision

to carry out an act of terror although the plans had not materialized in a concrete plan." The teen admitted curiosity made him buy the ingredients to make the poison but claimed he had no intention of hurting anyone. He confessed that he donated more than 1,250 kroner ($146) to a website supporting ISIS and that he posted a video on how to upload an ISIS propaganda video. The verdict noted that he also downloaded material on how to make and handle explosives. The court said that had he been over the age of 18, the sentence could have been 11 years.

October 13, 2021: The *Guardian, Reuters, TV2, Insider, NTB, NRK, Expressen, AFP, CNN,* and *AP* reported that Kongsberg police chief Oeyvdind Aas said that at 6:12 p.m., Espen Andersen Bråthen, variant Braathen, a Danish man, 37, wielding a bow and arrow killed four women and a man, aged between 50 and 70, and injured three people, including an off-duty officer, in a town 50 miles southwest of Oslo. The dead included an artist and a couple in their 70s. *BBC* reported that the individual first attacked a Coop Extra supermarket on Kongsberg's west side. With reports of sightings popping up throughout the city, police dispatched 22 patrols to find Bråthen. Police arrived at 6:18 p.m., but Bråthen shot arrows at them and escaped. Police eventually arrested him at 6:47 p.m. The *Washington Post* added that police believed it was a "terrorist act" by an Islamic convert. Regional police chief Ole B. Saeverud said police had received reports indicating that Bråthen may have been radicalized, although none came in 2021, and that police had earlier been in contact with Bråthen. The suspect was ordered to undergo a psychiatric examination. Police said the suspect had confessed. A court had granted a restraining order in 2020 for Bråthen to stay away from two of his family members for six months after he threatened to kill one of them. Police were temporarily ordered to carry weapons. Bråthen's attorney, Fredrik Neumann, said that his client had a Danish mother and Norwegian father. A relative told Danish newspaper *Ekstra Bladet* that Bråthen was mentally ill and said the family had suffered threats for several years. *AP* added on October 15 that a court in Kongsberg ordered Bråthen held in custody for four weeks, including two weeks in isolation, and banned him from communicating with others. He was held on five counts of preliminary murder and three counts of preliminary attempted murder. Norwegian media reported that he had earlier been convicted of burglary and drug possession.

AP reported on October 19 that police reported that the attacker stabbed the five victims to death, some in their homes. They were investigating "illness" as the motive.

AFP reported on October 27 that Norwegian police said that 24 people were being treated as victims. 21101301

November 9, 2021: AP and NTB reported that around 9 a.m., police shot to death a man, naked from the waist up and reportedly armed with a knife, who threatened passers-by on the streets of Oslo. A police officer was slightly hurt. Senior Police Chief Egil Joergen Brekke said, "We have so far no information that this is terror-related… To us, this appears to be a stand-alone act, so that there is no reason to fear for the safety of the city for others. This is a person who is known to us in the past and who has a history." Police had received reports about a man with a knife running after another person. A patrol car in the nearby Bislett neighborhood tried to stop the man by running him down before it drove into a building between a flower shop and a cafe to box him in. He opened the car door, whereupon witnesses heard six shots fired at him.

ROMANIA

March 28, 2021: Reuters reported that death threats were emailed to award-winning film and theater star Maia Morgenstern and her children at the start of Passover celebrations. Morgenstern portrayed Mary in Mel Gibson's *The Passion of the Christ* and runs the Jewish State Theater in Bucharest. The emailer also vowed to torch the Jewish theater and its staff. The email was signed "on behalf of the far right Alliance for Uniting Romanians (AUR)". AUR's leader George Simion said AUR was not involved.

RUSSIA

April 18, 2021: AFP reported Kurdish authorities in Qamishli in northeast Syria handed over to Anna Kuznetsova, Russian President Putin's envoy for children's rights, for repatriation 34 orphaned children, aged between three and 14, whose parents were suspected of ISIS membership. Fener al-Kait of the Syrian Kurdish foreign affairs department said that Moscow has repatriated at least 169 such children, with more orphans to come.

May 10, 2021: AP, CNN, Reuters, and ABC News reported that the head of the Republic of Tatarstan, Rustam Minnikhanov, said a "19-year-old terrorist" shot to death seven students—four boys and three girls—and a teacher and injured 18 children, six critically, in a shooting at School 175 in Kazan. Minnikhanov said the alleged gunman, who was detained, had a weapon registered in his name and that "no accomplices have been established". He also had a gun license. Students jumped from third-floor windows to escape the gunfire. RIA Novosti reported that two children died jumping from the windows. Lawmaker Alexander Khinshtein posted on Telegram that the suspect registered a Turkish-made Hatsan Escort shotgun on April 28. Russian media reported that on a Telegram channel created by the alleged shooter a few days earlier, a man in combat-style clothes posed in front of a mirror and referred to himself as "God", promising to soon kill "a large number of bio-trash". CNN had reported that eight children were killed by two gunmen; Tass reported that a second gunman was killed by officers from the Federal Security Services (FSB) who stormed the building. AP reported on May 12 that nine people—seven children and two school employees—had been killed and 23 people had been hospitalized. Russian media said the shooter was a former student at the school.

July 1, 2021: The FSB announced it had discovered a plot by ISIS followers to conduct terrorist attacks in Moscow and southern Russia. Authorities killed a suspected conspirator when he resisted arrest in the Astrakhan region, and arrested another in Moscow. The FSB added that two Russians were plotting the attacks with firearms and knives in crowded areas in Moscow and Astrakhan under the IS leaders' guidance. The FSB seized weapons and extremist literature during searches at the suspects' homes.

September 20, 2021: *AP, AFP, ABC News, Reuters,* and *BBC* reported that Timur Bekmansurov, 18, wearing black tactical gear and a helmet, fired a smoothbore hunting rifle at people in Perm State University, killing six and injuring 28 before being hospitalized with wounds received while resisting arrest. *Tass* reported that he purchased the rifle in May and also carried a knife. The first responders were local traffic police. The gunman fired several shots at them and was critically wounded by return fire from Officer Konstantin Kalinin. *ABC News* reported that he was a law student at the college and fired a shotgun. Russian state media reported that an account with Bekmansurov's name on the Russian social media network *VKontakte* published a lengthy post shortly before the attack which describes fantasizing about carrying out a mass killing at a public place. The poster wrote he has no religious or political motive and said he had dreamed of the killing "for years". A photo showed the suspected shooter in a helmet and with ammunition cartridges around his chest, giving the finger to the camera. Russian news sites showed video of students jumping out of second-story windows.

AFP reported the next day that the attacker killed one man and five women aged between 18 and 66. *AP* and *Tass* reported on September 21 that Minister of Science and Higher Education Valery Falkov said seven survivors were to be airlifted to Moscow for medical treatment.

December 7, 2021: A gunman opened fire in a Moscow government services center, killing two people and wounding three, including a girl, 10, after refusing to wear a face mask. Police arrested a Moscow resident, 45. *Interfax* reported that a Glock handgun was found.

December 13, 2021: *AP* and *BBC* reported that a former student, 18, was the chief suspect when a homemade bomb detonated in a school attached to the Orthodox Vladychny convent in Serpukhov, wounding 12 people, including

a 15-year-old. He tried to blow himself up, but survived, although in critical condition. *Interfax* said the attacker hated the students and nuns at the school. *Tass* reported that he was planning an attack during morning prayers, but his bomb went off at the entrance to the monastery.

SPAIN

March 24, 2021: The National Police detained and questioned the highest-ranking representative of the Muslim community in Spain, Aiman Adlbi, leader of the Islamic Commission of Spain (CIE), as part of a terrorism investigation.

April 23, 2021: *Reuters* reported that Interior Minister Fernando Grandes-Marlaska, the head of the Guardia Civil police force, and former Social Rights Minister Pablo Iglesias, leader of the left-wing Unidas Podemos party, received a death threat letter with four bullets enclosed in the envelope. The text read, "Your wife, your parents and you are sentenced to the capital punishment, your time is running out."

April 27, 2021: *Reuters* and *13 TV* reported that postal workers in a mail processing hub in Catalonia intercepted a death threat letter with two bullets enclosed that was mailed to Isabel Diaz Ayuso, the conservative head of the Madrid region's Popular Party and frontrunner in polling for the May 4 election to the 136-seat regional assembly. Another letter, with bullets, was sent to the chief of the Guardia Civil police.

July 31, 2021: *AP* reported on August 5 that the Guardia Civil's intelligence service announced the July 31 nighttime arrest on Mallorca of an Algerian man suspected of leading a gang that trafficked people from North Africa to Europe and sent fighters from Algeria, Morocco, and Tunisia to jihadist groups in Libya, using the revenue from the human trafficking activities. Authorities suspected the organization sent terrorists from Algeria to Spain.

September 16, 2021: *Reuters* reported that authorities evacuated the central part of Oviedo after an anonymous telephone call at 9:50 a.m. warned of an explosive device in an underground parking lot near the city courthouse. No bomb was found.

October 13, 2021: Police in the second phase of Operation ARBAC arrested five suspects—four in Barcelona and one in Madrid—believed to be part of a jihadist group that tried to recruit others and was attempting to acquire weapons, including a Kalashnikov assault rifle. Police seized machetes and ammunition. Police identified the group's leader as "Sheikh" who had been arrested in Turkey in 2016 when he had tried to join ISIS. He entered Spain in March 2021. In the first round of ARBAC, police in Barcelona arrested three Algerians in January 2021. Police then became aware of Sheikh as a person in Algeria who tried to help group members enter Spain without being detected. *AP* reported that police were assisted by Spain's intelligence services, the FBI, Europol, and Algerian security forces.

SWEDEN

March 3, 2021: *Al-Jazeera, Bloomberg, Vetlanda-Posten, NBC News, TT News Agency,* and *Reuters* reported that at 2 p.m., an Afghan, 22, armed with an axe wounded eight people at five crime scenes in Vetlanda. Police shot him in the leg, then arrested him. Prime Minister Stefan Lofven suggested a possible "terrorist" motive. *AFP* reported that the suspect arrived in Sweden in 2018, lived in the area, and had been accused of "petty crimes", such as cannabis use. On July 14, 2021, *Reuters* reported that a Swedish court sentenced him to life in prison for attempted murder. Although he suffered from a mental illness, he was judged fit to stand trial. 21030302

September 28, 2021: *CNN* and *AFP* reported that at 4:45 a.m., an explosion in an apartment building in Gothenburg, variant Goteborg, injured 16, four critically, and started a large fire that damaged 140 apartments. Stefan Gustafsson, a spokesman for Sweden's western regional police, said "The fire department has confirmed that there is no gas in that building, so we have ruled out a gas leak for the moment... There is no natural explanation for the explosion." Gang activity was suspected but later discounted as a motive. *Aftonbladet* reported that one of the

area's residents was involved in a witness protection program. On September 30, *AP* reported that Swedish police were seeking a man on suspicion of public destruction; Swedish media reported he was a man in his 50s who had lived with his mother in the building in Goteborg. *Aftonbladet* reported that the property owner had been trying to evict the man and his mother. The *Goteborg-Posten* newspaper said an eviction was planned for the day the explosion occurred. *Aftonbladet* noted that police had charged the man with several alleged crimes a week before the blast. *Reuters* reported that on September 30, Swedish police arrested the man in absentia. He was suspected of attempted murder, arson, and general destruction. *ABC News* reported on October 6 that the suspect was found dead in the waters of Goteborg's harbor, a few miles from the building. Police added that foul play was not suspected. Swedish media reported that he was born in Poland.

TURKEY

February 15, 2021: The Defense Ministry announced the arrest of S.A., an ISIS woman, 26, and two children who tried to cross illegally into the country from Syria at Reyhanli, in Hatay Province. She briefly held Australian and New Zealand citizenship. The leaders of the two countries argued over who should take responsibility for her if she was deported. Australia had stripped away her citizenship under anti-terrorism laws. New Zealand Prime Minister said S.A. had lived in Australia for most of her life and had traveled to Syria on her Australian passport, observing, "We believe Australia has abdicated its responsibilities in relation to this person and I have personally made that point to {Australian} Prime Minister Morrison. It is wrong that New Zealand should shoulder the responsibility for a situation involving a woman who has not lived in New Zealand since she was 6." Morrison countered, "We do not want to see terrorists who fought with terrorism organizations enjoying privileges of citizenship, which I think they forfeit the second they engage as an enemy of our country." He cited a 2015 Australian law that automatically cancels the citizenship of dual nationals who engage in terrorism. S.A. was wanted on an Interpol notice for allegedly belonging to ISIS.

April 28, 2021: *Demiroren* and *AP* reported that police in Istanbul's Atasehir district on the city's Asian side detained Afghan national Basim, a close aide of former ISIS caliph Abu Bakr al-Baghdadi. He had helped hide al-Baghdadi in Syria's Idlib Province. Basim entered Turkey with a false passport and identity card.

September 16, 2021: The U.S. Department of the Treasury imposed sanctions against five men, including three Turkish and two Egyptian nationals, in Turkey suspected of providing financial services and travel assistance to al-Qaeda. The designees included:

- Majdi Salim, an Egyptian-born lawyer accused of being one of the primary facilitators of al-Qaeda activities in Turkey. The U.S. said he had led the Egyptian Islamic Jihad, after taking over that role from al-Qaeda leader Ayman al-Zawahiri.

- Muhammad Nasr al-Din al-Ghazlani, an Egyptian

- Nurettin Muslihan, a Turk

- Cebrail Guzel, a Turk

- Soner Gurleyen, a Turk

October 11, 2021: The Gaziantep governor's office said three mortar shells fired from Syria fell into the Turkish town of Karkamış, across the border from Jarablus. One mortar fell near a train station, another in a park. No injuries were reported.

October 30, 2021: The Interior Ministry announced that it had deported 8,585 foreign terrorist suspects from 102 countries since the start of the Syrian civil war a decade earlier. They included 44 from the U.S. and 1,075 from European Union countries. Between January 1, 2021 and the end of October, 61 suspects from eight EU countries were deported.

December 28, 2021: *U.S. News and World Report* and *Reuters* reported that police detained 16 people accused of links to ISIS after protesters used sticks and stones against security forces trying to shut down an unlicensed religious bookshop in Bingol during the night. The suspects were held for assaulting a law enforcement officer, intentionally causing injury, and damaging public property.

UKRAINE

September 11-12, 2021: *Al-Jazeera* reported two Ukrainian soldiers were killed and ten others wounded in clashes with Russian-backed separatists in Ukraine's eastern Donetsk. Separatists fired large-caliber artillery, grenade launchers, and drones.

September 22, 2021: *CNN, Reuters, al-Jazeera,* and *Ukinform* state news reported that at 10 a.m., would-be assassins fired more than ten bullets at the car of Serhiy Shefir, first assistant to President Volodymyr Zelenskyy, in Lisnyky, a village on the outskirts of Kyiv, seriously wounding the driver with three gunshots from automatic weapons. Shefir was not hurt.

December 24, 2021: *Reuters* reported that the Russian foreign ministry said that someone had thrown a Molotov cocktail at the Russian consulate in Lviv, protesting the "act of terrorism" and demanding an apology. 21122401

UNITED KINGDOM

February 8, 2021: *The Hill* and *AP* reported Home Secretary Priti Patel said that the government's Joint Terrorism Analysis Center lowered the terrorist threat level from "severe" to "substantial", in the middle of the five-point scale. The threat level was raised in November after incidents in Austria and France.

March 22, 2021: *NBC News* reported that a would-be terrorist's manifesto included neo-Nazi tropes and a list of targets that included post offices, pubs, schools, and banks (for "obvious reasons", he wrote). He cited 19 firearms he wanted to obtain. He was 13 when he began radicalizing and 16 when he was convicted, in November 2019, of planning six terrorist attacks.

According to reports, at the time of his arrest he was the youngest person convicted of plotting a terrorist attack in the U.K.

March 24, 2021: *Bang Showbiz* reported that a man, 39, was arrested after a suspicious package was found and rendered safe at the Palace of Holyroodhouse, the Queen's official Scottish residence in Edinburgh.

April 1, 2021: *CNN* reported that a jury in London's Central Criminal Court convicted Metropolitan Police officer Benjamin Hannam, 22, of five charges, including membership in the banned neo-Nazi National Action group, making a false application to join the police force in 2018 by not disclosing his membership of the group, and the possession of indecent photographs of a child. Hannam was serving as a probationary officer in London's Metropolitan Police force. The *PA Media* news agency reported that he was the first police officer to be convicted of belonging to a far right terrorist group. Police found documents on a USB memory stick and other digital devices which linked Hannam to far-right groups. A folder on the memory stick was named "NA" and contained files related to National Action. He attended an NA meeting in a London pub in March 2016 and various other events until summer 2017. National Action was the first far-right group to be banned under British terrorism laws in December 2016. Membership is a criminal offense. Judge Anthony Leonard scheduled sentencing for later in April 2021. *Reuters* reported on April 30 that Hannam was sentenced to four years and four months in jail at London's Old Bailey court.

May 23, 2021: The *Washington Post*, the *Guardian, Fox News, SkyNews, Insider, UPI*, and *BBC* reported that British Black Lives Matter activist and mother of three Sasha Johnson, 27, was shot in the head at 3 a.m. at a house party on Consort Road in south London's Southwark borough. She had received numerous death threats. She was reported to be in critical condition at a local hospital. She was a leader of the Taking the Initiative party, which was founded in 2020. Police did not believe it was a targeted attack. *AP* reported on May 26 that British police had arrested five male suspects aged between 17 and 28 on suspicion of attempted murder and possession of drugs and weapons. London's Metropolitan Police force said she was in the back garden attending the house party when four Black men entered the premises and shot Johnson. A friend told *BBC* that gang violence at the party may have been involved. Authorities said four men had broken into the party and began firing.

AP and *Reuters* reported on May 29 that authorities at Westminster Magistrates' Court charged Cameron Deriggs, 18, with conspiracy to murder Johnson, who remained in critical condition. His next court appearance was scheduled for June 25. He was one of five people arrested in the case; the others were released on bail. Police believed she was an unintended victim.

AP and *CNN* reported that on June 11, 2021, a second person, Devonte Brown, 18, of Southwark, was charged at Westminster Magistrates' Court for conspiracy to murder over the shooting in south London of Sasha Johnson. Brown was remanded into custody with an order to appear at the Old Bailey courthouse on July 7. Five male suspects were arrested three days after the incident; four of them were released on bail until late June.

June 10, 2021: *The Hill* and *Reuters* reported that British police arrested a man, 20, at a hotel in Falmouth at around 3:15 a.m. after receiving a report of a suspicious package. The bomb hoax was near the site of the Group of Seven (G-7) Summit, which was to take place the following day. Most of the media covering the summit were staying in the hotel.

June 18, 2021: *CNN* reported that West Midlands Police were searching for a man who fired a BB gun and drove a silver Volvo into a crowd at Gigmill pub in Stourbridge, about 126 miles northwest of London, hospitalizing three women and a man, all in their 20s. A man and a woman sustained serious leg injuries. The driver fled on foot in what authorities called "a targeted attack" shortly after the Euro 2020 match between England and Scotland ended.

July 25, 2021: *AP* and *Newsweek* reported that an individual dressed in black with a hood and face mask slashed the throat and body of Christian woman proselytizer Hatun Tash, 39, with a knife at Speakers' Corner in London's Hyde Park. She was wearing a *Charlie Hebdo* T-shirt. Tash was injured in the face and hands. As of July 29, no arrests had been made. Tash, a former Muslim from Turkey, was represented by London's Christian Legal Centre, the legal services group of the not-for-profit advocacy group Christian Concern. Tash is a member of (Defend Christ Critique Islam) DCCI Ministries and the Free Speech Union.

August 6, 2021: The *Evening Standard* reported that at 7:20 p.m. an attacker stabbed a male social worker, 61, and slashed a police officer on Noel Park Road, Wood Green, in north London. Police arrested a man at the scene on suspicion of assault; two other people were arrested as part of the investigation. The Haringey Council social worker was trying to check on the welfare of vulnerable children. Two police officers joined him when residents refused him access. After the trio forced the door and entered a communal area of the building, the attacker, 33, rushed the social worker and stabbed him several times. He was arrested at the scene on suspicion of causing grievous bodily harm.

August 12, 2021: The *Washington Post, Reuters, CNN,* and *AP* reported that at 6:10 p.m., crane operator Jake Davison, 22, dressed in black, killed five people—two women and two men at the scene, and a woman who died in a hospital—before turning the pump-action shotgun on himself in a mass shooting in Plymouth. He initially fired shots in a house, killing his mother, Maxine Davison, aka Maxine Chapman, 51, before walking onto Biddick Drive in the Keyham area of Plymouth. A spokesman for the Devon and Cornwall Police said this was not "a terrorism-related incident". Most of the victims were strangers to the gunman. The *Times* and *Daily Mail* reported his next murder victim was a child, Sophie Martyn, 3, who was walking a dog with her father, Lee Martyn, 43, who also died. Davison badly injured two other passersby, then entered Henderson Place park, shooting dead Stephen Washington, 59, and walked to a nearby street, killing Kate Shepherd, 66. He then killed

himself. Police had no motive, and searched his computer for clues. He had no known contacts with extremist groups. He had a firearms license. *YouTube* removed his site. He had posted that he was a virgin as a teen and was an incel. He posted that he was beaten down by life.

August 25, 2021: *CNN* reported that Metropolitan Police arrested Leoaai Elghareeb, 37, a lawyer, on suspicion of contamination of goods with intention of causing public harm or anxiety after processed meat and microwaveable products were injected with needles at three supermarkets—Little Waitrose, Tesco Express and Sainsbury's Local—on Fulham Palace Road in southwest London. Police were called at 7:40 p.m. after a man shouted abuse at people in the street and started "throwing around" syringes filled with blood and injecting them into food items. He did not enter a plea during a preliminary hearing at Westminster Magistrates' Court; his next hearing was scheduled for September 24.

September 5, 2021: *Business Insider* and the *Sunday Mail* reported that the anti-vax Veterans 4 Freedom paramilitary group discussed attacking COVID-19 vaccine centers but disbanded after a newspaper exposed it the previous week. The group was founded by a former Royal Marine commando and included more than 200 former servicemen and servicewomen, some armed with crossbows. Some members formed the Global Veterans Alliance, whose leader used the name Bellzaac.

September 10, 2021: *Business Insider, Sky News,* and *BBC* reported that London transport staff had been warned about anti-mask posters, which bear the message "Masks don't work", that have razor blades on them. The posters were found in London's tube and rail stations. The Rail, Maritime, and Transport (RMT) union formally raised the issue with Transport for London (TfL) staff and called for police to take the "hardest possible line" against those found responsible. In July, a woman in Cardiff, Wales, injured her hand when taking down an anti-mask poster that had a hidden razor blade.

October 15, 2021: *AP, CNBC, CNN, Reuters,* and *Sky News* reported that at 12:05 p.m., Conservative Party Member of Parliament Sir David Amess, 69, who represented Southend West in Essex, was stabbed multiple times while meeting with constituents in his home district at the Belfairs Methodist Church on Eastwood Road North in Leigh-on-Sea in southeast England. Police arrested a male suspect, 25, on suspicion of murder and confiscated a knife. The *Washington Post* reported that Amess died hours later. The next day, the counterterrorism division of London's Metropolitan Police formally declared the incident an act of terrorism, observing, "The early investigation has revealed a potential motivation linked to Islamist extremism… We are not seeking anyone else in connection with the incident at this time… As part of the investigation, officers are currently carrying out searches at two addresses in the London area and these are ongoing."

Amess was a married father of five. He was a royalist, devout Roman Catholic, and supporter of Brexit. He called for a ban on fox hunting, supported animal-welfare legislation, opposed abortion, and supported Israel. Queen Elizabeth II knighted him in 2015. He hosted an annual tea for centenarians.

AP reported on October 16 that several British media outlets identified the suspect as Ali Harbi Ali, a British national of possible Somali heritage. The *BBC* reported that several years earlier, Ali had been referred to Prevent, the government's counter-extremism program. He was not on a terrorism watch list. The *Washington Post* reported on October 21 that Ali considered himself affiliated with ISIS. He was the son of a media adviser to a former prime minister of Somalia and grew up in Croydon, south London. The *Telegraph* reported that he had worked at King's College Hospital in London and trained in the radiography department, but that he had not worked for the hospital or Britain's National Health Service since at least 2019.

AP reported on October 21 that Nick Price of the Crown Prosecution Service charged Ali Harbi Ali with murder and preparing acts of terrorism. *Reuters* reported that British prosecutors said Ali had been planning similar attacks for years.

On December 21, 2021, Ali Harbi Ali pleaded not guilty to charges of murder and preparing acts of terrorism during a hearing at London's Central Criminal Court regarding the murder of MP David Amess. Ali was ordered detained until his trial, scheduled for March 21, 2022.

November 14, 2021: At 11 a.m., a taxi exploded in front of Liverpool Women's Hospital, killing one passenger and injuring the driver, David Perry. Counter-terrorism police were investigating the cause. The taxi driver picked up a passenger ten minutes away from the hospital. Liverpool Mayor Joanne Anderson said the taxi driver locked the doors of his cab so the passenger couldn't leave, thereby preventing further carnage. *CNN* added that Great Manchester Police tweeted "Officers in Merseyside have arrested three men—aged 29, 26, and 21—in the Kensington area of Liverpool under the Terrorism Act." *AP* reported the next day that British police said the explosion was a "terrorist incident". A fourth man, aged 20, was later arrested under terrorism legislation. The four were released late on November 15. *AP* and *Newsweek* reported on November 16 that the suspected bomber was Iraq-born Emad al-Swealmeen, alias Enzo Almeni, 32, an asylum-seeker claiming to be of Syrian and Iraqi background, who had converted from Islam to Christianity. He entered the UK in May 2014 with a Jordanian passport, falsely claiming to be a Syrian. He requested asylum in the UK in 2014, but was denied. Liverpool couple Malcolm and Elizabeth Hitchcott said that he had spent time in a psychiatric hospital several years ago and stayed with them for eight months after his release. A spokesman for Liverpool's Anglican Cathedral said al-Swealmeen was baptized there in 2015, confirmed by Bishop Cyril Ashton in 2017, then lost contact with the cathedral in 2018.

AFP added on November 17 that police said he had planned the attack for at least seven months, marking "relevant purchases" starting in April. The *Times of London* reported that his bomb contained TATP. *UPI* and *The Guardian* reported on December 30 that senior coroner Andre Rebello said during a hearing at Liverpool and Wirral coroner's court that Swealmeen had called his brother, who lives in the United States, with a warning two days before the explosion, asking if his family would be affected if he "did something bad". Swealmeen was earlier imprisoned in the Middle East for assault and was previously convicted for possession of an offensive weapon in Liverpool. Swealmeen had purchased 2,000 ball bearings and rented a flat on Rutland Avenue to manufacture the device.

November 15, 2021: The government increased the terror level from substantial to severe, meaning an attack is highly likely.

December 25, 2021: *AP, UPI,* the *Washington Post,* and *CNN* reported that British police arrested an intruder, 19, from Southampton armed with a crossbow at 8:30 a.m. on the grounds of Windsor Castle, where British monarch Queen Elizabeth II, 95, was celebrating Christmas. Thames Valley Police Superintendent Rebecca Mears said, "The man has been arrested on suspicion of breach or trespass of a protected site and possession of an offensive weapon." The man did not enter any buildings. He was detained under the Mental Health Act. The *Sunday Mirror* reported that he had used a rope ladder to scale a fence.

LATIN AMERICA

September 21, 2021: *NBC News* reported that *Global Witness* found that in 2020, Latin America experienced 165 deadly attacks on environmental activists. Leading locales included Colombia, with 65 deaths; Mexico, 30; Brazil, 20; and Honduras, 17.

BRAZIL

May 4, 2021: *O Globo, Folha de S. Paulo, G1, Reuters, CNN,* and *AP* reported that an attacker killed three children and a female teacher and an educational assistant at a day care center in Saudades in Santa Catarina State. Local school board official Silvia Fernandes dos Santos and police officer Ricardo Newton Casagrande said that an 18-year-old broke into the day care center at 10 a.m. with a knife. Other children were hospitalized. Police took the attacker into custody after he tried to kill himself.

COLOMBIA

January 22, 2021: *AFP* reported that the former Revolutionary Armed Forces of Colombia (FARC), which renamed itself the Common Alternative Revolutionary Force in 2017 when it became a political party led by Rodrigo Londono, alias Timochenko, had decided to adopt a new name less laden with memories of political violence. *Reuters* reported on January 25 that the group's second national assembly chose COMUNES.

January 25, 2021: *AFP* reported that authorities at Bogota Airport arrested former right-wing paramilitary commander Hernan Giraldo Serna, 72, alias The Boss, alias Lord of the Sierra, wanted in Colombia for numerous massacres, disappearances, and rapes. The U.S. deported him after he finished a 12-year prison sentence for drug trafficking. He was wanted under more than 40 warrants for crimes committed under his command by the Tayrona Bloc of the Self-Defense Units of Colombia, which operated in the north of Colombia, particularly in the mountainous region of Magdalena, where the Sierra Nevada de Santa Marta rise to 5,000 meters (16,404 feet) along the Caribbean coast, and where narco-plantations flourished. In 2008, he was extradited to the United States.

January 28, 2021: *AFP* reported that the government issued charges of war crimes against eight senior members of the secretariat of the now-defunct FARC, including serving politicians. Charges include crimes against humanity and "other war crimes related to the treatment of hostages, such as murder, torture, cruel treatment, attacks on personal dignity, sexual violence and forced displacement." Judge Julieta Lemaitre of Colombia's Special Jurisdiction for Peace announced that they were charged with kidnapping 21,396 people between 1990 and 2016. Nine percent of the hostages were never seen again; three percent were confirmed murdered—their remains were sent to their families. Among those charged were:

- Rodrigo Londono, head of Colombia's Common People's Party

- Pablo Catatumbo, who occupies one of the ten seats reserved for the militant group-turned-political party under the peace agreement

- Julian Gallo, who occupies one of the ten seats reserved for the militant group-turned-political party under the peace agreement

- Ermilo Cabrera, who died on January 27, 2021

February 8, 2021: *AFP* reported that Colombian Defense Minister Diego Molano announced that "the Colombian government received from the Cuban ambassador... Jose Luis Ponce a communication with an alleged terrorist attack that was being planned for Colombia by the ELN {National Liberation Army} group" in the "next few days". ELN representatives in Havana claimed "total ignorance" of the plot, adding that they have "no involvement in the military decisions or operations of the organization".

March 26, 2021: *Reuters* reported that a car bomb exploded in a rural town in western Colombia, injuring 16 people.

April 30, 2021: *Reuters* reported that leaders of the since-demobilized 13,000 FARC members accepted responsibility for tens of thousands of kidnappings during Colombia's long internal conflict. FARC kidnapped 21,396 people between 1990 and 2015.

June 15, 2021: After 3 p.m., men disguised as soldiers drove up a white pick-up and set off a car bomb inside a military base used by the 30th Army Brigade in Cúcuta in North Santander State on the Venezuelan border, injuring 36 people, three critically. The injured included members of the military and civilians. Defense Minister Diego Molano called the bombing a "vile terrorist attack" that sought to injure as many troops as possible. Two American military personnel at the base to conduct training exercises were slightly injured. Molano said the ELN or dissident members of the FARC were likely involved. The ELN denied involvement. *Reuters* reported that a Colombian soldier was in intensive care; two others underwent surgery. The defense ministry announced a 500 million peso ($135,000) reward for information leading to the terrorists' capture. 21061501

June 25, 2021: A Colombian Air Force helicopter carrying Colombian President Iván Duque, Defense Minister Diego Molano, Interior Minister Daniel Palacios, and the governor of Norte de Santander state, Silvano Serrano, came under fire in the Catatumbo region bordering Venezuela, while approaching Cúcuta. No one was injured. Shots hit the tail and main blade. The senior officials had attended an event in Sardinata titled "Peace with Legality, the Sustainable Catatumbo chapter". On June 26, *al-Jazeera* reported that the Colombian government offered a reward of 3 billion pesos ($796,000) for information leading to the capture of those involved. National police chief General Jorge Vargas said a search team found an AK-47 and a 7.62-caliber rifle "bearing the mark of the Venezuelan armed forces". *Reuters* and *al-Jazeera* reported on July 23 that Colombia arrested ten suspects in Norte de Santander Province for the helicopter attack and a June 15 car bombing at a military base in Cúcuta that wounded 44 people, including two U.S. military advisors. Military officials blamed former FARC 33rd Front rebel leaders based in Venezuela.

August 5, 2021: *Reuters* reported that Defense Minister Diego Molano said police had confiscated 148 pounds of pentolite explosives from dissident former FARC rebels who planned to carry out an attack in Bogota. Molano said Hernan Dario Velasquez, alias El Paisa, ordered the attack. He is a member of the Segunda Marquetalia group of former FARC, which is led by Ivan Marquez and whose leaders are hiding in Venezuela. Colombian police chief General Jorge Vargas said two people, including a former FARC combatant, were captured. Vargas said "El Paisa gave criminal instructions from Venezuela to commit attacks," adding that the government offered up to three billion pesos ($769,000) for information leading to the terrorist's arrest. On August 4, Colombia re-issued three Interpol Red Notices for Marquez's capture and requested his extradition from Venezuela.

August 10, 2021: The Special Jurisdiction for Peace, a Colombian tribunal that investigates war crimes, announced that the FARC recruited at least 18,600 children into its ranks between 1996 and 2016.

August 14-15, 2021: *AP* reported that during the weekend, 1,150 people fled their homes in the riverside village of Dipurdú del Guasimo in Choco Province when the rightwing paramilitary Gaitanista Self Defense Forces of Colombia clashed with the leftist ELN.

August 23, 2021: Gunmen on motorcycles killed student leader Esteban Mosquera as he walked home in Popayan. He lost an eye in clashes with police in 2018 and had participated in anti-government protests in April and May. He called for free tuition for university students and advocated for a basic income plan for Colombia's poorest residents. President Ivan Duque offered a $13,000 reward for information leading to Mosquera's killers.

August 30, 2021: A bomb exploded at a police station in a lower income neighborhood in Cúcuta, injuring 13 people.

September 12, 2021: *Reuters* reported two attacks at the La Cira Infantas oilfield run by majority state-owned Colombian oil company Ecopetrol caused a fire and a spill of crude onto vegetation but no injuries. The attacks affected a transport line between two areas of the field and a pipeline moving crude to a refinery in Barrancabermeja, halting production at some wells and blowing large holes into the side of pipeline tubing. The ELN was suspected.

September 27, 2021: *Reuters* reported that ten FARC rebel dissidents were killed in an armed forces bombing in the southeastern jungle in a rural area of Morichal Nuevo municipality in Guainia Province.

September 28, 2021: *Al-Jazeera* reported that Defence Minister Diego Molano announced that Angel Padilla Romero, alias Fabian, head of the ELN Western Front, died in a hospital in Cali of injuries sustained in a military bombing in the jungles of Choco Province ten days earlier.

Molano called Padilla "the most important leader of the ELN still in Colombia". Seven other ELN rebels died in the bombing.

October 21, 2021: *AFP* reported General Jonh Jairo Rojas said that the Colombian army killed ten FARC dissidents in a shootout in Micay Canyon in the Cauca Department. Rojas said that members of the smaller ELN participated in the fighting.

November 23, 2021: The Biden administration informed Congress that it planned to delist the former Revolutionary Armed Forces of Colombia as a designated terrorist group, but would list FARC splinters Segunda Marquetalia and FARC-People's Army (FARC-EP) and maintain U.S. indictments against individual members, including for drug trafficking. *Reuters* reported on November 30 that Secretary of State Antony Blinken announced the formal revocation of the designation of the FARC.

November 26, 2021: *Al-Jazeera* reported that Attorney General Francisco Barbosa charged Miguel Botache Santillana, leader of a breakaway faction of the former FARC rebel group with leading an "aggressive deforestation" campaign of vast portions of the Amazon rainforest for illegal purposes since 2016. Two associates were also charged with "invading an area of special ecological importance", damaging natural resources, financing coca plantations and criminal association.

December 14, 2021: Defense Minister Diego Molano blamed "terrorist" groups for setting off two explosions on the runway of Cucuta's Camilo Daza Airport in Norte de Santander Province at 5 a.m. that killed three people, including two policemen. Police said a man tried to hop a fence separating the runway from a nearby neighbor, but his bomb went off early. An hour later a second bomb went off while police inspected a package that had been left in the area, killing two members of the police's anti-explosives squad. *USNWR* and *Reuters* reported on December 28 that police captured three men and two women suspects in raids in Medellin and surrounding area. The five faced multiple charges, including for terrorism and aggravated homicide.

Costa Rica

September 11, 2021: *Reuters* reported that in an evening attack in Escazu, six miles west of San Jose, gunmen shot Nicaraguan political activist Joao Maldonado, 32, who opposes the government of President Daniel Ortega, critically injuring him. He led demonstrations in 2018 in Nicaragua's Jinotepe municipality. He was shot twice in the chest and once in the arm. Yefer Bravo of Unidad de Exiles Nicaraguan in Costa Rica said Maldonado was organizing a protest against Ortega's government for the next day in San Jose. The rally was sparsely attended.

Cuba

January 11, 2021: The *Washington Post* and *Bloomberg News* reported that Secretary of State Mike Pompeo re-designated Cuba as a state sponsor of terrorism. The Trump Administration cited Cuba's refusal to extradite to Colombia a group of ten leaders of Colombia's National Liberation Army (ELN), including commander Nicolás Rodríguez Bautista and chief ELN negotiator Israel Ramirez Pineda, accused in a car-bomb attack two years earlier on a police training school in Bogota in which 21 cadets were killed.

Guantánamo Bay

April 4, 2021: Miami-based U.S. Southern Command announced the closure of once-secret Camp 7 within the Guantánamo Bay detention center; prisoners were moved to Camp 5 on the American base to "increase operational efficiency and effectiveness". Among those held at Camp 7 were the five prisoners charged with war crimes for their alleged planning and providing logistical support for the 9/11 attacks.

April 18, 2021: *Military Times* and *AP* reported that the 40 Gitmo prisoners were to begin receiving COVID-19 vaccinations the next day.

April 23, 2021: The *New York Times* reported on May 9, 2021 that the federal appeals court in Washington agreed on April 23, 2021 to re-hear as a full court the case of detainee Abdul-salam Ali Abdulrahman al-Hela, a Yemeni tribal sheikh, and vacated a decision by a three-judge panel in August 2020 that had rejected his habeas corpus petition and held that due process does not apply to Gitmo detainees. The full court was scheduled to hear the case on September 30, 2021.

May 17, 2021: *AP* and *al-Jazeera* reported that the Pentagon approved the release of three men, including Pakistani detainee Saifullah Paracha, 73, the eldest Gitmo detainee, who had been held for more than 16 years on suspicion of being a wealthy "facilitator" for al-Qaeda but never charged with a crime. He was represented by attorney Shelby Sullivan-Bennis at his November 2020 hearing, his 8th before the review board. Paracha owned property in New York City. He was captured in Thailand in 2003 and held at Gitmo since September 2004. He has diabetes and a heart condition.

In 2005, a federal court in New York convicted his son, Uzair Paracha, of providing support to terrorism, based in part of the same witnesses against Saifullah. In March 2020, a judge threw out those witness accounts and the government decided not to pursue the case against Uzair, who was released and sent back to Pakistan.

Attorney Beth Jacob said that her client, Uthman Abd al-Rahim Uthman, a Yemeni who had been held without charge at Guantánamo since it opened in January 2002, was cleared for release.

July 3, 2021: *The Guardian* reported that Ravil Mingazov, 52, a Muslim Tartar who was held at Guantánamo Bay for 15 years without charge before being transferred to the United Arab Emirates in January 2017, faced forced repatriation to Russia. His family and lawyers said that the former Red Army ballet dancer fled Russia fearing religious persecution. He was detained on the battlefield in Afghanistan at age 33. His wife, son, and other family members settled in the U.K.

July 19, 2021: The *Washington Post, AP, AFP,* and *UPI* reported that the Biden administration transferred Abdul Latif Nasir, variant Abdullatif Nasser, 56, from Gitmo to Morocco. Nasir's release had been advised in 2016 by the Periodic Review Board but his detention continued under Donald Trump. Nasir, a former al-Qaeda fighter who came to Gitmo in May 2002, was never charged with a crime. Moroccan police took him into custody and the public prosecutor at the Court of Appeal in Rabat said the National Division of the Judicial Police in Casablanca would investigate him on suspicion of committing terrorist acts.

Nasir's Pentagon file listed him as a member of a nonviolent but illegal Moroccan Sufi Islam group in the 1980s. In 1996, he was recruited to fight in Chechyna but went to Afghanistan, where he trained at an al-Qaeda camp. He was captured after fighting U.S. forces.

His attorney said he studied math, computer science, and English at Gitmo and wrote a 2,000-word Arabic-English dictionary.

October 7, 2021: The Periodic Review Board approved the transfer out of Gitmo of Afghan national Asadullah Haroon Gul. On October 19, *CNN* reported that U.S. D.C. District Court Judge Amit Mehta ruled that the detention was unlawful and granted Gul's petition for a writ of habeas corpus. Gul was represented by attorney Tara Plochocki, who filed the case in 2016 with co-counsel Mark Maher, who works for Reprieve U.S.

Gul grew up largely in a refugee camp in Shamshato, Pakistan. He was accused of membership in Hezb-e-Islami/Gulbuddin (HIG), now known as Hezb-e-Islami Afghanistan (HIA), which the U.S. government dubbed an "associated force" of al-Qaeda. Gul entered Guantánamo in June 2007.

The court rejected a motion for release on the basis that the Geneva Convention requires release at the end of hostilities.

October 29, 2021: *AP* and *ABC News* reported that an eight-officer military jury sentenced Pakistani citizen Majid Khan, 41, to 26 years in a plea deal in which he admitted to joining al-Qaeda and involvement in several terrorist plots. He could be released in February 2022 and resettled in a third country with his wife and a daughter born after his capture in Pakistan. He came to the U.S. in the 1990s and graduated

from high school near Baltimore, Maryland. He had pleaded guilty to war crimes charges including conspiracy and murder for his involvement in al-Qaeda plots such as the August 2003 bombing of the J.W. Marriott hotel in Jakarta, Indonesia, that killed 11, and planning al-Qaeda attacks in the U.S. after 9/11 and a failed plot to kill former Pakistan President Pervez Musharraf. Seven jurors wrote a letter to Pentagon legal authorities recommending clemency. His defense team included Wells Dixon, a lawyer for the Center for Constitutional Rights, and Army Maj. Michael Lyness.

December 3, 2021: The *Guardian* reported that attorneys for Gitmo detainee Zayn al-Abidin Muhammad Husayn, alias Abu Zubaydah, 50, petitioned the U.S. district court in Washington, D.C. for his release on grounds that America's wars in Afghanistan and with al-Qaeda are over, thus removing any remaining legal justification for keeping him captive under the 2001 Authorization for Use of Military Force (AUMF), passed by Congress soon after 9/11. His lead attorney was Mark Denbeaux.

GUATEMALA

October 4, 2021: *ABC News* reported anti-vaccine residents of Nahuila village in Alta Verapaz Province held hostage for seven hours nurses who were trying to administer coronavirus shots. The villagers blocked a road, let the air out of the nurses' tires, then destroyed a cooler and 50 vaccine doses. Police and local officials negotiated their release.

HAITI

April 11, 2021: *AFP* reported that gunmen kidnapped ten people, including seven Catholic clergy, in Croix-des-Bouquets, northeast of Port-au-Prince. The clergy abducted were four priests and a nun from Haiti, plus a priest and a nun from France. *AP* identified the nuns as Anne-Marie Dorcelus and Agnès Bordeau, the priests as Michel Briand, Evens Joseph, Jean-Nicaise Millien, Joël Thomas, and Hugues Baptiste and three relatives of another priest. Briand was French. The five priests belong to the France-based Society of Priests of St. James. The three laypeople were members of the family of a Haitian priest, who was not taken. All were en route to the installation of a new parish priest in Ganthier. The kidnappers demanded a $1 million ransom. Three Haitian clergy were released on April 22. The government resigned and a new prime minister was appointed. Authorities suspected the 400 Mawozo armed gang. France's Central Office for the Fight against Organized Crime (OCLCO), which has jurisdiction over crimes committed against French citizens abroad, opened an investigation. *AP* reported on April 30 that the kidnappers had released five priests, two nuns, and two other people who had been held for nearly three weeks. One of the ill relatives was released earlier. It was not clear whether a ransom had been paid. 21041101

June 23, 2021: *Al-Jazeera* reported that gang leader Jimmy Cherizier, alias Barbecue, a former police officer, announced that he was launching a revolution against the country's business and political elites. He ran the G9 federation of nine gangs from his neighborhood in Lower Delmas, a district of Port-au-Prince.

June 29-30, 2021: *AP* and *al-Jazeera* reported that National Police Chief Leon Charles said 15 people, including journalist Diego Charles, who worked for *Radio Vision 2000*, and political activist Antoinette Duclaire died in a shooting rampage on a main street in the Delmas 32 neighborhood in Port-au-Prince. Duclair was dropping Charles off at his home. Hours earlier, a spokesman for the Fantom 509 group of disgruntled police officers was killed in the same area. The UN Office for the Coordination of Humanitarian Affairs (UNOCHA) attributed the violence to changing gang alliances and territorial disputes.

July 7, 2021: *AP*, *Reuters*, *CNN*, and *NBC News* reported that at 1 a.m., gunmen broke into the Port-au-Prince residence in the hilly Pelerin 5 neighborhood of former banana exporter President Jovenel Moïse, 53, and assassinated him, firing 16 bullets into him. Interim Premier Claude Joseph said First Lady Martine Moïse was hit by three bullets and was hospitalized in critical but stable condition. She was later evacuated to intensive care in Jackson Health System's Ryder Trauma Center in Miami. Joseph said some of the attackers spoke in Spanish or English. Some reports said the attackers tortured, then killed, the president, who suffered a broken leg and serious facial injuries. None of his 23 guards or residential staff were injured.

Succession was problematic. Moïse, sworn in on February 7, 2017, claimed he had another year to go, but the Constitution indicated that the term clock begins upon election, not swearing-in. He had been under pressure to step down on February 7, 2021 by oppositionists, who argued it would have been five years after he would have taken office if the first vote had been allowed. His first election in 2015 was annulled; he later was reelected. He had ruled by decree for more than a year after dissolving a majority of Parliament in January 2020 amid a delay in legislative elections.

Moreover, the government lacked a permanent prime minister since April 2021, when Joseph Jouthe resigned during an uptick in killings and kidnappings. Under the Constitution, the president of the Supreme Court would temporarily take over, but he died of COVID-19 in June 2021. The Constitution calls for the National Assembly to select a new leader, but the terms of the lower house members and two-thirds of those in the Senate had expired.

Acting Prime Minister Joseph had only an interim role. A day before the assassination, Moïse nominated neurosurgeon Ariel Henry, 71, as new prime minister, but he awaited confirmation. Joseph and Henry both claimed to be prime minister. The United Nations and United States acknowledged Joseph's legitimacy. Undaunted, eight of the ten remaining senators, sans quorum, recognized Joseph Lambert, head of the dismantled Senate, as provisional president and said Ariel Henry was prime minister.

The *Washington Post* reported on July 19 that Claude Joseph agreed to step down in favor of Ariel Henry "for the good of the nation".

To further muddy the waters, earlier in the year, opposition parties had declared Joseph Mécène Jean-Louis to be provisional president.

Reuters reported that Jimmy Cherizier, alias Barbecue, a former police officer who heads the G9 Family and Allies federation of nine gangs, said his followers would take to the streets to protest the assassination and practice "legitimate violence".

Moreover, the country apparently had two Constitutions.

Haitian Ambassador to the U.S. Bocchit Edmond blamed "foreign mercenaries and professional killers" masquerading as agents of the U.S. Drug Enforcement Administration.

NPR, The Hill, CNN, Reuters, the *Washington Post*, and *AP* reported on July 8 that police had killed four suspects (later raised to seven, still later reported as only three), arrested two others in Petionville, and freed three police officers taken hostage. The *Washington Post* noted that James Solages, a U.S. citizen of Haitian descent, was among six people who had been arrested. By July 9, some 17 suspects were in custody, including 15 retired Colombian army soldiers. Mathias Pierre, Minister of Elections and Interparty Relations, said that another detainee, Joseph Vincent, 55, was also believed to be a Haitian-American. Solages called himself a "certified diplomatic agent", an advocate for children, and budding politician on a website for a charity he established in 2019 in south Florida to assist residents. *AP* reported that Solages claimed he was a former bodyguard at the Canadian Embassy in Port-au-Prince. Haitian Communications Minister Pradel Henriquez said the other detainees and those killed were "foreigners". Police continued the search for two other suspects.

The *Washington Post* reported on July 9 that the Embassy of Taiwan said police had, with its approval, entered its grounds at 4 p.m. and detained 11 people who had broken into the compound and were holed up there. Authorities were searching for eight more Colombian suspects.

Minister Pierre released a video showing a jeering crowd dragging two bound suspects from a home. Mobs burned three of the five vehicles police had seized.

At a news conference, police displayed a cache of weapons, including assault rifles and machetes, plus passports.

Prosecutor Bed-Ford Claude requested the "interrogation" of Dimitri Hérard and Laguel Civil, senior figures in the president's security detail. On July 10, Colombian news website *Semana* reported that Hérard, head of Moïse's security detail, went to Colombia and Ecuador in May. *The Washington Post* reported on July 15 that police had taken Hérard into custody.

Le Nouvelliste newspaper reported that Solages and Vincent claimed to be interpreters for the attackers, who were to arrest Moïse, not to kill him. Schubert Dorisme, 63, Solages's uncle, said Solages had no military training.

CNN reported that Colombian National Police Chief General Jorge Vargas noted that two alleged attackers, killed in an operation by the Haiti Police, were retired Colombian Army officers. At least four detainees were retired soldiers.

The *Miami Herald* reported on July 8 that James Solages, 35, of Fort Lauderdale, was from Jacmel in southeast Haiti. Joseph Vincent, originally from Haiti, was from the Miami area. Minister Pierre said four of the Colombians were Alejandro Girardo Zapata, 41; John Jairo Ramirez Gomez, 40; Victor Albeiro Pinera Cardona, 40; and Manuel Antonio Groso Guarin, 41.

Reuters and *CNN* reported that Chief of Police Leon Charles said 28 people were involved in the assassination, including 26 Colombians and two Haitian-Americans. *Reuters* reported that unnamed sources in the Colombian army and national police said that the hit squad entered Haiti from the Dominican Republic, then spent more than a month preparing for the killing. Four of the men flew on an Avianca jet on June 4 to the resort of Punta Cana in the Dominican Republic, crossing the border two days later. Colombian newspaper *El Tiempo* reported that one Colombian who claimed former membership in the Colombian military's urban anti-terrorism special forces unit posted 16 photos on his *Facebook* account that appear to have been taken in the Dominican Republic. Another man on the same flight was a nurse at the naval hospital in Cartagena.

CNN reported on July 9 that Haiti had requested that the U.S. send circa 500 troops to assist in protecting infrastructure, ports, airports, and energy systems against a threat posed by mercenaries. The FBI and Department of Homeland Security were also sending investigators.

The *New York Times* reported that on July 9, prosecutors called in for questioning five senior businessmen and politicians, including Reginald Boulos, who had helped Moïse's election campaign but later split with him.

NPR reported that by July 10, twenty suspects were in prison.

Colombian police director General Jorge Luis Vargas Valencia said that four companies had recruited the suspects.

On July 10, *Reuters* and the *Miami Herald* reported that some of the detained Colombians claimed they were recruited to work in Haiti by Miami-based CTU Security, run by Venezuelan emigre Antonio Enmanuel Intriago Valera. Jenny Carolina Capador, sister of Duberney Capador, 40, a retired Colombian soldier killed in the firefight with Haitian police, said he had been offered work in security for high-profile people.

Another Colombian killed in the firefight was Mauricio Javier Romero, 45, a 21-year veteran of the Colombian military. His wife of 20+ years, Giovanna Romero Dussán, said that fellow former soldier Duberney Capador Giraldo invited him to work on a long-term "project".

The *LA Times* reported on July 11 that numerous conspiracy theories abounded, blaming Colombian mercenaries, presidential guards, and bodyguards who set up the mercenaries to take the blame.

NPR, CNN, and the *Washington Post* reported on July 12 that authorities had arrested Christian Emmanuel Sanon, 63, a Florida-based Haitian-born doctor who arrived in Haiti via private jet in June with "political intentions", according to the police. Police said he had recruited 26 mercenaries via a Venezuelan firm based in the U.S., and wanted to become president. The mercenaries were to serve as his bodyguards. The *Miami Herald* reported that Sanon had registered more than a dozen businesses in Florida. *CNN* added that the police chief said that after the assassination, Sanon was the first person one of the Colombians called. Police raiding Sanon's house found 20 boxes of 12 and 9 millimeter caliber ammunition, rifle and pistol holsters, 24 unused shooting targets, a cap labeled "DEA", two vehi-

cles, and four Dominican Republic license plates. Police said Sanon was born in Marigot, Haiti.

The U.S. Drug Enforcement Administration announced, "At times, one of the suspects in the assassination of Haitian President Jovenel Moïse was a confidential source to the DEA… Following the assassination of President Moïse, the suspect reached out to his contacts at the DEA. A DEA official assigned to Haiti urged the suspect to surrender to local authorities and, along with a U.S. State Department official, provided information to the Haitian government that assisted in the surrender and arrest of the suspect and one other individual." *CNN* reported that other detainees had been FBI informants.

The *Washington Post* reported on July 12 that a 2011 *YouTube* video suggested that Sanon could provide "Leadership for Haiti", and a since-closed website called "Haiti Lives Matter" listed him among a coalition "chosen to lead" the country. *NPR* reported that he was $400,000 in debt and earned $5,000/month. Sanon had filed for bankruptcy in Florida in 2013 and listed himself as a church pastor. The Florida Department of Health said there was no evidence that anyone with Sanon's name was ever licensed to practice medicine in Florida. Sanon claimed he was part owner of the Organisation Rome Haiti humanitarian foundation, and an evangelical church and telecommunications company based in Tabarre, Haiti.

AP reported on July 14 that Léon Charles, head of the Haiti's National Police, accused Venezuelan businessman Antonio Intriago, who owns CTU Security in Florida, of traveling to Haiti numerous times as part of the assassination plot. Colombia's national police chief added that CTU Security used its company credit card to buy 19 plane tickets from Bogota to Santo Domingo for the Colombian suspects.

Police were searching for five fugitives, including former Senator John Joël Joseph, a Haitian politician and opponent of Moïse's Tet Kale party, and Joseph Felix Badio, who allegedly rented a house near Moïse's home to help the suspects surveil the area. Badio had worked for the Ministry of Justice and joined a government anti-corruption unit in March 2013. He was fired in May 2021 for "serious breaches" of ethics rules. Also at large was John Joël Joseph, whom police accused of providing weapons used in the attack.

Police arrested Gilbert Dragon, a former police superintendent who led the National Revolutionary Front for the Liberation and Reconstruction of Haiti rebel group, seizing several weapons at his house, including a saber, two grenades, and an AR-15.

Police also arrested Haitian citizen Reynaldo Corvington on charges of providing the suspects with housing and giving them sirens to use on top of their cars with help from Haitian American detainee James Solages. Corvington established the Corvington Courier and Security Service in 1982, which provides tips on how to survive a kidnapping. Police seized nine pistols and an AR-15 at his home.

Police chief Charles noted that four senior officials who were in charge of the president's security detail were being held in isolation as authorities continued to track down other fugitives, including Haiti-born Rodolphe Jaar, alias Whiskey. Jaar speaks English and has a college degree in business administration. The *Miami Herald* and *Tribune News Service* reported that in 2013, a federal court in southern Florida indicted him for conspiring to smuggle more than 11 pounds of cocaine from Colombia and Venezuela through Haiti to the U.S. He pleaded guilty and was sentenced in 2015 to 51 months in prison, later reduced to 45 months. His attorney said he had been a confidential source for the U.S. government.

The *Post* added that Pentagon spokesman Lt. Col. Ken Hoffman announced that some of the detained Colombians had earlier been trained by the U.S. military.

CNN reported on July 27 that numerous threats were made against 20 court clerks investigating the murder.

AP reported on July 30, 2021 that National Police spokesperson Marie-Michelle Verrier said Haitian police arrested a fourth officer, Jean Laguel Civil, who served as general security coordinator for Moïse. Another 44 people, including nine officers, were held in isolation for questioning. Police named another at-large suspect: Superior Court Judge Windelle Coq Thelot.

AP reported on August 9 that Magistrate Bernard Saint-Vil, dean of the Court of First Instance in Port-au-Prince, announced that Judge Mathieu Chanlatte would be in charge of proceedings regarding the assassination. By that date, more than 40 people, including 18 former Colombian soldiers and 20 Haitian police officers, had been detained in the case. Authorities continued searching for an ex-senator, a judicial official, and a Haitian Supreme Court judge.

On September 13, 2021, Port-au-Prince prosecutor Bed-Ford Claude asked a judge to charge Prime Minister Ariel Henry, 71, regarding the assassination of President Jovenel Moïse and bar him from leaving the country. He said Henry was in telephone contact with Joseph Badio, a former Justice Ministry official and a key suspect, on the night of July 7, citing two calls lasting seven minutes made at 4:03 a.m. and 4:20 a.m., three hours after the killing. Claude sought indictment on charges including assassination, conspiracy against the state, and armed robbery. *NPR* and *AP* reported that Henry fired Claude within 24 hours, replacing him with Frantz Louis Juste.

Reuters reported on September 15 that Renald Luberice, who served more than four years as secretary general of Haiti's Council of Ministers, resigned, saying he could not serve a premier under suspicion in the assassination and who "does not intend to cooperate with justice, seeking, on the contrary, by all means, to obstruct it".

AP reported on October 21, 2021 that police Superintendent Stephanie Lindsay in Jamaica announced that authorities arrested a Colombian man they believe is a suspect in the assassination.

AP reported on November 15, 2021 that Haitian Foreign Minister Claude Joseph tweeted that Turkish authorities had arrested Samir Handal, a Haitian businessman considered a suspect in the assassination.

October 16, 2021: *AP, NPR,* and *CNN* reported that gangs were suspected when 17 missionaries and family members, including 16 Americans (among them five men, seven women, and a mother's five children, aged 3, 6, 14, 15, and 8 months) and one Canadian, and their Haitian driver were kidnapped in Ganthier while traveling on a bus to Titanyen after returning from a site visit to the Maison La Providence de Dieu orphanage in the Croix des Bouquets area. The adults ranged in age from 18 to 48. The Ohio-based Christian Aid Ministries issued a "prayer alert" via an audio recording. One of the abducted Americans posted a call for help on *WhatsApp* as the kidnapping was occurring. *AP* added that the 400 Mawozo Gang (translated as "inexperienced men") was blamed. They had been accused of kidnapping five priests, three relatives of one of the priests, and two nuns in April 2021.

CNN, the *Wall Street Journal, Newsweek,* and *BBC* reported on October 19 that the kidnappers demanded a $17 million ransom. *Newsweek* and the *Wall Street Journal* reported that the FBI and Haitian police were speaking with the kidnappers, who were holding the hostages in a safe house outside Croix-des-Bouquets.

The Center for Analysis and Research in Human Rights, a Port-au-Prince-based non-profit, reported that at least 628 kidnappings had taken place since January, of which 29 were of foreigners. *BBC* reported that 3,000 thugs belong to 162 gangs in Haiti.

On October 19, local unions staged a walk-out to protest rising levels of crime.

AP reported on October 21 that the gang's leader, Wilson Joseph, released a video in which he said, "I swear by thunder that if I don't get what I'm asking for, I will put a bullet in the heads of these Americans." He also threatened Prime Minister Ariel Henry and the chief of Haiti's National Police, Léon Charles. He spoke in front of open coffins that apparently held several members of his gang who were recently killed. "You guys make me cry. I cry water. But I'm going to make you guys cry blood."

Weston Showalter, spokesman for the Christian Aid Ministries, said that the families of the hostages are from Amish, Mennonite, and other conservative Anabaptist communities in Ohio, Michigan, Wisconsin, Tennessee, Pennsylvania, Oregon, and Ontario, Canada.

AFP reported on October 28, 2021 that Haitian police had received proof-of-life for the hostages.

On November 21, 2021, 400 Mawozo released two hostages.

On December 6, 2021, *AP* reported that Christian Aid Ministries said that on December 5, the kidnappers had released three more hostages. The *Washington Post* reported on December 16 that Haitian National Police spokesman Gary Desrosiers announced that the remaining hostages were released.

HONDURAS

July 27, 2021: *The Insider* reported on August 7 that on July 27, former presidential candidate Carolina Echeverría let three people disguised as doctors into her home in the belief that they were there to care for her husband, former police chief Andrés Urtecho, who was infected with COVID-19. Instead they shot her in the head, killing her, and attacked him. The motive was unclear. The killers—two men and a woman—escaped in a getaway vehicle. She was campaigning to win back her former seat. The attackers were dressed in full medical protective gear, including masks. Urtecho jumped out of his sickbed to try to save her, noting, "I went out into the hall with the gun in my hand and fired about 11 shots... My wife turned her face towards me and then they shot her in the left temple."

MEXICO

June 28, 2021: The National Institute of Indigenous Peoples condemned the murders of Oliverio Martinez and Flor de Jesús Hernández, two activists from the Triqui community, near the village of San Juan Copala in the mountains of southern Oaxaca State. The two worked as teachers.

July 26, 2021: *AP* and *Fox News* reported that in the afternoon, some 200 masked gunmen from the newly-formed El Machete vigilante group attacked Pantelho in Chiapas State, searching for Los Herreras drug traffickers. They burned three vehicles and a dozen homes, vandalized the town hall, and abducted 21 people, bringing them to San José Buena Vista Tercero, where the "self defense force" is allegedly based. El Machete appeared to include members of the Tzotzil Indigenous group.

October 19, 2021: *AFP* reported that authorities arrested former Colombian FARC chief diplomat Rodrigo Granda, 72, holding him under an Interpol "red notice" issued by Paraguay for kidnapping, criminal association, and intentional homicide.

NICARAGUA

October 6, 2021: *ABC News* reported that gunmen killed a man from a Mayangna Indigenous community on working in wildcat mining in the Bosawas nature reserve of Nicaragua's Caribbean coast. Three other men fled and were missing.

PERU

May 24, 2021: *AP* and *Deutsche Welle* reported that police chief César Cervantes, told local TV channel *N* that the Shining Path was suspected of killing 18 people in Vizcatan de Ene in remote central Peru two weeks before the presidential runoff election. General Oscar Arriola, the head of the police counter-terrorism unit, said that the victims included ten men, six women, and two children. The military said there were 14 victims. Local official Leonidas Casas said that the victims were inside two bars, one in front of the other, when armed men stormed into them and opened fire. Some women and at least one child tried to hide in a room, but were killed. Some of the bodies were burned. The Shining Path left leaflets vowing to "clean up" Peru of bars, "parasites", and "corrupts" and warning against participating in the election.

September 11, 2021: Manuel Rubén Abimael Guzmán Reynoso, alias Presidente Gonzalo, 86, founder of Sendero Luminoso (the Maoist Shining Path), died at 6:40 p.m. from an infection from bilateral pneumonia caused by a pathological agent while serving life in Callao Naval Base prison. The former philosophy professor was captured in 1992 and sentenced in life in prison for terrorism and other crimes. His wife, Augusta La Torre, alias Comrade Norah, about 15 years his junior and his deputy, died in 1988. She was replaced as No. 2 by Elena Iparraguirre, alias Comrade Miriam, who married Guzmán in

2010 at the maximum-security prison inside the naval base in Lima where he was serving a life term. She was captured in 1992 and was brought from the women's prison for the ceremony.

Guzmán was born in Tambo, Arequipa, in Peru's southern Andes on December 3, 1934. He studied law and philosophy at the University of San Agustin in Arequipa. He wrote two theses: *The Theory of Space in Kant* and *The Democratic-Bourgeois State*. He began teaching in 1963 at the state University of San Cristobal de Huamanga in Ayacucho, where he joined the pro-Chinese Bandera Roja (Red Flag) political party, heading its "military commission". He visited China in 1965.

The *Washington Post* reported on September 16, 2021 that the government was pondering what to do with his remains, fearing that burial would create a Shining Path shrine. A prosecutor turned down his wife's request, as she was serving a life sentence in prison. Attorney General Zoraida Ávalos Rivera sent to the Congress of the Republic a bill to allow for the cremation of the bodies of people whose "transfer, funerals or burial could seriously jeopardize security or public order". *AFP* reported on September 22, 2021, that survivors of an April 3, 1983 attack by SL members armed with machetes, axes, knives, kerosene, and guns who killed 69 civilians, among them 22 children, in Lucanamarca objected to any burial. On September 23, *AP* reported that the Peruvian prosecutor's office ordered the cremation of Guzmán's body, with the ashes to be scattered at an undisclosed date and place. The cremation was performed on September 24.

VENEZUELA

March 25, 2021: *AP* reported that Venezuelan Defense Minister Gen. Vladimir Padrino López announced that the army had clashed during the week with dissident remnants of the 10th Front of the Revolutionary Armed Forces of Colombia (FARC) in a community in Apure State along the nations' shared border. More than 3,900 people fled from Venezuela to northeast Colombia. Clashes began on March 21. To date, the government had arrested 32 people. The Colombian government earlier accused Venezuela of harboring members of the National Liberation Army and FARC dissidents. 21032502

April 23, 2021: *AP* reported on May 11 that the Colombian Martin Villa 10th Front rebel group, which had fought against the Venezuelan army since March, said that it had captured eight Venezuelan soldiers in Venezuela's Apure State on April 23 and wanted to hand them over to human rights groups. The group listed the names of the soldiers and their ranks, including sergeants and lieutenants. Venezuelan officials said 16 soldiers and nine rebels had died in the ongoing military clashes. The Front is part of a large group of FARC dissidents led by former FARC leader Gentil Duarte.

May 17, 2021: A Colombian army commando unit illegally entered Venezuelan territory and killed Seuxis Hernandez, alias Jesús Santrich, 53, who had been a chief negotiator for the FARC but dropped out of the 2016 peace accord in 2018 after the U.S. indicted him for trafficking ten tons of cocaine. His Second Marquetalia Movement said he was riding in a vehicle in Zulia State, Venezuela when Colombian soldiers attacked with grenades and gunfire. Colombian troops cut off Santrich's pinky finger before returning to Colombia in a yellow helicopter. Alternative reporting in the Colombian media said that mercenaries killed him while trying to detain Santrich and obtain the U.S. Department of State's Rewards for Justice $10 million reward. He had joined FARC in the early 1990s.

December 5, 2021: *BBC* and *Reuters* reported that former FARC dissident leader Hernán Darío Velásquez, alias El Paisa, was killed in an ambush in Apure State. The Colombian army said it had no knowledge of the killing. Local media speculated that mercenaries were responsible. Velásquez was behind a 2003 car bombing in Bogota that killed 36 people and wounded nearly 200.

MIDDLE EAST

September 11, 2021: *AP,* the *Independent,* the *Washington Examiner,* and *Fox News* reported that al-Qaeda leader Ayman al-Zawahiri, 70, appeared in a new 61-minute, 37-second video produced by AQ's as-Sahab Media Foundation entitled "Jerusalem Will Never be Judaized", marking the 20th anniversary of 9/11 as rumors of his death continued. He praised al-Qaeda attacks including one by Hurras al-Deen, a group aligned with al-Qaeda, that targeted Russian troops near Raqqa, Syria on January 1, 2021. He mentioned the American military withdrawal from Afghanistan. Observers noted that the Doha withdrawal agreement with the Taliban was signed in February 2020, so the video might not be recently made. He did not comment on the Taliban's takeover of Afghanistan in August.

September 11, 2021: *Newsweek* reported the pro-al-Qaeda *Wolves of Manhattan* magazine affiliated with the jihadist group Jaysh al-Malahim called for more attacks with planes. Jaysh al-Malahim is part of Guardians of the Religion, which was established in Syria and endorsed by al-Qaeda.

September 21, 2021: The *Washington Post* reported that al-Qaeda leader Ayman al-Zawahiri, 70, released an 852-page historical tome about failed governance in the Muslim world. An online excerpt referred to *The Book and the Sultan: Agreement and Separation — Reflections on Political Corruption and its Effects on the History of Muslims* as "Part I", which many took as a threat to release even more turgid prose. Al-Zawahiri thanked his followers for their "patience over long periods … it took me to write this book". He was silent on the Taliban's return to power. The book's introduction was dated April 2021, and included attacks on unnamed Islamist militant leaders and scholars for "demagoguery" and a "stream of bad morals".

AFGHANISTAN

January 2021: *AP* reported on March 26, 2021 that during the previous year, sticky bombs exploded in Kabul nearly daily. In January 2021, authorities arrested mechanic Abdul Sami, 30, in Kabul's poor Shah Shaheed area, on charges of putting sticky bombs inside newly repaired vehicles.

January 1, 2021: *NPR* reported that the Taliban denied involvement when gunmen attacked the car of the head of *Radio Sada-e-Ghor* and human rights activist Bismillah Adil Aimaq on the road near Feroz Koh in Ghor Province, killing him. Aimaq was returning home after visiting family. Others in the car, including Aimaq's brother, were unharmed.

January 14, 2021: The Afghan National Directorate for Security intelligence service announced that Afghan forces killed provincial council member Hazatullah Beg, who was suspected of ties with the Taliban, during a clash near the provincial capital of Faroz Koh in Ghor Province. An officer was killed and another wounded. NDS claimed Beg orchestrated the killing of another council member Ghor deputy council chief Abdul Rahman Atshan in mid-December 2020 and of Afghan journalist and human rights activist Bismillah Adil Aimaq in Ghor on January 1.

January 15, 2021: *Al-Jazeera, Reuters,* and *AP* reported that Herat police spokesman Abdul Ahad Walizada said two members of an Afghan militia fired on their fellow militiamen in Herat Province, killing 12, in an insider attack. The two then escaped with the dead militiamen's weapons and ammunition. Taliban spokesman Yousaf Ahmadi tweeted responsibility.

A suicide car bomber hit a police compound on the highway between Helmand and Kandahar Provinces in Lashkar Gah district in Helmand Province during the night, killing one policeman and wounding two others.

January 16, 2021: Kabul police spokesman Ferdaws Faramarz said a sticky bomb attached to an armored police Land Cruiser SUV exploded in western Kabul, killing two policemen. Two policemen said the bomb also wounded Kabul's deputy police chief Mawlana Bayan.

Provincial governor Rohullah Khanzada said a suicide car bomber and multiple gunmen attacked an auto workshop belonging to the Afghan intelligence agency in Kandahar Province. Four attackers died. No one claimed credit.

January 17, 2021: *AP* and *Reuters* reported that Supreme Court of Afghanistan spokesman Ahmad Fahim Qawim said that at 8:30 a.m., gunmen fired on a car in Kabul, killing two female judges who worked for Afghanistan's high court and wounding the driver. No one claimed responsibility. Taliban spokesman Zabihullah Mujahid denied involvement.

January 18, 2021: The Defense Ministry announced that during the night the Taliban attacked checkpoints in Kunduz Province, killing four soldiers. Fifteen Taliban were killed and a dozen were wounded. Kunduz Provincial Council member Ghulam Rabani Rabani said 25 security forces were killed in separate Taliban attacks in the Dasht-e-Archi district, including 13 soldiers and four policemen. Another eight soldiers were killed near Kunduz city. Taliban spokesman Zabihullah Mujahid claimed responsibility, adding that the Taliban seized weapons and ammunition.

In a nighttime attack, Abdul Nabi Elham, the provincial governor of Helmand, said gunmen killed Abdul Zahir Haqyar, administration chief in Washers district in Helmand Province and wounded two bodyguards. No one claimed credit.

Provincial governor Mohammad Omar Sherzad announced that a sticky bomb placed on a motorcycle exploded in Urozgan Province, wounding ten people, including women and children. He said that the target was a private car belonging to police officers.

January 28, 2021: Provincial Governor Ziaulhaq Amarkhil tweeted that a roadside bomb in Nangarhar Province killed three Pakistani militants, including Manghal Bagh, leader of Lashkar-e-Islam (Army of Islam), who carried a $3 million U.S. bounty issued in 2018 for alleged terrorist activities. LeI often attacked Pakistani troops in the country's northwest Tirah Valley bordering Afghanistan until the mid-2010s. 21012801

February 1, 2021: The Afghan Defense Ministry announced that army troops killed 48 Taliban fighters in operations in southern, northern, and western provinces. Ground and air forces killed 25 Taliban in Dand and Arghandab districts of Kandahar Province. Another 12 Taliban died in a gun battle in Kunduz Province's Imam Sahib district. Eleven insurgents died in fighting in Pusht Rod district in Farah Province.

February 2, 2021: Sticky bombs exploded on three vehicles in Kabul, killing two people, including cleric Mohammad Atef, who headed the Islamist nonprofit organization Jamiat-e-Eslah of Afghanistan, and wounding five people. One bomb, attached to a military vehicle in central Kabul, wounded two military personnel. An hour later, a bomb in northern Kabul killed two people, including Atef; ISIS-K claimed credit; the Taliban condemned his death. A third bomb wounded a person in western Kabul. A fourth bomb went off in Kabul.

Governor Mohammad Omar Shirzad announced that during the night, a car bomb went off at a military base in Uruzgan Province, killing four security personnel.

February 3, 2021: *Al-Jazee*ra reported that gunmen shot to death Judge Hafizullah as he headed to work in a motor trishaw in Jalalabad in Nangarhar Province.

A sticky bomb attached to a police vehicle in Kabul killed a policeman and wounded three others. Four other bombs went off.

February 6, 2021: Two bombs in Kabul killed three people, including members of the minority Sikh community, and wounded four others; other casualty reports conflicted. The first bomb caused a store to collapse, killing two Sikhs and wounding six. Kabul police spokesman Ferdaws Faramarz said a sticky bomb attached to a police car killed a police officer.

February 8, 2021: Three bombs went off in Kabul, killing one person.

February 9, 2021: *Al-Jazeera* and *Reuters* reported that four government employees and four policemen were killed in terrorist attacks. No one claimed credit.

Ferdaws Faramarz, spokesman for the city's police chief, said that gunmen in Kabul's Baghe-Daud neighborhood killed four employees of the Ministry for Rural Development.

A sticky bomb attached to a car in Kabul wounded a government employee.

Provincial governor Wahid Qatali said that a police vehicle hit a roadside bomb in the Zenda Jan district of Herat Province, killing four police officers and wounding one.

February 10, 2021: *AP, AFP,* and *al-Jazeera* reported that several sticky bombs aimed at Kabul police killed a district police chief and his bodyguard and wounded five people. No one claimed credit.

A bomb hit an armored police car in western Kabul, flipping the car upside down and killing District 5 police chief Mohammadzai Kochi and his bodyguard. The driver of the car was wounded in the morning rush hour attack.

Kabul police spokesman Ferdaws Faramarz said an hour earlier, two sticky bombs went off. One of them, 500 meters (yards) away from where the police car was targeted, wounded four civilians. There were no casualties in a bombing in Paghman district.

Ghazni provincial governor's spokesman Wahidullah Jumazada said an airstrike called in during fighting with the Taliban killed at least 22 insurgents, including foreign fighters. Taliban spokesman Zabihullah Mujahid tweeted that the Taliban have no foreign fighters in their ranks.

February 13, 2021: *AP, ISNA,* and *Reuters* reported that at 1:10 p.m., a fuel tanker exploded at the Islam Qala crossing in Afghanistan's Herat Province on the Iranian border, injuring at least seven people and causing a massive fire that destroyed more than 500 trucks carrying natural gas and fuel. Wahid Qatali, Herat's provincial governor, said it was not clear what caused the explosion. Sixty people were injured. Another explosion went off at 1:42 p.m. Wahidullah Tawhidi, spokesman for the Ministry of Power Supply, said that Afghanistan shut down its electrical supply from Iran, darkening 60% of Herat Province. Iran sent 21 ambulances and 20 fire trucks to the inferno. Younus Qazizada, the head of the Herat Chamber of Commerce and Industries, said "more than $50 million of damage has been caused by the fire so far."

February 18, 2021: A sticky bomb attached to a car exploded at noon, killing Mubasher Muslimyar and Marouf Rasikh, two lecturers at Kabul University's Islamic studies faculty. Two years earlier, the Afghan intelligence agency briefly arrested Muslimyar over allegations of promoting ISIS propaganda among university students. No charges were raised.

Earlier in the day, a bomb targeting police in Kabul's District 10 caused no casualties.

February 19, 2021: *Star and Stripes* reported that 30 Taliban died when a bomb they were making exploded prematurely.

February 20, 2021: *NBC News* reported that three sticky bombs attached to vehicles in Kabul killed five people and wounded two others. Two bombs went off within 15 minutes of each other; the first bomb hit a civilian car, wounding both travelers. A second bomb hit a car in which national army soldiers were traveling, killing two soldiers and a civilian passerby. Two hours later, a bomb targeted a police vehicle, killing two police officers. No one claimed credit.

February 21, 2021: *Al-Jazeera* reported that bombs killed three people, including a child, and wounded 20 others. Kabul police spokesman Ferdaws Faramarz said a roadside bomb hit a police car, killing the driver and a nearby child and wounding five civilians, including children. Five other civilians, including children, were wounded. Helmand provincial police spokesman Mohammad Zaman Hamdard said that a second bomb went off in a market in Helmand Province, killing a civilian and wounding 15 others, including two police. No group claimed credit.

February 25, 2021: Ghor provincial council member Hamidullah Mutahid said that gunmen killed three family members of assassinated journalist and activist Bismillah Adil Aimaq in western Afghanistan and wounded five children during an evening attack on the family home. Aimaq was shot to death in an unclaimed attack near Ghor on January 1. Ghor provincial governor Noor Ahmad Kohnaward blamed the Taliban. The Taliban denied involvement in the attack on Aimaq's family.

Earlier in the week, gunmen killed Khalil Narmgo, former head of a journalists association in Baghlan Province.

March 2, 2021: Shokrullah Pasoon, news editor of the privately owned *Enikass Radio and TV* station in Jalalabad, said terrorists shot to death three women, aged between 18 and 20, who worked for a local radio and TV station in eastern Afghanistan in separate attacks. One woman, Mursal Wahidi, was walking home when gunmen opened fire. The other two, whom Pasoon identified as Shahnaz and Sadia, were shot and killed in a separate incident as they walked home from work. Two passersby were wounded; one woman was critically injured. The three women dubbed popular and often emotion-laden dramas from Turkey and India into Dari and Pashtu. *NPR, Reuters,* and *AP* reported that ISIS-K later claimed credit, saying the three female journalists were targeted because they worked for one of the "media stations loyal to the apostate Afghan government" in Jalalabad. *AP* reported Afghan police in Jalalabad arrested the alleged killer of the three, Qari Baser, whom authorities claimed was a Taliban. Nangarhar police chief General Juma Gul Hemat said Baser had used a noise-suppressed pistol. Taliban spokesman Zabihullah Mujahid denied involvement.

During the March 3 funeral of Mursal Wahidi, 23, her father, Wahidullah Khogyani, said he had asked her to quit her job after the December 2020 murder of fellow employee Malala Maiwand.

March 6, 2021: In the evening, the Taliban attacked a police checkpoint in Balkh Province, killing eight policemen and wounding six policemen. Five Taliban fighters died and seven were wounded in the two-hour gun battle in Dawlat Shahi district.

March 7, 2021: Gunmen fired on the car of Malala, the former head of women police in Helmand Province, seriously injuring her and killing her husband, Abul Qayum, also a police officer, at Helmand police headquarters in Lashkar Gah. She served for 14 years and was working in a Helmand police section dealing with family domestic problems. No one claimed credit.

A bomb exploded on a minibus in Kabul in the afternoon, killing one person and injuring four. No one claimed credit.

March 12, 2021: A car bomb exploded during the evening, killing eight people, injuring 47, and destroying 14 homes in Herat Province. The dead included an Afghan Security Forces member and civilians, including women and children. Eleven Afghan Security Forces were injured. No one claimed credit.

March 15, 2021: Gunmen attacked a minibus in Kabul, wounding 15 people. The next day, three women and a 3-year-old child died of their injuries.

March 16, 2021: Jawed Basharat, spokesman for the police chief in Baghlan Province, said gunmen fired at a minibus belonging to a university, killing a student and the driver and wounding six university lecturers from the faculty of agriculture on the outskirts of Puli Khomri. Taliban spokesman Zabihullah Mujahid denied involvement.

In the morning, gunmen attacked a police outpost on the Pashdan Dam on the Hari River in Herat Province, killing three members of the Afghan security forces and wounding four security personnel. The government blamed the Taliban.

March 18, 2021: *Reuters* reported that a roadside bomb hit a bus carrying Afghan government employees in Kabul, killing four and injuring nine.

March 26, 2021: *Al-Jazeera* reported that the Taliban threatened to be "compelled to… continue its Jihad and armed struggle against foreign forces to liberate its country" by attacking foreign troops in Afghanistan if they did not meet the May 1 deadline to withdraw.

March 30, 2021: Gunmen killed three Afghan women carrying out polio vaccinations in two separate attacks in eastern Afghanistan. One woman was killed in Jalalabad in Nangahar Province. The others were murdered farther to the west. No group claimed credit.

March 31, 2021: Terrorist attacks killed four people, including a religious leader and an army officer.

A sticky bomb was attached to the vehicle of Mawlavi Abdul Samad Mohammadi, the head of Takhar Province's Ulema Council, in Taleqan, as he was returning home from attending a graduation ceremony, killing him and wounding three people.

A remotely-detonated bomb hidden in a cart killed two people, including a child, and wounded 16 in Balkh Province.

The Taliban claimed credit for an attack on a military convoy on a main highway linking Logar and Paktia provinces that killed an army officer. Colonel Faridoon Fayaz, unit commander of southeastern provinces, was en route to his office when he was fatally shot. One of his bodyguards was wounded.

April 1, 2021: Gunmen killed a policewoman en route to work in Jalalabad. Police arrested two suspects. ISIS-K claimed credit, saying that she was working with the "apostate" Afghan security services.

April 2, 2021: Omer Zwak, spokesman for the provincial governor in Helmand Province, said a roadside bomb killed five civilians traveling by car near Lashkar Gah.

A roadside bomb wounded seven women traveling in a minivan in Herat Province.

April 7, 2021: *Air Force Magazine* reported that the Taliban fired rockets at Kandahar Airfield, causing no casualties. 21040702

April 8, 2021: A plane flying Pakistani parliamentary speaker Assad Qaisar and a delegation of lawmakers was turned back from landing in Kabul's international airport after explosives, apparently years old, were found by NATO forces placed under a nearby building.

April 12, 2021: Hanif Rezaie, a spokesman for the Afghan army commander in the north, said that during the night, gunmen attacked an army checkpoint in the Chimtal district of Balkh Province, killing five soldiers and wounding two others. Rezaie added that seven insurgents, including a group commander, were killed. Taliban spokesman Zabihullah Mujahid claimed responsibility.

April 13, 2021: Tariq Arian, spokesman for the Interior Ministry, said a suicide car bomber set off his explosives near the police station in Farah's first district, killing three civilians, including a child, and wounding 24 others, including young children and six police. Most of the casualties were civilians.

Gunmen attacked a government checkpoint in the Daha-e Ghori district of Baghlan Province, killing five police officers and injuring another four. No one claimed credit.

April 20, 2021: *Reuters* reported that a suicide bomber hit an Afghan security forces convoy in Kabul.

April 21, 2021: *CNN* reported that the Taliban threatened to kill Afghans who had worked for the U.S. during the war.

April 25, 2021: *Reuters* reported that the Taliban killed eight members of a police public protection unit in Logar Province.

April 26, 2021: *Reuters* reported that a rocket hit the compound of Kunar Province Governor Iqbal Sayeed during a holy Koran recitation competition, wounding 16 children, three Afghan security force members, and religious affairs officials. Some children were critically injured. Local officials blamed the Taliban.

A roadside bomb hit an army vehicle in Jalalabad, wounding six people.

April 30, 2021: The *New York Times, Tolo News, BBC,* and *AP* reported that a suicide truck bomb went off at 7 p.m. near a school guest house in Pul-e-Alam, capital of Logar Province, killing 30 people, including students, injuring more than 100, and damaging a hospital and homes. The Interior Ministry blamed the Taliban. Hasib Stanikzai, head of the Logar provincial council, said that local police were staying at the guest

house, waiting for transportation home. The *New York Times* reported that the facility belonged to the family of a prominent member of the Afghan senate who had been assassinated by the Taliban. The truck driver had claimed that he was bringing supplies for the breaking of the Ramadan fast.

The *New York Times* reported that in a nighttime attack, the Taliban overran an army base near Ghazni, capturing 25 soldiers.

May 1, 2021: The *New York Times* reported that in the morning, a Kabul University professor was shot to death.

The Taliban fired rockets during the early afternoon at Kandahar Airfield.

May 3, 2021: *Reuters* reported that Farah Governor Taj Mohammad Jahid said the Taliban blew up an army outpost after digging a quarter-mile tunnel to it from a nearby house. The Taliban bomb killed seven soldiers. The Taliban captured another soldier. Two local officials claimed that dozens of soldiers, including elite commando forces, had been killed. Provincial council member Khayer Mohammad Noorzai said that around 30 had died.

A bomb exploded near a school in Farah, wounding 21 people, including ten students aged between 7 and 13. Farah Public Health Director Abdul Jabar Shayeq said three of the wounded were in critical condition.

May 5, 2021: In the morning, a bomb hit a minibus carrying doctors, nurses, and other medical workers in Kalakan district in Kabul Province to Panjsher Province, killing one person and hospitalizing three medics. No one claimed credit.

During the night, the Taliban attacked a security outpost in Ghazni Province, killing six Afghan security forces.

May 6, 2021: *AP* and *Reuters* reported that provincial spokesman Baheer Ahmadi announced that at noon, two gunmen killed former Afghan *Tolonews* TV presenter Nimat Rawan as he was travelling in Kandahar. The gunmen stole Rawan's cell phone. Rawan had been working in the Finance Ministry's media office. No one claimed credit, but Taliban spokesman Zabihullah Mujahid warned Afghan journalists against giving "one-sided news in support of Afghani-stan's intelligence" or "face the consequences".

Provincial police spokesman Jawed Basharat announced that the Taliban captured a second district in Baghlan Province.

May 8, 2021: *AP, BBC, UPI, CNN, Tolo News, Reuters, Washington Examiner, NPR,* the *New York Times,* and the *Washington Post* reported that a bomb exploded at 4 p.m. outside the Sayed Ul-Shuhada girls' high school in the Dasht-e-Barchi area of Kabul, killing 85 and injuring 165 civilians, many critically. *Reuters* reported that a car bomb and mortars were involved and that two more bombs had exploded when the students rushed out in panic. The attack target-ed Hazaras. No one claimed credit. The Taliban condemned the attack.

May 10, 2021: *Reuters* reported that a bomb hit a bus, killing 11 and wounding dozens.

May 11, 2021: Provincial Council spokesman Sharifullah Hotak said that the Taliban over-ran the Nirkh district headquarters in Maidan Wardak Province.

Taliban political spokesman Suhail Shaheen said the group released more than 100 govern-ment prisoners from across the country to com-memorate the Eid holidays.

May 12, 2021: *CNN* reported on July 22 that the Taliban stopped the car of Sohail Pardis, 32, a translator who worked for the U.S. Army for 16 months, as he was driving from his Kabul home to Khost Province to pick up his sister for Eid celebrations. He had earlier received death threats from the Taliban. He stomped on the gas, but the Taliban stopped his car, pulled him from it, and beheaded him.

May 13, 2021: *Reuters* reported that four bomb-ings killed 11 civilians and wounded 13.

May 14, 2021: *AP* and *Reuters* reported that a bomb exploded inside a mosque in Kabul's Sha-kar Dara district, killing 12 people, including the mosque's imam, Mofti Noman, and wounding 15, including a child, during Friday prayers on the Eid al-Fitr holiday. Worshipper Muhibullah Sahebzada said the bomb appeared to be hidden inside the pulpit at the front of the mosque. Au-thorities speculated that Noman was the target of the attack. The Taliban condemned the attack.

May 19, 2021: In the late evening, a car carry-ing a family of 12 en route to Lashkar Gah hit a roadside bomb in the Nad Ali district of Hel-mand Province, killing nine, including several children, and hospitalizing three children.

A roadside bomb in Ghor Province de-stroyed a motorcycle and killed a family of four who were riding it. No one claimed credit.

May 20, 202: Gunmen stopped a bus in west-ern Afghanistan, ordered three Hazara men to get out, and shot them to death. No one claimed credit. The government blamed the Taliban.

May 29, 2021: *AP* and *BBC* reported that pro-vincial police spokesman Shayeq Shoresh said that at 3:15 p.m., a remotely-detonated roadside bomb hit a minivan carrying university lecturers and students through Charikar in Parwan Prov-ince to Alberoni (variant al-Biruni) University in Kapisa Province, killing four, including three teachers, and wounding 15. Kapisa provincial hospital chief Abdul Qasem Sangin said that doctors were among the casualties. A ministry of higher education spokesman said that some of the teachers were in critical condition. The university's chancellor was also injured. No one claimed credit.

June 1, 2021: Three bombs went off in the eve-ning in Kabul, killing ten people. Deputy Interi-or Ministry spokesman Said Hamid Rushan said that two bombs targeting minivans exploded in quick succession in a mostly ethnic Hazara area in west Kabul, killing ten and wounding a dozen others. One bomb went off in front of a Shi'ite mosque near the home of prominent Hazara leader Mohammad Mohaqiq. Sangar Niazai, a spokesman for the government power supply de-partment, said that another bomb heavily dam-aged an electrical grid station in north Kabul. ISIS-K claimed credit.

Reuters reported that during the evening, two bombs hit two public transport buses in Ka-bul, killing 12 civilians and wounding ten. No one claimed credit.

June 3, 2021: Police spokesman Ferdaws Faramarz said that a bomb hit a minivan in a predominantly Hazara Shi'ite neighborhood in western Kabul, killing four people. No one claimed credit.

June 5, 2021: A roadside bomb hit a minivan carrying civilian passengers in Baghdis Province, throwing it into a valley and killing 11 passengers, including three children. The government blamed the Taliban.

June 6, 2021: Officials in Faryab Province said Taliban fighters took over the district of Qaisar after weeks of fighting in which provincial police chief Saifulrahman and seven other police officers were killed. The Taliban took 37 police hostage.

Kabul police spokesman Ferdaws Faramarz said a roadside bomb hit a civilian car and wounded three people.

June 8, 2021: *AP, NBC News, Reuters,* and *BBC* reported that at 9:50 p.m., masked gunmen killed 10 people, including three Hazaras, and wounded 16 others in an attack on the UK-based HALO Trust de-mining organization's camp in Baghlan Markazi district in Baghlan Province. The government blamed the Taliban, which the group denied. ISIS-K took credit on June 9. Some 110 local HALO employees were in camp after finishing their work on a minefield nearby. Survivors said the gunmen were looking for Hazaras, who in this area of Afghanistan tend to be Sunnis. Among the wounded was Sheikh Mohammad, who sustained leg injuries. He said that after the gunmen moved the deminers into two rooms, they asked, "Who is Hazara among you?" and "Who among you is working with the atheist Taliban?" Survivor Mohammad Zarif said some deminers fled while local villagers shot at the terrorists. 21060801

The Taliban claimed it had downed an MI-17 helicopter in the Jaghatu district of Maidan Wardark Province as it was delivering help to security forces in the battlefield. The government said it was an accident due to technical problems. Three crew died and one was wounded.

June 12, 2021: *AP* and *Reuters* reported that Interior Ministry deputy spokesman Ahmad Zia

Zia said that bombs hit two minivans on the same road two miles apart in a mostly Shi'ite Hazara neighborhood in Kabul, killing seven and wounding six. The first bomb killed six people, including Fatima Mohammadi and Tayiba Musavi, animators who worked for the state-run Afghan Film Organization on an animated film for children, and wounded two. Mohammadi and Musavi were returning home. The second bomb went off in front of Muhammad Ali Jinnah Hospital, where a majority of COVID-19 patients are admitted, killing one and injuring four. The next day ISIS-K claimed its operatives blew up two minivans carrying "disbeliever Shi'ites" using sticky bombs.

June 15, 2021: *AFP, Reuters, al-Jazeera,* and *AP* reported that gunmen shot to death five male polio workers and wounded one in the districts of Khoyani and Surkhrud in Nangarhar Province and wounded three in Jalalabad. Three were wounded critically. The Taliban denied responsibility.

June 16, 2021: The Taliban attacked a base in Dawlat Abad district in Faryab Province, killing 23 soldiers, including U.S.-trained Colonel Sohrab Azimi, 31, a retired Army general's son and field commander in the Afghan special forces that often rescues troops and retakes outposts from the Taliban. The Taliban released the bodies of Azimi and two other commandos after negotiations with the International Committee of the Red Cross. The slain commando leader was promoted posthumously to brigadier general.

CNN reported on July 13 that a video showed Taliban gunmen shooting to death a dozen unarmed members of an Afghan Special Forces unit who had surrendered in Dawlat Abad, near the border with Turkmenistan. The Red Cross said the bodies of 22 commandos were retrieved. Among the dead was Sohrab Azimi, 32, who spent two years at a U.S. military school and was to marry his American fiancée in August.

July 1-2, 2021: The *Washington Post, Fox News,* and *Slate* reported that the U.S. military vacated Bagram Air Base, turning it over to the Afghan National Security and Defense Force, nearly 20

years after the start of the Global War on Terror. Bagram was once the headquarters for U.S. Special Operations troops.

July 9, 2021: *UPI, New York Times,* and *Tolo News* reported that Afghan officials claimed that they had repelled a Taliban attack on Kandahar. But Taliban forces took control of at least two security outposts in District 7. *Tolo* added that authorities were fighting the Taliban in Kunduz, Baghlan, Herat, Ghazni, Faryab, and Maidan Wardak Provinces.

July 9, 2021: *Reuters* reported that during the U.S. military's withdrawal from Afghanistan, the Taliban conducted a campaign of assassinations of Afghan Air Force pilots, killing seven off base in several months.

The Taliban killed the realtor of Air Force Major Dastagir Zamaray, 41, who had decided to sell his home to move to a safer area of Kabul. A gunman walked into the realtor's office and fatally shot the real estate agent in the mouth. When Zamaray reached for his sidearm, the gunman shot him in the head. He collapsed on his son, 14, who was spared but rarely speaks. Zamaray left behind seven children.

On June 7, the Taliban shot down a Russian-made, U.S.-financed Mi-17 helicopter evacuating troops wounded during a surge of fighting against the Taliban insurgency, killing pilots Milad Massoud and Abdul Alim Shahrayari.

On December 30, 2020, two motorcycles flanked the gray Toyota Corolla on a Kandahar city highway of Black Hawk helicopter pilot Masood Atal. The gunmen shot him 11 times, once in the face, six times in his right arm and hand, the rest in his chest, killing him. He had received expletive-laced phoned death threats from the Taliban on December 28. The Afghan military rejected his request for bodyguards and a bullet-proof car. His parents had lost four other children. In 1984, a Taliban rocket landed in front of their children's school in Kandahar, killing another son and three daughters.

Taliban spokesman Mujahid said, "Targeting those who bombard civilians, who drop blind bombs on civilian houses, is an obligation for us and we will do this."

July 16, 2021: *Reuters, AP, Business Insider, CBS News,* and *ABC News* reported that *Reuters* photojournalist Danish Siddiqui, a Pulitzer Prize-winning photographer from India, was killed in a Taliban crossfire in the main market of the Spin Boldak district of Kandahar near the Pakistan border while covering an Afghan special forces unit's attempt to retake districts from the Taliban. He was embedded with the Afghan unit. He had tweeted on July 13 that a rocket had hit the armor plate on the roof of his Humvee. He died with a senior Afghan officer. He had been wounded in the arm by shrapnel earlier in the morning and was talking to shopkeepers when the Taliban attacked. The *New York Times* reported on August 1 that Siddiqi's body was mutilated while in Taliban custody. An Indian official said he was hit by nearly a dozen bullets and there were tire marks on his face and chest. Taliban spokesman Zabihullah Mujahid said the group had not been aware there was a journalist reporting from the site. Siddiqui won a Pulitzer Prize for Feature Photography for documenting the Rohingya refugee crisis in 2018. He joined *Reuters* in 2010, then covered the wars in Afghanistan and Iraq, the Rohingya refugee crisis, the Hong Kong protests, COVID-19 in India, and Nepal earthquakes. 21071602

July 20, 2021: *AP, Anadolu, Tolo TV, CNN,* and *NBC News* reported that three rockets hit outside the presidential palace grounds in Kabul's Green Zone during 8:30 a.m. prayers and shortly before Afghan President Ashraf Ghani was to give an address to mark Eid al-Adha. No injuries were reported. ISIS-K claimed credit on its *Aamaq* news channel. A car parked on a nearby street in Police District 4 was destroyed; police said it was used to launch the rockets, which landed in Police Districts 1 and 2. Abdullah Abdullah, the No. 2 official in the government who leads the High Council for National Reconciliation, was inside the palace during the rocket attack. *Reuters* reported that Taliban spokesman Zabihullah Mujahid denied involvement.

July 28, 2021: *Tolo News* and *AP* reported that the Taliban kidnapped and executed on video Kandahar police officer and online *TikTok* comedian Nazar Mohammad Khasha, alias Khasha

Zwan, the previous week, sparking widespread condemnation. *AP* reported on July 29 that Taliban spokesman Zabihullah Mujahid said the two killers were arrested and would be tried. He claimed Zwan was a member of the Afghan National Police and had been implicated in the torture and killing of Taliban.

July 29, 2021: The Special Inspector General for Afghanistan Reconstruction (SIGAR) and American military officials announced that Taliban offensives between April 1 and June 30 included more than two dozen insider attacks that killed 81 Afghan troops and wounded 37 Afghan troops.

July 30, 2021: *AFP* reported that gunmen fired rocket-propelled grenades at a U.N. compound in Herat, killing an Afghan police guard. 21073001

July 31, 2021: *Reuters* reported that during the night, the Taliban fired three rockets at Kandahar Airport, hoping to thwart government air strikes.

August 1, 2021: *Military Times* and *AP* reported that a mortar shell hit a taxi in Kandahar Province, killing five civilians, including two children. Provincial police spokesman Jamal Naser Barekzai blamed the Taliban, which denied involvement.

August 3, 2021: *AP* and *CNN* reported that Interior Ministry spokesman Mirwais Stanekzai said a car bomb went off in the upscale Sherpur neighborhood in an evening attack on the Kabul guesthouse of acting Defense Minister Bismillah Khan Mohammadi, killing eight people and wounding 20. The minister was not in the guesthouse and his family was safely evacuated. Gunmen entered the area after the explosion. Security personnel killed four attackers. *The World* reported that the Taliban claimed credit. *KETV* reported that the Kabul office of the University of Nebraska at Omaha, two houses down the street from Mohammadi's guest house, was damaged in the car bombing. 21080301

The Defense Ministry tweeted that 41 Taliban were killed in "joint clearing operations" on the outskirts of Herat.

August 5, 2021: The *Omaha World Herald* reported that a car bombing in Kabul badly damaged the nearby offices of the University of Nebraska at Omaha's Center for Afghanistan Studies. 21080501

August 6, 2021: The Taliban shot to death Dawa Khan Menapal, the director of Afghanistan's Government Information Media Center, while he was in his car. He had previously been a deputy spokesman for Afghan President Ashraf Ghani.

August 7, 2021: *BBC* reported the Taliban claimed to have captured a prison in Sheberghan in Jawzjan Province and freed all of the hundreds of prisoners.

Reuters reported that Afghan Air Force pilot Hamidullah Azimi was killed when a Taliban sticky bomb attached to his vehicle detonated in Kabul. Five civilians were wounded. Azimi was trained to fly U.S.-made UH60 Black Hawk helicopters and had served with the Afghan Air Force for almost four years. He and his family had moved to Kabul a year earlier due to security threats.

August 15, 2021: President Ashraf Ghani fled the country, the government collapsed, and the Taliban completed its takeover of Afghanistan. On August 17, 2021, *Business Insider* and the *New York Times* reported Gholam Ruhani, who was held at Gitmo for six years before being repatriated to Afghanistan in December 2007, was filmed celebrating at the Afghan presidential palace. He had told a prison guard in April 2005, "We will get you on the outside." He entered Gitmo the first day it opened in January 2002. He had worked for the Taliban's Ministry of Intelligence before his capture in December 2001. He had claimed to be a simple shopkeeper.

August 16, 2021: *Reuters* reported that in separate incidents within 24 hours, U.S. forces protecting Kabul's airport in Kabul killed two gunmen who fired into the crowds trying to flee.

August 23, 2021: The *Washington Post, Business Insider, Washington Examiner, Deseret News, Politico, Slate, BBC, NBC News, CBS News, Yahoo! News,* and *CNN* reported that CIA Director

William J. Burns met face-to-face in Kabul with Taliban co-founder and deputy leader Abdul Ghani Baradar.

August 26, 2021: *AP* and *Reuters* reported that a suicide bomber set off his 25-pound explosive vest at the Abbey Gate entry gate to Kabul's Hamid Karzai International Airport at 5:48 p.m., while thousands of Americans and Afghans were attempting to evacuate the country via the "Digital Dunkirk" airlift, in what the Pentagon called a complex attack, with terrorists then opening fire on the crowd. *NPR* and the *Washington Post* said 12 U.S. soldiers—11 Marines and a Navy corpsman—and dozens of civilians died; *Tass* said Russian government officials claimed 13 people were dead. Several Americans were injured. *Military Times* reported that 18 American soldiers were injured. *CNN* reported that an Afghan health official put the toll at 90+Afghans dead and 140 injured. *Reuters* put the death toll at 85. *Business Insider* quoted an Afghan interpreter as saying that a baby girl died in his arms. A 13th soldier died later that day. By August 27, the *Washington Post* put the casualty numbers at 170 dead and 155 injured; the figure did not include U.S. service members. Two British nationals and the child of a third were killed. The *New York Times* on January 2, 2022 reported that nearly 200 people were killed.

ISIS-K claimed credit. Reports had been circulating of an ISIS-K terrorist threat against the airlift. Additional warnings suggested that ISIS-K could strike again as the airlift continued.

The *New York Times* reported on January 2, 2022 that ISIS-K identified the bomber as Abdul Rahman al-Logari, a former engineering student at Manav Rachna University in New Delhi. His father, an Afghan merchant, often visited India and Pakistan for business. Al-Logari went to India in 2017. The *Times* reported that in 2017, the CIA warned Indian intelligence that he was plotting a suicide bombing in New Delhi. Indian intelligence detained him. He was sent to Afghanistan, serving time at the Parwan prison in Bagram Air Base. When the Taliban overran the base, he was among thousands of prisoners who were freed. 21082601

The Pentagon later withdrew an announcement that a second bomb went off at the nearby Baron Hotel.

Newsweek, Sky 24 TG, ANSA, and *Reuters* reported that an unknown individual fired shots at an Italian military C-130 transport carrying 100 Afghan former NATO workers as it was departing Kabul airport. 21082602

In an address from the White House, President Biden said, "Know this. We will not forgive. We will not forget. We will hunt you down and make you pay."

The Pentagon released the names of the murdered soldiers; *CNN, Fox News,* and *AP* provided biographic details:

- Marine Corps Lance Cpl. David L. Espinoza, 20, of Rio Bravo, Texas, enlisted after graduating from Lyndon B. Johnson High School in Laredo, Texas. He was assigned to the 2nd Battalion, 1st Marine Regiment, 1st Marine Division, I Marine Expeditionary Force, Camp Pendleton, California.

- Marine Corps Sgt. Nicole Gee, 23, of Roseville, California, was one of the soldiers photographed cradling a refugee baby; the *Instagram* photo was captioned "I love my job." The Sacramento native was assigned to Combat Logistic Battalion 24, 24th Marine Expeditionary Unit, II Marine Expeditionary Force, based out of Camp Lejeune in North Carolina. She was promoted three weeks earlier in Kuwait.

- Marine Corps Staff Sgt. Taylor Hoover, 31, 2nd Battalion, 1st Marine Regiment, 1st Marine Division, I Marine Expeditionary Force, Camp Pendleton, California. He was from Utah, and graduated from high school in 2008. He also was known as Darin Hoover.

- Army Staff Sgt. Ryan Knauss, 23, of Knoxville, Tennessee, while in second grade, wrote in his yearbook, "I want to be a Marine" and drew himself in uniform. He joined a JROTC program in high school. Upon graduating, he enlisted in the Army. The Corrytown resident was assigned to the 9th PSYOP Battalion, 8th PSYOP Group, based in Fort Bragg, North Carolina.

- Marine Corps Cpl. Hunter Lopez, 22, 2nd Battalion, 1st Marine Regiment, 1st Marine

Division, I Marine Expeditionary Force, Camp Pendleton, California. He was from Indio, California, and came from a family in law enforcement. His mother is a deputy sheriff and his father is a sheriff's captain in Riverside County. He had planned to join them as a sheriff's deputy following his deployment.

- Marine Corps Lance Cpl. Rylee McCollum, 20, of Bondurant, Wyoming, who was married on February 14, 2021 before going on his first overseas deployment to Jordan in April. He was assigned to the 2nd Battalion, 1st Marine Regiment, 1st Marine Division, I Marine Expeditionary Force, Camp Pendleton, California. Two weeks before the blast, he was transferred to Afghanistan to help with the evacuation. He and wife Jiennah, who lives in San Diego, were expecting their first child in three weeks. The couple met while he was in boot camp. He joined the infantry the day he turned 18, a childhood dream since he was a 2-year-old. He attended Jackson Hole High School and Summit Innovations School in Jackson. He was a decorated wrestler, once dropping 30 pounds in five months before a state wrestling tournament. He hoped to become an American history teacher and coach wrestling.

- Marine Corps Lance Cpl. Dylan R. Merola, 20, of Rancho Cucamonga, California, was assigned to the 2nd Battalion, 1st Marine Regiment, 1st Marine Division, I Marine Expeditionary Force, Camp Pendleton, California. He had planned on becoming an engineer. He had attended Los Osos High School.

- Marine Corps Lance Cpl. Kareem Nikoui, 20, of Norco, California, who was assigned to the 2nd Battalion, 1st Marine Regiment, 1st Marine Division, I Marine Expeditionary Force, Camp Pendleton, California, near where his extended family lived. The day before his death, Kareem had sent his father a video showing Marines giving candy to Afghan children.

- Marine Corps Cpl. Daegan William-Tyeler Page, 23, of Omaha, Nebraska, was a diehard Chicago Blackhawks fan and animal lover. He planned to attend a local trade school, perhaps becoming a line man. He was a member of the Boy Scouts. He graduated from Millard South High School and joined the Corps in 2019. He was assigned to the 2nd Battalion, 1st Marine Regiment, 1st Marine Division, I Marine Expeditionary Force, Camp Pendleton, California.

- Marine Corps Sgt. Johanny Rosariopichardo, 25, assigned to the 5th Marine Expeditionary Brigade, Naval Support Activity Bahrain, was from Lawrence, Massachusetts. She went by Rosario for short.

- Marine Corps Cpl. Humberto Sanchez, 22, Logansport, Indiana, was assigned to the 2nd Battalion, 1st Marine Regiment, 1st Marine Division, I Marine Expeditionary Force, Camp Pendleton, California

- Marine Corps Lance Cpl. Jared Schmitz, 20, of Wentzville and St. Charles County, Missouri, joined the Marines in 2019 and assigned to the 2nd Battalion, 1st Marine Regiment, 1st Marine Division, I Marine Expeditionary Force, Camp Pendleton, California. He was on his first deployment.

- Navy Hospital Corpsman Maxton Soviak, of Berlin Heights, Ohio, planned to be a Navy careerist. He graduated from Edison High School in 2017. He was on the state champion wrestling team and played in consecutive semifinal trips with the football team. He was assigned to the 1st Marine Regiment, 1st Marine Division, based out of Camp Pendleton, California. He was survived by Kip and Rachel Soviak and 12 of their other children.

The *Washington Post* reported on August 29 that the Afghan victims—170 dead and 200 wounded—included young and old, women and men, doctors, journalists, athletes, and tailors. They included:

- Ali Reza Ahmadi, 36, who in 1996, had escaped as a child to Iran, where he grew up as a refugee and graduated from high school. He returned to Kabul in 2001. He enrolled at Kabul University, graduating with a degree in journalism in 2013. Ahmadi co-founded the *Raha News Agency*, and worked as a freelance reporter for local media outlets. His brother, Mujtaba, 33, went with him to the airport and also died.

- Wasiq Ehsan, 21, attended Kabul University, studying Spanish, hoping to become a graphic designer and a professional soccer player. He, his sister, 19, and another family member were killed and another relative was wounded.

- Qurban Ali Faiazy, 21, lived in Paris. He graduated from high school in 2018. He borrowed money and snuck into Iran, then Turkey. He worked as a tailor and sent money back to his family in Kabul every month. His application for asylum through the Office of the U.N. High Commissioner for Refugees fizzled. He returned to Kabul in May 2021. He and his family were at the Abbey Gate. He died in a wheelbarrow.

- Najma Sadeqi, 20, was in her last semester in journalism school. Her brother and a cousin who had escorted her to the airport to ensure her safety also died. She had worked for two private broadcasters and ran a *YouTube* channel. Her sister, Freshta, said Najma received threatening phone calls and text messages from unknown men who objected to her appearing in public.

- Mohammed Jan Sultani, 25, who won national Taekwondo championship certificates. His wife and two children, Zahid, 4, and Zahra, 2, survived.

CNN reported that the Pentagon said a nighttime drone strike on August 27 on a house in the 7th district of Jalalabad killed two ISIS-K terrorists, including an "ISIS-K planner", and wounded another ISIS-K terrorist.

The *Washington Post* reported on August 28 that the Taliban claimed to have arrested two members of ISIS-K. A resident claimed that two people were killed and three other injured in a strike on a house in the Naghrak neighborhood.

August 27, 2021: The *Washington Post* reported that Amazon disabled a website used by ISIS's *Nida-e-Haqq* media group that distributes Islamist content in the Urdu language. The *Nida-e-Haqq* app on August 26 carried what it claimed was a photo of the Kabul Airport bomber wrapped in a suicide vest.

August 29, 2021: The U.S. military announced that it had carried out a strike on a vehicle carrying ISIS-K suicide bombers that posed an "imminent" ISIS-K threat to Kabul's international airport. Navy Capt. Bill Urban, a spokesman for U.S. Central Command, added "Significant secondary explosions from the vehicle indicated the presence of a substantial amount of explosive material."

Taliban spokesman Bilal Karimi said that a "rocket" had struck a home in the Khawaja Bughra neighborhood, northwest of Hamid Karzai International Airport. Afghan police said that at least one child was killed. Local media channel *Rukhshana* reported that up to six civilians had been killed. *Al-Jazeera-English* reporter Ali Latifi told *NPR* that ten members of a family including people aged 2, 3, 4, and 40, were killed getting out of a car in front of their home; they were awaiting the paperwork for their Special Interest Visas (SIV) to join the evacuation.

CNN reported on September 17, 2021 that Gen. Frank McKenzie, the seniormost general of U.S. Central Command, announced that a United States military investigation into the drone strike on a vehicle near the Hamid Karzai International airport in Kabul found it killed ten civilians, including seven children, and the driver and that the vehicle targeted was likely not a threat associated with ISIS-K. McKenzie said, "This strike was taken in the earnest belief that it would prevent an imminent threat to our forces and the evacuees at the airport, but it was a mistake and I offer my sincere apology." The Pentagon had earlier claimed that at least one ISIS-K facilitator and three civilians were killed in what Chairman of the Joint Chiefs Gen. Mark Milley had previously called a "righteous strike". Secretary of Defense Lloyd Austin offered condolences to the family of Zamarai Ahmadi, the driver of the car targeted in the strike.

August 30, 2021: *NPR* reported that the U.S. military Counter-Rocket, Artillery, and Mortar System (C-RAM) missile defense system intercepted five rockets that were fired at Kabul airport from a sedan whose back seats had been replaced by rocket tubes. Other rockets landed in residential neighborhoods but did not cause injuries. ISIS-K claimed credit. 21083001

August 31, 2021: The last U.S. military flight left Kabul airport one minute before midnight, officially ending the 20-year American involvement in the war in Afghanistan.

September 7, 2021: *CNN* reported that the Taliban interim government included individuals on the Most Wanted Terrorist list and four Gitmo alumni who had been traded for Bowe Bergdahl in 2014. They included:

- Mohammad Hassan Akhund, a close aide of the Taliban's late founder Mohammad Omar and under UN sanctions, acting prime minister. He had led the group's Shura (Leadership Council) for two decades.

- Abdul Ghani Baradar, one of the group's co-founders, deputy prime minister

- Mohammed Yaqoob, a son of Mohammad Omar, acting defense minister

- Zabihullah Mujahid, spokesman

- Sirajuddin Haqqani, leader of the Haqqani Network, acting interior minister. Haqqani had been one of two deputy leaders of the Taliban since 2016. He appeared on the FBI's Most Wanted Terrorist List. The U.S. offered a $10 million bounty for his arrest.

- Khalil Haqqani, Sirajuddin's uncle, acting minister for refugees. He has a $5 million bounty for his past relationship with al-Qaeda.

- Two other members of the Haqqani clan were also named to the interim government.

- Gitmo alumni included:
  - Noorullah Noori, acting minister of borders and tribal affairs
  - Abdul Haq Wasiq, acting intelligence director

- Khairullah Khair, acting minister of information and culture

- Mohammad Fazil Mazloom, deputy minister of defense

A fifth detainee released in the 2014 trade, Mohammed Nabi Omari, was appointed governor of Khost Province in August.

September 18-19, 2021: *Reuters* and the *Washington Post* reported that ISIS-K, via the *Aamaq News Agency's Telegram* account, claimed "More than 35 Taliban militia members were killed or wounded, in a series of explosions that took place" in Jalalabad on September 18-19. *Reuters* quoted eyewitnesses and hospitals that indicated that three people were killed and about 20 were wounded in blasts in Jalalabad on September 18. Taliban spokesman Bilal Karimi said a September 19 bombing in Jalalabad targeted a Taliban vehicle, killing one child and injuring two people, including a Taliban member.

September 22, 2021: ISIS-K was suspected of firing on a Taliban vehicle at a gas station in Jalalabad, killing two fighters and three civilians, including a child and the gas station attendant.

In a separate bombing of another vehicle, a child was killed and two Taliban were wounded. Another bombing of a Taliban vehicle in Jalalabad wounded a person nearby.

October 1, 2021: The Taliban raided an ISIS-K hideout in Charikar in Parwan Province, killing and arresting several terrorists.

The Taliban had arrested two ISIS-K members linked to a roadside bombing that targeted their vehicle in Kabul, wounding four fighters. Their questioning provided information about the hideout.

October 3, 2021: *AP* and *ABC News* reported that ISIS-K claimed credit for a roadside bomb that exploded outside Kabul's Eidgah mosque that killed five civilians and injured several others during a memorial service for the mother of the Taliban's acting deputy information minister and main spokesman, Zabihullah Mujahid. The *Montreal Gazette* reported that gunfire was heard on the outskirts of the city. Taliban spokesman Bilal Karimi said three suspects were arrested and no Taliban fighters were harmed. An Italian-funded emergency hospital tweeted it had received four injured people.

October 5, 2021: ISIS-K claimed it targeted a vehicle carrying Taliban members in Kunar Province during the night, killing and wounding "many" members of a Taliban reinforcement patrol.

October 6, 2021: *ABC News* reported that the Taliban arrested four ISIS-K members north of Kabul, seizing documents and weapons.

Two Taliban fighters were shot and killed and three civilians wounded when gunmen fired on a Taliban patrol in a vegetable market in Jalalabad. ISIS-K did not claim responsibility.

October 8, 2021: *AP* reported that at 1:15 p.m., an ISIS-K suicide bomber set off his explosives in the male section of the Sayed Abad mosque in Kunduz during Friday prayers involving more than 300 worshipers. Deputy Taliban spokesman Bilal Karimi said that the bomb killed 46 worshipers and injured 143. Shi'ite community leader Sayed Ahmad Shah Hashemi told the *New York Times* that more than 70 people were killed. The Doctors Without Borders hospital received 21 bodies and 99 wounded, all of them men. The Islamic State-Khorasan claimed credit on its *Amaq* news channel.

The U.N. reported that no one claimed credit for attacking a religious school in Khost Province.

October 9, 2021: *Newsweek* and *Military Times* reported that the Taliban announced that it could handle ISIS-K on its own and would not work with the U.S. against the group.

October 15, 2021: *NPR, AP, CNN,* and the *Washington Post* reported that four suicide bombers at the Shi'ite Imam Bargha Fatimiya mosque in Kandahar Province killed 47 and injured 70. Local eyewitness Murtaza Khaledi, 26, said two terrorists hit the security gate, while another two ran inside to hit the congregation during Friday prayers. ISIS-K claimed on *Aamaq* that two ISIS-K members, Anas al-Khurasani and Abu Ali al-Baluchi, both Afghan nationals, shot and killed security guards manning the entrance of the mosque. Victim family members dug 63 graves, although the Taliban's chief for the provincial department of culture and information said the official death toll was 47.

October 18, 2021: Interior Ministry spokesman Saeed Khosty tweeted that the Taliban's acting interior minister, Sirajuddin Haqqani, promised plots of land to dozens of relatives of suicide bombers who attacked U.S. and Afghan soldiers. Haqqani called them "heroes of Islam and the country". He gave 10,000 afghanis ($112) per family and promised each a plot of land.

October 23, 2021: Two roadside bombs targeting a Taliban vehicle killed two civilians, including a child, and wounded four people in Nangarhar Province. District police chief Ismatullah Mubariz said that no Taliban fighters were harmed. No one claimed credit. ISIS-K was suspected.

October 29, 2021: Taliban deputy spokesman Bilal Karimi said that in a nighttime attack, two gunmen on a motorcycle lightly injured Ali Reza Sharifi, a journalist for *Islamic Republic of Iran Broadcasting*, as he was driving home in Kabul. Sharifi said, "A bullet fired from the left just touched my lip... shredded window pieces hit my left eye... They started firing from the front and I escaped to the back seat." No one claimed credit. 21102902

November 2, 2021: Taliban deputy spokesman Bilal Karimi announced that two suicide bombers set off their explosives, followed by gunmen firing at the main Sardar Mohammad Daud Khan military hospital in the former diplomatic zone in the Wazir Akbar Khan area of central Kabul. The Taliban and a doctor at military hospital, Habib Rahman, told the *Washington Post* that 20 were killed and 37 wounded. *Al-Jazeera* said 19 were killed and 43 wounded. The *Wall Street Journal* said 23 died. *Reuters* put the numbers at 25 dead and more than 50 wounded. No one claimed credit. In 2017, ISIS-K claimed credit for an attack on the hospital when gunmen disguised as medics opened fire on patients and staff, killing 30 people. Reports differed as to whether the attackers were suicide car bombers or on a motorcycle. The official *Bakhtar News Agency* cited witnesses who indicated that

ISIS-K fighters entered the hospital and clashed with authorities.

November 3, 2021: A roadside bomb struck a Taliban patrol in ISIS-K stronghold Jalalabad, capital of Nangarhar Province, killing two people and wounding three. Taliban district commander Mubariz said four Taliban fighters were wounded. No one claimed credit.

November 6, 2021: The government arrested two suspects in connection with the murders of civil society activist Frozan Safi 29, and three other women whose bodies were found in a house in Mazar-e-Sharif. The duo confessed to luring the women to the house. Safi had worked at a local cultural center. She wanted to join her activist fiancé, who had already fled the country.

November 10, 2021: Khalil Hamraz, spokesman for the Taliban intelligence service, announced the arrests of nearly 600 ISIS-K members, including key figures and financial supporters. He added that 33 ISIS-K members died in gun battles with Taliban security forces.

November 12, 2021: *Reuters, al-Jazeera, AFP, AP,* and *CNN* reported that at 1:30 p.m., a bomb went off during Friday prayers in a mosque in Traili in the Spin Ghar district of Nangarhar Province, wounding 15 people, including the imam. Qari Hanif, director of Nangarhar's information and culture department, said that there were no fatalities after a mine was placed inside the mosque. The attack targeted Sunnis. Walli Mohammed, a local elder and activist, said a bomb appeared to have been hidden in a loudspeaker near the imam's rostrum. When the speaker was switched on to sound the *azaan* call to begin the prayer ritual, the bomb went off. *CNN* reported that social media photos showed three dead bodies and *AFP* quoted a doctor saying three were killed.

November 13, 2021: A bomb exploded in the back of a mini-bus on a busy commercial street in Kabul's Dashti Barchi neighborhood, which is mainly populated by members of Afghanistan's minority Hazara community, killing Hamid Sighyani, a journalist with *Ariana TV*, and injuring five. ISIS-K said it was targeting Shi'ites.

November 15, 2021: A roadside bomb exploded as a taxi was passing by in the Kota-e Sangi district of western Kabul, wounding two people, including a woman in the taxi and a man passing by. No one claimed credit.

November 17, 2021: A bomb hit a minivan in a Shi'ite neighborhood in western Kabul, killing one person and wounding three others. No one claimed credit.

November 19, 2021: Two months after he was kidnapped in Mazar-i-Sharif, the body of prominent psychiatrist Mohamed Nader Alemi was found in a street. His son Roheen Alemi said the family had paid a $350,000 ransom, less than half of what was originally demanded. He added "My father was badly tortured, there are signs of harm on his body." Alemi had worked for the government's provincial hospital in Mazar-i-Sharif and owned the city's first private psychiatric clinic. Taliban Interior Ministry spokesman Saeed Khosty said Taliban forces arrested eight suspected kidnappers who were behind the abductions of three people, including Alemi, in Balkh Province. He said two of those abducted were rescued. Police were searching for two associates of the detainees.

November 30, 2021: *Reuters* and *Ariana News* reported that a roadside bomb in Kabul injured five people.

December 23, 2021: *AFP* reported that Mobin Khan, spokesman for Kabul's police, announced that police shot dead a would-be suicide bomber at a checkpoint outside Kabul's main passport office as 200 Taliban fighters lined up for travel documents on a day reserved exclusively for their applications.

ALGERIA

August 19, 2021: *Al-Jazeera* reported that police arrested 22 people for starting recent deadly fires and blamed the Islamist Rashad group and the MAK autonomy movement for the mostly Amazigh-speaking Kabylie region. It deemed both groups as "terrorist" organizations, claiming that MAK was backed by Morocco and Israel.

September 10, 2021: Salah Goudjil, a National Liberation Front (FLN) political leader and Speaker of the Council of the Nation, announced the death of Saadi Yacef, variant Yacef Saadi, 93, guerrilla leader of the FLN that fought for and eventually obtained independence from France in 1962. He led the group in the Battle of Algiers, a campaign of urban guerrilla warfare in his native, labyrinthine Casbah district of the city in 1956-57. French paratroopers captured him in 1957. He was sentenced to death by guillotine, but his sentence was reduced to life. French President Charles de Gaulle pardoned him in 1958. Yacef starred as himself in the *Battle of Algiers* movie, which was nominated for three Academy Awards and won the 1966 Golden Lion at the Venice Film Festival. At the time of his death, he had been serving as a senator for the FLN, which became a political party at independence, in the Council of the Nation, the Algerian Senate. His 1962 memoir was *Souvenirs de la Bataille d'Alger*.

He was born on January 20, 1928 to illiterate ethnic Berber parents who had moved from the Kabylia region of northern Algeria. At age 17, while working as an apprentice baker, he joined the leftist Algerian People's Party (PPA) until it was outlawed by the French colonial authorities. He then joined the Movement for the Triumph of Democratic Liberties (MTLD). Between the ages of 21 and 24, he lived in France. Returning to Algiers, he joined the FLN when the War of Independence started in 1954. By 1956, he was the group's military chief in the capital.

He participated in killings and bombings against French soldiers and civilians and Algerian pieds noirs.

ARABIAN SEA

May 8, 2021: *AP* and *NPR* reported that the guided missile cruiser *U.S.S. Monterey* seized an arms shipment of thousands of assault weapons, machine guns, and sniper rifles hidden aboard a stateless dhow, apparently en route to Yemen to support Houthi rebels. The crew was released. The Navy's initial investigation found the vessel came from Iran. The shipment included nearly 3,000 Chinese Type 56 assault rifles, a variant of the Kalashnikov; hundreds of other heavy machine guns and sniper rifles; dozens of advanced, Russian-made anti-tank guided missiles; several hundred rocket-propelled grenade launchers; and optical sights for weapons.

July 29, 2021: U.S. Navy Mideast-based 5th Fleet explosive experts suggested that a nighttime "drone strike" hit the Liberian-flagged oil tanker *Mercer Street* northeast of the Omani island of Masirah in the Arabian Sea, killing two crewmen, one from the UK, one from Romania. Israel blamed Iran, which denied the charge. No one claimed credit. The nuclear-powered aircraft carrier *USS Ronald Reagan* and the guided missile destroyer *USS Mitscher* escorted the *Mercer Street* to a safe port. The explosion created a hole through the top of the oil tanker's bridge. The London-based Zodiac Maritime, part of Israeli billionaire Eyal Ofer's Zodiac Group, manages the *Mercer Street*. British maritime security firm Ambrey said one of its team members on board the vessel was killed. The *Mercer Street* was deadheading from Dar es Salaam, Tanzania, to Fujairah, United Arab Emirates. Zodiac Maritime said the ship's owners are Japanese. Lloyd's List identified the vessel's owner as Taihei Kaiun Co., which belongs to the Tokyo-based Nippon Yusen Group.

BAHRAIN

November 22, 2021: *Al-Jazeera* reported that the Interior Ministry announced that Bahrain security forces arrested several suspects and confiscated weapons and explosives ahead of a planned attack. The Ministry tweeted that "Terrorists (were) arrested for plotting terrorist operations against security and civil peace… linked with terrorist groups in Iran".

EGYPT

January 1, 2021: A remotely-detonated roadside bomb hit an armored vehicle on patrol in Bir al-Abd in the Sinai Peninsula, killing two members of the country's security forces and wounding five. IS was suspected.

January 21, 2021: At dawn, a remotely-detonated Islamic State roadside bomb hit an armored vehicle carrying forces on patrol in Sheikh Zuweid in the Sinai Peninsula, killing a member of the security forces and injuring three others. IS claimed credit.

February 8, 2021: IS gunmen killed a conscript on duty in Gifgafa village in central Sinai.

February 9, 2021: IS gunmen killed six Bedouins from the nomadic Arab Trabin tribe in an ambush at a fake checkpoint for their alleged collaboration with the Egyptian military in the mountainous Maghara area in the Sinai Peninsula. The Bedouins had been riding in two vehicles. A seventh Bedouin was missing. The Sinai Tribes Union provides intelligence to the military and police forces, joining patrols and raids searching for weapons caches.

June 8, 2021: Islamic State gunmen kidnapped five Egyptians–three engineers, a laborer and their driver—who were driving to work in Bir al-Abed in the Sinai Peninsula. The five work at the el-Salam canal project that moves Nile Delta drainage water to be reused in agriculture in the peninsula. No one claimed credit.

July 31, 2021: Islamic State-affiliated gunmen ambushed a checkpoint in Sheikh Zuweid in the Sinai Peninsula, killing five troops and wounding six other security forces, who were taken to a military hospital in el-Arish. Three terrorists died in the clash.

August 12, 2021: *AP* and *al-Jazeera* reported that in the evening, a roadside bomb killed eight members of the security forces, including an officer, and seriously wounded six others riding in an armored vehicle in New Rafah in the Sinai Peninsula, on the border with the Gaza Strip. ISIL claimed credit.

    Lt. Col. Gharib Abdel Hafez Gharib, spokesman for Egypt's armed forces, said that nine troops were killed and wounded in clashes with militants in Sinai. He added that the armed forces had killed 13 militants and confiscated 15 automatic rifles and ammunition in Northern and Central Sinai.

October 27, 2021: EgyptAir flight MS728, an Airbus A220-300 en route to Moscow, returned to Cairo's airport 22 minutes after takeoff after a threatening message was found on a seat on the plane.

Gaza Strip

January 18, 2021: In response to two rockets being fired toward Ashdod from the Gaza Strip, the IDF conducted air strikes into Gaza. The Israeli Army said the rockets landed in the Mediterranean Sea and caused no injuries. Palestinians said the morning strikes hit an agricultural field in Rafah and landed near the al-Furqan mosque in al-Qarara, northeast of Khan Younis.

April 24, 2021: *AP, al-Jazeera,* and *NPR* reported that Palestinians fired three dozen rockets into Israel during the night. The IDF intercepted six rockets; most of the other 30 fell into open areas. There were no reports of injuries or serious damage. IDF fighter jets and helicopters attacked Hamas targets in retaliation, hitting an underground facility and rocket launchers.

May 10-11, 2021: Hamas fired more than 500 rockets into southern Israel, killing two in Ashkelon, and wounding ten Israelis. Israeli airstrikes into Gaza killed 26 Palestinians, including nine children and a woman, and wounded 122. The IDF said at least 16 militants were killed. The Islamic Jihad said a strike on an apartment building in Gaza City killed three of its commanders. A dawn airstrike on high-rise killed a woman, her 19-year-old disabled son and another man. IDF said the military hit 130 targets in Gaza, including two tunnels militants were digging under the border with Israel.

May 18, 2021: As rocket attacks from Gaza into Israel and IDF retaliatory air strikes continued, a rocket attack from Gaza killed two Thai workers in their 30s and injured seven inside a packaging plant in southern Israel. As of May 18, Hamas had fired more than 3,400 rockets at civilian targets in Israel. 21051801

May 20, 2021: Israel and Hamas agreed to an Egyptian-brokered ceasefire after Hamas had lobbed some 4,000 rockets into Israeli territory and Israeli airstrikes had leveled numerous buildings and killed dozens in Gaza in retaliation.

July 1, 2021: Militants sent incendiary balloons into Israel. The IDF retaliated with air strikes against a Hamas weapons R&D site.

July 25, 2021: Hamas-linked activists sent incendiary balloons into southern Israel, causing three fires. On one of the balloons was the message: "Time is running out."

August 1, 2021: Hamas announced that its Shura Council had given a new four-year term as supreme leader to Ismail Haniyeh, who has been living in exile for the past two years. He served as the Palestinian prime minister after Hamas won parliamentary elections in 2006. He had been living in Turkey and Qatar.

August 7, 2021: *Reuters* reported that Israeli aircraft bombed Hamas sites in the Gaza Strip in retaliation for the launch of incendiary balloons from the Palestinian enclave. The balloons caused four brush fires.

September 4, 2021: Hamas sent more than a dozen incendiary balloons into Israel.

September 10, 2021: Palestinians fired a rocket toward Israel that was intercepted by Israeli air defenses. No Palestinian group claimed credit.

September 12-13, 2021: *The Hill* reported that Hamas fired three rockets into Israel during the night of September 12 and into the next morning, spurring Israeli rocket launches on Hamas targets in the Gaza Strip. The Iron Dome defense system intercepted two Hamas rockets.

IRAN

January 12, 2021: In a speech to the National Press Club, outgoing U.S. Secretary of State Mike Pompeo accused Iran of having secret ties with al-Qaeda and imposed new sanctions on several senior Iranian officials. He claimed Tehran had given safe haven to the group's deputy, Abu Muhammad al-Masri, who was killed on August 7, 2020. Two unnamed senior officials

indicated that Iran had facilitated al-Masri's stay in Tehran, including by sending security guards with him on shopping excursions and granting him access to a swimming pool.

March 2, 2021: State television blamed the al-Qaeda-linked Sunni Jaish al-Adl for assaulting a vehicle carrying members of Iran's Revolutionary Guard paramilitary force in Sistan and Baluchestan Province, injuring an officer. Another went missing.

April 22, 2021: *AP* and *IRNA* reported that gunmen killed two members of the paramilitary Revolutionary Guard, Osman Jahani and Nasser Amini, in a nighttime ambush. IRGC members fired back, killing two gunmen and wounding several accomplices near the Kurdish town of Marivan near the border with Iraq. Several terrorists fled.

April 24, 2021: *AP* and *Tasnim* reported that the Revolutionary Guard shot to death three gunmen and dismantled their cell in Sistan and Baluchistan Province near the Afghan border. IRGC troops seized explosives and weapons, noting that the gunmen were planning attacks.

May 11, 2021: *IRNA* reported that a "group of terrorists" snuck into Iran illegally from Turkey and conducted a gun battle with Revolutionary Guard forces around noon in Salmas in West Azerbaijan Province. *IRNA* said the IRGC killed seven militants and dismantled their cell, but two Guard members also died.

June 7, 2021: *IRNA* reported that Shi'ite cleric Ali Akbar Mohtashamipour, 74, who as Iran's ambassador to Syria in 1982 helped found Lebanese Hizballah and lost his right hand and two fingers of his left hand to a book bombing on February 14, 1984 reportedly carried out by Israel, died of COVID-19. He was a close ally of Iran's late Supreme Leader Ayatollah Ruhollah Khomeini. He also helped found the paramilitary Revolutionary Guard. He also became Iran's Interior Minister and was a hard-line parliamentarian before joining reformists in 2009.

June 23, 2021: State television, *AP*, and *Nournews* reported that authorities claimed to have thwarted a "sabotage attack" on a civilian Atomic Energy Organization nuclear facility at Karaj near Tehran, causing no casualties. The same day, Iranian social media ran unconfirmed reports that authorities had prevented an unmanned aerial vehicle from targeting a COVID-19 vaccine production facility.

July 10, 2021: *IRNA* and state TV reported that a stun grenade went off at 12:52 a.m. in the Mellat public park near state television headquarters in Tehran, causing no casualties or damage.

August 9, 2021: *Iran's Labor News Agency (ILNA), Reuters,* and the *Daily Beast* reported that an angry driver yelled at two women for being "un-Islamic" for not wearing full hijab, then crashed his Peugeot into them, critically injuring them on the busy Kashani Street. The driver fled, but was arrested later that night. Iran's Vice President for Women's Affairs, Masoumeh Ebtekar, requested that the charges include attempted murder.

IRAQ

January 14, 2021: *Newsweek* reported that U.S. Secretary of State Mike Pompeo deemed Popular Mobilization Forces deputy commander Abdulaziz al-Muhammadawi, alias Abu Fadak, a Specially Designated Global Terrorist. Pompeo said Abu Fadak earlier led the Iran-backed Kataib Hizballah. The U.S. Department of the Treasury initially linked him to ISIS.

January 21, 2021: *NPR, CNN,* and the *Washington Post* reported that two pedestrian suicide bombers killed 32 people and wounded 110 at a market in Baghdad's Tayaran Square. One bomber pretended to be sick, and asked people in the market for help. People gathered around him to help; he then blew himself up. The second bomber arrived on a motorbike and targeted people responding to the initial mid-morning incident. Military spokesman Yahya Rasool gave a differing account, saying that security forces had chased the bombers. ISIS was suspected.

January 24, 2021: *AFP* reported that an official from Iraq's presidency announced that more than 340 execution orders "for terrorism or crim-

inal acts" were ready to be carried out and that "We are continuing to sign off on more." A second official said that all the orders were signed after 2014, most of them under ex-president Fuad Massum, when jihadis occupied a third of the country.

January 25, 2021: *AFP* reported that the government hanged three Iraqis at Nasiriyah Central Prison who were convicted under Article 4 of the anti-terror law.

January 27, 2021: *Military Times* and *AP* reported that Prime Minister Mustafa al-Kadhimi tweeted that an "intelligence-led" operation by the Counter-Terrorism Service and Iraqi intelligence near Kirkuk killed Abu Yasar al-Issawi, born Jabbar al-Issawi, alias Abu Yasir, 39, deputy commander and ISIS chief in Iraq.

Military Times reported that Col. Wayne Marotto, spokesman for Combined Joint Task Force-Operation Inherent Resolve, tweeted that the air strike killed 10 ISIS terrorists.

February 10, 2021: *AP* and *Reuters* reported on February 14 that Turkish Defense Minister Hulusi Akar said troops found the bodies of 13 Turkish citizens abducted by Kurdistan Workers' Party (PKK) insurgents in a cave complex in the Gara region in northern Iraq near the Turkish border. Twelve victims were shot in the head; the other died of a shoulder bullet wound. The ongoing Turkish Operation Claw-Eagle 2 led to the deaths of 48 PKK militants, including three senior members, and the capture of two insurgents. Malatya Governor Aydin Barus later said ten of the dead had been identified and named them as soldiers or police officers, as well as two civilians, kidnapped inside Turkey in the last six years. Three Turkish troops died and three others were wounded during the operation. 21021002

February 15, 2021: *AP* and *AFP* reported that 14 107mm rockets landed at 9:30 p.m. outside Irbil international airport near where U.S. forces are based, killing a coalition Filipino contractor, wounding several Iraqi and Kurdish civilians, eight civilian contractors, a U.S. National Guard soldier, and four U.S. civilian contractors, and damaging cars. Two rockets hit residential neighborhoods. Delovan Jalal, head of Irbil's health directorate, told *AFP* five civilians were wounded, one critically. The Shi'ite group Saraya Awliya al-Dam (Guardians of Blood Brigade) claimed credit. 21021501

February 20, 2021: Four rockets struck Balad airbase in Salahaddin Province during the night, wounding a South African who works at the base, where the American defense company Sallyport services Iraq's F-16 combat aircraft. The little-known Shi'ite Saraya Awliya al-Dam (Guardians of Blood Brigade) claimed credit. 21022001

February 22, 2021: Three rockets hit Baghdad's Green Zone, causing no casualties but causing minor property damage, including a damaged vehicle. Two Iraqi security officials said one fell within the perimeters of the U.S. Embassy complex. 21022202

March 3, 2021: *CNN, UPI, Military Times,* and *AP* reported that at 7:20 a.m., ten Grad missiles hit the Ain al-Asad air base near al-Baghdadi, killing a U.S. civilian contractor, who suffered a heart attack while sheltering. Authorities found a rocket launcher on a truck in the al-Bayader agricultural area near the town in Anbar Province. No one claimed credit. Pope Francis was to visit Iraq on March 5. 21030301

March 10, 2021: Jasb Hattab Aboud, father of Ali Jasb, a missing Iraqi anti-government activist and attorney who waged a public campaign trying to bring to account Ansar Allah al-Awfia, an Iran-backed militia suspected of abducting him in October 8, 2019 in Amara in Missan Province, died of a gunshot wound to the head at 6 p.m. in Amara.

March 12, 2021: *CNN* reported that ISIS claimed credit for shooting to death eight people, including six family members, in three attacks in Albu-Dour's predominantly Sunni village in Salah al-Din Province north of Baghdad. ISIS said some of those related to the dead were "spies" working for the Shi'a Popular Mobilization Units. ISIS also killed a local police officer and an attorney in the same village. Investigations "concluded that the perpetrators of the crime were elements of ISIS terrorist group

who infiltrated the village on foot while wearing military uniform under the pretext of searching homes of the victims".

March 15, 2021: *Reuters* reported that five rockets hit the Iraqi military air base of Balad north of Baghdad, causing no casualties. Two other rockets fell outside the Balad air base, damaging a civilian house. No group claimed credit.

April 2021: *AP* reported on May 8 that in mid-April, an early Saturday morning drone strike targeted a military base in Irbil that hosts U.S. troops, causing only minor damage and no casualties but damaging a hangar. No one claimed credit. 21049901

April 4, 2021: *Military Times* reported that Major General Tahseen al-Khafaji said two rockets landed near Balad Air Base, where U.S. trainers are present, after noon, causing no casualties or damage. 21040401

April 8, 2021: The *Washington Post* reported the Pentagon released 53 declassified interrogation reports showing that Amir Muhammad Sa'id Abd-al-Rahman al-Mawla, alias Abu Ibrahim al-Hashimi al-Qurashi, the current leader of ISIS, had been an informer against al-Qaeda in Iraq for the U.S. military while he was Iraqi prisoner M060108-01 for months in an American detention camp in Iraq in 2008. The *Post* said he helped with artists' sketches of senior terrorism suspects, and identified restaurants and cafes where his at-large comrades ate. Christopher Maier, assistant secretary of defense for special operations and low-intensity conflict, observed, "He did a number of things to save his own neck, and he had a long record of being hostile—including during interrogation—toward foreigners in ISIS."

April 14, 2021: During the night, three rockets were fired at a Turkish military base in the northern Bashiqa region, killing a soldier and wounding a child in a nearby village. One rocket hit the base; two others landed in the village. No one claimed credit. 21041401

AP and *Military Times* reported that a drone attack targeted U.S.-led coalition forces near Irbil's international airport, causing no injuries but sparking a fire that damaged a building. Coalition spokesman Col. Wayne Marotto said the drone landed on a storage hangar at Irbil Air Base. No one claimed credit. 21041402

April 15, 2021: *The Hill, AP,* and *Reuters* reported that a bomb hit a second-hand equipment market in the Habibiya neighborhood of Baghdad's Sadr City area, killing four, injuring 17, and damaging five cars. No one claimed credit.

April 18, 2021: *Military Times* and *AP* reported that Maj. Gen. Diaa Mohsen, commander of the Balad airbase north of Baghdad, said that several rockets hit the base, wounding two Iraqi security forces, one seriously. Two rockets exploded inside the base, which houses U.S. trainers. 21041801

April 22, 2021: *Al-Jazeera* reported that three rockets landed in the perimeter of Baghdad International Airport near the area of the airport housing United States forces during the night. No one claimed credit. No casualties were reported. Security forces defused unfired rockets placed on the rooftop of an empty house that was used as the staging area. 21042201

AFP reported that it was the 23rd bomb or rocket attack against U.S. interests in Iraq since President Biden took office.

May 3, 2021: *Reuters, AP,* and *al-Jazeera* reported that at 8 p.m., between two and six Katyusha rockets hit Balad Ain al-Asad Air Base, which houses U.S. contractors. *Al-Jazeera* said a foreign contractor working for Sallyport, a U.S. company that maintains F-16 aircraft purchased by Iraq from the U.S., was slightly injured. No one claimed credit. The missiles were fired in two tranches of three apiece, within 15 minutes of each other. 21050301

May 8, 2021: *The Hill* and *AP* reported that in the morning, a drone attacked Ain al-Asad Air Base, an Iraqi facility that hosts U.S. troops, damaging a hangar but causing no injuries. 21050801

May 9, 2021: Protesters set fire to trailers belonging to Iran's consulate in Karbala following the nighttime shooting death of Ehab Wazni, variant Ihab al-Wazni, a prominent activist, outside his Karbala home. *AFP* added on May 24 that Wanzi's funeral was held at the Imam Hussein Shrine in Karbala. No one claimed credit. 21050802

May 10, 2021: Prominent journalist Ahmed Hassan was shot in southern Iraq. After undergoing brain surgery, he was in a coma as of May 24.

May 24, 2021: *Military Times* reported that at 1:35 p.m., a rocket struck close to Ain al-Asad Air Base hosting U.S. troops in Anbar Province. No injuries were reported. No one claimed credit. *Reuters* reported on May 27 that Iraqi security forces arrested militia commander Qasim Muslih in Baghdad at dawn for several assaults on Ain al-Asad Air Base. Muslih heads the Popular Mobilization Forces (PMF) in Anbar Province. 21052401

June 3, 2021: A gas cylinder exploded in the morning at a crowded restaurant in Baghdad's northwestern Kadhmiyah district, killing three and injuring 16, some critically. The café was near the shrine of Imam Musa al-Kadhim, revered by Shi'ites.

June 6, 2021: *CNN* reported that the Iraqi military shot down two drones aimed at al-Asad Air Base, which houses US troops and Iraqi and coalition forces, in Anbar Province. 21060601

Hours earlier, a rocket crashed near the Baghdad Diplomatic Support Center (BDSC), causing no injuries or damage. 21060602

June 9, 2021: *AP* and *Newsweek* reported that at 4 p.m., three rockets hit Balad Air Base, which hosts U.S.-led coalition troops and foreign contractors, causing no damage or casualties. Hours later, a missile landed near a military base next to Baghdad's airport, setting alight a coalition trailer but causing no casualties. No one claimed credit. 21060901-02

June 20, 2021: A Katyusha rocket launched from the al-Baghdadi area did not explode when it landed near the perimeter of Ain al-Asad Air Base in Anbar Province, causing minor damage to a fence. 21062001

June 30, 2021: A bomb placed under a kiosk detonated in the Maridi market area of Sadr City in

Baghdad's suburbs, wounding 15 people. No one claimed credit. ISIS was suspected.

July 6, 2021: In the evening, the counter-terrorism unit in the northern Kurdish-run region reported a drone attack on Irbil airport, which caused no damage. The missiles fell in open fields and set fires.

July 7, 2021: In the afternoon, 14 rockets landed on al-Asad Air Base and its perimeter, which houses U.S. troops, causing two minor injuries. The Security Media Cell, affiliated with Iraq's security forces, found a mobile rocket launcher hidden in a truck loaded with bags of flour and parked in Baghdadi village. Other rockets exploded on the truck, damaging some homes and a mosque. The Brigades To Avenge al-Muhandis said it fired 30 rockets toward the base "run by American occupiers". It warned U.S. troops, "We will force you to leave our lands defeated." 21070701

July 8, 2021: *Newsweek* reported that the Kataib Hizballah militia forbid its fighters from attacking the U.S. embassy in Baghdad. KH spokesperson Abu Ali al-Askary said, "Targeting diplomatic missions is rejected by the Iraqi resistance, and its decision is to not even strike the evil American embassy military camp."

Newsweek added that the Security Media Cell of the Iraqi Prime Minister's Office said that in the early morning, rockets landed near the headquarters of the National Security Service, Grand Festivities Square, and a residential neighborhood of the Sheikh Omar area in Baghdad. *AP* said that before daybreak, two Katuysha rockets fell near the national security building, and in an open courtyard inside the Green Zone. A third rocket fell in a nearby residential area, damaging a civilian vehicle.

July 19, 2021: The *Washington Post* and *Reuters* reported that in the early evening, a roadside bomb in the busy Wahailat market of Sadr City in Baghdad killed 35 people and hospitalized 60 others a day before the Eid al-Adha holiday. Children and women were among the victims. *CNN* reported that ISIS credited a suicide bomber wearing an explosive vest.

July 23, 2021: *Al-Jazeera* reported that in the morning, rockets hit a military base that hosts U.S. troops near al-Harir, 45 miles northeast of Erbil, Kurdistan. No casualties were reported. 21072301

July 30, 2021: An Iraqi security official said ISIS terrorists killed eight people, including police and civilians, in an attack on a funeral procession in Salahaddin Province.

August 12, 2021: *Al-Jazeera* reported that Kurdish PKK rebels fired mortar rounds at a Turkish military base in northern Iraq, wounding a Turkish soldier who later died in a hospital. The Turkish defense ministry said three terrorists were "neutralized". 21081301

August 15, 2021: *Al-Jazeera* reported that PKK mines exploded in northern Iraq, killing three Turkish soldiers and wounding two who were conducting a cross-border operation.

September 4, 2021: During the night, gunmen fired at a federal police checkpoint in Satiha village in Kirkuk Province in rural northern Iraq, killing 13 police and wounding five police during an hour-long clash blamed on ISIS.

September 11, 2021: *AP* reported that Kurdistan's Counter-Terrorism Service said two drones carrying explosives targeted Irbil international airport. There were no reports of casualties. *Fox News* added that U.S. forces used the counter-rocket, artillery, and mortar system (C-RAM) to shoot down the pair of Iranian drones.

September 12, 2021: *AP* and *Reuters* reported that the Turkish Defense Ministry said "separatist terrorists" (a term usually referring to the Kurdistan Workers' Party (PKK)) fired on a military vehicle leaving a base in northern Iraq, killing a Turkish soldier and injuring a second. 21091201

September 27, 2021: *Rudaw* reported that the Popular Mobilization Forces (PMF) thwarted an "infiltration attempt" by ISIS in Tarmiyah district, killing an ISIS member during a security operation. The PMF also stymied an ISIS "terrorist plot" in al-Hussainiya village, southwest of Mosul. The force found explosive devices.

In its weekly propaganda magazine *al-Nabaa*, ISIS claimed it conducted six attacks in Iraq from September 17 to 23, killing and injuring 11 people.

October 11, 2021: *AP, al-Jazeera,* and *AFP* reported that Prime Minister Mustafa al-Kadhimi announced that security forces, apparently in Turkey, had detained Sami Jasim al-Jaburi, alias Haji Hamid, who had been a deputy of ISIS founder Abu Bakr al-Baghdadi and was ISIS's finance chief. Al-Jaburi pledged allegiance to al-Qaeda in Iraq leader Abu Musab al-Zarqawi in 2003. He met al-Baghdadi in 2012, rising to positions in the ISIS judiciary, finance, and industry ministries. The U.S. Rewards for Justice Program had offered $5 million for his capture, saying he "reportedly served as the equivalent of... finance minister (for IS), supervising the group's revenue-generating operations from illicit sales of oil, gas, antiquities and minerals". In September 2015, the U.S. Department of the Treasury deemed al-Jaburi a Specially Designated Global Terrorist.

October 26, 2021: ISIS gunmen firing machine guns attacked the predominantly Shi'ite village of al-Rashad northeast of Baqouba in Diyala Province, killing 11 civilians and wounding six. ISIS had kidnapped two villagers earlier and raided the village when their demands for ransom were not met.

The Hill, AFP, and Reuters reported that ISIS claimed credit on *Telegram* for an attack on al-Hawasha village that killed 11 and injured 13. The villagers were part of the Bani Tamim tribe. Many security service members lived in the area.

November 7, 2021: *NPR, AP,* and the *Washington Post* reported that three explosives-laden drones in the early morning attacked the home in Baghdad's Green Zone of Prime Minister Mustafa al-Kadhimi, 54, injuring seven bodyguards. Two drones were shot down. Al-Kadhimi sustained a light cut to his left hand. Iran-backed militias, which had rejected the results of Iraq's October 10 parliamentary elections, were suspected. Al-Kadhimi ran Iraqi intelligence before becoming prime minister in May 2020.

November 26, 2021: *Rudaw* reported that ISIS set off a roadside bomb that killed five Kurdish peshmerga fighters and wounded four in the Garmian district in Kurdish-run northern Iran.

December 2, 2021: Christian Ritscher, head of a U.N. Investigative Team to Promote Accountability for Crimes committed by the Islamic State group in Iraq, told the U.N. Security Council that ISIS committed "crimes against humanity of murder, extermination, torture, enforced disappearances, persecution and other inhumane acts" and "war crimes of willful killing, torture, inhumane treatment, and outrage upon personal dignity" in June 2014 at Badush Central Prison in Mosul, where at least 1,000 predominantly Shi'ite prisoners were systematically killed.

December 3, 2021: *Reuters* reported that ISIS was suspected in an early morning attack in the mountainous Makhmour area of the autonomous Kurdish region that killed three villagers and ten Kurdish soldiers.

December 5, 2021: *Reuters* reported that a day after ISIS overran Luhaiban village, Iraqi forces and Kurdish Peshmerga fighters had recaptured it. ISIS booby-trapped some homes with explosive devices.

ISIS killed four Peshmerga soldiers and a civilian and wounded six in Qara Salem village in northern Iraq.

December 7, 2021: *AP* and *Reuters* reported that a bomb on a motorcycle exploded in the morning near a major hospital in central Basra, killing four and wounding 20. The governor of Basra, Asaad al-Idani, blamed ISIS. No one claimed credit.

December 19, 2021: *Military.com* and *AP* reported that two rockets hit Baghdad's Green Zone, causing property damage but no casualties. The U.S. embassy's C-RAM defense system destroyed one rocket. Another fell near a national monument, damaging two civilian vehicles.

ISRAEL

March 23, 2021: *Storyful, AFP,* and *al-Jazeera* reported that a rocket was fired from Gaza into Israel. The IDF retaliated the next morning at 2:30 a.m. with aerial attacks into Gaza, hitting a Hamas rocket manufacturing site and military post. No deaths or injuries were reported.

April 15, 2021: The Israeli Defense Force announced that a projectile fired from the Gaza Strip during the evening landed in Sderot in the Negev Desert, but caused no casualties or damage. No Palestinian group claimed credit from the Hamas-controlled enclave.

April 16, 2021: The IDF reported that Palestinian militants fired a rocket from Gaza into the Negev Desert town of Sderot in southern Israel during the evening, causing no damage or injuries. Israeli aircraft hit three facilities operated by Hamas in response.

May 10, 2021: *NPR* and *AP* reported that Hamas claimed credit for firing rockets at Jerusalem during the early evening of Jerusalem Day. There were no immediate reports of injuries or damage. The IDF said it had intercepted one of seven rockets in the initial barrage.

May 12, 2021: Israeli airstrikes killed several senior Hamas military figures, including the senior commander for Gaza City, and hit three multistory towers in the Gaza Strip in retaliation for continuing rocket barrages which killed an Israeli soldier and six Israeli civilians, including three women and two children, one age 6, who was in an apartment in Sderot. An Arab Israeli citizen, 52, and his daughter, 16, died when a rocket from Gaza hit the courtyard of their Lod home. The Israeli military said between May 10 and 12, Hamas fired more than 1,050 rockets. A Jewish gunman shot to death an Arab.

May 24, 2021: *UPI, Reuters,* and *AP* reported that a Palestinian man stabbed and injured two people, including a civilian man, 23, and a male soldier, 21, at a light-rail train station near Israeli Police headquarters near the Sheik Jarrah neighborhood in east Jerusalem. The civilian was stabbed in the back. The soldier, who was wearing an Israeli Air Force uniform, was stabbed in the back when he tried to help the victim. The attacker was shot dead.

June 15-16, 2021: *CNN* reported that the Israeli military blamed Hamas for sending dozens of incendiary helium balloons over the border fence from Gaza into Israel during the night, setting 20 fires on June 15 and four more on June 16. *AFP* reported that the perpetrators were Palestinian Islamic Jihad supporters. The IDF reported that since 2018, more than 10,400 acres had been burned by the devices.

June 16, 2021: The *Washington Post* reported that incendiary balloons floated into Israel from Hamas-controlled territory in Gaza. Israel conducted retaliatory airstrikes against Hamas military compounds, including a site east of Khan Younis, in the early morning.

July 4, 2021: The Jerusalem District Court sentenced Palestinian woman Yasmine Jaber from east Jerusalem to 30 months in prison starting August 4, twelve months of probation, and a 5,000-shekel ($1,500) fine after she acknowledged aiding Lebanon's Hizballah over several years. She admitted to charges of association with a foreign agent, membership in a terrorist organization, and other terror-related charges. The charge sheet said that she was in contact with two Hizballah agents on *Facebook, Instagram,* and *WhatsApp.* One of them invited her to a conference on the Palestinian cause in Beirut. She traveled there in 2015 and again in 2016 in violation of Israeli law.

July 11, 2021: The Security Cabinet froze roughly $200 million in tax transfers to the Palestinian Authority that it said had been transferred to the "martyrs fund" for families of alleged attackers.

August 11, 2021: The IDF announced it had intercepted an unarmed Hizballah drone that crossed the border from Lebanon.

August 16, 2021: Israeli air defense batteries over Sderot intercepted a rocket launched from the Gaza Strip. No one claimed credit.

August 21, 2021: Israeli police announced that Israeli border police officer Barel Hadaria

Shmueli, 21, who was shot in the head by a Palestinian gunman at point-blank range during a violent protest staged by Hamas on August 21 on the Gaza border, died of his injuries on August 30.

August 24, 2021: *AP, Reuters,* and *NBC News* reported Hamas-backed Palestinian activists sent incendiary balloons into Israel. Israeli warplanes conducted airstrikes against Hamas targets.

August 29, 2021: *The Hill* reported Israel announced it struck a Hamas military compound and tunnel entrance in the Gaza Strip in response to clashes along the border and the launching of incendiary balloons.

September 6, 2021: *AP, CNN,* the *Jerusalem Post,* the *Times of Israel,* and *UPI* reported that six Palestinian prisoners escaped overnight through a tunnel at the high-security Gilboa facility. The escapees were believed to have been headed for Jenin. The Palestinian Prisoners' Club, which represents former and current prisoners, said the men were aged 26 to 49 years old and included Zakaria Zubeidi, 46, a leader in Fatah's al-Aqsa Martyrs Brigade, who has been detained since 2019. Four of the other prisoners had been serving life sentences. The Israel Prison Service said the fugitives were Mondal Ainfaat, variant Monadel Yacoub Nafe'at, 26, Mahmad Aardiya, variant Mahmoud Abdullah Ardah, variant Mahmoud Aradeh, 46, Muhammed Aardiya, variant Mohammed Aradeh, Yakub Kadari, variant Yaqoub Mahmoud Qadri, 49, and Iham Kamagi, variant Ayham Nayef Kamamji, 35, of the Palestinian Islamic Jihad group and Zakaria Zubeidi of Fatah. *Al-Jazeera* identified one of the escapees as Yaqoub Qassem.

Al-Jazeera reported on September 7 that surveillance cameras recorded the moment the men exited the tunnel, but none of the guards in the control room noticed. One watchtower guard fell asleep.

AP and *Haaretz* reported on September 10 that Israeli police caught Mahmoud Aradeh and Yakub Kadari in the Arab-majority city of Nazareth in northern Israel during the night. The duo showed no resistance. A civilian alerted police to two suspicious figures. The duo were serving life

sentences. Kadari was serving two life sentences for attempted murder and planting bombs.

AP and *Haaretz* reported on September 11 that two other escapees, including Zakaria Zubeidi and Mohammed Aradeh, were recaptured while hiding in a truck parking lot in the Arab town of Umm al-Ghanam in northern Israel. They had been hiding outdoors for some time. *Haaretz* quoted a defense official who said that the duo appeared to have received no assistance during their escape and had no plan on where to go. Local residents had turned in the prisoners.

AP reported on September 19 that before dawn, the IDF arrested Munadil Nafayat and Iham Kamamji without resistance from a house in Jenin. The IDF, the Israeli Security Authorities, and the Israeli Police Counterterrorism Unit also apprehended two men who helped the men to hole up in the house.

September 10, 2021: Israeli police in Jerusalem's Old City said an officer was lightly injured by a firearm in an attempt to thwart a suspected stabbing attack against police by a Palestinian, who was arrested and later died of his gunshot wounds. Palestinian media reported the attacker was Hazem Joulani, 50, a doctor living in Jerusalem.

September 13, 2021: *Reuters* reported that a Palestinian stabbed and moderately wounded two people in a cosmetics shop near Jerusalem's central bus station before being shot and critically wounded by a policewoman.

September 14, 2021: The *Washington Examiner* reported that Israeli journalist Roy Sharon tweeted a video showing a silver car pulling off a road in Gush Etzion. Two people exited. One pushed a tire toward a wire fence; the other threw a Molotov cocktail but caught his shirt on fire and entered the car while still on fire. The driver turned the car around and sped off. The duo were believed to be Palestinians.

September 30, 2021: *AP, al-Jazeera,* and *AFP* reported that police officers shot to death a Palestinian woman, 30, who allegedly attempted to stab them at Bab al-Silsila, also known as Chain Gate, in east Jerusalem's Old City. She approached officers outside an entrance known to Muslims as the Al-Aqsa Compound and to Jews as the Temple Mount. The Palestinian health ministry identified the woman as Isra Khzamiah, variant Israa Khuzaima, a mother of three from Qabatiya, a northern West Bank town near Jenin.

A Palestinian "terrorist", 22, fired on Border Police involved in a dawn arrest raid in Burqin, a northern West Bank town. *WAFA* reported that troops returned fire, killing the man and wounding two people. Two other men were arrested. Palestinian Islamic Jihad said Alaa Nasser Mohammed Zayyoud, from the village of al-Silah al-Harithiya, northwest Jenin, in the occupied West Bank, was a member of its military wing. No Israeli forces were wounded. Local media said dozens of military jeeps and special forces were involved.

October 22, 2021: Israel declared six Palestinian non-governmental human rights groups terrorist organizations. The groups included

- al-Haq, a human rights group founded in 1979
- Addameer rights group
- Defense for Children International-Palestine
- Bisan Center for Research and Development
- Union of Palestinian Women's Committees
- Union of Agricultural Work Committees

The Israeli Defense Ministry said they were secretly "controlled by senior leaders" of the Popular Front for the Liberation of Palestine, and served as a "central source" of PFLP financing.

November 17, 2021: Police officers shot to death a Palestinian, 16, from east Jerusalem who stabbed two Israeli border police officers who were patrolling near a section of the Via Dolorosa in Jerusalem's Old City. The Israeli police officers were hospitalized, one in moderate condition and another with minor injuries.

November 21, 2021: *AP, UPI*, and *Reuters* reported that a Palestinian man fired a Beretta M12 submachine gun on Israelis near the Chain

Gate entrance to the Temple Mount/Noble Sanctuary holy site in Jerusalem's Old City in the morning, killing Eliyahu David Kaye, 26, and injuring four others, one seriously. Police fatally shot the assailant within 32 seconds of the start of the incident. Israeli Minister of Public Security Omer Bar-Lev said the gunman, 42, was an Islamic preacher and known member of Hamas's political wing. Official Hamas media said Fadi Abu Shkhaydam, variant Shkhaidem, a teacher at a nearby high school, was "the leader of the Hamas movement" in the Shuafat refugee camp in East Jerusalem. The shooter's wife traveled overseas three days ago, and some of his four children were also abroad. Kaye recently immigrated to Israel from South Africa and worked as a tour guide at the Western Wall. He lived in Modiin. One victim, Rabbi Zeev Katzenelnbogen, was taken to Shaare Zedek Medical Center for emergency surgery.

Two female police officers fired at Shkaydam. Two male officers then ran in to assist them.

Shkhaydam had posted in Arabic on *Facebook*: "God determines our destiny, but most people do not know. The question of our destiny is a question that God determines, God in His wisdom and greatness, He chooses whoever He wants and presents them to their destiny."

Hamas, while not taking credit, announced "The message of the heroic operation is a warning to the criminal enemy and its government to stop the attacks on our land and our holy sites… {Israel} will pay a price for the iniquities it commits against Al-Aqsa Mosque, Silwan, Sheikh Jarrah, and elsewhere."

December 3, 2021: In the morning, paramilitary Border Police in Umm al-Fahm fired on a vehicle speeding toward them, killing one man, 16, and hospitalizing the passenger, who was later arrested. Two officers were injured. Authorities found a gun and ammunition in the car. The two men were suspected of involvement in violent family disputes.

December 4, 2021: Israeli Border Police shot a Palestinian who had stabbed and severely wounded an ultra-Orthodox Jew in his 20s on near Damascus Gate outside Jerusalem's Old City. The attacker, 25, from Salfit in the West

Bank, had tried to stab a police officer. Hamas praised the attack but did not take credit for it.

December 8, 2021: *AP,* the *Washington Post,* and the *Jerusalem Post* reported that in the morning, a Palestinian girl, Nofoud Jad Araf Hamad, 14, stabbed in the back with a 12-inch knife and lightly wounded an Israeli woman, Moriah Cohen, 26, who was walking her children to school on a street in Sheikh Jarrah in east Jerusalem. The attacker fled and was arrested inside the nearby al-Ruda girls' school; authorities also arrested the school's principal, another staff member, and a student who is a relative of Hamad. Authorities raided Hamad's home and detained her mother. The victim was taken to the trauma unit of the nearby Hadassah Mt. Scopus Hospital, the knife still in her back. Cohen and her family are among the few Jewish residents living in Sheikh Jarrah. Dvir Cohen, Moriah's husband, said, "The stabber is our neighbor… She lives right in front of us. She followed her, got close to her, then stabbed her." He added that 11 Molotov cocktails had been thrown at their home. Hamad's family had faced eviction. Hamas said that "the heroic operations in the West Bank and Jerusalem, the last of which was at dawn today, with the stabbing of a settler in Sheikh Jarrah, prove the greatness of our rebellious people and that their resistance is unbreakable."

December 14, 2021: The *Jerusalem Post* reported that IDF and Shin Bet uncovered "terrorist infrastructure" at the largest Palestinian university, An-Najah National University, arresting 11 Islamic Bloc student activists involved in Hamas operations in Judea and Samaria on campus in Nablus. IDF Spokesperson for Arab Media Avichay Adraee tweeted the suspects were involved in the "transfer of funds, organizing rallies in support of Hamas, in addition to incitement campaigns under the supervision and direction of senior Hamas officials". He added that Hamas paid the students' tuition.

LEBANON

February 3, 2021: Prominent Shi'ite political activist and researcher Lokman Slim, 58, a frequent critic of Hizballah, was found dead in his

rental car on a rural road in Addoussieh before midnight with four gunshots at close range in his chest, head, and neck. He had been missing for hours. Slim's ID, phone, and gun were missing.

May 11, 2021: The U.S. Department of the Treasury imposed new sanctions on seven Lebanese linked to the Iran-backed Hizballah group and its al-Qard al-Hasan financial arm. Six of the seven sanctioned were the group's "shadow bankers", who used personal accounts at certain Lebanese banks to evade sanctions against Hizballah's financial arm and transfer $500 million over the past decade. The seventh sanctioned person was Ibrahim Daher, one of Hizballah's chief financial executives who oversaw the group's overall budget, including the funding for its operations. The Treasury said he leads Hizballah's Central Finance Unit, overseeing its income and budget and coordinating payments of its members.

July 20, 2021: *Al-Jazeera, UPI,* and *AP* reported that two rockets fired from Lebanon landed in Israeli territory. U.N. peacekeeping force in Lebanon (UNIFIL) radar detected rockets fired from southern Lebanon toward Israel just before 4 a.m. The Israeli Defense Forces retaliated with artillery barrages. The IDF claimed that the Iron Dome Aerial Defense System intercepted a rocket; the second fell in an open area. No injuries or damage were reported. Lebanon's army claimed Israel fired 12 artillery shells at the Wadi Hammoul area. The army found three launching pads for Grad rockets in the al-Qulaylah area, one with a rocket ready for firing. 21072001

August 1, 2021: Gunmen fired rocket-propelled grenades on the funeral of Hizballah commander Ali Chebli, who was killed on July 31. Two people, his brother-in-law and a friend, died and one soldier was injured in the attack in Khaldeh. Chebli's family, from a Sunni Arab tribe, said Ali was killed during a wedding party at a club the previous night. The killer was apprehended. The latter's Sunni Arab family said Chebli shot to death one of their relatives, 15, a year earlier.

August 4, 2021: Three rockets were fired from Lebanon into northern Israel. *Channel 12* reported that one rocket exploded in an open area and the Iron Dome missile defense system downed another. The IDF fired artillery in retaliation. No one claimed credit.

August 6, 2021: Hizballah announced that it had fired ten rockets near Israeli positions across the Shebaa Farms enclave in the disputed Golan Heights and Upper Galilee close to the Lebanese border, calling it retaliation for Israeli airstrikes on southern Lebanon the previous day. Israel said 19 rockets were fired; three fell into Lebanese territory; the Iron Dome missile defense system intercepted ten. No casualties were reported.

October 14, 2021: *AP* and *NPR* reported that gunmen fired at a Hizballah-organized demonstration around the Tayyooneh roundabout in Beirut, killing seven people and wounding 30 who were calling for the replacement of Judge Tarek Bitar, the investigating judge in the August 4, 2020 Beirut port explosion. Hizballah blamed the Lebanese Forces, a right-wing Christian movement. Local media reported that one sniper and the building caretaker were caught. Around noon, five small explosions believed from rocket-propelled grenades went off nearby.

December 10, 2021: The *National News Agency* and *AP* reported that arms stored in a mosque for Hamas exploded in a refugee camp in the Burj Shamali camp in Tyre during the night, killing a dozen people. Hamas said that the explosion was caused by an electrical short-circuit in a storage area for oxygen bottles used to treat coronavirus patients.

AP and *NNA* reported on December 12 that between two and four Palestinians were killed and seven injured, one critically after gunfire broke out during the funeral of Hamza Chahine, a Hamas member killed in the explosion.

LIBYA

February 21, 2021: *AP, AFP,* and *Reuters* reported that at 3 p.m., gunmen in an armored Toyota truck in Tripoli fired a machine gun on the motorcade of Interior Minister Fathi Bashagha, 58, wounding one of his guards. His guards chased the assailants, killing one, injuring another, and arresting two. Bashagha was returning to his res-

idence in the Janzour neighborhood. No group claimed credit.

March 24, 2021: *AP* and *AFP* reported that gunmen in Benghazi shot to death Mahmoud al-Werfalli, a commander in the Libyan Arab Armed Forces militia. He was wanted by the International Criminal Court for his alleged role in executing or ordering the executions of 33 captives in Benghazi in 2016 and 2017. The ICC noted that videos of the executions were posted on social media. Al-Werfalli's brother was wounded when the terrorists fired on Mahmoud's car in a busy street. *AFP* reported that his cousin, Ayman, was killed in the attack. No group claimed credit.

In August 2017, the ICC issued a first warrant for al-Werfalli's arrest for having personally shot hooded and bound prisoners, or ordering a firing squad to shoot them, in seven separate rounds of executions of 33 people in 2016 and 2017. In July 2018, a second ICC arrest warrant charged al-Werfalli for his "alleged responsibility for murder as a war crime" when he "allegedly shot dead 10 persons in front of the Bi'at al-Radwan Mosque" in Benghazi on January 24, 2018. He served as a lieutenant colonel in militia strongman Khalifa Hiftar's militia. Born in 1978, al-Werfalli was a commander of the al-Saiqa Brigade that defected from Libya's military during the 2011 uprising that toppled and killed Mu'ammar Qadhafi.

AFP reported on March 27 that Colonel Ali Madi, the head of Benghazi's military prosecution, announced the arrest of two suspects, Mohamad Abdeljalil Saad and Hanine al-Abdaly. The latter is the daughter of lawyer and rights activist Hanan al-Barassi, who was shot to death in daylight hours in November 2020 in Benghazi. Abdaly was arrested while "threatening a fellow citizen with a handgun".

April 8, 2021: Gunfire inside the al-Mabani Collection and Return Center, which houses 1,500 migrants in Tripoli, killed one migrant and hospitalized two others, aged 17 and 18. Doctors Without Borders said authorities opened an investigation.

August 3, 2021: *AP* reported on August 17 that Rida Faraj Fraitis, chief of staff for the first deputy prime minister, and his colleague were released in Benghazi two weeks after gunmen kidnapped the duo in Tripoli. It was not clear which group was responsible.

Morocco

July 20, 2021: Authorities arrested Uighur exile activist Yidiresi Aishan, 33, based on a Chinese terrorism warrant distributed by Interpol, upon landing at Mohammed V International Airport in Casablanca after flying from Istanbul. Morocco's General Directorate for National Security said he "was the subject of a red notice issued by Interpol due to his suspected belonging to an organization on the lists of terrorist organizations". China sought his extradition. Aishan, a computer engineer and father of three, was based in Turkey since 2012, where he worked as a web designer and activist and has residency papers. He worked on a Uighur diaspora online newspaper and assisted other activists in media outreach and collecting testimonies of abuse in China's Xinjiang Province. He was arrested several times in Turkey. A human rights group said it was part of a pattern of Chinese harassment of Uighur dissidents.

December 16, 2021: *Reuters* reported on December 29, 2021 that the trial began of a Moroccan, 24, suspected of involvement in IS who was active in Sala al-Jadida in the advanced stages of planning terrorist attacks, according to police. He was arrested on December 16.

Gulf of Oman

February 26, 2021: *AP* and *NPR* reported that several mysterious explosions hit the *Helios Ra*, an Israeli-owned Bahamas-flagged freighter loaded with vehicles in the Gulf of Oman. The ship's owner speculated that missiles or mines were responsible for leaving holes above the waterline on both sides of the hull. None of the crew was injured. The ship traveled under its own power to Dubai for repairs. On February 28, Israeli Prime Minister Benjamin Netanyahu blamed Iran, vowing to retaliate.

Red Sea

April 6, 2021: *Reuters* cited *al-Arabiya TV* in reporting that the *Iran MV Saviz* cargo ship affiliated with Iran's Revolutionary Guards was attacked in the Red Sea off the coast of Eritrea. The semi-official Iranian news agency *Tasnim* said the vessel was targeted by a limpet mine. *Tasnim* added that "The vessel *Iran Saviz* has been stationed in the Red Sea for the past few years to support Iranian commandos sent on commercial vessel (anti-piracy) escort missions." *AP* reported that the ship was believed to be a base for the Revolutionary Guards and had anchored for years off the coast of Yemen. Observers suspected Israeli involvement, although Iran did not blame anyone.

Saudi Arabia

January 23, 2021: *AP* reported on February 25, 2021 that three bomb-carrying drones were launched from Iraq by a little-known Iran-backed faction in Iraq at Saudi Arabia's royal palace in Riyadh on January 23, 2021. Houthi rebels in Yemen denied involvement in the attack on Yamama Palace. The Awliya Wa'ad al-Haq (The True Promise Brigades) said the attack was retaliation for a suicide bombing claimed by ISIS in a main Baghdad shopping district on January 21. An Iraqi militia official said the drones came "in parts from Iran and were assembled in Iraq, and were launched from Iraq".

February 10, 2021: *Newsweek, Saudi Press Agency, al-Arabiya Television,* state-run *al-Ekhbariya Television,* and *AFP* reported that Yemen-based Houthi fighters launched a drone attack on Abha International Airport, setting fire to a passenger plane. The Houthis claimed they sent four drones. 21021003

The US State Department said it would remove the terrorist designation of the Houthis, announced in the final days of the Trump Administration, on February 16.

February 11, 2021: *AFP* and *SPA* reported Saudi forces intercepted an armed drone fired by Yemen-based Houthi rebels at the garrison town of

Khamis Mushait in southern Saudi Arabia that hosts a key airbase.

February 27, 2021: *AP* and the state-owned *al-Ekhbariya TV* reported that the government announced its Patriot missile batteries had intercepted a nighttime missile attack over Riyadh and three bomb-laden drones targeting Jizan Province. A fourth missile was sent toward another southwestern city. Riyadh blamed Yemen's Houthi rebels. The state-run *Saudi Press Agency* reported that civil defense spokesman Mohammed al-Hammadi said scattered debris damaged a house, but no one was hurt. 21022701

March 4, 2021: The *Washington Post* reported Brig. Gen. Yahya Sarea, the spokesperson for Yemen's Houthi rebels, tweeted that they hit an Aramco oil facility in Jiddah with a winged Quds 2 missile. 21030401

March 5, 2021: *Reuters*, the Saudi state news agency *SPA*, and *Ekhbariya TV* reported that the Saudi-led coalition said it intercepted six explosive drones fired towards the kingdom. Saudi civil defense officials said said parts of the destroyed drones fell and injured a 10-year-old boy plus a man who was driving near Khamis Mushait. Houthi military spokesman Yahya Sarea tweeted that three drones had been fired at dawn, and five in the afternoon, hitting Abha International Airport and King Khalid Air Base in the Khamis Mushait area. 21030501

March 7, 2021: The *Washington Post* reported that Yemeni Houthi rebel spokesman Brig. Gen. Yahya Sarea claimed that the group's ballistic missiles and drones hit an Aramco oil facility in the port of Ras Tanura on Saudi Arabia's Persian Gulf coast, one of its largest refineries, and military positions in nearby Dammam. An Energy Ministry official said that one petroleum tank farm was attacked in the morning. Shrapnel from a ballistic missile fell near Aramco's residential area in Dhahran. No casualties were reported. *AP* reported the next day that oil prices had risen to $70 per barrel for the first time in over a year, gaining $1.14 to $70.47 a barrel. 21030701

March 19, 2021: *Bloomberg* reported that Yahya Saree, spokesman Yemen's Iran-backed Houthi

rebels, claimed they attacked Saudi Aramco in Riyadh using six bomb-laden drones. 21031901

March 25, 2021: *Reuters* and Saudi state television reported that Saudi-led coalition forces intercepted and destroyed several explosive-laden drones Houthis had aimed at Saudi Arabian universities in Najran and Jazan, Saudi cities near the Yemeni border. The coalition destroyed the one targeting Najran and six other explosive-laden drones fired by the Houthis. 21032503

March 26, 2021: Houthi rebel military spokesman Yahya Sarea tweeted that the group had fired drones at King Abdelaziz military base in Dammam military sites in Najran and Asir, and Aramco facilities in Ras al-Tanura, Rabigh, Yanbu, and Jizan. State news agency *SPA* reported Saudi Arabia's energy ministry said one of the projectiles struck a petroleum products distribution station in Jazan that resulted in a fire in a tank, causing no casualties. 21032601

April 6, 2021: *Reuters* quoted Saudi state television as saying that the Saudi-led coalition fighting in Yemen intercepted and destroyed an explosive-laden drone launched by Iran-aligned Houthis towards Khamis Mushait in Saudi Arabia. Houthi military spokesman Yahya Sarea tweeted that Houthis have targeted "sensitive sites" at King Khalid air base in Khamis Mushait with two drones. He claimed that the "hit was precise".

April 15, 2021: Saudi authorities blamed Yemeni Houthi rebels for sending five ballistic missiles and four bomb-laden drones from Saada, Yemen, that damaged Jizan University's campus. No casualties were reported. The kingdom's Patriot air defenses intercepted many of the missiles. The Houthis' *al-Masirah* television reported that Houthi military spokesman Brig. Gen. Yehia Sarie tweeted that Houthis had launched 11 missiles and drones at Saudi Arabia, targeting the kingdom's Patriot defense system, oil sites, and other "critical" areas in Jizan. *Al-Jazeera* reported that the Houthis claimed that a site belonging to state oil giant Aramco caught fire in the attack. Riyadh told *AP* that since the war began in 2014, the Houthis had fired more than 550 bomb-laden drones and more than 350 ballistic missiles toward Saudi Arabia. 21041501

April 17, 2021: *Reuters* reported that Yemeni Houthis claimed to have attacked King Khalid air base in Khamis Mushait with explosive drones. 21041701

April 27, 2021: *AP* and the *Saudi Press Agency* reported that Saudi military spokesman Colonel Turki al-Maliki said that a remotely-piloted boat carrying explosives targeted the oil shipping port of Yanbu in the Red Sea. Saudi officials said the military intercepted and destroyed the attacking craft. Private security firms suggested commercial traffic was hit in the assault. Houthis did not immediately claim credit and did not respond to a request for comments. 21042701

June 13, 2021: A Yemeni Houthi-launched bomb-laden drone crash-landed in the premises of a school in Asir Province near the kingdom's southern border. The *Saudi Press Agency* said no injuries were reported.

August 30, 2021: The government said it downed an explosives-carrying drone at Abha Airport, which sprayed shrapnel across the tarmac but caused no injuries. Yemeni Houthi rebels were suspected. 21083002

August 31, 2021: The military downed a drone carrying explosives over Abha Airport in southwestern Saudi Arabia. The drone's fragments wounded eight people, including citizens of Bangladesh, Nepal, and India, and damaged a civilian plane. One Bangladeshi man was critically injured. Yemeni Houthis were suspected. 21083101

September 5, 2021: The *Saudi Press Agency* reported that the military intercepted a ballistic missile fired by Yemeni Houthi rebels. Debris fell on a neighborhood near Dammam, wounding two children and damaging 14 homes. Brig. Gen. Turki al-Malki said the Houthis launched three bomb-carrying drones and three ballistic missiles. The rebels claimed they sent at least eight explosive-laden drones and one ballistic missile on Aramco facilities in the city of Ras Tanura, about 34 miles north of Dammam, and fired five ballistic missiles and two drone bombs at Aramco facilities in Jeddah, Jizan, and Najran. 21090501

October 8-9, 2021: *Reuters* reported that two drones carrying explosives attacked King Abdullah airport in Jizan late on October 8 and on early October 9. The evening attack injured six Saudis, three Bangladeshi nationals, and one Sudanese, and shattered some of the airport façade's windows. The second drone was intercepted. Yemen-based Houthis were suspected but did not immediately claim credit. 21100801

November 20, 2021: *Reuters* reported that Yemeni Houthi rebels claimed they had fired 14 drones at several Saudi Arabian cities, including at Saudi Aramco facilities in Jeddah.

December 24, 2021: *Reuters* reported that Houthi rebels in Yemen fired a projectile that hit Jazan, Saudi Arabia, killing a Saudi citizen and a Yemeni resident, injuring six Saudis and a Bengali resident, and damaging 12 cars and two shops. A second rocket fired by the Houthis hit Najran in Saudi Arabia, causing material damage. 21122402-03

SYRIA

January 2021: *AP* reported on February 18, 2021 that 20 men and women were murdered in the al-Hol camp housing 62,000 people belonging to ISIS families. They included five female Syrian and Iraqi residents, and an Iraqi man who was beheaded. 21019901

January 2, 2021: *Reuters* and *SANA* reported that a car bomb exploded in a vegetable market in Ras al Ain, close to the border with Turkey, killing several people, including several Turkish-backed fighters and two children, and wounding their mother.

January 9, 2021: A gunman using a noise-suppressed pistol killed a policeman in the al-Hol ISIS refugee camp. He then threw a hand grenade at pursuing police, seriously wounding the patrol commander. Later that day, an official with a local council dealing with Syrian civilians in the camp was shot to death; his son was critically wounded.

January 30, 2021: *Reuters* reported that a car bomb exploded at an industrial site in central

Afrin, killing eight, including four children, and wounding 22. The Turkish Defense Ministry blamed the Syrian Kurdish YPG militia.

January 31, 2021: *AFP* and *AP* reported car bombs exploded in Aleppo Province in Turkish-held north Syria, killing 13 people, including seven civilians. The first bomb hit near a culture center in Azaz, killing seven civilians, including a young girl, and wounding 30 people. Another car bomb hit a checkpoint of pro-Ankara rebels near Al-Bab, killing six fighters.

February 8, 2021: *AFP* reported that a morning ISIS ambush killed 26 pro-regime fighters, including seven Syrian troops, in Deir Ezzor Province. Eleven jihadis died.

Kurdish officials reported 14 killings, including three beheadings, in the al-Hol displacement camp housing 62,000 alleged ISIS relatives since January 1. The dead included ten Iraqis and four Syrians. Some had been shot by noise-suppressed guns.

February 20, 2021: *AFP* reported that 130 Russian Air Force Sukhoi-25 fighter jet airstrikes killed 21 ISIS members in the Badia desert during a 24-hour period.

February 20, 2021: The *New York Times* and *Pittsburgh Post-Gazette* reported that ten Frenchwomen who joined ISIS and were being held in detention camps in Syria began a hunger strike to protest Paris's refusal to repatriate them for trial. Meanwhile, in northern France, the mother of a Frenchwoman detained in Syria began a similar hunger strike on February 1. The ten women were represented by attorneys Marie Dosé and Ludovic Rivière.

February 22, 2021: *Al-Mayadeen TV, AP, SANA,* and *AFP* reported that former Palestinian terrorist Anis Naccache, 69, who participated in the December 21, 1975 Arm of the Arab Revolution barricade-and-hostage attack on OPEC oil ministers in Vienna, Austria, died of COVID-19 in a private hospital in Damascus. The Lebanese citizen spent his last two decades running a Beirut-based think tank and frequently appeared on TV shows as an analyst on Middle Eastern affairs. He was born in June 1951. He joined Yass-

er Arafat's Fatah group in the early 1970s, later working with the Popular Front for the Liberation of Palestine. He recruited Imad Mughniyeh to Fatah; the latter eventually became Hizballah's operations chief, believed behind the bombings of the U.S. Embassy and U.S. Marine barracks in Lebanon in the 1980s that killed hundreds of Americans. Naccache also befriended Venezuelan-born Ilich Ramirez Sanchez, alias Carlos the Jackal, who ran the OPEC operation. Naccache and four other men were convicted in the July 1980 attack in France on Shahpour Bakhtiar, Iran's prime minister before the 1979 Islamic Revolution. In 1990, French President Francois Mitterrand pardoned Naccache and his four accomplices were expelled to Tehran. Iran-backed terrorists conducted a bombing campaign in Paris in 1986 to obtain his release.

Coincidentally, former Saudi Oil Minister Sheikh Ahmed Zaki Yamani, who was among the 1975 OPEC hostages, died on February 23, 2021.

February 25, 2021: The *Washington Post, AP,* and *Military Times* reported that a U.S. airstrike on the border-crossing station of Boukamal facing Qaim in eastern Syria killed several alleged Iranian-linked fighters. *USA Today* reported that the airstrikes were in retaliation for rocket attacks on U.S. targets in Iraq. The Pentagon said targets included a "number of Iranian-backed militant groups including Kataib Hizballah and Kataib Sayyid al-Shuhada". The UK-based Syrian Observatory for Human Rights reported that 22 pro-Iranian Popular Mobilization Forces fighters were killed, many more were wounded, and several trucks carrying munitions were destroyed. An aide to a senior commander in Kataib Hizballah said one of its soldiers was killed in the attack.

March 31, 2021: Kurdish-led forces arrested 71 suspected ISIS terrorists, including a religious leader, a communications expert, a security officer, and a recruiter, inside al-Hol refugee camp, home to 62,000 people from more than 50 countries. All four were Iraqis, aged between 18 and 62. The religious leader hailed from Iraq's Anbar Province and had joined terrorists long before ISIS was formed in 2014. He later became an

ISIS judge. After hiding among residents of the camp, he issued fatwas on who was to be killed inside the camp.

April 4, 2021: *Reuters* reported that the UK Ministry of Defense announced that an RAF Reaper drone, armed with Hellfire missiles, struck a small group of ISIS forces in northern Syria, 50 miles west of al-Hasakah.

May 10, 2021: In the evening, rockets were fired on a Turkish military supply convoy in Idlib Province, killing one soldier and wounding four others. 21051001

The UK-based Syrian Observatory for Human Rights said a roadside bomb exploded when a Turkish convoy of seven vehicles was passing on a road between the Bab al-Hawa border crossing point and the Syrian border village of Kfar Lousin, causing some injuries. 21051002

June 27, 2021: The *Washington Post* reported that the U.S. conducted airstrikes in Iraq and Syria following drone attacks on U.S. troops by Iran-backed militias. The Pentagon said airstrikes hit two locations in Syria and one in Iraq. The sites were used by the Iran-linked Kataib Hizballah and Kataib Sayyid al-Shuhada groups. Kataib Sayyid al-Shuhada said that four of its militiamen were killed in the attack in Iraq.

June 28, 2021: *CNN* reported that rockets hit a U.S. military base at an eastern oil field site the U.S. calls "Green Village". No injuries were reported. Iranian-backed militias were suspected. 21062801

June 29, 2021: *NBC News* reported that U.S. Col. Wayne Marotto, military spokesman for Operation Inherent Resolve, said that at 7:44 p.m., rockets were fired on its forces a day after the U.S. carried out defensive airstrikes in Iraq and Syria against Iran-backed militia groups. No injuries were reported. U.S. forces fired artillery at rocket-launching positions. 21062901

July 4, 2021: *SANA*, Siyamend Ali, a spokesman for the U.S.-backed and Kurdish-led Syrian Democratic Forces (SDF), and a human rights organization reported that in the evening, two rockets were fired at a facility housing U.S. troops at al-Omar field in Deir el-Zour Province, caus-

ing no injuries. The UK-based Syrian Observatory for Human Rights said the rockets were fired from areas controlled by Iran-backed fighters in Mayadeen in Deir el-Zour. SDF denied reports that another base housing U.S. troops was hit, explaining that the sounds of explosions at the Conoco facility were from training with live ammunition. But coalition spokesman Col. Wayne Marotto tweeted "There is no truth to the reports that U.S. forces in Syria were attacked by rockets today." 21070401

July 7, 2021: U.S.-backed Syrian Democratic Forces and American troops foiled a drone attack on the al-Omar oil field in Deir el-Zour Province. No damage was reported. 21070702

July 7, 2021: State television and *AFP* reported the death from illness in a Damascus hospital of Ahmed Jibril, 83, leader of the Popular Front for the Liberation of Palestine-General Command, a terrorist group responsible for hijackings, bombings, and other attacks against Israeli targets in the 1970s and 1980s. Jibril suffered from a heart condition.

Jibril was born in Jaffa in 1938 to a Palestinian father and a Syrian mother. His family later moved to Syria, where he served as a Syrian army officer and became a Syrian citizen.

He founded the Popular Front for the Liberation of Palestine (PFLP) in the late 1950s, later leaving over ideological disputes. In 1968, he founded the pro-Syrian PFLP-GC, which briefly joined the Palestine Liberation Organization. PFLP-GC left the PLO in 1974, following disagreements with PLO leader Yasser Arafat.

Among the group's major attacks were

- hijacking an El Al jetliner in 1968
- machine gunning an El Al plane at Zurich airport in 1969
- setting off a time bomb in 1970 on Swissair SR330 that blew up en route from Zurich to Tel Aviv, killing all 47 on aboard
- capturing three Israeli soldiers in Israel's 1982 invasion of Lebanon, negotiating for the release of 1,100 jailed Palestinian, Lebanese, and Syrian prisoners in 1985

- conducting a 1987 hang-glider attack by two terrorists who killed six Israeli soldiers, sparking the first intifada

His son, Jihad, head of the PFLP-GC military wing, was killed in an attack in 2002 in Beirut. The group blamed Israel.

Ahmed Jibril was survived by four daughters and three sons.

On July 18, the PFLP-GC announced Talal Naji was elected to replace Jibril during a meeting in Damascus, Syria. Naji was born in Nazareth in 1946, studied in Syrian schools, and joined the Palestinian Liberation Front faction in 1962 before joining the PFLP-GC. He lost an arm and an eye in a grenade explosion reportedly while training. He was the deputy chief of the PFLP-GC since 1973. He received a doctorate in political science from Moscow in 1984. Khaled Jibril, the son of the late leader, was named as his deputy.

July 24, 2021: The Turkish defense ministry said "terrorists" attacked a Turkish armored vehicle in the Euphrates Shield area between the Turkish border and northern Aleppo, killing two Turkish soldiers and wounding two others. 21072401

August 4, 2021: An explosion in the gas tank of a bus at the entrance of the military barracks near Qudsaya, west of Damascus, killed its driver and hospitalized three other people. State-owned *al-Ikhbariya TV* called it a terrorist attack.

August 24, 2021: *AP* and *ABC News* reported that Syrian opposition activists claimed that an explosion at the base of the al-Qaeda-linked Hayat Tahrir al-Sham (Levant Liberation Committee), near the village of Ram Hamadan in Idlib Province, killed eight gunmen and wounded ten. The UK-based Syrian Observatory for Human Rights suggested a shell exploded as fighters trained.

September 11, 2021: *AP* and *al-Jazeera* reported that a roadside bomb hit a convoy of Turkish troops following a search and screening operation in Idlib Province's de-escalation zone on the road between Idlib city and Binnish, killing two non-commissioned infantry officers and wounding three soldiers. The Supporters of Abu Bakr al-Siddiq Company claimed credit. 21091101

September 12, 2021: *AP* and *Reuters* reported that gunmen fired on a Turkish patrol conducting a search and screening operation in the Idlib de-escalation zone. Two soldiers died and three were injured. An injured soldier later died of his wounds. 21091202

September 17, 2021: Electricity Minister Ghassan al-Zamel announced that explosive devices went off along a natural gas pipeline southeast of Damascus, knocking out power in parts of the country. No one claimed credit. The Oil Ministry deemed it a "terrorist attack that targeted the Arab Natural Gas pipeline" in the Haran al-Awamid area.

September 19, 2021: The *Washington Post* reported that since January, 70+ people were killed in the al-Hol detention camp, likely by hard-line ISIS Iraqi women.

September 20, 2021: The *Washington Examiner* and *Newsweek* reported that U.S. Central Command spokesperson Lt. Josie Lynne Lenny announced a successful "kinetic counterterrorism strike" against a "senior al-Qaeda leader" in a vehicle on a rural road near Idlib. No civilians were hurt. *Newsweek* and *Military Times* quoted CENTCOM spokesman Army Major John Rigsbee that "Salim Abu-Ahmad was responsible for planning, funding, and approving trans-regional al-Qaeda attacks."

October 10, 2021: The Turkish Interior Minister said a missile fired from Tal Rifat, east of Afrin, struck an armored car, killing two Turkish special operations police officers and wounding three others. 21101001

October 11, 2021: *AP* and *al-Jazeera* reported that a car bomb exploded in a market in Afrin, which is controlled by Turkey-backed Syrian opposition fighters, in Aleppo Province, killing four people, including a woman. The UK-based Syrian Observatory for Human Rights said six, including suspected opposition fighters, died and 12, including two children, were wounded in the streets near the Kawa Roundabout, where several government offices are located.

October 20, 2021: *AP* and *SANA* reported that at 6:45 a.m., two bombs exploded on a military bus as it crossed the President Hafez al-Assad Bridge, around the corner from the Four Seasons Hotel, in Damascus, killing 14 people and wounding three. Authorities found and dismantled a third device that had fallen off. ISIS was suspected. The little-known Qasioun Brigades claimed credit, saying the bombs were attached under the bus.

October 22, 2021: *UPI* reported that CENTCOM announced that an MQ-9 Reaper drone strike near Suluk, in Raqqa Governorate's Tell Abyad district, near the border with Turkey, killed senior al-Qaeda leader Abdul Hamid al-Matar.

December 2, 2021: *SANA* blamed a "terrorist attack" when a bomb hit a bus carrying oil field workers in a government-held area, killing ten and injuring one. The employees worked at the government-controlled Kharata oil field in Deir el-Zour Province. Authorities did not announce whether the device was placed on the side of the road or thrown at the bus.

December 13, 2021: A Kurdish Syrian Democratic Forces anti-terrorism unit killed five suspected ISIS fighters in a raid near Busayrah in Deir el-Zour Province. The team had targeted an ISIS member who fled on his motorcycle but was shot dead. The SDF then captured and later shot his father and his brother outside their home.

West Bank

January 5, 2021: *Reuters* reported that a Palestinian suspect threw a knife toward an Israeli community security officer, who shot and killed him at a road junction near a cluster of Israeli settlements southwest of Bethlehem.

April 5, 2021: *AP* and *Reuters* reported that in the late night, Israeli troops shot and killed a Palestinian man at a temporary vehicle checkpoint near Jerusalem. The military said the soldiers thwarted an attempted car-ramming attack in Bir Nabala village. The Palestinian Authority

identified the man as Osama Mansour, 42. The man's wife, Sumaya Mansour, 35, who was in the car with him and was wounded by the gunfire, said the couple followed the soldiers' instructions and posed no threat and had been waved through. She told *Palestine TV*, "They told us to stop the car and we stopped and turned it off... Then they looked at us and told us to go. We turned the car on and moved and all of them started shooting at us." Salem Eid, mayor of Biddu village, where Mansour lived, said Palestinians could raise the incident at the International Criminal Court. Eid noted that Mansour was the father of five.

May 2, 2021: In a drive-by shooting, gunmen fired at Israelis standing at Tapuah junction, a major intersection, injuring three people in their 20s, two seriously. Troops fired at the car, which had Palestinian license plates, but two assailants escaped. No one claimed credit. On May 5, Yehuda Guetta, 19, who was shot in the head, died of his injuries. On May 6, the armed forces and Shin Bet raided a building in Silwad in the West Bank, and arrested Muntasser Shalaby, 44, a Palestinian from nearby Turmus Ayya, who had no known ties to militant groups. Local media reported that he held U.S. citizenship.

AP and *Newsweek* reported on June 23, 2021 that Israel's Supreme Court upheld the decision to demolish Shalaby's family home in Turmus Ayya village, rejecting a claim by his estranged wife, Sanaa Shalaby, who lives in the house with their three children, aged 17, 12, and 9, that she knew nothing about the attack. Sanaa said that they were estranged for several years and that he spent most of his time in Santa Fe, New Mexico, where he had married three other women in unofficial Islamic ceremonies. The entire family are U.S. citizens. She said Muntasser visited for a month or two every year. HaMoked, an Israeli rights group representing her, said he had a history of mental illness. The Supreme Court held that Muntasser had lived in the home continuously from 2006-2012 and had resided there for weeks before the attack. An interim injunction was to lapse on June 30. *AP* reported on July 8, 2021 Israeli army troops using controlled explosions demolished the two-story family home. 21050201

May 6, 2021: Israeli authorities in a West Bank military court charged Spanish woman Juana Ruiz Sánchez, 62, with sending large donations from European governments to the banned Popular Front for the Liberation of Palestine. The group is listed by Israel, the United States, Canada, and European Union as a terrorist organization. Ruiz lives in the West Bank and had worked for Health Work Committees, a Palestinian non-governmental organization that provides medical services in the territory. Shin Bet said the NGO's senior accountant, former accountant, and former purchasing department manager were expected to be charged with similar offenses. Ruiz was arrested on April 13 at her home near Bethlehem. Her defense attorney was Israeli human rights lawyer Gaby Lasky.

On November 10, 2021, Juana Ruiz Sánchez, also known by her married name of Juana Rishmawi, and who is married to a Palestinian, admitted under a plea bargain reached in an Israeli military court that she raised hundreds of thousands of dollars that were diverted to the PFLP. She was convicted of "performing a service for an outlawed organization" and illegal money transfers into the West Bank. She was represented by prominent Israeli defense attorney Avigdor Feldman, who said his client had admitted to lesser charges in order to go free. The Ofer military court sentenced her to a 13-month prison term and fined her 50,000 shekels, roughly $16,000, on November 17.

May 7, 2021: Three Palestinians fired on an IDF base near Jenin. An Israeli soldier returned fire, killing two and wounding a third, who was evacuated to a hospital.

June 12, 2021: *AP* and *Wafa* reported that a private security guard shot and killed a Palestinian woman, 28, a resident of a West Bank camp, who carried a knife and ran toward the Israeli military's Qalandia checkpoint north of Jerusalem. She had ignored calls by the guard to stop. The Palestinian Prisoners Club advocacy group said Ibtissam Kaabneh had served 18 months in an Israeli prison after being arrested in 2016 for an attempted stabbing.

June 16, 2021: The Israeli military shot and killed Palestinian woman Mai Afaneh, 28, who it said had tried to ram her car into a group of soldiers guarding a West Bank construction site in Hizmeh, north of Jerusalem, after she exited the car and pulled out a knife. One soldier was slightly injured while jumping away from the car. The official Palestinian news agency *Wafa* and *AP* reported that she lived a half hour away in Abu Dis, a West Bank town on Jerusalem's eastern suburbs. *AP* reported that she had health problems, having just left the hospital but still was weak and needing colon surgery. She had posted on *Facebook* about Palestinians killed by Israel but otherwise was not politically active. She had earned a doctorate in psychology in Jordan, taught at a local university, and was married and raising a daughter, 5.

August 9, 2021: Israeli soldiers shot and wounded in the lower body a Palestinian woman who attacked them with a knife in the night in Nablus. No Israeli soldiers were wounded.

August 16, 2021: Israel's paramilitary border police attempting to arrest a suspect in Jenin came under heavy fire from close range. The IDF returned fire, killing four suspects and seriously wounding another. None of its officers were injured.

September 13, 2021: *Reuters* reported that a Palestinian armed with a screwdriver tried to stab an Israeli soldier. Troops shot the man, who was hospitalized.

September 26, 2021: In two clashes sparked by Israeli raids against suspected Hamas gunmen, five Palestinians died and two Israeli soldiers were seriously injured. Israeli Prime Minister Naftali Bennett said the gunmen were about to carry out attacks "in real time". The Palestinian Health Ministry said two Palestinians were shot dead near Jenin and three others were killed in Biddu. An officer and soldier suffered serious injuries during the arrest in Burqin, near Jenin.

September 28, 2021: Dozens of Israeli settlers from Avigayil and Havat Maon attacked Mufaqara, a Palestinian village in the South Hebron Hills, throwing stones at cars and homes and injuring several people, including Palestinian toddler Mohammed Bakr, 4, who was hospitalized with a head injury. Police arrested three people, including a minor, suspected of assault and damaging property.

October 13, 2021: During the night, a Palestinian driver, 22, from Qalqilya in the West Bank, struck and moderately wounded a member of Israel's paramilitary Border Police at a major checkpoint north of Jerusalem. Officers fired on the vehicle, which hit a wall, then arrested the suspect.

A Jewish settler attacked an Israeli military officer and a soldier with pepper spray near a settlement outpost in the West Bank. The two soldiers received medical treatment at the scene.

October 14, 2021: Israeli troops shot and killed a Palestinian, one of two of whom were spotted throwing firebombs at cars on a main highway near Beit Jala, a Palestinian town south of Jerusalem. The second was detained.

November 15, 2021: Jewish settlers attacked Palestinian farmers in the northern West Bank area of Burqa with stones, clubs, and pepper spray, injuring three people.

November 24, 2021: Jewish settlers threw rocks at a car driving near the West Bank village of al-Mughayir, critically injuring Palestinian man Raid Kharaz who veered off the road and crashed after rocks smashed through the windshield. *Wafa* reported that his son, who was also in the vehicle, sustained lighter injuries.

December 13, 2021: *Reuters* reported that Israeli paramilitary border police killed a Palestinian during a raid in Nablus in which Palestinians threw bombs at them at close range after they detained a wanted militant. Islamic Jihad mourned his death, but did not claim his as a member. Israeli undercover forces seized an assault rifle.

December 21, 2021: *Reuters* and *U.S. News and World Report* noted that Israeli soldiers shot to death a Palestinian motorist they suspected of attempting to crash through a military checkpoint near a West Bank settlement. The car crashed into an Israeli army vehicle, setting both on fire. No soldiers were injured.

The attack happened near the site of a December 16 ambush in which Palestinian gunmen killed an Israeli motorist leaving yeshiva in the former Homesh settlement outpost.

Hamas praised the latest incident but did not take responsibility.

December 31, 2021: *Reuters* and *AP* reported that troops shot and killed Amir Atef Reyan, a Palestinian man running toward a bus stop and brandishing a knife in an attempted stabbing attack at a junction near the settlement of Giti Avishar in the West Bank. He exited a car and advanced on Israeli civilians and soldiers at the bus stop.

YEMEN

January 10, 2021: *AP, UPI,* and *Reuters* reported that Secretary of State Mike Pompeo announced that he would designate Yemen's Iran-backed Houthi rebels (also known as Ansarallah) as a "foreign terrorist organization", effective January 19. Pompeo added, "I also intend to designate three of Ansar Allah's leaders, Abdul Malik al-Houthi, Abd al-Khaliq Badr al-Din al-Houthi, and Abdullah Yahya al-Hakim, as Specially Designated Global Terrorists."

January 26, 2021: Gunmen kidnapped security official Brig. Ibrahim Harad outside of his house in Aden's Buraiqeh district during the night. His body, with multiple bullet wounds, was found the next day in the same district. No one claimed credit. Harad headed political security in Hodeida.

February 4, 2021: *CNN* reported that the U.N. Security Council announced that Khalid Batarfi, leader of al-Qaeda in the Arabian Peninsula (AQAP), was arrested and his deputy, Saad Atef al-Awlaqi, died during an "operation in Ghayda City, Al-Mahrah Governorate, in October". Batarfi, in his early 40s, was born in Riyadh, Saudi Arabia. He became AQAP's leader after his predecessor, Qassim al-Rimi, died in a U.S. airstrike in Yemen in February 2020. He had trained with al-Qaeda in Afghanistan before 9/11 and later oversaw AQAP's external operations. *AFP* reported on February 11, 2021 that

AQAP's *al-Malahem Media* released a 20-minute video titled "America and the Painful Seizure" on which he talked about the January 6, 2021 attack on the U.S. Capitol. Batarfi observed "storming the Congress is only the tip of the iceberg of what will come to them, God willing".

February 6, 2021: The *Washington Post* reported that the Biden Administration revoked the terrorist designation of Yemen's Houthi rebels.

February 19, 2021: Houthi rebels led by Abu Khalid al-Raei shot to death tribal leader Sheikh Ali Abu Nashtan and three of his sons and a sister outside their house in the Arhab district in northern Sanaa.

February 26, 2021: Clashes between Iranian-backed Houthi rebels and government forces in the Marib killed 27 people, most of them Houthis.

March 2, 2021: *Al-Monitor* reported the U.S. announced sanctions on two military leaders of Yemen's Houthi rebels: Mansur al-Saadi, the head of the Houthis' naval forces, and Ahmad Ali Ahsan al-Hamzi, head of the rebels' air force, for "procur[ing] weapons from Iran and oversee[ing] attacks threatening civilians and maritime infrastructure".

May 24, 2021: Two aid workers and their driver, all Yemenis, were injured in a crossfire at a checkpoint in the south as they were en route to Aden. They were taken to a hospital, where Oxfam worker Fathi al-Zurigi died the next day. The driver remained in intensive care; the other worker was discharged on May 26.

June 5, 2021: Ali al-Ghulisi, the provincial governor's press secretary, announced that Houthi rebels fired a ballistic missile that hit a gas station in the Rawdha neighborhood of the government-held city of Marib, killing 14 people, including a girl, 5, and wounding dozens. The government-run *SABA* news agency added that Houthis fired an explosive-laden drone shortly after the missile attack, destroying two ambulances tending to the wounded.

June 10, 2021: *AP* and *SABA* reported that Iran-backed Houthi rebels fired four ballistic missiles and flew drones that dropped explosives on Marib, hitting a mosque and a women's prison, killing eight people, and wounding 27.

AP reported that the U.S. imposed sanctions against a Yemeni network, including 11 Yemeni individuals, alleged front companies, intermediaries, and vessels cooperating with Iran's Revolutionary Guard to illicitly transfer tens of millions of dollars to Houthi rebels. They included Jami' 'Ali Muhammad, a Houthi and alleged Iranian Revolutionary Guard associate who the United States says helped "procure vessels, facilitate shipments of fuel, and transfer funds for the benefit of the Houthis".

June 11, 2021: An explosion of indeterminate origin went off after a convoy of the secessionist Southern Transitional Council arrived at a market in Abyan that sells khat leaves. Six separatist troops died and 15 people, including civilians, were wounded. No group claimed credit.

August 29, 2021: *NPR* and *AP* reported that Houthis were suspected regarding a missile and drone attack on the al-Anad Air Base in Lajh Province that killed 30 troops and wounded 65. A missile landed in the base's training area, where dozens of troops were doing morning exercises. No one claimed credit.

August 30, 2021: The government said Houthi rebels attacked the city of Rahbah, killing 12 government troops.

September 11, 2021: *Al-Jazeera* reported that Houthi rebels fired a ballistic missile and five explosive-laden drones at al-Makha port on the Red Sea, destroying humanitarian aid warehouses. No casualties were reported.

September 18, 2021: Houthi rebels announced that a firing squad in Sanaa executed nine people, including a 17-year-old boy, for their alleged involvement in the killing of a senior Houthi official in an airstrike in Hodeida by the Saudi-led coalition in April 2018. The nine were among more than 60 people the Houthis accused of involvement in the killing of Saleh al-Samad, president in the Houthi-backed political body.

October 2, 2021: Ten people, including four civilians, died and a dozen fighters were wounded in gun battles between UAE-backed Southern Transitional Council separatists and a rival armed religious splinter group that was once part of the council in Aden's residential Crater neighborhood, where the presidential palace and other government buildings are located. The splinter is led by Salafi officer Brig. Imam al-Noubi, who commanded a faction of the separatist militia known as the Security Belt. He fell out with and left the council two years ago.

October 3, 2021: *ABC News* reported that Houthi rebels fired three ballistic missiles at Marib, a government-held central city, killing two children—Ghozlan Feisal, 4, and her sibling Radad, 2—in the residential Rawdha neighborhood and wounding 32 people, including five children and four women. Among the seriously wounded were a mother and her seven-month-old child. The missiles destroyed two houses, damaged 10 others, and burned eight vehicles.

October 10, 2021: Information Minister Moammar al-Iryani announced that a car bomb targeted the convoy of Agriculture Minister Salem al-Socotrai and Aden's Governor Ahmed Lamlas in the district of Tawahi in Aden, killing six of Lamlas's companions and hospitalizing seven others who had been passing by. Lamlas and al-Socotrai survived. Several buildings were damaged. No one claimed credit. Prime Minister Maeen Abdulmalik Saeed deemed the explosion a "terrorist attack".

October 28, 2021: A ballistic missile fired by Houthi rebels hit a family's house in a residential neighborhood of al-Aumd in Marib Province, killing 11 family members of a key tribal leader, including women and children, wounding 16 civilians, and damaging 12 houses.

October 30, 2021: *AP* and the government-run *SABA* news agency reported that Moammar al-Iryani, information minister of the internationally recognized government, claimed that Houthi rebels fired a howitzer shell into the Camp residential neighborhood in the Taiz suburbs, injuring six people, including three children from the same family.

In the afternoon, a car bomb went off at a security checkpoint in the Khormaksar neighborhood outside Aden's international airport, killing eight people, injuring 11, and damaging buildings and an Internet café. No group claimed responsibility.

October 31, 2021: Houthi rebels fired two ballistic missiles, hitting the Dar al-Hadith religious school and mosque in the residential neighborhood of al-Aumd in Marib Province during the night, killing ten civilians and wounding 25. Moammar al-Iryani, information minister, said the casualties included women and children. The madrassa is attended by 1,200 students from across the country.

November 2, 2021: *AFP* reported the Saudi-led military coalition said that air strikes in al-Jawba, 30 miles south of Marib, and al-Kassara killed 115 Houthi rebels. The *Saudi Press Agency* added that 14 military vehicles were destroyed. The next day, *AP* and *ABC News* reported that security officials claimed that more than 200 Houthi fighters had been killed and hundreds were wounded.

November 9, 2021: A bomb exploded inside the family vehicle of Yemeni journalist Rasha Abdalla in Aden's Khormaksar neighborhood, killing her and her child, Jawad. No group claimed credit. The family were en route to see a doctor. Abdalla, who was pregnant, worked for the UAE-based *Asharq* satellite television channel. Her husband, journalist Mahmoud al-Attomy, was hospitalized in critical condition. Three passersby were wounded.

November 11, 2021: Houthis breached the compound that housed the U.S. Embassy in Sana'a and detained Yemeni employees of the U.S. government. A State Department spokesperson said that a "majority" of the U.S. Embassy staff that were detained have been released and that the Washington was engaging in "unceasing" diplomatic efforts to free the employees still in custody. The detained Yemeni employees are security personnel who had guarded the exterior of the compound. The American diplomatic mission suspended operations in 2015.

November 18, 2021: *Reuters* reported that the U.S. Department of the Treasury imposed economic sanctions against senior Houthi military officer Saleh Mesfer Alshaer, citing his "unlawful tactics".

NORTH AMERICA

CANADA

January 25, 2021: *Newsweek* reported that the House of Commons voted unanimously to classify the extremist far-right group Proud Boys as a white supremacist terrorist organization.

February 3, 2021: Public Safety Minister Bill Blair announced that the government had declared the Proud Boys a terrorist entity, calling the group one of the country's "most serious threats". The Canadian terrorist list includes al-Qaeda, ISIS, al-Shabaab, seven other entities affiliated with al-Qaeda and the Islamic State; Hizbul Mujahideen, a militant Kashmiri liberation group; neo-Nazi groups Blood and Honor and Combat 18. Also added to the list were the Atomwaffen Division, a neo-Nazi group whose members participated in the violent 2017 Unite the Right rally in Charlottesville; The Base, another neo-Nazi group; and the Russian Imperial Movement, a Russian nationalist group. Gavin McInnes, a Canadian and Vice Media co-founder, formed the Proud Boys in 2016 as a far-right, male-only group of self-described "Western chauvinists".

March 27, 2021: *Reuters, UPI,* and the *Canadian Broadcasting Corporation* reported that a woman in her late 20s was killed and five others were wounded in a mass stabbing at 1:45 p.m. at the Lynn Valley Library near a busy shopping area in North Vancouver, British Columbia. Police arrested a lone suspect, who had injured himself with a knife before his arrest. He had a criminal record. *Reuters* reported on March 29 that Canadian authorities charged Yannick Bandaogo, 28, with second-degree murder.

May 2, 2021: The Canadian chapter of the Proud Boys announced that it had been "officially dissolved", posting on *Telegram*, "there is officially no longer any Proud Boys in Canada… As a fraternity of men we had thought of pursuing the case legally but we have no financial support, given we are not funded by the rich."

June 6, 2021: Police said that during the evening, Nathaniel Veltman, 20, of London, Ontario, crashed his black pickup truck at an intersection into a family of five Muslims, killing four and hospitalizing one. Canadian police said he deliberately attacked Muslims. He did not know the victims—Salman Afzaal, 46; his wife Madiha Salman, 44; their daughter Yumna Salman, 15; and her grandmother, Talat Afzaal, 74. The couple's son, Fayez, 9, was in serious condition but was expected to recover. Police arrested Veltman in the parking lot of a nearby mall four miles away and held him on four counts of first degree murder and one of attempted murder. Detective Superintendent Paul Waight said Veltman was "wearing a vest that appeared to be like body armor". *Reuters* reported that he was remanded to custody on June 7 and appeared virtually in court on June 10 at 9:15 a.m. He did not enter a plea and had not found a lawyer. The case was adjourned until June 14. *Reuters* added that Veltman worked part-time at an egg-packing plant in Strathroy, Ontario, near London. He enjoyed video games and distance running.

Newsweek and *AP* reported that Yellow London Taxi President Hasan Savehilaghi said that one of his company's drivers was having a cigarette and coffee by his taxi in an empty strip mall parking lot during the evening when Veltman pulled up behind him and demanded that the cabbie call police so he could surrender because he had killed someone. The cab driver noticed heavy damage and much blood on the front of the pickup truck. While on a phone call with the 911 dispatcher, the cabbie chased down a police officer going by. The driver wore a military helmet and an armored vest, along with a t-shirt with swastikas. Veltman asked the cabbie to record the arrest and make a movie of him.

AP reported on June 14 that prosecutors laid terrorism charges against Veltman, observing that four counts of first-degree murder constitute an act of terrorism. His next court date was scheduled for June 21.

The *World* reported on June 22 that it would be the first time an individual involved in an Islamophobic act would be charged with terrorism.

June 21, 2021: The *Washington Post, Penticton Western News, Vancouver Sun, Global News,* and *UPI* reported that arson was suspected in suspicious fires at two hundred-year-old Catholic churches, including Sacred Heart Church of the Penticton South Okanagan Band reserve and St. Gregory's Church on the Osoyoos Indian Band reserve, on First Nations reserves in British Columbia. The fires occurred on National Indigenous Peoples Day, a Canadian holiday. The Sacred Heart fire was spotted at 1:22 a.m.; the St. Gregory's fire at 3:10 a.m.

CNN reported on June 29 that on the morning of June 26, fires damaged St. Ann's Catholic Church on Upper Similkameen Indian Band land and the Chopaka Catholic Church on Lower Similkameen Indian Band land.

In late May, the Tk'emlupste Secwépemc First Nation found the remains of 215 children at the former Kamloops Indian Residential School, which was operated by the Catholic Church from 1890 to 1969 before it was taken over by the Canadian government until it was closed in 1978.

June 25, 2021: Public Safety Minister Bill Blair announced that the government had declared the Three Percenters a terrorist entity, citing "ample reason" to believe the U.S.-based right-wing, anti-government, self-styled militia group was active in Canada. The group was linked to bomb plots targeting U.S. government buildings and Muslim communities. Weeks earlier, four Three Percenters from California were arrested and charged with conspiracy and aiding and abetting the obstruction of a joint session of Congress after participating in the riot at the U.S. Capitol on January 6. Canada also designated as terrorists the Aryan Strikeforce, a UK-based neo-Nazi group that it said aims to "start a race war and eradicate ethnic minorities" and the Islamic State in the Democratic Republic of the Congo. James Mason, an American neo-Nazi, was also listed.

Newsweek and the *Canadian Broadcasting Corporation* reported that assailants yelling about Muhammad Kashif's religious clothing stabbed him in the arm and cut his beard in the morning in Saskatoon in an unprovoked attack. He was near his parked car when another person drove up behind him, stabbed him in the back, and yelled, "Why you are here? We don't like you are Muslim, why are you wearing this dress?" One assailant then held his hands and a second cut Kashif's beard. They then knocked him unconscious by hitting him over the head with his walking cane, fleeing with his keys and phone. He needed 14 stitches on his arm. Kashif said one of the attackers had previously verbally abused him.

June-July 2021: *Fox News* reported on July 4 that nine Catholic and Anglican churches had been torched amid indigenous anger over the country's use of church-run residential schools to forcibly assimilate indigenous children from the late 19th century until the 1970s. Hundreds of unmarked graves were found at the former schools within the last month. Most of the arsons occurred on First Nations land. They included:

- June 21: Sacred Heart Catholic Church, located in Penticton Indian Band in British Columbia, was destroyed. A few hours later, St. Gregory Catholic Church, on Osoyoos Indian Band lands, also in British Columbia, was torched.

- June 26: Our Lady of Lourdes Chopaka and St. Ann's Church, two Catholic churches on indigenous land, were destroyed. Also that day, St. Paul, an Anglican church in British Columbia, was set on fire.

- June 28: A fire caused major structure damage to Siksika First Nation Catholic Church.

- June 30: St. Jean Baptiste Paris Church in Alberta was leveled by flames.

- July 1: A second fire destroyed the Anglican St. Paul church in British Columbia. A Molotov cocktail thrown into St. Patrick Co-Cathedral in Yellowknife in the Northwest Territories caused minor structural damage.

- July 2: Firefighters doused a morning blaze at St. Columba, an Anglican church in British Columbia.

August 26, 2021: *Newsweek* reported on September 2 that the Langley Islamic Center mosque received a threatening letter using letters cut out from newspapers, posted onto *Facebook,* and signed by someone claiming membership in the Ku Klux Klan. The posting read "You have two month to shut [this] place down and leave or I will go [Brenton] Tarrant on you mudslimes. Invaders must die. Heil Hitler 1488. KKK". White supremacist Brenton Tarrant killed 51 people during two mosque shootings in Christchurch, New Zealand in March 2019. The number 14 is a reference to the "14 Words" slogan "We must secure the existence of our people and a future for white children" used by white supremacists, while 88 is code for "Heil Hitler"; the letter H is the eighth letter of the alphabet.

October 2, 2021: Windsor news media reported a bomb threat temporarily closed the Ambassador Bridge to Detroit. At 9 a.m., patrol officers and the Explosive Disposal Unit were dispatched to the 2600 block of Wyandotte Street West after receiving a report that two grenades were located inside a vehicle. The *Detroit News* reported on October 5 that the Windsor Police Service found two inert grenades and an unknown white powdery substance during a secondary inspection by officers with the Canadian Border Service Agency at the crossing in Windsor. The American driver was taken into custody, questioned by the CBSA, then turned over to U.S. Customs and Border Protection.

UNITED STATES

January 6, 2021: *CNN* and the *Washington Post* reported that at 1 p.m., Trump-supporting rioters, urged by his call to action at a local rally, stormed the U.S. Capitol building, breaking windows, climbing inside, entering the well of the U.S. House of Representatives and taking over the office of House Speaker Nancy Pelosi. Vice President Mike Pence, who was presiding over the ceremonial counting of the ballots from the Electoral College establishing the election of President-Elect Joe Biden, was evacuated from the area. Initial reports indicated that pipe bombs were discovered at the D.C. headquarters of the Republican National Committee, the Democratic National Committee, and on the grounds of the Capitol complex. U.S. Capitol Police shot Ashli Elizabeth Babbitt, 35, in the shoulder as she was entering the Capitol through a smashed window; the rioter later died of her wounds. Three others—Rosanne Boyland, 34, of Kennesaw, Georgia; Kevin Greeson, 55, of Athens, Alabama; and Benjamin Philips, 50, of Ringtown, Pennsylvania—died of unspecified medical emergencies. *CNN* reported that at least 14 D.C. Metropolitan Police officers were injured. Apologists for the right-wingers soon claimed that the attack was the work of antifa instigators. After challenges to electors from Arizona and Pennsylvania were overwhelmingly defeated, Pence formally declared Biden the winner of the 2020 Presidential election.

The *Washington Post, San Diego Tribune,* and *military.com* reported that the dead rioter, Ashli Babbitt, had a Trump flag tied around her waist. Her ex-husband said she was an Ocean Beach, San Diego, California native who had served in the Air Force in Afghanistan and Iraq with National Guard deployments to Kuwait and Qatar. She had posted on social media many of Trump's conspiracy theories and false claims of voter fraud. Ex-husband Timothy McEntee said he met Babbitt in the Air Force. They were married in April 2005 and were together for 14 years, before divorcing in May 2019. *WTTG* and *KUSI* reported that Babbitt had remarried and owned Fowler's Pool Service and Supply, Inc. in Spring Valley with her husband, CFO Aaron Babbitt, who did not accompany her to Washington. In early September, she tweeted a photo from a Trump boat parade in San Diego wearing a shirt that said, "We are Q," referring to QAnon, and the hashtag "#WWG1WGA, (Where we go one, we go all)" an acronym used by supporters who believe in the claims that Trump was fighting "deep state" satanic child abusers. She had retweeted messages calling for Vice President Pence to resign and be charged with treason. In one of her final tweets, she said, "Nothing will stop us ... they can try and try and try but the storm is here and it is descending upon DC in less than 24 hours ... dark to light!"

CNN reported on January 8 that U.S. Capitol Police officer Brian D. Sicknick, 42, died of his injuries on January 7 at 9:30 p.m. Sicknick enlisted in the National Guard after graduating from the Middlesex County Vocational and Technical School in East Brunswick, New Jersey in 1997, then deployed to Saudi Arabia and Kyrgyzstan. He had joined the Capitol Police in July 2008, and recently served in the First Responders Unit. He was hit in the head with a fire extinguisher. *NPR* reported that he lay in state in the Capitol Rotunda on February 2-3.

Newsweek reported on January 8 that QAnon supporters claimed Babbitt was still alive.

Health officials suggested that the Capitol insurrection would be a COVID-19 superspreader event.

The *Washington Post* reported on January 8 that the FBI was investigating whether some of the rioters intended to take hostage or kill lawmakers and their staffers. Some rioters were carrying zip ties; one man was carrying a pistol. Authorities arrested dozens of people on various charges.

Authorities arrested Derrick Evans, a recently elected state lawmaker from West Virginia, for unlawfully entering restricted grounds after allegedly live-streaming a video of himself on his *Facebook* page in which he said, "Bring the tear gas. We don't care... We're taking this country back, whether you like it or not. Today's a test run. We're taking this country back." He was represented by attorney John H. Bryan. *NPR* reported that Evans resigned on January 9.

Prosecutors charged Lonnie Leroy Coffman, 70, of Falkville, Alabama, with one federal and one local count of possessing an unregistered or unlicensed firearm. He was the registered owner of a red GMC pickup truck with Alabama plates parked near the Capitol in which officers allegedly found 11 Molotov cocktails and an M4 carbine assault rifle. Prosecutor Kenneth C. Kohl said police determined that Coffman was carrying two handguns.

The *Washington Post* reported on January 9 that federal prosecutors in the District of Columbia charged two more people for taking part in the riot inside the Capitol. Adam Johnson, 36, of Bradenton, Florida, accused of stealing the lectern of House Speaker Nancy Pelosi (D-California), was charged with one count of knowingly entering or remaining in any restricted building or grounds without lawful authority; one count of theft of government property; and one count of violent entry and disorderly conduct on Capitol grounds. Johnson was arrested on January 8.

Prosecutors charged Jacob Anthony Chansley, 33, alias Jake Angeli, of Arizona, with knowingly entering or remaining in any restricted building or grounds without lawful authority, and with violent entry and disorderly conduct on Capitol grounds. He was arrested on January 9. He appeared in numerous videos of the attack as wearing a fur-lined headdress and face paint who stood on the dais in the Senate chamber next to Vice President Pence's chair. Some media sources identified him as the QAnon Shaman. *Navy Times* reported that he had served as a Navy supply clerk seaman apprentice for 25 months in September 2005-October 2007. On September 3, 2021, *CNN* reported that Jacob Chansley pleaded guilty during a virtual hearing before District Judge Royce Lamberth in D.C. District Court to a felony for obstructing the Electoral College proceedings. He had called Vice President Mike Pence a "child-trafficking traitor". Chansley agreed to pay $2,000 in restitution for damage to the Capitol. He faced a fine of up to $250,000 and 20 years in jail. Sentencing was scheduled for November 17. Prosecutors agreed to seek a punishment between three and four years in prison. He was represented by defense attorney Al Watkins, who argued that his client had mental health issues that were exacerbated by confinement.

Military Times reported on January 10 that authorities arrested retired Air Force Lt. Col. Larry Rendall Brock, Jr., who was photographed on the Senate floor clad in tactical gear and holding zip-tie flex cuffs. He had told *New Yorker* magazine reporter Ronan Farrow, "The President asked for his supporters to be there to attend, and I felt like it was important, because of how much I love this country, to actually be there." Brock reportedly served as a chief operations inspector and flight commander within the 706th Fighter Squadron, claiming to have received three Meritorious Service Medals, six Air Medals, and three Aerial Achievement Medals from service in Afghanistan and non-combat service in Iraq.

CNN and *KCCI* reported on January 10 that a man who chased a Black Capitol Police officer up the stairs was Doug Jensen, 41, who faced five federal charges of unlawfully entering the Capitol, disrupting government business, violent entry, parading in a Capitol building, and blocking law enforcement during the riot. Jensen twice tweeted that he was in one of the pictures that was circulating online after the riot and insurrection. He was wearing a QAnon t-shirt. FBI officials presented Jensen to Polk, Iowa, County Jail for processing. Forrest & Associate Masonry terminated his employment; company President and CEO Richard Felice told *KCCI* the company does not agree with Jensen's actions.

NPR reported on January 11 that 80 arrests had been made.

CNN reported on January 11 that Army secretary Ryan McCarthy told Democratic Representative Jason Crow (D-Colorado), a member of the House Armed Services committee, that at least 25 domestic terrorism cases had been opened after authorities seized long guns, Molotov cocktails, explosive devices, and zip-ties. Crow expressed concern regarding "reports that active duty and reserve military members were involved in the insurrection". *CNN* noted that 20 people faced federal criminal charges.

The *Washington Post* reported on January 11 that cancer survivor Representative Bonnie Watson Coleman (D-New Jersey), 75, tested positive for the coronavirus after sheltering in a room with lawmakers who refused to wear masks during the riot. Representatives Pramila Jayapal (D-Washington) and Brad Schneider (D-Illinois) later announced their positive tests.

Acting D.C. Police Chief Robert J. Contee, III, said 56 of his officers were injured by the rioters. Rioters tasered and beat an officer in an attempt to steal his gun. He was hospitalized. The *Washington Post 202* said the head of the police union claimed about 140 officers were injured.

On January 11, *CNN* ran video showing rioters dragging a police officer down Capitol steps and beating him with a flagpole that held a U.S. flag.

USA Today reported that two Capitol Police officers were suspended. One wore a MAGA hat and was "directing some people around", according to Representative Tim Ryan (D-Ohio). The other took a selfie with one of the rioters inside the Capitol building.

On January 13, the U.S. House of Representatives impeached President Donald Trump for inciting the insurrection. It was the second time he was impeached, a U.S. record.

CNN reported that federal filing documents on January 15 indicated that some of the rioters planned "to capture and assassinate elected officials" including Vice President Mike Pence. Prosecutors soon withdrew that language, saying there was "no direct evidence of kill and capture teams".

USA Today reported that as of January 21, authorities had arrested residents of 32 states and the District of Columbia. Among them were 85 men and 11 women. Six had been charged with assaulting an officer; three with possession of firearms. Those facing charges including current and former police officers, a fashion student, grandparents, former athletes, and elected officials. Three were members of the Oath Keepers, charged with planning the attack. The trio—Thomas Caldwell of Virginia and Jessica Watkins and Donovan Crowl of Ohio—allegedly were wearing helmets, reinforced vests, and military-style insignia and coordinated via radios and *Facebook* in their search for legislators in hiding. A 22-year-old woman was believed to have stolen a laptop from Speaker Nancy Pelosi's office, intending to sell it to the Russians.

CNN reported on January 23 that the Department of Justice revealed five criminal charges against Garret Miller of Texas, including trespassing and posting online death threats against U.S. Representative Alexandria Ocasio-Cortez (D-New York) and a US Capitol Police officer. Court documents indicated that Miller allegedly tweeted, "assassinate AOC" and that a police officer who shot QAnon supporter Ashli Elizabeth Babbitt as she entered the Capitol through a smashed window "deserves to die" and won't "survive long" because it's "huntin[g] season". The complaint held that he posted on *Instagram* that he would "hug his neck with a nice rope". He also had posted before and during the attack that a "civil war could start" and "next time we bring the guns." He was arrested on January 20.

The *Washington Post* reported on January 29 that investigators believed that the two pipe bombs were planted around 8:13 p.m. on January 5, citing video footage. Authorities had increased the reward for tips leading to the bomber's arrest to $100,000.

AP reported on January 30, 2021 that federal authorities indicted two members of the Proud Boys from New York for conspiracy for orchestrating the riot. Former Marine Dominic Pezzola was seen on video smashing a Capitol window with a stolen Capitol Police riot shield. William Pepe was photographed inside the building. The duo were arrested earlier on federal charges including illegally entering a restricted building. The indictment noted "the object of the conspiracy was to obstruct, influence, impede and interfere with law enforcement officers engaged in their official duties in protecting the U.S. Capitol and its grounds." As of January 30, federal authorities had charged more than 150 people.

During the U.S. Senate impeachment trial of former President Donald John Trump, House impeachment managers noted that the mob beat police officers; some had their eyes gouged. One officer lost three fingers. Rioters brought a gallows outside the Capitol, chanting, "Hang Mike Pence" and "Bring out Pence." At the end of February 12, the Senate unanimously awarded the Congressional Gold Medal to U.S. Capitol Police Officer Eugene Goodman, who directed the mob away from the Senate chamber and redirected Senator Mitt Romney (R-Utah) to safety. On February 13, the Senate failed, by a vote of 57-43, to convict Trump of inciting the insurrection.

The *Washington Post* and *USA Today* reported on March 16, 2021 that federal authorities arrested and charged Julian Elie Khater, 32, of State College, Pennsylvania and George Pierre Tanios, 39, of Morgantown, West Virginia, with assaulting U.S. Capitol Police officer Brian D. Sicknick, 42, with an unknown chemical spray during the January 6 Capitol riot. Officer Sicknick died on 9:30 a.m. a day after the riot. The duo, who were arrested on March 14, grew up together in New Jersey. In a video recorded at 2:14 p.m. during the assault, Khater said to Tanios, "Give me that bear sh--". Arrest papers allege that nine minutes later, after Khater said he had been sprayed with something, Khater was seen on video discharging a canister of a toxic substance into the face of Sicknick and two other officers. The duo were each charged with nine counts, including assaulting three officers with a deadly weapon—Sicknick, U.S. Capitol Police officer C. Edwards and D.C. police officer B. Chapman—civil disorder and obstruction of a congressional proceeding. They faced 20 years in prison and a $250,000 fine.

CNN reported on April 16, 2021 that Jon Ryan Schaffer, 53, who was believed to have had ties with the Oath Keepers, became the first pro-Trump rioter to plead guilty to charges stemming from the U.S. Capitol insurrection. Schaffer pleaded guilty to obstruction of an official proceeding during the formal certification of the Electoral College votes and entering a building with a dangerous weapon (bear spray). Prosecutors and defense attorneys recommended to federal Judge Amit Mehta that Schaffer get between 3.5 and 4.5 years in prison. He was initially charged with six federal crimes. Ryan was a rhythm guitarist and principal songwriter for the Florida-based heavy metal band Iced Earth.

The *Washington Post* reported on April 19, 2021 that District Chief Medical Examiner Francisco J. Diaz ruled that Capitol Police officer Brian D. Sicknick suffered two strokes and died of natural causes a day after he confronted rioters at the January 6 insurrection. The official cause was "acute brainstem and cerebellar infarcts due to acute basilar artery thrombosis". Two men—Julian Elie Khater, 32, of Pennsylvania, and George Pierre Tanios, 39, of West Virginia—were earlier accused of assaulting Sicknick by spraying a powerful chemical irritant at him during the siege; prosecutors did not link that action to Sicknick's death. They were both charged with nine counts, including three of assaulting an officer of the U.S. with a deadly weapon, conspiracy to injure an officer, and physical violence on restricted grounds. Each assault charge carried a 20-year prison sentence and a $250,000 fine. Tanios was represented by federal public defender Beth Gross. Diaz also found no evidence of internal or external injuries. Sicknick suffered two strokes at the base of the brain stem caused by a clot in an artery that supplies blood to that area of the body. He was sprayed with bear spray at 2:20 p.m., collapsed at 10 p.m., and died in a hospital at 9:30 p.m. the next day.

The *Washington Post* reported that on June 2, Tampa crane operator Paul Allard Hodgkins, 38, pleaded guilty to one felony count of obstructing Congress's joint session to confirm the 2020 presidential election results. He faced a 15-to-21-month recommended sentence under advisory federal guidelines. Sentencing was set for July 19.

On June 14, 2021, the *Washington Post* reported real estate agent Joshua Bustle, 35, and vaccine critic Jessica Bustle, 36, of Northern Virginia, became the first defendants to plead guilty to Class B misdemeanor charges in the Capitol riot. They accepted a federal criminal conviction, would pay $500 in restitution, and agreed to let a judge decide the possibility of prison time. Jessica Bustle was represented by attorney Nabeel Kibria; Joshua by Tim Anderson.

Some 480 defendants were federally charged in the riot.

Prosecutors logged $1.5 million in damages to the Capitol.

The *Florida Times-Union* on June 21, 2021 ran an extensive analysis of Floridians who were charged in the insurrection. It noted in passing:

- Some 472 people were arrested; 47 were from Florida. Texas also had 47 arrests; Pennsylvania was third with 44. The *Florida Times-Union* and *USA Today* reported on June 29 that Florida's arrest number had risen to 53, making it number one in the country.

- Florida had the most arrests of members of the Oath Keepers and Proud Boys.

- Nearly half of the arrested Oath Keepers were from Florida; a quarter of the Proud Boys arrestees were Floridians.

- Detainee occupations included firefighter, messianic rabbi, car dealership manag-

er, ride-share driver, nurse's assistant, small business owner, bail bondsman, corrections officer, child day care owner, chiropractor, vocal coach, and Circle K convenience store worker.

- Five served in the military.

- Two had run for office as Republicans—Jody Tagaris of Palm Beach and Miami Proud Boy Gabriel Garcia.

- Arrestees were from 24 of Florida's 67 counties. Marion County had the most arrests with four.

- Some 42 men and five women were arrested.

- Ages ranged from 21 to 67; most were in their 30s or 40s.

The U.S. Department of Justice listed the Florida-based arrestees as:

- Tristan Stevens, 25, Escambia County

- Jesus Rivera, 36, Escambia County

- Andrew Griswold, 28, Okaloosa County

- Bradley Weeks, 43, Baker County

- Jeffrey Register, 39, Jacksonville, Duval County

- Daniel Paul Gray, 41, Jacksonville, Duval County

- Adam Honeycutt, 39, Clay County

- Jonathan Carlton, 45, Union County

- Rachael Pert, 40, Clay County

- Dana Winn, 45, Clay County

- John Anderson, 61, St. Johns County

- Joseph Biggs, 37, Ormand Beach, Volusia County, a member of the Proud Boys. The Army veteran deployed twice to Iraq, earning two Purple Hearts. He worked for conservative media outlets such as *InfoWars*. His attorney said he suffered from "combat-related PTSD, depression, and some related alcohol problems."

- Kenneth Kelly, 58, Marion County

- Connie Meggs, 59, Dunnellon, Marion County, a member of the Oath Keepers

- Kelly Meggs, 52, Dunnellon, Marion County auto dealership manager, a member of the Oath Keepers
- Michael Curzio, 35, Marion County
- Howard Adams, 57, Volusia County
- Andrew Williams, Seminole County
- John Nassif, 54, Orange County
- Grady Owens, 21, Orange County
- Arthur Jackman, 30, Orange County, with a Proud Boys tattoo on his left wrist, is married to a sheriff's deputy.
- Kenneth Harrelson, 41, Titusville, Brevard County, a member of the Oath Keepers
- William Isaacs, 21, Kissimmee, Osceola County, a member of the Oath Keepers
- Audrey Southard-Rumsey, 52, Hernando County
- Steve Maldonado, 40, Brevard County
- Corrine Montoni, 31, Polk County
- Paul Hodgkins, 38, Hillsborough County
- Matthew Council, 49, Hillsborough County
- Michael Stepakoff, 55, Pinellas County
- Robert Palmer, 53, Pinellas County
- Paul Rae, 38, Largo, Pinellas County, a member of the Proud Boys
- Daniel "Milkshake" Scott, 28, Bradenton, Manatee County, with a Proud Boys arm tattoo, was charged with assaulting an officer. Video showed him pushing two Capitol police officers backward up a set of steps.
- Steve Maldonado, 40, Brevard County
- Anthony Mariotto, St. Lucie County
- Joseph Hackett, 50, Sarasota County chiropractor, a member of the Oath Keepers
- Graydon Young, 54, Englewood child daycare owner, a member of the Oath Keepers
- Christopher Worrell, 49, East Naples, Collier County, a member of the Proud Boys who was charged with assaulting an officer
- Vitali Gossjankowski, 31, Collier County

- Jason Dolan, 44, Wellington, Palm Beach County, a member of the Oath Keepers and former security guard at the Four Seasons Resort in Palm Beach
- Nicholes (sic) Lentz, 41, Palm Beach County
- Felipe Marquez, 25, Broward County
- Samuel Camargo, Broward County
- William Reid, 35, Miami-Dade County
- Richard Harris, Broward County
- Gabriel Garcia, 40, Miami-Dade County, a member of the Proud Boys

The June 29 report by *USA Today* and the *Florida Times-Union* listed six other arrestees:

- Jamie and Jennifer Buteau, Ocala QAnon adherents. Jamie was charged with assaulting a police officer.
- Brian Bingham, Port Charlotte, charged with assaulting a police officer.
- Jim Cusick, Jr., and his son, Casey Cusick, of Brevard County; they lead a church in Melbourne.
- David Lesperance, Brevard County, a member of the Cusicks' church

NBC News reported on June 23, 2021 that Anna Morgan-Lloyd, 49, from Indiana, pleaded guilty to a charge of illegally demonstrating in the Capitol building. As part of the plea deal, the government dropped three other misdemeanor charges. She had come to Washington with her hairdresser friend, Dona Sue Bissey, who also faced misdemeanor charges. Judge Royce Lamberth sentenced Morgan-Lloyd to three years of probation, and ordered her to perform 120 hours of community service and pay $500 in restitution. It was the first sentence related to the insurrection. Morgan-Lloyd said, "I would just like to apologize to the court, the American people, and my family… I went there to show support for President Trump peacefully, and I'm ashamed that it became a savage display of violence." She was represented by attorney Heather Shaner of Washington, D.C.

AP reported on June 24 that House Speaker Nancy Pelosi (D-Calif.) announced that House

Democrats would form a select committee to investigate the attack on the Capitol, one month after Senate Republicans blocked an effort to form an independent, bipartisan commission.

The *Washington Post* added on June 30 that the Department of Justice announced or unsealed 13 new arrests, including charges against alleged supporters of extremist right-wing groups including the Oath Keepers, Proud Boys, and Boogaloo Bois, and individuals accused of attacking the property of news media. Defendants included George Tenney, III, of Anderson, South Carolina, accused of being the first to open the east Capitol Rotunda doors from the inside, allowing the mob to enter. Tenney administers *Facebook*'s PowerHouse Patriot page.

Also charged were Gabriel Brown and Zvonimir Jurlina, both of Long Island, accused of destroying media equipment, and Army veteran Steven Thurlow from St. Clair Shores, Michigan, who allegedly posted images of himself in the Capitol and wearing a "Boogaloo" patch on social media. In 1988-1991, he served in the 101st Airborne Division.

Meanwhile, alleged Oath Keeper Mark Grods, 54, of Mobile, Alabama, reached an unexpected plea deal with prosecutors, admitting to two federal counts of conspiracy and aiding and abetting the obstruction of an official proceeding.

Defense lawyer Christopher DeLaughter said his client, Michael Perkins, 37, of greater Tampa, was accused of beating a police officer with a flagpole.

The *Washington Post* reported on July 4, 2021 that the Department of Justice began arresting individuals who attacked reporters or damaged their equipment as journalists documented the violence of the insurrection.

- On June 24, Shane Jason Woods, 43, of Illinois, was charged with engaging in violence on the Capitol grounds by knocking down a cameraman and assaulting a law enforcement officer.
- On June 28, the Department of Justice charged Sandra Pomeroy Weyer of Mechanicsburg, Pennsylvania, with disorderly conduct and trespassing after videos showed her egging on an attack on a *New York Times*

photographer inside the Capitol. Investigators said that a video showed her calling the photographer a traitor and urging others to "get her out" and "mace her".

- On June 28, authorities arrested Gabriel Brown and Zvonimir Joseph Jurlina for destroying media equipment. Jurlina posted a video in which he said: "Donald Trump, please pay for my legal fees because this all happened because of you … and I did nothing wrong."
- On June 30, authorities arrested Chase Kevin Allen, 25, of Seekonk, Massachusetts, for engaging in violence and destroying property on the grounds of the Capitol. FBI papers indicated that he was seen on video stomping on reporting equipment as a large group of individuals swarmed several reporters and drove them away.
- On July 1, the FBI arrested Joshua Dillon Haynes, of Covington, Virginia, for allegedly destroying journalists' equipment and bragging about it in a text to a friend. He became the fifth person arrested in connection with attacks on the media in roughly a week. Court papers indicated that he messaged, "We attacked the *CNN* reporters and the fake news and destroyed tens of thousands of dollars of their video and television equipment here's a picture behind me of the pile we made out of it."

The *Washington Post* reported on July 19 that U.S. District Judge Randolph D. Moss sentenced Tampa crane operator Paul Allard Hodgkins, 38, to eight months in prison. Hodgkins was the first person to be sentenced for a felony in the Capitol riot. He was represented by attorney Patrick Leduc, who noted that his client is an Eagle Scout who volunteered at a Tampa food bank. Hodgkins pleaded guilty in June to one count of obstructing a joint session of Congress meeting to confirm the results of the 2020 presidential election. He had carried a red-and-white "Trump 2020" flag into the well of the Senate. Judge Moss said, "The symbolism of that act was unmistakable… He was staking a claim on the floor of the U.S. Senate not with an American flag, but declaring his loyalty to a single individual over the nation. In that act, he captured the threat to democracy that we all witnessed that day… left a stain that will remain on our nation for decades… It means it will be harder for all of us to tell our children and grandchildren that democracy stands as the immutable foundation of our nation. It means we are all fearful of the next attack in a way we never were, and it makes us question whether our democracy is less secure than we believed just months ago." U.S. prosecutors had called for 18-month prison term. Special Assistant U.S. Attorney Mona Sedky said, "January 6 was genuinely an act of terrorism … The need to preserve respect for the law is really at its pinnacle in a crime like this."

The *Washington Post* reported on July 20 that Caleb Berry, 20, of Tampa, pleaded guilty to one count of conspiracy and one count of obstructing an official proceeding by joining a "stack formation" of Oath Keepers members and associates who breached the Capitol. He was the first among the formation to specify that he intended to hinder Congress that day using intimidation and coercion. Prosecutors agreed to request lowering an estimated prison term of 51 to 63 months. The case was heard by U.S. District Judge Amit P. Mehta. Two other Oath Keepers associates — Graydon P. Young, 55, of Florida, who also admitted being part of the "stack", and Mark Grods, 54, of Mobile, Alabama, who said he entered minutes later—had also pleaded guilty and agreed to testify against others. Berry was represented by attorney Daniel J. Fernandez of Tampa. Berry had been charged under seal on July 9.

On July 20, the *Washington Post* reported that probationary Drug Enforcement Administration special agent Mark Ibrahim, of Orange County, California, was arrested for trespassing with his government-issued firearm on the Capitol grounds and then lying about his actions. Prosecutors said he had falsely claimed he was there to help the FBI. He was represented by attorney Darren Richie.

Magistrate Judge G. Michael Harvey ruled that former Army Ranger Robert Morss was too dangerous to release. Court records indicated that Morss, a substitute social studies teacher from Shaner, Pennsylvania, and Afghanistan

veteran, wore body armor and carried a knife at the Capitol. Judge Harvey noted videos in which Morss directed others to use riot shields against police.

The U.S. House of Representatives panel investigating the insurrection began its first hearing on July 27, with testimony by four Metropolitan and Capitol Police officers—Aquilino Gonell, Michael Fanone, Daniel Hodges, Harry Dunn—about being electrocuted, tortured, beaten, being called "traitor" and "n----ger", bashed in the head with a weapon, and otherwise attacked by the Trump supporters.

The *New York Times* reported on August 1, 2021 that retired New York City police officer Thomas Webster turned himself in to the FBI on February 22. He was charged with assaulting police and carrying a dangerous weapon (a flagpole) onto Capitol grounds. He was denied bond. He was seen on video wearing body armor, grabbing a policeman's gas mask, choking him, and was given the hashtag #EyeGouger for his attack on a downed policeman.

The *Washington Post* and *AP* reported on August 7 that Scott Kevin Fairlamb, 44, the owner of Fairlamb Fit gym in Pompton Lakes, New Jersey and former mixed martial arts competitor of Sussex, New Jersey, and Devlyn D. Thompson, 28, of Puyallup, Washington, became the first people to plead guilty to assaulting police in the attack. Fairlamb admitted to shoving and punching a D.C. police officer, Z.B., yelling on video, "Are you an American? Act like it!" Fairlamb pleaded guilty to two of 12 indicted counts: assaulting an officer and obstructing an official proceeding of Congress. The first charge is punishable by up to eight years and the obstruction charge by 20 years. As part of the plea deal, prosecutors agreed to drop the other counts, which included rioting, trespassing, and violent disorder. Fairlamb's recommended sentencing range is 41 to 51 months in prison. Fairlamb, whose brother is a U.S. Secret Service agent, was arrested on January 22 at his home in Stockholm, New Jersey. He had prior convictions for illegal possession of a handgun and simple and aggravated assault. He was represented by attorney Harley Breite. Thompson admitted to using a baton to strike at an officer deploying pepper spray inside the archway and tunnel of the West Terrace's ceremonial entrance. Thompson admitted to being in the tunnel for 13 minutes, and left seven minutes before Capitol Police Officer Daniel Hodges was crushed in a doorway. Thompson surrendered to authorities via a lawyer in January and cooperated in three interview sessions with the FBI and U.S. prosecutors between February 2 and April 1. He apologized to D.C. police sergeant W.B. Thompson was represented by defense attorney Thomas Durkin. On July 11, prosecutors charged Thompson with one count (to which he pleaded guilty) of assaulting police with a dangerous weapon, punishable by up to 20 years. Thompson faced an advisory range of 46 to 57 months in prison. U.S. District Judge Royce C. Lamberth set their sentencing for September 27.

CNN reported on August 26 that attorneys for seven U.S. Capitol Police officers filed suit against former President Donald Trump, Stop the Steal rally organizers, and members of far-right extremist groups, including the Proud Boys and Oath Keepers, for spreading lies, using White supremacist sentiments to attempt to overthrow the 2020 election, and ultimately bearing responsibility for the riot that injured more than 140 officers. The 71-page lawsuit, filed in U.S. District Court for the District of Columbia, noted that "Plaintiffs and their fellow law enforcement officers risked their lives to defend the Capitol from a violent, mass attack—an attack provoked, aided, and joined by Defendants in an unlawful effort to use force, intimidation, and threats to prevent Congress from certifying the results of the 2020 Presidential election... Because of Defendants' unlawful actions, Plaintiffs were violently assaulted, spat on, tear-gassed, bear-sprayed, subjected to racial slurs and epithets, and put in fear for their lives... Plaintiffs' injuries, which Defendants caused, persist to this day." The defendants also "incited violence against members of Congress and the law enforcement officers whose job it was to protect them". A few days earlier, the U.S. Capitol Police's Office of Professional Responsibility determined that Capitol Police Lieutenant Michael Byrd, the officer who shot and killed pro-Trump rioter Ashli Babbitt on January 6, will not face

disciplinary action. His exclusive interview ran on *NBC Nightly News* on August 26.

CNN reported on September 11, 2021 that seven defendants pleaded guilty to charges related to the January 6 insurrection, including one man who threatened to shoot House Speaker Nancy Pelosi. A key defendant was Cleveland Meredith, Jr., who drove from Colorado to Washington, D.C., with two guns and 2,500 rounds of ammunition. He missed the January 6 incident because of car troubles. He texted a relative on January 7 that he was thinking about attending an event with Pelosi and "putting a bullet in her noggin on Live TV". He also texted that he was considering shooting the Washington, D.C. mayor and others. Meredith pleaded guilty in September to sending threatening communications and faced a five-year sentence. Sentencing was scheduled for December 2021.

CNN added on September 11, 2021 that the United States Capitol Police (USCP) announced that disciplinary action was recommended in six cases against officers following internal investigations into the attack. Violations included three cases for conduct unbecoming, one for failure to comply with directives, one for improper remarks, and one for improper dissemination of information.

The *Washington Post* reported on September 15, 2021 that 20-year Marine veteran and former marksmanship instructor Jason Dolan, 45, of Wellington, Florida, became the second defendant to plead guilty and agree to cooperate fully with prosecutors in hopes of reducing his prison term. He pleaded guilty to two federal counts of conspiracy and aiding and abetting the obstruction of Congress, felonies punishable by up to 20 years in prison. Both sides agreed that Dolan, who had no prior convictions, could face 63 to 78 months under advisory federal sentencing guidelines. The government agreed to request a lower term at sentencing in exchange for his "substantial assistance". He had been a security guard at the Four Seasons resort in Palm Beach. He was an alleged associate of the Oath Keepers extremist anti-government group. He admitted bringing a rifle to Washington with others in the group who were stashing weapons beforehand at a Ballston hotel in case a "Quick Reaction Force" was needed. He had been charged on May 27 with five counts, including rioting and destruction of federal property. Prosecutors agreed to dismiss the other three charges. Dolan was represented by attorneys Michael van der Veen—who represented Trump in his second impeachment trial—and Libbey Van Pelt. U.S. District Judge Amit P. Mehta in Washington accepted Dolan's plea, left him on conditional release, and gave prosecutors until December 17 to provide an update on the investigation and whether the case is ready for sentencing.

USA Today and the *Florida Times-Union* reported on September 29 that his attorney told the court that John Steven Anderson, 61, died on September 21, 2021 at Baptist Medical Center South in Jacksonville, Florida. He had been indicted and was awaiting trial on charges of civil disorder and assaulting or resisting officers. His obituary, posted by St. Johns Family Funeral Home and Crematory, noted that he started and ran Coastal Automotive and Diesel Service, Energy-Foam of North Florida, and EMP Provisions. He had received medical treatment at the U.S. Capitol for an asthma attack. He was born in Michigan and served in the Marines for four years. He had faced decades in prison.

On September 29, U.S. District Judge James Boasberg sentenced Ohioans Derek Jancart and Erik Rau to 45 days in jail. Prosecutors had asked for four months. Air Force veteran Jancart brought a gas mask and two-way radios to the riot. Steel mill worker Rau brought a medical kit and Kevlar-lined gloves.

On October 15, 2021, U.S. Capitol Police Officer Michael Angelo Riley, 50, a 25-year force veteran and canine officer, was charged with two counts of obstructing justice in the Capitol breach investigation after allegedly telling a riot participant to erase self-incriminating *Facebook* posts and then deleting his own messages with the man. He faced 20 years in prison. A federal court released him on personal recognizance on the condition he not contact certain people to be named by prosecutors. He was represented by defense attorney David Benowitz, who did not enter a plea. The next hearing was scheduled for October 26. The charge sheet said he emailed, "Hey [Person 1] im a capitol police officer who

agrees with your political stance. Take down the part about being in the building they are currently investigating and everyone who was in the building is going to charged. Just looking out!" *AP* reported that at least 49 defendants were accused of trying to erase incriminating photos, videos, and texts from social media and phones.

On October 15, 2021, Jeffrey Register, 39, of Fernandina Beach, Florida, pleaded guilty to parading, picketing, or demonstrating in the Capitol as part of a plea deal for prosecutors dropping other charges. Video showed him inside the Capitol, wearing a hoodie with "God, Guns and Trump" on the back. Sentencing was scheduled for January 18, 2022. He faced six months behind bars.

The *Washington Post* reported on October 21 that U.S. District Judge Tanya S. Chutkan of Washington sentenced Troy Smocks, 59, of Dallas, Texas to 14 months in prison after pleading guilty to a felony count of making an interstate threat based on social media posts from his Washington hotel room on January 6 and 7. He posted on *Parler* as ColonelTPerez on January 7 that was viewed at least 54,000 times: "Prepare our weapons, and then go get'em. Lets hunt these cowards down like the Traitors that each of them are. This includes RINOS, Dems, and Tech Execs. We now have the green light." Prosecutors and defense attorneys had requested a time-served sentence at the low end of eight to 14 months recommended by federal guidelines. The judge noted that Smocks had 17 convictions since age 18, many of them involving deception or fraud and the impersonation of the military or police.

The *Washington Post* and *BuzzFeedNews* reported on November 3, 2021 that seven people who attended the pro-Trump rally on January 6 that preceded the attack on the U.S. Capitol were elected to public office. Thirteen Republicans who traveled to D.C. to protest the results of the 2020 election had run for office. None were charged with crimes, and all denied being part of the pro-Trump mob that attacked the Capitol. *HuffPost* reported that Dave LaRock, John McGuire, and Marie March were elected to the Virginia House of Delegates. Philip Hamilton and Maureen Brody lost their races for the

Virginia House of Delegates. Other winners included Christine Ead for the Watchung, N.J., city council; Natalie Jangula for the city council in Nampa, Idaho; Matthew Lynch for the local school committee in Braintree, Massachusetts; and Susan Soloway for reelection to the board of directors in Hunterdon County, New Jersey.

UPI and the *Washington Post* reported on November 8 that Evan Neumann, wanted by the FBI for violent entry and disorderly conduct on the Capitol grounds; assaulting, resisting, and obstructing law enforcement during civil disorder; and other charges, appeared to be seeking asylum in Belarus, according to its state-run news media. He said that he "lost almost everything and is being persecuted by the U.S. government" after he "sought justice and asked uncomfortable questions" about the election. He claimed he had stayed in the Ukraine until security service agents started following him and he escaped to Belarus, where Belarusian border guards detained him on August 15. He sold his Mill Valley, California home in April for $1.3 million after charges were filed against him.

The *Washington Post* reported on November 10 that federal Judge Royce Lamberth sentenced Sussex, New Jersey gym owner Scott Kevin Fairlamb, 44, who punched a D.C. police officer, Z.B., during the riot, to 41 months in prison. Judge Lamberth called Fairlamb's actions "an affront to society and to the law" and said he was smart to plead guilty rather than take his chances with a jury that would see numerous videos of his actions. Fairlamb trained as a mixed martial arts fighter. The bar bouncer in New Jersey had two prior assault convictions. Fairlamb was the third felon to be sentenced. Prosecutors had played videos of Fairlamb assaulting the D.C. police officer and shouting at him, "Are you an American? Act like ... one. You guys have no idea what the ... you're doing!" He was represented by attorney Harley Breite. Fairlamb pleaded guilty in August to assaulting an officer and obstructing an official proceeding of Congress. He was ordered to pay $2,000 in restitution for damages to the building.

On November 12, a grand jury in Washington, D.C. charged former White House adviser Stephen K. Bannon, 67, with two counts of contempt of Congress after refusing to comply with a September 23 subpoena from the House committee investigating the January 6 attack. Each misdemeanor charge carried a one-year maximum sentence and $1,000 fine. Bannon surrendered to authorities on November 15.

On November 17, the *Washington Post* reported that U.S. District Judge Royce Lamberth sentenced Jacob Chansley, 34, self-described QAnon Shaman, to 41 months in prison. Chansley was represented by attorney Albert S. Watkins, who argued that a psychological evaluation earlier this year found that his client suffered from schizotypal personality disorder, anxiety, and depression.

On December 14, *CNN* reported Judge Amy Berman Jackson sentenced Meredith, a QAnon believer from Georgia, to 28 months in prison. He was given credit for 11 months time served.

The *Washington Post* reported on December 17, 2021 that U.S. District Judge Tanya S. Chutkan sentenced Robert S. Palmer, 54, of Largo, Florida, to 63 months in federal prison for attacking police with a fire extinguisher, a plank, and a long pole. He had pleaded guilty in October to assaulting law enforcement officers with a dangerous weapon.

On December 20, 2021, *CNN* reported that Judge Royce Lamberth of the federal district court in Washington, D.C. sentenced Devlyn Thompson of Washington State to 46 months in jail for assaulting a police officer with a dangerous weapon in a tunnel at the U.S. Capitol. Court documents noted that he helped move police shields up a line of rioters in the tunnel, attempted to throw a speaker at police officers but hitting and injuring a fellow rioter and hitting a police officer in the hand with a metal baton. Thompson pleaded guilty earlier.

Scott Fairlamb received 41 months for punching an officer.

CNN reported on December 21, 2021 that Judge Royce Lamberth, 78, of the federal district court in Washington, D.C. sentenced Army veteran Gary Wickersham, 81, to three years of probation, 90 days of home detention, and payment of a $2,000 fine and $500 for damage done to the building when he illegally breached the Capitol.

AP reported on December 22 that Matthew Greene, 34, a New York man who was a member of the Proud Boys, pleaded guilty to obstructing Congress and conspiring to obstruct law enforcement. He admitted coordinating with other members of the extremist group at the front of the Capitol mob. Greene agreed to pay a $2,000 fine. Sentencing was scheduled for March 10, 2022. He was represented by defense attorney Michael Kasmarek. Greene served in Afghanistan with the National Guard and works in graphic design. He had no prior criminal history.

January 12, 2021: The FBI issued a warning that armed far-right extremist groups planned to march on all 50 state capitals during the upcoming weekend. *ABC News* reported that courthouses and administrative buildings were also potential targets. On January 13, the *Washingtonian* reported that there were more U.S. troops protecting the U.S. Capitol than were in Afghanistan or Iraq.

January 15, 2021: The *Washington Post* and *New York Times* reported that Capitol Police arrested Wesley Allen Beeler, 31, of Front Royal, Virginia after finding a firearm and 509 rounds of ammunition, including hollow-point bullets, in his Ford F-150 truck as he tried to enter an inauguration security checkpoint on E Street Northeast near the Capitol during the evening with an unauthorized credential. He faced charges of carrying a pistol without a license, possession of an unregistered firearm, and possession of unregistered ammunition. He had told his mother that he was helping secure downtown Washington; his parents said he worked in private security. He had a badge from MVP Protective Services. He appeared in D.C. Superior Court the next day, and was ordered released on personal recognizance. The judge issued a stay-away order from the District, able to return only to appear in court or meet with his lawyer. Police noted that bumper stickers on the truck's windows included "Assault Life" and "If they come for your guns giv 'em your bullets first." He admitted to having a 9mm Glock in the center armrest. The Glock was loaded with a high-capacity magazine and 17 rounds of ammunition, including one round chambered and ready to fire. Court documents indicated that 21 shotgun shells were "located in plain sight in the rear cargo area of the vehicle". "I pulled up to a checkpoint after getting lost in D.C. because I'm a country boy," he said. "I showed them the inauguration badge that was given to me."

January 19, 2021: *CNN* reported that authorities in Georgia arrested Army Private Cole Bridges, 20, of Stow, Ohio, on terrorism charges after federal prosecutors said he allegedly attempted to assist ISIS efforts to plan attacks on targets in New York City and on U.S. soldiers in the Middle East. He was charged with one count of attempting to provide material support to ISIS and one count of attempting to murder U.S. military service members. Each charge carries a 20-year prison term. He was based at Fort Stewart. Prosecutors alleged that in October 2020, Bridges began communicating with an FBI covert employee online who was posing as an ISIS supporter in contact with ISIS fighters in the Middle East. Prosecutors alleged that he provided training and guidance to purported ISIS fighters, as well as advice about possible targets in New York City, such as the 9/11 Memorial. He allegedly gave the FBI employee portions of a U.S. Army training manual and "guidance about military combat tactics, for use by ISIS". In December 2020, Bridges began supplying the covert FBI employee with "instructions for the purported ISIS fighters on how to attack U.S. forces in the Middle East", such as diagramming specific military maneuvers to help ISIS fighters "maximize the lethality of attacks on US troops", which included advice on fortifying an ISIS encampment by wiring certain buildings with explosives to kill American troops. Manhattan U.S. Attorney Audrey Strauss said, "Cole Bridges betrayed the oath he swore to defend the United States by attempting to provide ISIS with tactical military advice to ambush and kill his fellow service members... Our troops risk their lives for our country, but they should never face such peril at the hands of one of their own."

January 22, 2021: *CNN* reported that police responded at 1 a.m. to a report of vandalism and an explosion at the First Works Baptist Church in El Monte in the San Gabriel Valley of Los Angeles County, California. El Monte Police Department Lt. Christopher Cano explained that smoke was coming out of the church's window, which apparently was blown out by the explosion. No injuries were reported. Obscenities and the words "get out" had been spray-painted on the front of the church. The FBI Los Angeles field office, El Monte police, and the Los Angeles County Sheriff's Department investigated a suspected improvised explosive device attack. *KCAL* reported that the self-described "independent, fundamental" Baptist church, part of the New Independent Fundamental Baptist Movement, which calls for police to round up and execute gays, had attracted local protests against its condemnation of same-sex relationships. Its website noted, "We believe that homosexuality is a sin and an abomination which God punishes with the death penalty." The *New York Times* reported that it had also railed against women, Jews, and the Black Lives Matter movement.

January 26, 2021: The *Washington Post* reported that federal prosecutors charged that Ian Benjamin Rogers, 44, of Napa, California, who had believed that Donald Trump had won the November 2020 election, built pipe bombs and planned to go to "war" against Democrats and others to keep him in power. Rogers was arrested on January 15, 2021 on state charges after Napa County authorities and the FBI searched his home and business and found 49 guns and five pipe bombs. He was held on $5 million bail on the state charges. Rogers claimed the bombs were for entertainment. The FBI also found a U.S. Army Special Forces Guide to Unconventional Warfare, and a U.S. Army Guerrilla Warfare Handbook, plus a gag "White Privilege Card" with allusions to Trump. His vehicle had a sticker associated with the Three Percenters, a group that holds anti-government and pro-gun beliefs and whose name is a reference to the incorrect belief regarding the number of American colonists who fought against the British during the American Revolution. He was represented by attorney Jess Raphael, who said that Rogers was betrayed by a September 2020 letter from Mr. X, who had been fired from Rogers's British marque auto repair shop.

On July 15, 2021, federal prosecutors in San Francisco federal court charged Rogers, now 45, and Jarrod Copeland, 37, of Vallejo, California, with conspiracy to destroy by fire or explosive a building used in or affecting interstate commerce by plotting to use incendiaries against the John L. Burton Democratic Party Headquarters in Sacramento, which was to be the first in a series of politically-motivated attacks. The duo used several messaging apps. Rogers was also charged with one count of possession of unregistered destructive devices and three counts of possession of machine guns. Copeland was also charged with one count of destruction of records. Authorities arrested Copeland on July 14, 2021. The duo faced 20 years in prison.

January 27, 2021: *Voice of America* reported that the Department of Homeland Security issued a National Terrorism Advisory System (NTAS) Bulletin, cautioning that a "heightened threat environment" was likely to persist through April. The Bulletin added, "Violent riots have continued in recent days and we remain concerned that individuals frustrated with the exercise of governmental authority and the presidential transition, as well as other perceived grievances and ideological causes … could continue to mobilize." DHS suggested that violent domestic extremists "may be emboldened by the Jan. 6, 2021, breach of the U.S. Capitol in Washington, D.C., to target elected officials and government facilities". However, DHS "does not have any information to indicate a specific, credible plot".

January 29, 2021: The *Daily Mail* reported that at 1:10 a.m. U.S. Customs and Border Protection agents assigned to the El Centro Station in the Calexico area of California arrested an unarmed Yemeni man, 33, on the terrorist watch list who illegally entered the U.S. about three miles west from the Calexico Port of Entry at the Mexican border. He had a cellular phone sim card hidden inside the insole of his shoe.

February 5, 2021: *CNN* reported that a computer hacker got inside the water treatment system of Oldsmar, Florida and tried to increase the levels of sodium hydroxide—lye—in the city's water. Pinellas County Sheriff Bob Gualtieri said an operator noticed the intrusion and watched the hacker access the system remotely, adjusting the level of sodium hydroxide to more than 100 times its normal levels, putting thousands at risk of being poisoned. He added that the operator immediately reduced the level back and the public was never in danger. Authorities had not determined whether the intrusion was by an individual in the area, in the U.S., or from overseas. The University of Florida Health System reported that symptoms of sodium hydroxide poisoning include breathing difficulties, lung inflammation, throat swelling, burning of the esophagus and stomach, severe abdominal pain, vision loss, and low blood pressure. *Al-Jazeera* and *AFP* added on February 8 that the intruder was in the TeamViewer software system for three to five minutes.

March 2, 2021: In testimony before the Senate Judiciary Committee, FBI Director Christopher A. Wray said the Bureau had 2,000 ongoing investigations against domestic terrorists. The *Washington Post* reported that Director Wray added that the FBI had sent a warning about a likely attack on the Capitol on January 6 in three ways—sent by email to the FBI's Joint Terrorism Task Force, which includes the D.C. and Capitol Police; posted on a law enforcement web portal; and mentioned in a command center briefing in D.C. He added, "We have not to date seen any evidence of anarchist violent extremists or people subscribing to antifa in connection with the 6th. That doesn't mean we're not looking and we'll continue to look. But at the moment, we have not seen that."

March 2, 2021: The *Washington Post* and the *Des Moines Register* reported that a special unit from the Iowa State Fire Marshal Division, along with agents from the Bureau of Alcohol, Tobacco, Firearms and Explosives and the FBI, disarmed a live pipe bomb at the Lakeside community center in Ankeny, Iowa where voting was taking place for a school district election. A pair of dog walkers had reported a suspicious-looking package in the parking lot around 9:30 a.m.

March 3, 2021: The *Washington Post* and *al-Jazeera* reported that the U.S. House of Representatives rescheduled a March 4 session to the evening of March 3 after security officials warned of a possible plot by right-wing extremists to breach the Capitol, find Democrats, and celebrate "true Inauguration Day" when former president Donald Trump would be sworn in for a second term.

March 16, 2021: *BBC, Reuters, CNN, USA Today*, and the *Florida Times-Union* reported that a gunman opened fire at three spas in Georgia, killing eight people, including six Asian women. Four people died at a massage parlor in Acworth, a suburb north of Atlanta; four more died at two Atlanta spas across the road from each other.

The first shooting occurred at 5 p.m. at Young's Asian Massage Parlor in Acworth, Cherokee County. Two died at the scene; three more were hospitalized—two of them soon died. Sheriff's office spokesman Captain Jay Baker said that the victims were two Asian women, a white woman, and a white man. The dead were identified as

- Delaina Ashley Yuan, variant Yaun, 33, of Acworth, was at the spa to get a couple's massage with her husband, who survived by locking himself in a room when gunfire broke out. She left behind a son, 13, and a daughter, 8 months. She and her husband wed in August 2020. Husband Mario Gonzalez said that he was held in handcuffs for four hours in a patrol car outside the spa. He suggested to *Mundo Hispanico* that he was held because he is Mexican.

- Paul Andre Michels, 54, of Atlanta, owned an alarm company and was interested in owning a spa. He and his wife, Bonnie, had lived in Atlanta for 26 years. He grew up with ten siblings in Detroit. He and his brother, John, served in the Army at the same time in the 1980s. Paul was with the infantry.

- Ziaojie Yan, variant Xiaojie Tan, often known as Emily, 49, of Kennesaw, owner of an LLC associated with Young's and another spa. She emigrated to the U.S. from the Nanning region of southern China about 20 years ago, according to ex-husband Jason Wang, 47. She had separated from her first husband, and met Wang in 2012. Tan owned Young's Nail Salon, where she met Wang. They married in 2013. In 2017, Tan opened Young's Asian Massage and Wang's Feet and Body Massage. Her adult daughter recently graduated from the University of Georgia. Tan was a naturalized U.S. citizen. Tan sent money to her family in China along with other gifts for her parents.

- Daoyou Peng, 44

WGCL reported that Elcias Hernandez-Ortiz, a Hispanic father with a daughter, Yoseline, 9, was shot in the forehead while on his way to a business next door to the spa. His wife Flora Gonzalez Gomez said the bullet traveled down into his lungs and into his stomach. He often sent money to family members back in San Marcos, Guatemala, where the couple was from. He came to the U.S. nearly a decade earlier. His wife and daughter joined him in Georgia in 2015.

At 6 p.m. and 30 miles away, the gunman fired at Gold Spa on Piedmont Road in northeast Atlanta, killing three women. Across the street, police found the body of another woman at Aromatherapy Spa. *CNN* and *AP* reported on March 19 that the Fulton County Medical Examiner identified the four Korean-origin women killed as:

- Soon Chung Park, 74, who died of a gunshot wound to the head, had moved more than 800 miles to Atlanta from her family in the New York/New Jersey area, according to the *Washington Post*. She helped manage one of the spas, cooking lunch and dinner for the employees. When she was younger, she was a dancer.

- Hyun Jung Grant, 51, a single mother who died of a gunshot wound to the head, left behind two children without other family members in the U.S., according to *CNN* and the *Washington Post*. Her son, Randy Park, 23, set up a GoFundMe page which raised more than $2.5 million from 67,000 donors within a day. He said the rest of the family was in South Korea. Park told *NBC News* that she worked so much that he and his brother, Eric, stayed with another family for a year. Randy Park and his brother were

raised in Seattle, later moving to Atlanta 13 years ago for more opportunities. She had worked as an elementary school teacher in South Korea, according to the *Daily Beast*.

- Suncha Kim, 69, who died of a gunshot wound to the chest, did not speak English when she arrived in the U.S. in 1980, according to the *Washington Post*. She worked, including washing dishes at a restaurant at an army station in Texas, at a convenience store, at George Washington's Mount Vernon property, and cleaning office buildings. The naturalized U.S. citizen left behind two children, three grandchildren, and her husband of more than 50 years. Her mother died when she was in middle school in Korea, leaving her to care for three younger sisters and her father, who worked in local government. While in her 20s, she married a Korean man; they had a daughter and son. Around 1980, she and her son moved to the United States; her husband and daughter arrived a few years later. Kim was Catholic, and she volunteered by cooking and fundraising for various organizations, such as the Global Children Foundation, a nonprofit established in 1998 after the economic crisis in South Korea to help children going hungry due to their families' financial hardship. The organization later expanded to help children around the world. She was given the President's Volunteer Service Award during President Barack Obama's term for the volunteer work she did in the D.C. area to help feed the homeless. Her granddaughter set up a GoFundMe page to raise money for her funeral and a memorial.

- Yong A. Yue, 63, who died of a gunshot wound to the head, died across the street from Gold Spa at the Aromatherapy Spa after she opened the door reportedly believing the shooter might be a customer, according to the *Washington Post*. One son, Robert Peterson, 38, told the *Atlanta Journal-Constitution* that she lost her job during the pandemic. She had come to Georgia in the 1980s after meeting his father, an American soldier.

South Korean Foreign Minister Chung Eui-yong said four of the victims were women of Korean descent. Police said two others were of Asian descent.

At least four of the Asian-origin victims had become U.S. citizens. Two divorced their American husbands. Two were grandmothers.

Acting on the family's identification of a suspect on CCTV footage, police arrested Robert Aaron Long, 21, of Woodstock, Georgia, 150 miles away in Crisp County, apparently en route to continue his attacks in Florida. Although the media was quick to point out that the country had experienced thousands of anti-Asian racist attacks, blaming Asians for the coronavirus pandemic, Long said that he was motivated by "sex addiction" and was trying to remove the spas as a source of temptation. Police suggested that he had earlier frequented the businesses. Long was charged with four counts of murder and one count of assault in Cherokee County and four counts of murder in Atlanta.

The *Atlanta Journal-Constitution* reported that Long had legally purchased a firearm from Big Woods Goods in Holly Springs, Georgia that day.

The *Washington Post* reported on March 20 that Long graduated from Sequoyah High School in Canton, Georgia in 2017. He was raised in a one-story gray ranch-style house in the woods of Woodstock, 30 miles north of downtown Atlanta. Real estate records showed that his parents, Robert and Diane Long, bought the home in 2002 for $127,500. Hobbies included drumming, reading the Bible, and participating in a Christian student club. He also hunted deer, played video games, and traveled with the youth group at Crabapple First Baptist Church in Woodstock, Georgia. He was involved with outreach to younger children and took summer mission trips to Costa Rica, Pittsburgh, and Brunswick, Georgia. He left the University of North Georgia campus in Cumming after a year. His girlfriend ended their relationship over his visits to massage parlors. His parents threw him out of the house the night before the attacks. Video showed that he entered the first massage parlor an hour before he opened fire.

The evangelical congregation's minister, the Rev. Jerry Dockery, preached a socially conservative brand of Christianity that, per church bylaws, views "adultery, fornication, homosexuality, bisexual conduct, bestiality, incest, polygamy, pedophilia, pornography, or any attempt to change one's sex, or disagreement with one's biological sex" as "sinful and offensive to God". The *Washington Post* reported on March 22 that the conservative Baptist church expelled Long from its congregation because he is no longer considered a "regenerate believer in Jesus Christ".

In August 2019, Long lived for six months at Maverick Recovery, a 12-step transitional-housing facility in Roswell, Georgia, but also frequented massage parlors, including the ones he attacked. He later moved on to an intensive inpatient addiction facility, HopeQuest Ministry Group, which uses counseling "integrated with Christian principles". HopeQuest is a mile from Young's Asian Massage.

Robert Aaron Long, 21, pleaded guilty on July 27, 2021 to four murder charges in Cherokee County and faced four consecutive life sentences without the possibility of parole. He faced four additional murder charges in Fulton County, where the prosecutor was seeking the death penalty.

March 17, 2021: *CNN* reported that at 12:12 p.m., U.S. Secret Service Uniformed Division officers arrested Paul Murray, 31, of San Antonio, Texas, outside Vice President Kamala Harris's official residence, the U.S. Naval Observatory on the 3400 block of Massachusetts Avenue, NW on weapons and ammunition charges. Washington Metropolitan Police found an AR-15 semi-automatic rifle, 113 rounds of unregistered ammunition, and five 30-round magazines in his vehicle. He was charged with carrying a dangerous weapon, carrying a rifle or shotgun outside of a business, possession of unregistered ammunition, and possession of a large capacity ammunition feeding device.

March 21, 2021: *USA Today* reported that the Office of the Director of National Intelligence assessed that domestic terrorists "will almost certainly" try to attack again during 2021.

March 22, 2021: *AP, CNN, al-Jazeera*, the *Washington Post*, and *BBC* reported that police said Ahmad al-Aliwi Alissa, 21, from the Denver suburb of Arvada, shot at shoppers with an AR-15 pistol inside a crowded King Soopers supermarket in a busy shopping plaza in southern Boulder, Colorado, killing ten people, including an officer. The gunman engaged in a shootout with police, who shot him in the leg, arrested him, and brought him to a local hospital. He was charged with ten counts of first-degree murder. Boulder County District Attorney Michael Dougherty said authorities believed he was the only shooter. *USA Today* reported that Alissa was held without bail pending an assessment "to address his mental illness". He was represented by attorney Kathryn Herold, who requested that the next hearing be delayed for two months. Authorities said he had passed a background check by the Colorado Bureau of Investigation before he purchased the firearm at the Eagles Nest Armory gun store in Arvada six days before the attack. He did not use a second weapon he had at the scene. Alissa faced life in prison; Colorado had abolished the death penalty in 2020. He reportedly was not talking with police. A defense attorney said he had an unspecified mental illness. Ali Alissa, his brother, said Ahmad was paranoid and believed he was being watched and followed.

The *Florida Times-Union* reported that supermarket employees said Alissa shot an elderly man several times outside the store before going inside. Another person was shot in a vehicle next to a car registered to Alissa's brother.

The dead included:

- Tralona Bartkowika, 49, known to her friends as Lonna, ran the Boulder clothing shop Umba Love, which she and her sister, Lisa, founded after a trip to Bali. They sold clothing at music venues, festivals, and local fairs. She was engaged. She took Zumba and Middle Eastern dance classes. Umba dedicated its profits to an organic farm in Oregon.

- Suzanne Fountain, 59, a community actress who worked for many years as the front house manager at eTown Hall, a Boulder music venue.

- Teri Leiker, 51, had worked King Soopers for 30 years, and was dating a colleague since 2019. He survived. A friend said she may have gotten her job through a program for people with special needs; she met several friends through Best Buddies. She enjoyed attending sporting events and singing "Frozen" songs.

- Kevin Mahoney, 61, died while shopping in his home town. His daughter, Erika Mahoney, was pregnant with his granddaughter.

- Lynn Murray, 62, from Ohio, a former photo editor/producer for Condé Nast and Hearst. She supervised shoots for the nation's top fashion magazines, including *Cosmopolitan* and *Marie Claire*, before she left to raise her children. She befriended New York's "Soup Nazi", subject of a "Seinfeld" episode. She left behind a husband, John R. Mackenzie, 59, and two children, Pierce and Olivia. The couple met at a photography studio in the late 1980s while she was supervising a shoot involving French photographer Jacques Malignon and Mackenzie was working for an apparel firm. They dined with their friend, the late Anthony Bourdain. The couple wed in 1995 in Mauritius and moved to Long Island and later to Florida, where Murray quit her job to devote herself to parenting. They moved to Colorado to be near Olivia.

- Rikki Olds, 25, was a manager for King Soopers. She attended Centaurus High School in Lafayette, Colorado, and attended Front Range Community College. Her grandparents raised her. She left behind a boyfriend, Jordan Arthur. She had worked for Kroger grocery stores for six years. She died on her grandmother's birthday.

- Neven Stanisic, 23, was viewed as a role model by members of St. John the Baptist Serbian Orthodox Church in Lakewood, west of Denver. His family fled the war in Bosnia in the 1990s, leaving everything behind. He worked a teenager, helping to support his family. He was fixing the coffee machines inside King Soopers when the shooting began.

- Denny Strong, 20, lived in Boulder and was training to become a professional pilot. He started work at King Soopers in December 2018 to earn money for airplane fuel. He was stocking shelves when he died. He said on *Facebook* that he was a fan of old muscle cars, motorcycles, dirt bikes, airplanes, and Pink Floyd. He participated in the 77-member Boulder Aeromodeling Society; members design, build, and fly model aircraft. On March 8, he asked people to celebrate his birthday by donating to the National Foundation for Gun Rights, which its website says works "to expand pro-gun precedents and defend gun owners".

- Police officer Eric Talley, 51, joined the force in 2010 at age 40, moving from an IT job. He was the first to respond to a call about shots fired and someone carrying a rifle. Talley was the father of seven children. Fellow officers recalled that when one of his children swallowed a coin, another performed CPR after learning the technique from his dad. The Boulder Police Department gave the child a Life Saver award. In 2013, the *Boulder Daily Camera* newspaper reported that Talley and other officers waded out into knee-deep cold water to save ducklings caught in a drainage ditch. He was learning to be a police drone operator. He had earned a black belt in karate.

- Jody Waters, 65, loved working in retail. She brought Beanie Babies to Boulder when she co-owned the Applause boutique in Boulder's downtown Pearl Street Mall pedestrian district, in the 1990s. She worked for six years at the Island Farm clothing store before recently taking time off to care for her new grandson. The *Denver Business Journal* published a feature on her boutique to mark Applause's 20th anniversary in 1999.

An assault weapons ban in Boulder, aimed at halting mass shootings, was blocked ten days earlier.

The *New York Times* reported on March 28 that the Alissa family had left Syria two decades earlier, settling in the Rocky Mountains and opening the Sultan Grill restaurant, where he worked. The family also opened the Amir Grill in Golden, Colorado. The King Soopers was 15 miles from their home in the Westwoods subdivision of Arvada. He had posted on *Facebook* that he moved to the United States in 2002. His family said they had lived in Aleppo and Raqqa. Ahmad had six siblings. Some of his older brothers had driven food trucks, which later became restaurants. They had also worked in a car service business and junk removal.

Ahmad had initially attended Denver South High School, but when the family moved, he finished at Arvada West High School, joining the wrestling team and practicing martial arts. He was bullied early on, developing a temper. As a senior in November 2017, he pummeled a bully without warning after being called a "terrorist". He was suspended from school for two weeks, and pleaded guilty to misdemeanor assault. He was sentenced to a year of probation and 48 hours of community service. By the time of the shooting, he was obese. Police dragged him out of the store shirtless.

On March 16, Alissa bought a Ruger AR-556 pistol from a gun store three miles from his home.

CNN reported on April 22, 2021 that Boulder County District Attorney Michael Dougherty amended the criminal complaint and filed 43 more charges against Alissa, including 32 additional counts of attempted murder, one count of first-degree assault, and ten counts of unlawful possession of a large-capacity magazine during the commission of a crime. The next court hearing was scheduled for May 25.

March 24, 2021: *Newsweek* reported that authorities arrested Benjamin Carpenter, alias Abu Hamza, 31, of Knoxville, Tennessee, for making English translations of propaganda for ISIS. On April 5, a federal grand jury indicted Carpenter for allegedly leading *Ahlut-Tawhid Publications*, an international organization that translates and publishes ISIS and pro-ISIS materials, and that he shared some translated materials with an undercover FBI agent posing as an ISIS affiliate. Carpenter's trial was scheduled to begin on June 1. He faced up to 20 years in prison.

March 26, 2021: The *Washington Examiner* reported that the Department of Justice announced that Mariam Taha Thompson, 63, a female linguist who worked for a U.S. Special Operations Task Force in Erbil, Iraq, pleaded guilty to handing over classified information about on-the-ground human sources who were assisting the United States to a Hizballah-linked foreign national with whom she was romantically linked. Authorities arrested her in February 2020. She was charged in May 2020 in a federal court with "transmitting highly sensitive classified national defense information to a foreign national". The DOJ said she provided her co-conspirator with the identities of at least 10 clandestine human assets, including their true names and photographs as well as cables showing the intelligence these assets provided to the U.S., and at least 20 U.S. targets. Thompson signed an extensive statement of facts in late January 2021 admitting to the plot. She faced life in prison.

During a February 2020 search of her residence, the FBI found a handwritten note in Arabic concealed under Thompson's mattress which contained classified information from Pentagon computers, naming assets, and warning a "target who is affiliated with a designated foreign terrorist organization with ties to Hezbollah".

On June 23, 2021, the *Washington Post, UPI,* and *AP* reported that U.S. District Judge John D. Bates sentenced Thompson, of Rochester, Minnesota, to 23 years in prison for passing classified national defense information to a man that was linked to Lebanese Hizballah. On March 26, 2021, she had pleaded guilty to one count of delivering defense information classified at the secret level to aid a foreign government, which carries a maximum sentence of life imprisonment. She was born in Lebanon and became a naturalized U.S. citizen in 1993. A family member introduced her in 2017 to the man, whom she believed to be a wealthy, well-connected Lebanese national. They never met, but she agreed to marry him. She had worked as a linguist since 2006, was assigned to Erbil in mid-December 2019. The individual asked her to provide information on the human assets who helped the U.S. plan airstrikes, including the one that killed a Hizballah leader and Iranian IRGC general Soleimani. Prosecutors said she identified eight undercover human assets, including their real names and photographs, ten U.S. targets, and "multiple" tactics, techniques, and procedures human assets use to retrieve information for the United States. With good time credit and credit for time served, she could complete her term at age 81.

March 30, 2021: The *Washington Post* reported that Judge J. Harvie Wilkinson, III, writing for a three-judge panel of the U.S. Court of Appeals for the 4th Circuit, upheld the constitutionality of the FBI Terrorist Screening Database watch list of more than 1 million "known or suspected terrorists", holding that it falls under the government's power to guard its borders. Gadeir Abbas, an attorney with the Council on American-Islamic Relations, said the group would appeal to the full 4th Circuit.

The *Daily Mail* reported that at 11:30 p.m., U.S. Customs and Border Protection agents assigned to the El Centro Station in the Calexico area of California arrested an unarmed Yemeni man, 26, on the terrorist watch list and a no-fly list who illegally entered the U.S. at the Mexican border.

March 31, 2021: *CNN* reported that the New York Police Department Hate Crime Task Force and the Manhattan DA's Hate Crimes Unit were investigating an attack on a Jewish family in Manhattan. An attacker with a knife slashed a man, woman, and their 1-year-old child who was in a stroller. Although the family was wearing traditional Hasidic garb, no anti-Semitic slurs were heard during the attack. Police arrested Darryl Jones, 30, who was charged by the Manhattan District Attorney's office with one count of attempted murder, three counts of assault in the second degree, three counts of attempted assault, endangering the welfare of a child, and criminal possession of a controlled substance in the seventh degree. Jones was paroled in February 2021 after a seven-year period of incarceration for attempted murder. He was represented by attorney Edward McGowan.

March 31, 2021: *Newsweek* reported that the FBI arrested James Bradley, alias Abdullah, 20, of the Bronx, New York, and his wife, Arwa Muthama, 29, of Hoover, Alabama, at a New Jersey seaport while attempting to travel to Yemen via cargo ship to join and fight for ISIS. If they could not make the trip, they allegedly planned to attack military cadets at West Point and another area university where Bradley knew military recruits trained. The duo appeared before U.S. Magistrate Judge Debra Freeman in Manhattan federal court on April 1. The Department of Justice complaint said Bradley had confided in and planned their journey with an undercover officer. He told the officer that he might be on a terrorism watch list. The duo were charged with one count of attempting to provide material support to a designated foreign terrorist organization, and one count of conspiring to provide material support to a designated foreign terrorist organization. Both counts carry 20-year sentences. The couple wed in an Islamic marriage ceremony in January 2021. Bradley told a second undercover officer that in a dream he gave "bay'ah," Arabic for oath of allegiance, to ISIS leader Abu Ibrahim al-Hashimi al-Qurashi. Upon arrest, Muthana waived her Miranda rights and said during an interview that she was willing to fight and kill Americans for Allah.

April 2, 2021: The *Washington Post* and *CNN* reported that at 1 p.m., Noah Green, 25, of Virginia, rammed his dark blue Nissan sedan into Capitol Police officers on Constitution Avenue at the North Barricade of the U.S. Capitol, killing 18-year veteran officer William F. "Billy" Evans, and wounding a second officer. Green wielded a wood-handled knife and lunged at other police, who shot him to death. *AP* added that the attack occurred 100 yards from the Senate entrance to the building. Green was not known to either D.C. or Capitol Police. Acting D.C. police chief Robert J. Contee, III said, "It does not appear to be terrorism related," although Green's motive was unknown. Evans was a member of the US-CP's First Responders Unit. *Al-Jazeera* reported on April 6, 2021 that Evans's body would lie in honor in the Capitol Rotunda on April 13. Evans was the father of two children, Logan and Abigail. Investigators determined that Green had been experiencing delusions, hallucinations, heart palpitations, headaches, paranoia, and suicidal thoughts. He had posted that he was under

government thought control and being watched. He claimed to be a follower of the Nation of Islam and its longtime leader, Louis Farrakhan. He donated $1,085 to the Nation of Islam's Norfolk chapter for Saviours' Day, the birthday of the group's founder.

USA Today and the *New York Times* reported that West Virginia-born Green grew up in Covington, Virginia with nine siblings. He played basketball, ran track, and was named Alleghany High School's most valuable football player. After studying at Glenville State College in West Virginia, he graduated as a business major in 2019 from Christopher Newport University, where he was #21, a defensive back. He had worked at the school's gym. Friends said he focused on Black economic empowerment and financial management. He lost a job during the pandemic. He had moved from Virginia to Indiana, later moving to Botswana, where he jumped in front of a car. In Indiana, he applied in December 2020 to legally change his name to Noah Zaeem Muhammad. He had earlier used the name Noah X. Family members speculated that his difficulties might have come from head injuries from playing football.

April 7, 2021: *AFP* reported that the U.S. Department of Justice announced that neo-Nazi leader Cameron Shea, 25, admitted to federal hate crimes charges for threatening journalists and activists campaigning against anti-Semitism. He was among four people arrested in early 2020 for conspiring in an encrypted online chat group to threaten reporters and advocates, mostly Jewish individuals or people of color. DOJ said the group "created posters, which featured Nazi symbols, masked figures with guns and Molotov cocktails, and threatening messages, to deliver or mail to the journalists or advocates the group targeted". Shea said he wanted a "show of force" from his Atomwaffen organization against the targets. One poster showed a Grim Reaper and a Molotov cocktail with the text: "Our Patience Has Its Limits... You have been visited by your local Nazis." Five others were charged in Alexandria, Virginia, for organizing "SWATting" attacks that falsely call police to target victims' homes. Shea admitted conspiracy and hate crimes charges in federal court in Washington

State. Sentencing was scheduled for June 28; he faced up to 15 years in prison. Roman Garza was given 16 months in prison and Taylor Ashley Parker-Dipeppe was sentenced to time served. Kaleb Cole pleaded not guilty; his trial was scheduled for September 2021.

April 8, 2021: The *Washingtonian* and *Patch.com* reported that a Department of Justice complaint indicated that the FBI, acting on a citizen tip, arrested Seth Aaron Pendley, 28, of Wichita Falls, Texas, after a confidential informant reported that in January Pendley had posted on MyMilitia.com about a "little experiment" that would to "kill off about 70% of the internet" by destroying an Amazon Web Services data center on Smith Switch Road in Ashburn, Virginia. Pendley used the screen alias Dionysus. Pendley exchanged emails with another informant regarding his plans. Pendley ordered a topological map of Virginia and painted his silver Pontiac black with Plasti Dip rubber, thinking that he could peel off the new color and elude police. In a March 31 meeting with the informant and an undercover FBI employee, Pendley described 24 buildings in an Amazon Web Services complex that he claimed accounted for "70 percent of the Internet", including CIA and FBI servers. "So we f*** those servers, and it's just gonna piss all the oligarchy off." Pendley claimed he was at the January 6, 2021 U.S. Capitol riot, but that he had left his sawed-off AR rifle in his car. Pendley was charged with a malicious attempt to destroy a building with an explosive. He faced 20 years in prison.

On April 8, the undercover FBI officer gave Pendley what he said were plastic explosives and detonation cord. DOJ noted that the substances were inert. The FBI arrested Pendley after he placed the materiel in his car. A search warrant led to investigators to maps, an AR "receiver" with the barrel sawed off, flashcards, notes, a pistol painted to look like a toy gun, and a machete with the name Dionysus on it.

April 23-25, 2021: *CNN* reported that six attacks were conducted against four separate Bronx synagogues over three days. NYPD Detective Francis Sammon said that the New York Police Department's Hate Crimes Task Force investigated four incidents as possible hate crimes. Two attacks occurred on April 23, three on April 24, one on April 25. Video surveillance suggested that the same person was involved in the attacks on the Conservative Synagogue Adath Israel of Riverdale, the Young Israel of Riverdale, Chabad Lubavitch of Riverdale (also known as Riverdale Jewish Synagogue), and the Riverdale Jewish Center. The Riverdale Jewish Center and Riverdale Jewish Synagogue were both attacked twice. Video showed an individual throwing rocks, breaking windows in doors, in the late night and early morning. No injuries were reported.

April 27, 2021: The *Washington Post* reported that Brendan Hunt, 37, a Trump supporter who called for killing members of Congress two days after the January 6 insurrection, was found guilty in U.S. District Court in Brooklyn of making a death threat against elected officials. The jury deliberated for three hours. He faced 10 years in prison. The jury held that menacing social media posts he made in 2020—including one directed at Sen. Charles E. Schumer (D-N.Y.), then the Senate minority leader, House Speaker Nancy Pelosi (D-Calif.), and Rep. Alexandria Ocasio-Cortez (D-N.Y.)—did not rise to the level of criminality. He was arrested on January 19 and charged with one count of making a threat to assault and murder a United States official. The FBI received a tip about his video, titled "KILL YOUR SENATORS: Slaughter them all.", which was posted on BitChute, a site popular with the far-right. He was represented by attorneys Jan Rostal and Leticia Olivera. U.S. District Court Judge Pamela Chen presided over the case involving the Fordham University graduate, former actor, and amateur documentarian who had an administrative job in the New York state court system. Assistant U.S. Attorney David Kessler noted that he had saved Internet memes with Nazi propaganda-like depictions of Jews that mocked the Holocaust. Hunt called immigrants "low I.Q. mongoloids". He sent a message to his cousin in December 2020 threatening to "stick a knife" in the relative's newborn baby after the cousin defriended Hunt on *Facebook*.

May 3, 2021: *CNN* reported that in the morning, an individual drove up to the gates of the Central

Intelligence Agency in McLean, Virginia and suggested that there was a bomb in the vehicle. After a day-long standoff, an FBI agent shot the individual at 6 p.m. after he emerged from his car with a weapon.

May 7, 2021: *CNN* reported that a ransomware attack forced Colonial Pipeline to shut down its 5,000 miles of fuel pipelines that daily transport more than 100 million gallons of gasoline and other fuel from Houston to New York City. As of May 11, operations were still suspended. The DarkSide Russian hacker consortium claimed it was just trying to make money, not aiming for social dislocation. Colonial restarted operations the evening of May 12. Panic buying had shuttered thousands of gas stations along the east coast; 74% of North Carolina gas stations reported having sold out. *NBC News* reported on May 13 that CP paid nearly $5 million in ransom.

May 13, 2021: The *Florida Times-Union* and *USA Today Network* reported that Romeo Xavier Langhorne, 31, of St. Augustine, Florida, pleaded guilty to attempting to provide material support and resources to ISIS. He faced 20 years in federal prison. He pledged his allegiance to ISIS in 2014, reaffirming his support in 2018 and 2019 on social media. He posted ISIS-produced videos to his *YouTube* account. Prosecutors said that in 2018-2019, he said he wanted to create a video showing how to make an explosive while on a chatroom. In February 2019, he started communicating with an undercover FBI agent posing as an ISIS operative. The FBI posted a fake explosives formula for him. Langhorne was arrested on November 15, 2019.

June 13, 2021: The *Washington Post* reported that a man crashed his car into a group of protestors in the Uptown neighborhood of Minneapolis at 11:30 p.m., killing Deona M. Knajdek, 31, and injuring three people. Demonstrators pulled him from his vehicle and police arrested him. Garrett Knajdek said, "She was using her car as a street blockade, and another vehicle struck her vehicle and her vehicle struck her." Deona left behind 11- and 13-year-old daughters.

June 16, 2021: *Newsweek* and the *New York Post* reported that Judge Sterling Johnson sentenced

Noelle Velentzas, 33, of Queens, New York to 198 months in federal prison for her role in a bomb-making plot and teaching other women bombmaking techniques. She had called Osama bin Laden her "hero". She was arraigned in federal court in Brooklyn on April 2, 2015. She and co-defendant Asia Siddiqui had in-depth discussions about making bombs with an undercover federal agent who they knew as "Mel". Federal authorities investigated them between 2013 and 2015. When federal authorities searched their homes in 2015, they found jihadi literature, instructions on making car bombs, propane gas tanks, and weapons, including machetes. The two pleaded guilty to teaching and distributing information pertaining to the making and use of a weapon of mass destruction with the intention of committing a federal crime in August 2019. Siddiqui, also of Queens, was sentenced to 15 years in prison in January 2020. Acting U.S. Attorney for the Eastern District of New York Mark J. Lesko said Velentzas "expressed her support for foreign terrorist organizations like al-Qaeda and the Islamic State of Iraq and al-Sham by learning how to build bombs and other explosive devices and targeting members of law enforcement for terror... Today's sentence imposes a just punishment on the defendant for her planned horrific crimes." Assistant Attorney General John C. Demers of the U.S. Department of Justice's National Security Division added that "As part of her planned goal to wage violent jihad, Velentzas and her co-defendant Asia Siddiqui researched and taught each other how to construct bombs to be used on American soil against law enforcement and military targets." Velentzas had also lauded Mohamad Shnewer, who is currently serving life in prison for a failed terror plot to murder soldiers at Fort Dix Army base in New Jersey.

June 30, 2021: *AP, KABC,* and *KTTV* reported that a Los Angeles Police Department bomb-disposal truck exploded at 6:40 p.m. after officers removed explosives from a South Los Angeles home from which they had seized between 3,000 and 5,000 pounds of illegal fireworks. Nine LAPD police officers, one officer with the Bureau of Alcohol, Tobacco, Firearms and Explosives, and seven residents were injured when the truck transporting the materials exploded about 6:40 p.m. Three of the civilian bystanders were seriously injured. LAPD Chief Michel R. Moore said that the bomb squad removed nearly 40 "Coca-Cola can-sized" improvised explosive devices and 200 similarly-made smaller devices. The fireworks filled three box trucks and a 53-foot trailer. Authorities arrested Arturo Cejas, 27, on charges of possession of a destructive device. Police planned to pursue child-endangerment charges against Cejas because his brother, 10, was in the home with the fireworks and explosives.

July 2-3, 2021: *CNN* and *NBC News* reported that Massachusetts State Police arrested 11 people after a nine-hour overnight standoff in the woods with several heavily-armed men following a traffic stop on Interstate 95. The Wakefield Police Department announced that several men carrying rifles and handguns ran into the woods after refusing to comply with orders during a motor vehicle stop around 1:30 a.m. Two large trucks were by the side of the road. The men claimed to belong to a group that "does not recognize our laws". The 11 were scheduled to appear in district court on a variety of firearms charges on July 6. State Police Col. Christopher Mason said the men were not carrying gun licenses and wore camouflage jackets, bulletproof vests, and body cameras. They carried long rifles, pistols, or a combination, he said. They told police they were traveling from Rhode Island to Maine for "training". They appeared to be adherents of the Moorish Sovereign Citizens, which holds to conspiracy theories that they are part of a sovereign nation and are thus not subject to U.S. law. The Anti-Defamation League and the Southern Poverty Law Center deem the Sovereign Citizens as an extremist movement. One of the men broadcast a video in which he said he was a member of Rise of the Moors, observing, "We are not anti-government. We are not anti-police, we are not sovereign citizens, we're not Black identity extremists... As specified multiple times to the police that we are abiding by the peaceful journey laws of the United States federal courts." Police seized several firearms from the men, who claimed to be from Rhode Island. They were later discovered to be from Rhode Island, New York, and Michigan.

CNN reported on July 4 that the Middlesex District Attorney's office announced that the 11 suspects, aged 17 to 40, were charged with six offenses, including eight counts of unlawful possession of a firearm, unlawful possession of ammunition, use of body armor in commission of a crime, possession of a high capacity magazine, improper storage of firearms in a vehicle, and conspiracy to commit a crime. Police confiscated three AR-15 rifles; two pistols; a bolt-action rifle; a shotgun; and a short-barrel rifle. The juvenile defendant was to be released to parental custody; the ten adults were held at the Billerica House of Correction on $100,000 cash bail, pending arraignment in Malden District Court.

July 7, 2021: *CNN* reported that the FBI arrested a "Bible study" group in Virginia whose members discussed surveilling the U.S. Capitol and wanted to secede from the U.S. Court records indicated that one member, Fi Duong, alias "Monkey King" and "Jim", of Alexandria, Virginia, told an undercover FBI officer of his plans to build and test Molotov cocktails. He was arrested the previous week, charged with four federal crimes, including entering the restricted grounds of the Capitol and obstruction of an official proceeding related to his alleged participation in the attack on January 6, 2021. On January 6 in downtown Washington, Duong spoke with an undercover Metropolitan Police officer. Investigators said he dressed in black, in an alleged effort to disguise himself as an antifa member. Investigators found an AK-47 and five boxes full of materials to make and test Molotov cocktails at Duong's residence.

July 16, 2021: The *Florida Times-Union* and *USA Today Network* reported that the U.S. Attorney's Office in Jacksonville unsealed an indictment against 16 members of a Florida white supremacist group, the Unforgiven, including two from Jacksonville and one from Orange Park, on charges of assault, kidnapping, and other violent crimes as part of a racketeering scheme. One of the charges was assault on protesters at a Peace Walk for Black Lives on June 5, 2020. The northeast Florida detainees included:

- Ryan McLaughlin, alias Pretty Boy, 35, of Jacksonville, charged with two counts of conspiracy to commit assault

- William Walker, alias The Duke, 38, of Jacksonville, charged with conspiracy to commit assault

- Levi Sharp, alias Sketch, 38, of Satsuma, charged with kidnapping and assault in the aid of racketeering

- Joshua Williamson, alias Chain Gang, 36, of Live Oak, charged with assault in aid of racketeering

Other Floridians included:

- Steve Anderson, 28, of Bristol, charged with two counts of conspiracy to commit assault in aid of racketeering

- George Andrews, II, alias Shrek, 51, of Pensacola, charged with assault in aid of racketeering and conspiracy to commit assault in aid of racketeering

- Jarrett Arnold, alias Jit, 31, of Zephyrhills, charged with kidnapping in aid of racketeering activity and assault in aid of racketeering

- Joshua Fisher, alias Hammer, 27, of Brooksville, charged with three counts of conspiracy to commit assault in aid of racketeering, assault in aid of racketeering, and kidnapping in aid of racketeering

- Joshua Hall, alias K9, 42, of Wildwood, charged with kidnapping in aid of racketeering and assault in aid of racketeering

- David Howell, 35, of Laxahatchee, charged with two counts of conspiracy to commit assault in aid of racketeering and assault in aid of racketeering

- Maverick Maher, alias Saxon, 39, of Pensacola, charged with four counts of conspiracy to commit assault in aid of racketeering and threats of violence in aid of racketeering

- James Mapoles, alias Matt Mapoles, alias Matt Criston, 40, of Panama City, charged with three counts of conspiracy to commit assault in aid of racketeering and threats of violence in aid of racketeering

- Scott Marshall, alias Solo, 45, of Port Richey, charged with kidnapping in aid of racketeering and assault in aid of racketeering

- Darrin Terranova, alias Nova, 51, of Beverly Hills, charged with conspiracy to commit assault in aid of racketeering

- Branch Welcome, alias Scumbag, 34, of Milton, charged with assault in aid of racketeering

August 5, 2021: The *Washington Post* and *Business Insider* reported on August 7 that Myanmar citizens Phyo Hein Htut, 28, and Ye Hein Zaw, 20, were arrested on August 5 and the U.S. Attorney's Office for the Southern District of New York charged them in U.S. District Court in White Plains with conspiring to injure or kill Myanmar's Ambassador to the United Nations, Kyaw Moe Tun. The two men were charged with conspiracy to assault and make a violent attack upon a foreign official. They faced five years in prison for planning to tamper with his car tires. Myanmar's military leaders tried to oust Tun from his post in New York and charged him with treason. Prosecutors said Htut accepted $4,000 in two payments from an unnamed arms dealer in July, using the money transfer app Zelle. Court papers say he was to receive another $1,000 after completing his part of the mission. Officials said that the conspiracy transpired between July 2021 and August 5, 2021. The attack was to occur in Westchester County.

August 19, 2021: At 9:15 a.m., a man drove his black pickup truck onto the sidewalk outside the Library of Congress at First Street and Independence Avenue, SE, near the U.S. Capitol in Washington, D.C. He claimed to have a sound-activated bomb and ammonium nitrate in the toolbox of the truck. He surrendered to police in the afternoon after a five-hour standoff during which the Cannon, Jefferson, and Madison office buildings were evacuated. Officers identified the man as Floyd Ray Roseberry, 49, of North Carolina. A man in a pickup livestreamed, talking about a revolution, calling on "other patriots", and trying to get President Biden on the phone, saying, "If you blow my truck up, It's on you, Joe, I'm ready to die for the cause." He claimed four other "patriots" were in vehicles that contained bombs. He claimed the bomb was built by someone with military experience who had lost two legs. He suggested Biden was not democratically elected. He called for airstrikes on Afghanistan to push out the Taliban. He said Democratic Senators "should step down because the people don't want you there… Democrats, you're killing America… You're making people want to leave America. This is supposed to be a place people want to come." He claimed he had a wife, two children, and a grandchild.

September 1, 2021: Federal intelligence agencies warned Capitol Police that right-wing extremist groups like the Proud Boys and Oath Keepers were planning to attend the September 18 Justice for J6 rally scheduled for the perimeter of the Capitol. Counterprotests were reportedly being planned.

CNN added on September 15 that Look Ahead America, a nonprofit led by former Trump campaign staffer Matt Braynard, was behind the rally. Its website said the group was "dedicated to standing up for patriotic Americans who have been forgotten by our government". White Lives Matter was also planning global demonstrations for September 18.

September 2, 2021: *AFP* and *AP* reported that Alexanda Kotey, 37, a British member of the ISIS "Beatles" kidnapping cell, pleaded guilty in federal court in Alexandria, Virginia, to charges of conspiring to murder four American hostages. He and fellow Beatle El Shafee Elsheikh, 33, were flown to the U.S. from Iraq in October 2020 to face trial for involvement in the murders of American journalists James Foley and Steven Sotloff and relief workers Peter Kassig and Kayla Mueller. Syrian Kurdish forces captured them in Syria in January 2018. The Kurds turned them over to U.S. forces in Iraq. The UK withdrew their British citizenship and did not want to try them. U.S. authorities assured London they would not seek the death penalty. They pleaded not guilty from prison before Judge T.S. Ellis by video link on October 9, 2020. Kotey changed his plea in September 2021, apparently having reached a deal with the prosecution. The Beatles were allegedly involved in abducting American, European, and Japanese hostages in Syria from 2012 to 2015, torturing and killing their victims, including by beheading, and releasing propaganda videos of the murders. Kotey faced a mandatory life sentence. Prosecutors agreed that after Kotey serves 15 years in a U.S. prison, he may seek to serve the rest of his sentence in the UK.

September 13, 2021: *CNN* reported that early in the morning, U.S. Capitol Police arrested Donald Craighead, 44, of Oceanside, California, who had multiple knives, a bayonet, and a machete in his Dodge Dakota pickup truck, which had a swastika and other White supremacist symbols painted on it, near the Democratic National Committee headquarters. He had substituted a picture of an American flag for the truck's license plate. The bayonet and machete are illegal in the District. It was unclear whether he had intended to participate in the rightwing Justice for J6 demonstration, scheduled for September 18.

September 18, 2021: The rightwing Justice for J6 demonstration at Union Plaza in Washington, D.C. fizzled, with only 400-450 attending—and many of them were journalists or bystanders. Four people were arrested, one with a knife, another with a gun. Police also stopped a vehicle on the morning of September 18 on Louisiana Avenue and arrested two people wanted in Texas on outstanding felony warrants, one for possession of a firearm. The Proud Boys had discouraged its members from participating. Turnout at local demonstrations was also small—15 in Seattle, 20 in Charlotte. A counterprotest at Freedom Plaza attracted only 100 people.

September 20, 2021: Authorities arrested QAnon supporter Enrique Figueroa, 47, for threatening to kill Dominican Republic President Luis Abinader after he tracked him down in New York City where he was staying for the United Nations General Assembly. Figueroa made several threats on *Facebook* and *Instagram* in recent weeks, posting photos of Abinader's motorcade in New York City. He was represented by attorney Amy Gallicchio. U.S. Magistrate Judge James L. Cott ordered Figueroa held without bond. He recently tried to travel to the Dominican Republic to find Abinader but was stopped at Newark International Airport because his passport had expired. Dominican newspaper *Diario Libre* said Figueroa was a Dominican who claimed to be a presidential candidate for 2024 and who has previously threatened Dominican activists and public figures.

September 21, 2021: *CNN* reported that while *San Francisco Chronicle* reporter Jack Epstein was going through old letters in his attic from readers of his budget travel book on Latin America in August, he found two letters from 1979 from Unabomber Ted Kaczynski. The letter read, "I'm looking for a refuge in South America, where the closest person is five miles away, you seem to know South America well, can you give me some advice." A second letter thanked Epstein for his advice and being "helpful and courteous".

October 2, 2021: The *Montreal Gazette* reported that U.S. prosecutors charged Saudi-born Canadian man Mohammed Khalifa with aiding ISIS, alleging that he threw grenades in battle and worked with propagandists to publicize beheading hostages. The Department of Justice called him a "leading figure" in the English-language media unit of ISIS. He was captured in 2019 by the Syrian Democratic Forces and was arrested recently by the FBI.

October 8, 2021: *UPI* reported that a federal grand jury in New York indicted former Taliban commander Haji Najibullah, 45, on charges connected to the killing of U.S. soldiers in Afghanistan and the downing of a U.S. military helicopter. The grand jury unsealed the superseding indictment listing 13 terrorism-related charges, including murder, attempted murder, destruction of U.S. military aircraft, hostage-taking, and kidnapping. He was charged in October 2020 regarding the November 2008 abduction of an American journalist. U.S. Attorney Audrey Strauss for the Southern District of New York said he was a Taliban commander from 2007, overseeing more than 1,000 fighters who attacked and killed U.S. and NATO troops and Afghan allies with automatic weapons, improvised explosive devices, rocket-propelled grenades, and other anti-tank weapons. Ten of the 13 charges carry a maximum sentence of life imprisonment. The indictment said Najibullah

commanded Taliban fighters who on June 26, 2008, attacked a U.S. military convoy in Wardak Province, killing Sgt. First Class Matthew L. Hilton and Joseph McKay, Sgt. Mark Palmateer, and their Afghan interpreter. On October 27, 2008, Najibullah's Taliban fighters shot down a U.S. military helicopter. Prosecutors accused him of kidnapping a New York journalist and two Afghan nationals in Pakistan on November 19, 2008. Ukraine arrested and extradited him to the U.S. in October 2020.

November 7, 2021: The *Washington Post* reported that Cornell, Columbia, and Brown universities evacuated campus buildings after receiving bomb threats. None were credible. Cornell evacuated Goldwin Smith Hall, Upson Hall, Kennedy Hall, and the law school at 2:15 p.m. Columbia received bomb threats at 2:30 p.m. Brown issued an all-clear at 5:45 p.m. A bomb threat against multiple buildings at Yale was received on November 5. Similar threats were made the previous week against Ohio University's Athens campus and Miami University of Ohio.

November 16, 2021: *Newsweek* reported that an immigration judge ruled that Iraqi refugee Omar Abdulsattar Ameen, accused of killing for ISIS, is eligible for deportation to Iraq or Turkey because he lied on his refugee application when entering the U.S. The Iraqi government and the U.S. Department of Homeland Security claimed that Ameen was part of an ISIS group that killed Police Officer Ihsan Abdulhafiz Jasim in Rawah in 2014 and kept his membership in two terrorist groups a secret before gaining refugee status and resettling in Sacramento, California. He was represented by attorney Siobhan Waldron.

November 21, 2021: *AP* and the *Washington Post* reported that Darrell E. Brooks Jr., 39, fleeing a domestic disturbance (initially reported as a knife fight), crashed through police barricades and drove his speeding red Ford Escape SUV into Wisconsin's 58th Annual Waukesha Holiday Parade at 4:39 p.m., hitting a marching band and other participants and attendees, killing five people and injuring 48, including a dozen children, among them three sets of siblings. *CNN* reported that he faced five counts of first-degree intentional homicide. Among the dead were members of the Milwaukee Dancing Grannies. *Fox News* and *NPR* reported that the dead were Wilhelm Hospel, 81; Virginia Sorenson, 79; LeAnna Owen, 71; Tamara Durand, 52; and Jane Kulich, 52. A police officer had fired at the suspect's vehicle in an attempt to stop it. Waukesha Police Chief Dan Thompson said, "There is no evidence this is a terrorist incident." Brooks had been released on $1,000 bail on November 11 in relation to charges including domestic abuse regarding a November 2 incident in which Brooks was accused of running over a woman with his car while she was walking through a gas station parking lot. Prosecutors filed five charges related to the incident including obstructing an officer; second-degree recklessly endangering safety with domestic abuse assessments; disorderly conduct with domestic abuse assessments; and misdemeanor battery with domestic abuse assessments. He was also charged with bail jumping; he was out on bail following a July 24, 2020, incident during which he was accused of firing a handgun during an argument. During his arrest, police found a stolen handgun and three "multi colored pills", which tested "presumptively positive" for methamphetamines. He was charged with two counts of second-degree reckless endangering safety while using a dangerous weapon and one count of possession of a firearm by a felon. Brooks had an outstanding arrest warrant in Nevada issued on August 15, 2016, in an unrelated case for which he was arrested and allegedly jumped bail. The *Washington Post* reported on November 23 that a child died from injuries from the crash. During his court appearance, bail was set at $5 million.

November 30, 2021: *CNN* and the *Detroit Free Press* reported that around 1 p.m., sophomore Ethan Crumbley, 15, was arrested after a mass shooting at Oxford High School. He walked out of a restroom, firing more than 30 shots at people in a school hallway and through classroom doors, killing four and injuring six students and a teacher. He was to be tried as an adult and pleaded not guilty to 24 charges: one count of terrorism causing death—a rare charge for a school shooting, four counts of first-degree murder, seven counts

of assault with intent to commit murder and 12 counts of possession of a firearm in the commission of a felony. District Court Judge Nancy Carniak denied bond.

The victims were

- Tate Myre, 16, a star football player and honor student. An online petition with 48,000 signatures called for the school's football stadium to be renamed after him.

- Hana St. Juliana, 14, a women's basketball team member

- Madisyn Baldwin, 17, had several scholarship offers from universities

- Justin Shilling, 17, co-captain of the bowling team, he worked at Anita's Kitchen

A 14-year-old girl was placed on a ventilator after surgery. A teacher, 47, was discharged from the hospital after treatment. A 14-year-old boy sustained a gunshot wound to the jaw and head.

Authorities found a video made on November 29 when he threatened to shoot and kill students. They also found a journal in which he discussed murdering classmates. School authorities called in his parents three hours before the attack because of concerning behavior. He used a 9 mm Sig Sauer SP 2022 pistol his father had purchased on November 26.

On December 3, Oakland County Prosecutor Karen McDonald said prosecutors would file four counts of involuntary manslaughter against James, 45, and Jennifer Crumbley, 43, Ethan's parents. After the parents skipped a court hearing, police and U.S. Marshals issued a BOLO for the couple. Authorities were tipped off that they were hiding inside the studio of artist Andrez Sikora near a parking lot on Bellevue near Jefferson in Detroit and arrested them. On December 4, Oakland County Judge Julie A. Nicholson announced a bond of $500,000 each, citing a likely second flight risk. The duo were represented by attorneys Shannon Smith and Mariell Lehman. The parents faced up to 15 years in prison.

December 10, 2021: *Deutsche Welle* reported that the U.S. Department of Justice announced that Saudi Arabia-born Canadian citizen Mohammed Khalifa, 38, pleaded guilty and admitted to "conspiring to provide material support to a designated foreign terrorist organization, resulting in death" at a hearing in U.S. District Court in Alexandria. He narrated 15 violent ISIS videos, including the 2014 "Flames of War" and its 2017 sequel. He traveled to Syria to join ISIS in 2013, inspired by the lectures of Anwar al-Aulaqi. Sentencing was scheduled for April 15, 2022. After fighting on the battlefield, the Syrian Defense Forces captured him in 2019. Khalifa told *CBC* he wanted to return to Canada to be with his wife and their three children, but not be tried.

UPDATES OF PRE-2021 INCIDENTS

AFRICA

BURKINA FASO

December 2018: *AP* reported on September 22, 2021 that jihadis captured Canadian Edith Blais and her Italian companion Luca Tacchetto while they were touring eastern Burkina Faso and planning to cross into Benin. They were held in the northern Malian desert for 15 months before escaping one night on foot. In September 2021, Blais, now 37, released a memoir, *The Weight of Sand: My 450 Days Held Hostage in the Sahara*. The duo converted to Islam at the behest of their kidnappers.

CAMEROON

October 24, 2020: *AFP* reported on September 10, 2021 that a court sentenced to death by public firing squad four suspected Anglophone separatists for the killing of seven schoolchildren, aged between nine and 12, in Kumba in the Southwest Region, on October 24, 2020. A military tribunal found them guilty of "acts of terrorism, hostility towards the motherland, insurrection and murder."

CENTRAL AFRICAN REPUBLIC

November 16, 2020: *AFP* reported on April 2, 2021 that Return, Reclamation and Rehabilitation (3R), a rebel group which is part of a coalition seeking to overthrow President Faustin Archange Touadera, announced that its leader, Bi Sidi Souleymane, alias Sidiki Abass, died in a hospital on March 25, 2021 of wounds suffered during an attack on Bossembele on November 16, 2020. 3R is made up largely of members of Fulani nomadic herders. In December 2020, 3R joined with the Coalition of Patriots for Change, an alliance of armed groups. U.N. and security sources claimed that Abass had been wounded in fighting in December during an ambush on his convoy. His group had been accused of war crimes and he was a target of an investigation by CAR's Special Criminal Court, set up to probe serious human rights violations committed since 2003. In 2019, Human Rights Watch said 3R had killed 46 civilians in Ouham Pende Province, a few months after Abass had signed a peace deal in Khartoum with the CAR government and 13 other armed groups.

CONGO

January 16, 2001: *Al-Jazeera* and *AFP* reported on January 8, 2021 that on December 31, 2020 President Felix Tshisekedi pardoned and released from Makala central prison Colonel Eddy Kapend, 61, who had been sentenced to death for his role in the January 16, 2001 assassination of President Laurent-Desire Kabila by one of his bodyguards. Tshisekedi had pardoned all 22 Congolese prisoners who had been sentenced to 20 years or more (initially death sentences) on political charges. Eleven of Kapend's co-defendants died in prison before the pardon was granted. Kapend had been Kabila's cousin and aide-de-camp, and denied involvement in the assassination. Laurent-Desire was the father of Joseph Kabila, Tshisekedi's predecessor. Former intelligence chief Georges Leta and Cesaire Muzima were freed with Kapend on January 8. A Kinshasa court in 2003 sentenced 26 people to death in connection with the killing. Another 64 were sentenced to terms ranging from six months to life.

KENYA

August 7, 1998: On March 31, 2021, *AFP* reported that Sudan had paid $335 million as part of an agreement to compensate survivors and victims' families of past anti-US terrorist attacks, including al-Qaeda's August 7, 1998 bombings of the U.S. embassies in Kenya and Tanzania, that removed Sudan from the U.S. list of terrorist sponsors. The agreement also covered the October 12, 2000 al-Qaeda attack on the *U.S.S. Cole* off Yemen's coast and the killing of U.S. development worker John Granville in Khartoum in 2008.

BBC reported on April 28, 2021 that Kenyans complained that they were not to receive the same compensation as Americans injured in the al-Qaeda bombing of the U.S. Embassy in Nairobi on August 7, 1998. Among the injured Kenyans were

- civil servant Diana Mutisya, 60, who needed 15 metal plates inserted to hold her spine together. One of her lungs no longer functions and she needs an orthopedic chair to work. She spends $750/month for therapy. Four other people who were in the bank with her when the bomb went off perished. The U.S. media reported that each American victim or family of the attacks will receive $3 million, while locally employed staff will receive $400,000.

- Douglas Sidialo, who was blinded by the blast

A photo of the Nairobi memorial included the names Doreen Namchu Mbayaki, Rachel Kebendi Mboya, Francis Ndungu Mbugua, Samuel Thuo Mbugua, Lucy Waruthi Mbuiya, Stephen Waweru Mburu, Elizabeth Anyango Mito, Ahmed Warku Mohammed, Edward Mokaya, Juliet Veronica Morrison, Luciano Mugami, Edward Mokaya, Rachel Pussy Mugasia, Peterevans Rungu Mugo, Sharon Wangeci Mugo, Josephat Mutua Muai, Emmanuel Mujyambere, Isaac Mwaria Mukera, Samuel Vondo Mulalya, Francis Mukenye Mulehi, Edward Miwea Mungai, John Amos Mungai, Benson Wathiga Munyir, Tommy Knurume Munzala, Caroline Mumbi Muraguri, and Riddie Wambui Muritu.

January 5, 2020: *AP* reported on April 12, 2021 that U.S. Secretary of Defense Lloyd Austin ordered an Army review of the U.S. Africa Command investigation into the January 5, 2020 pre-dawn attack by 30-40 al-Shabaab terrorists on the Manda Bay military base in Kenya that killed three Americans, wounded three others, and destroyed six aircraft.

MALI

November 2013: *AP* and *AFP* reported on June 11, 2021 that French Defense Minister Florence Parly said French troops on June 5, 2021 killed Baye ag Bakabo, variant Bayes ag Bakabo, an al-Qaeda-linked Malian jihadi leader believed to have helped in the kidnapping and killing of Ghislaine Dupont and Claude Verlon, French journalists working for *Radio France Internationale*, in November 2013. The two French journalists, both in their 50s, were captured in Kidal after interviewing a separatist Tuareg leader. Al-Qaeda in the Islamic Maghreb (AQIM) claimed credit for the killings. The weekend anti-terrorist Operation Barkhane raids killed another three terrorists around Aguelhok in northern Mali. The group was suspected of plotting an attack on U.N. forces in the area. *RFI* reported that drug trafficker ag Bakabo drove the beige pick-up truck used for the kidnapping. In recent months he had headed an armed group aiming to eliminate "all people suspected of collaborating" with French forces operating in Africa's Sahel region. *RFI* reported that only one kidnapper remained alive. As of November 2020, Agnes Callamard, the U.N. Special Rapporteur on extrajudicial, summary, or arbitrary executions, noted that "the alleged perpetrators have been named but are yet to be arrested and prosecuted." Amada Ag Hama, a senior AQIM figure linked to the murder of the *RFI* journalists, was killed in a May 2015 raid in Mali.

February 7, 2017: On October 9, 2021, *AP* reported that Colombian nun Sister Gloria Cecilia Narvaez, who was kidnapped in February 2017 near Mali's border with Burkina Faso by al-Qaeda in the Islamic Maghreb, was freed. AQIM had released several videos in which she asked for help from the Vatican. She said on state television, "I first thank God, who is the light and the peace, I thank the Malian authorities, the president for all the efforts made so that I am free. May God bless you, may God bless Mali. I thank you very much... I thank the people of Karangasso very much for their prayers and all the efforts they made to obtain my release. And I ask forgiveness from all the Malians, all the people who were not well perhaps (because of me)." *AFP* reported on November 17, 2021 that Sister Gloria Narvaez, 59, returned to Colombia on November 16, 2021. Her mother died in September 2020 while awaiting the release. Before returning to Bogota, Sister Gloria visited Pope Francis at the Vatican.

October 2020: *AFP* reported on April 5, 2021 that former jihadi Ahmada Ag Bibi, who helped secure the release of four hostages in October 2020, told *Radio France Internationale (RFI)* that Mali's government paid €two million ($2.36 million) for the release of the late Malian opposition leader Soumaila Cisse, who died of COVID-19 in December 2020 at age 71. France denied paying a ransom for the release of septuagenarian NGO humanitarian worker Sophie Petronin. Bibi added that Mali did not pay ransom for three other foreign hostages—Petronin and Italians Nicola Chiacchio and Pier Luigi Maccalli—although he did not rule out that external funds changed hands. Bibi, an ethnic Tuareg, had served several terms as a member of Mali's parliament. While a jihadi, he fought alongside Iyad Ag Ghaly, leader of the al-Qaeda-affiliated Group to Support Islam and Muslims (GSIM) in the Sahel.

NIGER

October 2016: On November 17, 2021, *AP* and *ABC News* reported that Els Woodke, wife of American Christian humanitarian worker Jeff Woodke who was kidnapped from his home in Abalak, Niger in October 2016, said that the kidnappers had demanded a multimillion-dollar ransom but U.S. government "restrictions" have hindered her ability to raise the money. He had worked for decades aiding nomads in the Sahel. He was believed to have been kidnapped by the Islamic State in the Greater Sahara (IS-GS). She believed he was transferred to the al-Qaeda-affiliated JNIM and that he was alive as of the summer of 2021. She pleaded in a video to JNIM leader Sheik Iyad Ag Ghali to release him, saying in English and French, "You are the only one with the power to make that happen. Releasing Jeff will require compassion and mercy, but these are the characteristics of a strong and courageous leader." Els Woodke, a teacher's assistant in McKinleyville, California appeared in the *ABC News* documentary *3212 Un-Redacted* on *Hulu*.

NIGERIA

April 14, 2014: On January 29, 2021, *CNN* and *ABC News* reported that some of the 276 Chibok schoolgirls kidnapped by Boko Haram on April 14, 2014 escaped from their captors. Among them was Halima Ali Maiyanga, whose sister escaped in 2016.

Reuters reported on August 7, 2021 that one of the Chibok girls had been freed and was reunited with her parents. Governor Babagana Zulum said the girl and someone she married during her captivity surrendered themselves to the military ten days earlier.

CNN reported on August 16, 2021 that Chibok hostage Hassana Adamu and her two children were freed and reunited with her parents.

Asia

Bangladesh

August 24, 2002: *Al-Jazeera* and *AFP* reported on February 4, 2021 that the Satkhira district court jailed 50 opposition activists for up to ten years for an attack on the leader of the then-opposition party Awami League and now current Prime Minister Sheikh Hasina's motorcade on August 24, 2002. Several of her Awami League followers and journalists were injured; she was unharmed. The defendants included a former Member of Parliament for the Bangladesh Nationalist Party (BNP), which was in power at the time of the attack, which involved rocks, batons, and machetes. Prosecutor Shaheen Mirdha announced, "Three men, including the ex-MP, were given 10 years in jail and the rest got various jail terms from four and a half years." Twelve convicts remained at large. BNP leader Khaleda Zia, prime minister at the time of the attack, is serving a 17-year jail term for corruption imposed in 2018. Tarique Rahman, Zia's son who lives in London, was sentenced in 2018 to life for a grenade attack on a Hasina rally in 2004.

February 26, 2015: On February 16, 2021, *AP* reported that Anti-Terrorism Special Tribunal Judge Majibur Rahman sentenced five members of a banned militant group to death and a sixth man to life in prison for the February 26, 2015 killing of Avijit Roy, a prominent Bangladesh-born U.S. citizen and blogger known for speaking out against religious fundamentalism. He was hacked to death in the streets of Dhaka when he was walking with his wife near an annual book fair. His wife, also a blogger, was injured and fled to the United States. Four defendants were in the courtroom. The other two, including sacked military official Sayed Ziaul Haque Zia, were at large.

October 31, 2015: *AP* and *al-Jazeera* reported on February 10, 2021 that Anti-Terrorism Special Tribunal Judge Majibur Rahman announced that the court had sentenced to death eight jihadis for hacking to death on October 31, 2015 Faisal Abedin Deepan, variant Faysal Arefin Dipon, of the Jagriti Prokashoni publishing house in a market near Dhaka University. Deepan specialized in books on secularism and atheism. He was killed in his office in Dhaka's Shahbagh area. Six defendants—Moinul Hasan Shamim, Md Abdus Sabur, Khairul Islam, Md Abu Siddique Sohel, Md Mozammel Hossain Saimon, Md Sheikh Abdullah—were in the courtroom; the other two, including sacked Army Major Sayed Ziaul Haque Zia, variant Ziaul Haque, and Akram Hossain, alias Hasib, were in hiding. Prosecutors said they belonged to the banned Ansar al-Islam, a local affiliate of al-Qaeda. On the same day, publisher Ahmed Rashid Tutul was severely wounded but survived a near-simultaneous attack also in Dhaka. Tutul flew to Nepal and on to asylum in Norway with his family. Deepan and Tutal had published the works of Bangladeshi-American writer and blogger Avijit Roy, who also was hacked to death in February 2015 when he was returning from an annual book fair in Dhaka. Defense attorney Md Kahirul Islam vowed to appeal. Judge Rahman added, "If the criminals involved in this heinous act survive, other members of Ansar al-Islam will be motivated to commit such crimes." Only a death penalty will "ensure justice and it will be an exemplary punishment".

April 25, 2016: Terrorists hacked to death Xulhaz Mannan, an editor of *Roopbaan*, Bangladesh's first gay rights magazine, who had worked for the U.S. Agency for International Development and as a U.S. Embassy protocol officer, and his friend Mahbub Rabbi Tonoy. Mannan was a cousin of former Foreign Minister Dipu Moni of the governing Awami League party. *AP* reported on August 31, 2021 that a Bangladesh anti-terrorism tribunal sentenced six jihadis to death for the murders. Judge Mojibur Rahman of the Anti-Terrorism Special Tribunal acquitted two others. Four of the defendants were present; the two others were at large. Prosecutors said all of them were members of Ansar-al-Islam. Defense lawyers planned to appeal to the High Court.

Several groups had claimed a wave of killings, including Ansar-al-Islam and al-Qaeda in the Indian Subcontinent (AQIS). The domestic groups Jumatul Mujahedeen Bangladesh and Harkatul Jihad were also blamed for some attacks.

CHINA

June 2017: *BBC* reported that in June 2017, China Southern Airlines announced that a passenger, 80, threw nine coins at the engine of a plane at Shanghai Pudong International Airport as she was boarding. One of the coins hit the engine, delaying the flight. The unnamed woman was questioned at a police station, where she said that she threw the coins to "pray for safety". Police did not charge her.

February 2019: *BBC* reported that in February 2019, Chinese man Lu Chao, 28, threw coins into a Lucky Air plane's engine as he embarked for his first-ever flight at Anqing Tianzhushan Airport in Anhui Province. Authorities charged Lu with disturbing public order and detained him for ten days. Lu argued in court that airlines should make it clear to passengers not to throw coins at the engine. A judge later fined Lu $17,600 to compensate the airline for the incident.

INDIA

2013: On November 2, 2021, *AFP* reported that a court convicted and sentenced to death four people accused of bombing a 2013 election rally for Indian Prime Minister Narendra Modi. Two others received life sentences in the bombing in a park in Patna before then-opposition leader Narendra Modi was due to address a large crowd at a campaign event. The terrorists also attacked a nearby train station. The attacks killed six and injured nearly 100 people. The National Investigation Agency said that the accused were all from the banned Students Islamic Movements of India group. Public prosecutor Lalan Kumar Sinha said they were convicted for conspiring to "wage a war against the government". Three others were sentenced to between seven and 10 years. An attorney planned to challenge the sentences in a higher court.

February 14, 2019: *Reuters* reported on July 31, 2021 that Mohammad Ismail Alvi, commander of Jaish-e-Mohammad India and mastermind behind the February 14, 2019 attack that killed 40 Indian paramilitary troops, died in a shootout with security forces south of the regional capital Srinagar in Kashmir. Kashmir police chief Vijay Kumar said, "Mohammad Ismail Alvi alias Lamboo alias Adnan was from the family of Masood Azhar. He was involved in conspiracy and planning of Lethpora Pulwama attack" in which a suicide bomber rammed a car into a bus carrying Indian paramilitary police in Kashmir. The Pakistan-based Jaish-e-Mohammad (JeM) claimed responsibility.

INDONESIA

October 12, 2002: *AP, UPI,* and *AFP* reported on January 21, 2021 that the Pentagon announced plans to move ahead with a military trial for three men held at Guantánamo Bay who are suspected of involvement in bombings in Indonesia in 2002 and 2003. The non-capital charges include conspiracy, murder, attempted murder, intentionally causing serious bodily injury, terrorism, attacking civilians, attacking civilian objects, destruction of property, and accessory after the fact, all in violation of the law of war. The trio had been held for 17 years for their alleged roles in the bombing of Bali nightclubs on October 12, 2002 that killed 202 people and of a J.W. Marriott Hotel in Jakarta on August 5, 2003 that killed 12 and wounded 150. Military prosecutors filed charges against Indonesian Riduan Isamuddin, alias Encep Nurjaman, alias Hambali, leader of Jemaah Islamiyah, and Mohammed Nazir Bin Lep, alias Lillie, and Mohammed Farik Bin Amin, alias Zubair, who are from Malaysia, in June 2017. The trio were captured in Thailand in 2003.

Al-Jazeera reported on August 30, 2021 that the trial at the U.S. military detention facility was to begin of Indonesian terrorist Riduan bin Isomudin, who was captured in Thailand on August 11, 2003, in connection with a series of nightclub and hotel bombings in Indonesia in the early 2000s, including the Bali bombing of October 12, 2002 and the 2003 attack on the J.W. Marriott Hotel in Jakarta. Some 213 people were killed and 109 wounded in the al-Qaeda-affiliated Jemaah Islamiyah (JI) bombings. He faced a military commission on charges of war crimes, including murder, terrorism, and conspiracy. Two

Malaysian men, Mohammed Nazir bin Lep and Mohammed Farik bin Amin, accused of being accomplices, were to stand trial with him. The JI leader was also accused of involvement in a series of foiled plots in Singapore, Australia, and the Philippines. Hambali was represented by military attorney Major James Valentine.

May 28, 2005: *AP* reported on December 8, 2021 that Presiding Judge Sutikna of the East Jakarta District Court sentenced Jemaah Islamiyah jihadi Taufiq Bulaga, alias Upik Lawanga, alias "Professor", 43, to life in prison after finding him guilty of making bombs used in a May 28, 2005 market attack at Tentena market in Poso district that killed 22 people and injured 91, mostly Christians. He was also accused of fabricating bombs used in a 2004 passenger minibus attack that killed six people and a 2006 attack using a flashlight bomb that killed a Christian woman. After eluding capture for 16 years, he was arrested at Soekarno-Hatta International Airport in Tangerang, on Sumatra Island, Indonesia, on December 16, 2020. Lawanga said he would appeal claiming that he helped make the bombs but did not carry out the attacks, and did not know how they would be used. He said he was obeying orders from other senior JI members to build bombs to avenge Christians for the massacre of Muslims at an Islamic boarding school in May 2000. He said he was avenging the deaths of relatives and friends and the burning of mosques and his brother's house. He admitted joining JI in Poso in 2002 and learned how to assemble bombs from Azahari bin Husin, a Malaysian bomb-making mastermind who was killed in a police raid in Indonesia in 2005. He said that after leaving Poso in 2005, he lived with his wife and children in Lampung as a duck farmer. Police found a bunker at Lawanga's house with handmade guns and explosive materials.

MALAYSIA

January 2020: Abu Sayyaf gunmen kidnapped eight Indonesians off Malaysia. The men were working for a Malaysian fishing firm. The gunmen brought the hostages to Sulu Province. AS freed three hostages but shot and killed another who tried to escape while troops were attempting a rescue operation. AS demanded a ransom, which the hostages' poor fishing families could not afford. Indonesia's government has a no-ransom policy, according to the *DZMM* radio network.

Philippine police rescued three captives on March 18, 2021 after an AS speedboat was hit by huge waves and overturned off Pasigan Island in Tawi Tawi Province during the night. Villagers found the Indonesian men along the shore of South Ubian town. Police captured a 45-year-old kidnapper. Other AS members in a separate speedboat got away. A fourth hostage went missing. A military spokesman said the terrorists were trying to get to Tambisan Island in Malaysia's Sabah State to release the captives in exchange for a ransom of five million pesos ($104,000), but the Philippine military got wind of the plan and launched covert assaults.

On March 21, 2021, Philippine troops wounded Abu Sayyaf rebel commander Amajan Sahidjuan, who soon died from loss of blood on Kalupag Island in Tawi Tawi Province. He was blamed for years of ransom kidnappings. Regional military commander Lt. Gen. Corleto Vinluan Jr. said that two other AS terrorists dragged their hostage away, but soldiers soon rescued him. 20019901

PAKISTAN

January 23, 2002: On January 6, 2021, *AP* reported Mehmood A. Sheikh, lawyer for Ahmed Omar Saeed Sheikh, the key suspect in the kidnap/beheading of American journalist Daniel Pearl in 2002, said he would petition the Supreme Court to free his client from custody from a Karachi jail. The Sindh High Court had acquitted him in April 2020; Pearl's family and the Pakistani government appealed the acquittal to the Supreme Court. Three others—Fahad Naseem, Adil Sheikh and Salman Saqib—were acquitted on all charges.

AP reported on January 27, 2021 that in a handwritten letter dated July 25, 2019, Ahmad Saeed Omar Sheikh admitted to a "minor" role in Pearl's killing. Pearl family lawyer Faisal Siddiqi said that the letter was submitted to Pakistan's Supreme Court nearly two weeks ago. Sheikh's lawyers confirmed their client wrote it on January 27, 2021. Sheikh did not explain his "minor" role and admitted that he knew who killed Pearl—Pakistani extremist Atta-ur-Rahman, alias Naeem Bokhari, who has since been executed in connection with an attack on a paramilitary base in southern Karachi. Sheikh's lawyer Mehmood A. Sheikh claimed that his client wrote the letter under duress.

CNN, Reuters, AFP, CBS News, and the *Washington Post* reported on January 28, 2021 that Pakistan's Supreme Court ruled 2-1 in ordering the release of the four men convicted of Pearl's kidnap/murder and dismissing the appeal by Pearl's family and the Pakistani government. The Interior Ministry said that the four were placed on Pakistan's exit control list, barring them from leaving the country. *Reuters* reported on January 29 that the Sindh government appealed to the Supreme Court to review its decision.

Reuters, AP, Deutsche Welle, and *AFP* reported on February 2, 2021 that Pakistani Supreme Court Justice Omar Ata Bandyal ordered the release from prison of Ahmad Omar Saeed Sheikh to a government safe house as a stepping stone to his full release, saying, "He should be moved to a comfortable residential environment, something like a rest house where he can live a normal life."

AP and *AFP* reported that on March 22, 2021 Punjab Counter-Terrorism police announced that Ahmad Saeed Omar Sheikh, a Pakistani-British man who was on death row for 18 years before his acquittal in the beheading of Daniel Pearl, was transferred from Karachi to a government safe house in Lahore, his home city, for security reasons.

The *Washington Post* reported on July 30, 2021 that Ruth Pearl, nee Eveline Rejwan, 85, mother of Daniel Pearl, had died ten days earlier. In 1941, at age 5, she survived the deadly Farhud pogrom against the Jews of Baghdad. Ruth Pearl and her husband, the eminent computer scientist Judea Pearl, established the Daniel Pearl Foundation, that seeks to promote cross-cultural understanding.

November 2020: *AP* reported on July 1, 2021 that an anti-terrorism court in Khusab district of Punjab Province issued a death sentence to former security guard Ahmad Nawaz, who in November 2020 shot and killed his bank's manager, Malik Imran Hanif, after accusing him of insulting Islam's Prophet Mohammad. Prosecution lawyer Mian Rizwan said that a day earlier the court sentenced him to two years in prison for assaulting police during his arrest. Police later determined that Nawaz had a personal feud with Hanif.

SRI LANKA

April 21, 2019: *AP* reported on February 4, 2021 that Sri Lankan President Gotabaya Rajapaksa had received the final report of an inquiry commission investigating the 2019 Easter Sunday bomb attacks that killed 290 people and wounded more than 500 in three churches and three hotels. He issued instructions to implement its recommendations. *CNN* and *AFP* reported on February 24, 2021 that the investigation called for Sri Lanka's former President Maithripala Sirisena and senior police and intelligence officials to be prosecuted. It added that then-Prime Minister Ranil Wickremesinghe had a "lax approach" towards Islamic extremism, "one of the primary reasons for the failure". The commission recommended criminal proceedings against former Defense Secretary Hemasiri Fernando, former Police Chief Pujith Jayasundera, former Chief of National Intelligence Sisira Mendia, and other senior police officers.

AP reported on March 2, 2021 that Archbishop of Colombo Cardinal Malcolm Ranjith and other Sri Lankan Roman Catholic Church officials declared a "Black Sunday" for the coming weekend to demand justice for the victims. Church leaders asked their parishioners to attend Mass on Sunday dressed in black. Church bells tolled at 8:45 a.m., the time of the near-simultaneous attacks.

AP reported on August 10, 2021 that on the previous day, prosecutors filed 23,270 charges against 25 people in connection with the six Easter Sunday suicide bomb attacks on three churches and three hotels. Charges filed under the country's anti-terror law included conspiring to murder, aiding and abetting, collecting arms and ammunition, and attempted murder.

AUSTRALIA-NEW ZEALAND

NEW ZEALAND

March 15, 2019: *Reuters* reported on April 14, 2021 that Australian white supremacist Brenton Tarrant, who was sentenced in August 2020 to life without parole for the murder of 51 people and attempted murder of 40 others at two mosques in Christchurch on March 15, 2019, sought a review of his prison conditions and his status under the Terrorism Suppression Act as a "terrorist entity", the only person in New Zealand with that designation. The High Court in Auckland was scheduled to review those issues on April 15, but Tarrant, who was to represent himself, missed the teleconferenced hearing. Justice Geoffrey Venning adjourned the proceedings.

AP reported on June 14, 2021 that producer Philippa Campbell pulled out of a FilmNation Entertainment movie project "They Are Us" which lauded Prime Minister Jacinda Ardern's response to the Christchurch terrorist attacks. Rose Byrne was to play Ardern.

EUROPE

AUSTRIA

July 2020: On August 6, 2021, the trial in Korneuburg began of a Russian man, 48—an ethnic Chechen—for the execution-style shooting death of a Chechen, 43, at an industrial estate in Gerasdorf, a Vienna suburb, in July 2020. Austrian public broadcaster *ORF* reported that prosecutors could not establish whether the killing was politically motivated or resulted from an argument the men had over a gun deal. The defense attorney blamed the victim's bodyguard for shooting him six times, including once in the head from a short distance. The defendant faced a life sentence. The trial ended that day, with jurors unanimously finding the Russian guilty of murder. The regional court sentenced him to life in prison. The defense planned to appeal.

November 2, 2020: *AP* reported on July 7, 2021 that German investigators raided the Osnabrueck and Kassel homes of Kosovo citizen Blinor S. and German citizen Drilon G., two acquaintances of Kujtim Fejzulai, an ISIS sympathizer who shot to death four people and injured another 20, including a police officer, in Vienna on November 2, 2020. Federal prosecutors suggested that the duo might have known about his plans for the attack and failed to inform authorities. Prosecutors added that they visited him in Vienna in July 2020, shortly after he acquired the weapon used in the attack, and met other radicals from Austria and Switzerland. They erased material on their cellphones and social media platforms to cover up their connections to him. Fejzulai, a dual national of Austria and North Macedonia, was earlier convicted of trying to join ISIS in Syria.

BELGIUM

March 22, 2016: *AFP* reported on January 5, 2021 that Belgian judges were scheduled to decide whether to send a dozen suspected jihadis to trial for their alleged roles in the March 22, 2016 bombings of the Brussels airport and a Maaleek-Maelbeek city center metro station that killed 32 people and wounded 340. Several of the 13 defendants were alleged members of the ISIS cell that carried out the November 2015 attacks in France that killed 130. The best known defendant was Salah Abdeslam, 31, who was sentenced in 2018 to 20 years for shooting at Brussels police in the days before his 2016 arrest.

The *Florida Times-Union* reported on July 31, 2021 that equestrian Beatrice de Lavelette, who lost her lower legs at age 17 in the ISIS suicide bombing at Brussels Airport, was to participate on the U.S. Para Dressage Team in the Paralympic Games in Tokyo, Japan on August 28, 2021. She lives and trains in Palm Beach County, Florida. She grew up in France and Belgium to a French-American father and an American mother. She began riding at age 3.

2018: The *Washington Examiner* reported on February 4, 2021 that an Antwerp court convicted Iranian operative Assadollah Assadi, 49, of attempting to bomb a 2018 gathering of the

Free Iran exiled opposition group near Paris organized by the National Council of Resistance of Iran, the political arm of Mujahedeen-e-Khalq (MEK). He was sentenced to 20 years for attempting terrorist murder and participating in the activities of a terrorist group. Belgian authorities were tipped off by Mossad and pulled over the Mercedes of Amir Saadouni, 40, and Nasimeh Naami, 36. Police found a detonator and more than a pound of triacetone triperoxide (TATP) explosive. Prosecutors alleged that Assadi recruited the couple. He was detained in Germany the following day, accused of smuggling the TATP from Iran on a commercial flight to Austria, where he was attached to the Iranian mission in Vienna. Assadi traveled to Luxembourg, dressed as a tourist, where he gave the TATP to Saadouni and Naami two days prior to their arrests in Germany. The *Guardian* reported that Assadi was denied diplomatic immunity because he was on vacation at the time of his arrest. Saadouni was sentenced to 15 years; Naami to 18 years. *AP* reported that Mehrdad Arefani was sentenced to 17 years.

DENMARK

February 2020: *AP* reported on April 15, 2021 that authorities charged three members of the London-based Iranian separatist Arab Struggle Movement for the Liberation of Ahwaz with financing and promoting terror in Iran with an unnamed Saudi intelligence service. The trio were arrested in February 2020 in Ringsted, and charged with illegal intelligence activity. Chief prosecutor Lise-Lotte Nilas said the men faced up to 12 years in jail. Their trial was scheduled to begin on April 29, 2021.

The arrests were linked to the arrest in the Netherlands of a man, 40. Dutch police said ASMLA's armed wing conducts attacks in Iran, mainly against the Iranian Revolutionary Guard, plus oil and gas fields.

FRANCE

October 3, 1980: *AFP* and *CBS News* reported on May 19, 2021 that France's Court of Cassation upheld an order that Lebanese-Canadian academic Lars Hagberg Hassan Diab, 67, who spent years fighting claims of planting a bomb in a Paris synagogue on Rue Copernic on October 3, 1980 that killed four people and injured 46, stand trial. It was first fatal attack on Jews in France since World War II. The RCMP arrested him in November 2008. Canada extradited him to France in 2014. He was released and returned to Canada in January 2018 when French magistrates deemed handwriting evidence against him "not convincing enough". In January 2021, the Paris appeals court overturned the dismissal and ordered he stand trial. He was represented by Canadian attorney Don Bayne. Diab had been a professor of sociology at the University of Ottawa. The attack, in which a bomb was hidden in the saddle bag of a motorbike, was attributed to the Special Operations branch of the Popular Front for the Liberation of Palestine (PFLP). Diab said he was taking exams in Beirut at the time. He spent nine years either in jail or under strict bail conditions in Canada and France, awaiting trial. In 2020, he sued the government of Canada for $90 million for extraditing him.

November 13, 2015: *Reuters, La Repubblica, La Gazzetta del Mezzogiorno,* and *AFP* reported on March 8, 2021 that police in Bari, Italy, arrested an Algerian man, Athmane Touami, 36, on suspicion of belonging to ISIS and helping the perpetrators of the coordinated attack in Paris and elsewhere that killed 130 people and wounded 350 on November 13, 2015. Police said he was believed to have provided counterfeit documents to the gunmen and bombers who attacked the Bataclan concert hall, restaurants, and the vicinity of the Stade de France sports stadium. *La Repubblica* said he was suspected of being part of an ISIS cell operating in France and Belgium with his two brothers, Medhi and Lyes, and to have been in contact with Belgian Abdelhamid Abaaoud, ISIS mastermind of the Paris attacks, his accomplice Chakib Akrouh, and Khalid Zerkani, the jihadist preacher in Brussels who recruited scores of young Muslims as jihadist fighters to Syria. Touami was serving a two-year term in Bari for possession of fake documents and was due to be released in June 2021. French investigating magistrates said that the Paris attackers had 14 fake Belgian identity documents from the same manufacturer. The police said that since 2010, Touami and his brothers had contact with Amedy Coulibaly and Cherif Kouachi, the terrorists in the Paris attacks on a Jewish supermarket and the *Charlie Hebdo* newsroom in January 2015. Prosecutor Federico Perrone Capano said Touami's brother Medhi was serving a 16-year prison sentence in Belgium for association with terrorists; Lyes was killed in Syria.

AP, BBC, NPR, UPI, Reuters, France Inter Radio, and *AFP* reported on September 8, 2021 that the trial began of 20 alleged perpetrators and accomplices in the November 13, 2015 ISIS attacks. Five suspects were presumed dead and another was imprisoned in Turkey. Only one of the ten direct perpetrators—Belgian-born French-Moroccan citizen Salah Abdeslam, 32—survived and was in court in a specially built, temporary courtroom inside the Palais de Justice in central Paris. The eight-month case was scheduled to involve 330 lawyers and 1,800 civil parties, including survivors. Abdeslam told the court he was "a soldier of the Islamic State".

AP and *Reuters* reported on September 15, 2021 that Salah Abdeslam told the court that "We fought France, we attacked France, we targeted the civilian population. It was nothing personal against them... I know my statement may be shocking, but it is not to dig the knife deeper in the wound but to be sincere towards those who are suffering immeasurable grief." Mohammed Abrini, also on trial in Paris, acknowledged his role in a subsequent attack in Brussels, saying, "In this evil that happened in France, I am neither the commander nor the architect. I provided no logistical nor financial help." *BBC* and *BFMTV* reported that Abdeslam said the attackers were retaliating for French military action against ISIS.

The other defendants included:

- Mohamed Amri, who admitted taking Salah Abdeslam by car from Paris to Belgium after the attacks but denied any link to terrorism

- Hamza Attou, accused of driving Abdeslam away

- Yassine Atar, accused of holding the keys to Abdeslam's Brussels safe house, condemned the attacks and claimed innocence.

The *New York Times* reported on November 14, 2021, that more than 300 survivors and bereaved family members testified in the trial of individuals accused of the 2015 terrorist attacks. Sophie Dias, 39, said her father, Manuel Dias, a bus driver who had taken fans to the national soccer stadium, was the only person who was killed there. Gaelle, 40, said her cheek was blown off by a bullet in Bataclan. She underwent her 40th surgery in August 2021. Maya, 33, lost her husband and two of her best friends at the Carillon café. She was hit in the legs. Guillaume Valette killed himself two years after the attack, and was officially recognized as the 131st victim.

Reuters reported on December 31, 2021 that the trial of Salah Abdeslam was to be recessed because he caught Covid-19.

April 4, 2017: Malian emigre Kobili Traore, 27, while yelling "Allahu Akbar", brutally beat retired Jewish teacher and doctor Dr. Sarah Attal-Halimi, 65, in her Belleville apartment in Paris, then threw her through a third-floor window, killing her. He later yelled "I killed the Shaitan." In 2019, the government declared him not criminally responsible because he was in a state of psychosis from ingesting cannabis. The Supreme Court of Cassation in late April 2021 upheld the lower court's ruling. He remained in a psychiatric institution. He was upset by her mezuza. President Emmanuel Macron had called for a trial of the attacker.

March 28, 2018: Two men stabbed to death Mireille Knoll, 85, a French Holocaust survivor, in her Paris apartment, which they then torched. Prosecutors called it an antisemitic attack. The trial of the accused duo charged with killing a vulnerable person based on religious motives, and aggravated theft, began on October 26, 2021. The defendants accused each other of the killing. Their lawyers denied antisemitism. One suspect grew up in her neighborhood; she often hosted him.

June 30, 2018: *AFP* reported on May 5, 2021 that the February 4, 2021 conviction and 20-year sentence in an Antwerp court of Iranian diplomat Assadollah Assadi, 49, for plotting to bomb an opposition rally outside Paris, was confirmed after he failed to appeal. The court convicted him of supplying explosives for the planned June 30, 2018 attack on the exiled opposition National Council of Resistance in Iran (NCRI). Assadi was represented by attorney Dimitri de Beco, who said Assadi contested the right of Belgian courts to judge him and put him behind bars. Three others sentenced to between 15 and 18 years in prison as accomplices maintained their appeals of their convictions.

October 16, 2020: On January 12, 2021, *AP* reported that anti-terrorism police detained seven people suspected of having communicated via social media with Chechen refugee Abdoullakh Anzorov, 18, the killer of schoolteacher Samuel Paty, who was beheaded outside his Paris-region school after showing caricatures of the Prophet Muhammad during a class discussion of free expression. The seven were picked up in the Paris region, western France, Lyon, and Toulouse. Some 14 people were already being formally investigated and faced preliminary terrorism- and murder-related charges in the investigation. Seven had been denied bail.

GERMANY

December 19, 2016: *BBC* and *Reuters* reported on October 26, 2021 that Tunisian Anis Amri, a known jihadist threat, drove a lorry into the crowded market on Breitscheidplatz in Berlin on December 19, 2016, initially killing 11 people. Sascha Hüsges was badly injured when he was apparently hit on the head by a beam as he rushed to help victims. He needed 24-hour care ever since. His husband, Hartmut Hüsges, told *Tagesspiegel* that in October 2021, he died of his wounds, making him the 13th fatality.

August 27, 2018: *AP* and *DPA* reported on September 8, 2021 that the trial began for Kevin A., 30, a right-winger charged with severe aggravated assault, breach of the peace, and property damage for an anti-Semitic attack by ten people on the Jewish Schalom restaurant in Chemnitz on August 27, 2018 that injured the owner, Uwe Dziuballa, and damaged the restaurant.

June 2, 2019: *Al-Jazeera, Reuters,* and *AP* reported on January 28, 2021 that the Oberlandesgericht Frankfurt (Frankfurt State Court or Higher Regional Court) sentenced German neo-Nazi Stephan Ernst, 47, to life in prison for murdering pro-migration Christian Democratic Union politician Dr. Walter Luebcke, 65, in Kassel on June 2, 2019. Markus Hartmann was cleared of accessory to murder but found guilty of weapons possession charges and received a suspended sentence of 18 months. *DPA* reported that because the court noted the "particular severity" of the crime, Ernst would likely not be eligible for release after 15 years as is typical under German law. Ernst was represented by attorney Mustafa Kaplan.

August 23, 2019: *Reuters, BBC, Tass, CNN, RIA Novosti,* and *AP* reported on December 15, 2021 that Judge Olaf Arnoldi announced that a Berlin court convicted Vadim Krasikov, 56, a former colonel in the Russian intelligence service, of the murder of Zelimkhan "Tornike" Khangoshvili, 40, a Georgian Muslim of Chechen ethnicity in broad daylight on August 23, 2019 and sentenced him to life in prison. Federal prosecutors called it a political murder ordered by Russia. Khangoshvili died from three gunshots in the central Berlin park Kleiner Tiergarten after Krasikov tailed him on a bicycle. He was shot with a suppressed Glock 26 twice in the body and once in the back of the head. The court ruled that the crimes were particularly grave, likely preventing an early release after 15 years. Khangoshvili commanded a militia in Chechnya from 2000 to 2004 and fought the Russians, who called him a "terrorist". Germany expelled two Russian diplomats in December 2019 over the case. At the start of his trial, Krasikov claimed to be Vadim Sokolov, 50, an engineer with no connections to the Russian government.

Khangoshvili was buried in Duisi village in the Pankisi Gorge valley, Georgia, on August 29, 2019. *BBC* reported that he had lived under the alias Tornike Kavtarashvili. He became an asylum seeker in Germany in 2016.

Judge Arnoldi said, "This was not an act of self-defence by Russia. This was and is nothing other than state terrorism… Four children lost their father, two siblings, their brother."

October 4, 2020: *AP* reported on April 12, 2021 that the trial began in Dresden of Abdullah A.H.H., 21, a Syrian man from Aleppo charged with murder, attempted murder, and causing serious bodily harm by killing a German man and seriously injuring another in an attack motivated by Islamic extremist ideology. He used a kitchen knife against the 53- and 55-year old men, believing they were a gay couple and considering this to be a "grave sin". He was arrested three weeks later. Abdullah A.H.H. had been released from prison in September 2020 after serving a sentence for promoting ISIS and attacking a prison guard. Prosecutors said Abdullah A.H.H. came to Germany as a refugee in 2015 and had planned to carry out another attack.

AP and *AFP* reported on May 21, 2021 that presiding judge Hans Schlueter-Staats of the state court in Dresden convicted and sentenced Abdullah A.H.H. to life in prison for murder, attempted murder, and bodily harm for stabbing with an eight-inch blade a gay couple who were outside Dresden's Palace of Culture. Thomas L., 55, died from his injuries in a hospital. Oliver L., 53, sustained serious wounds. Prosecutors blamed his Islamic extremist beliefs which included seeing homosexuality as a "grave sin". Judges ruled that H. bears "particularly severe guilt", which generally means he would not be released for at least 15 years. H. came to Germany as a refugee in 2015. He had served a three-year juvenile sentence for promoting ISIS and attacking a prison guard, and had been released for a month before the attack. He was arrested on October 20, 2020 with a large knife in his backpack. He was represented by attorney Peter Hollstein.

GREECE

June 14, 1985: *AP* reported on October 9, 2021 that Hizballah announced that Ali Atwa, a senior Hizballah operative believed to be in his early 60s, who was on the FBI's Ten Most Wanted Fugitives list since 2001 with two other alleged participants for his role in the June 14, 1985 hijacking of TWA Flight 847, died of complications related to cancer. The hijacking lasted 16 days and included the murder of U.S. Navy diver Robert Stethem, 23. The hijackers de-manded the release of Lebanese and Palestinian prisoners held by Israel. The FBI had offered a $5 million reward for information leading to Atwa's arrest on charges of conspiring to take hostages, committing air piracy that led to the slaying of an American, and placing explosives aboard an aircraft. Atwa had failed to get a seat on the flight and was arrested at Athens airport; he later joined the hijackers on the ground in Algeria.

September 8-9, 2020: *AFP* reported on June 11, 2021 that four young Afghan asylum-seekers were convicted on the island of Chios of intentional arson leading to a risk to human life and membership of a criminal group for starting the fires that burnt down Europe's largest migrant camp, the Moria camp on the Aegean island of Lesbos, home to more than 10,000 people, on September 8-9, 2020. The four were sentenced to 10 years in prison. In March 2021, two other Afghan youths were jailed near Athens for five years.

October 7, 2020: *Al-Jazeera* reported on January 15, 2021 that despite the court ruling on October 7, 2020 against the neo-fascist Golden Dawn members that they were guilty of forming and running a criminal organization, two key defendants remained at large. Ioannis Lagos remained a Member of the European Parliament and Brussels had not removed his diplomatic immunity from extradition. Christos Pappas, number two in Golden Dawn, disappeared in October, hours before police arrived at his home to arrest him. Meanwhile, in early January, authorities arrested Sotiris Develekos, a Golden Dawn fugitive wanted for attempted murder, in a seaside town outside Athens.

MALTA

October 16, 2017: On February 23, 2021, *Reuters* reported that Vince Muscat, one of three men accused of the October 16, 2017 car bomb murder of Maltese anti-corruption journalist Daphne Caruana Galizia, pleaded guilty to the killing during pre-trial compilation of evidence. He was jailed for 15 years. He had been under arrest since December 2017. A self-confessed middleman in the plot, Melvin Theuma, turned state's evidence in 2019 in return for a pardon. Muscat was denied a pardon in January 2021, but accepted a reduced sentence in a plea bargain. He is not related to Joseph Muscat, the former prime minister who was in office when Caruana Galizia was killed and resigned in December 2019.

BBC and *Reuters* reported on July 29, 2021 that a public inquiry into the assassination concluded that the state was responsible for her death by failing to recognize the risks to her life and take reasonable steps to protect her. The 437-page report concluded that the government had "created an atmosphere of impunity, generated by the highest echelons" and developed an "unwarranted closeness" between big business and government.

AP reported on August 18, 2021 that Malta's attorney general indicted hotelier Yorgen Fenech on charges of complicity in the murder and for criminal conspiracy. Fenech was arrested in November 2019.

NETHERLANDS

May 2020: *AP* reported on June 30, 2021 that a man, 32, vandalized the kosher HaCarmel restaurant in Amsterdam in May 2020, smashing a window and ramming an Israeli flag through the hole. On June 30, 2021, prosecutors said he acted with terrorist intent and asked a court in Amsterdam to order him to undergo psychiatric treatment at a secure facility and impose a sentence of 418 days' imprisonment, i.e., time served. It was the sixth attack targeting the restaurant in recent years. The suspect was convicted two years ago of vandalism at the same restaurant. A bureau that analyzed him added that he is "radicalized, holds extremist ideas and acted based on that ideology". Prosecutors said he held a pro-Palestinian sentiment. The verdict was scheduled for July 14.

NORTHERN IRELAND

April 1972: *AP* reported on May 4, 2021 that Belfast Crown Court acquitted A. and C., two former British paratroopers now in their 70s, accused of the April 1972 murder of an Official

IRA leader in Belfast. Paratroopers shot Joe McCann, 24, as he was evading arrest in the Markets area of Belfast in April 1972. A judge ruled that evidence implicating the veterans was inadmissible. Among the attorneys was Philip Barden, senior partner at the law firm representing A. and C.

August 15, 1998: *AP* and the *Evening Standard* reported on July 23, 2021 that Northern Ireland High Court Justice Mark Horner in Belfast recommended that authorities in the U.K. and Ireland open an investigation into the August 15, 1998 Omagh bombing that killed 29 people, arguing that there was plausible evidence that authorities could have prevented the attack with a more "proactive" security approach to intelligence sharing.

BBC reported on July 28, 2021 that the three-judge Irish Court of Appeal dismissed Liam Campbell's appeal against extradition to Lithuania, ending a 12-year battle. Campbell, 58, was one of four men held liable for the Omagh bombing. Lithuania wanted him to face charges related to weapons smuggling for the Real IRA between late 2006 and early 2007. The High Court in June 2020 had approved his extradition. Authorities had arrested him in Upper Faughart, Dundalk, County Louth, on December 2, 2016, on the second European Arrest Warrant (EAW) issued by Lithuanian authorities to be endorsed by the High Court in Northern Ireland. He was wanted for preparation of a crime, illegal possession of firearms, and terrorism, the latter carrying a 20-year sentence. The EAW alleged that Campbell "made arrangements with Seamus McGreevy, Michael Campbell (his brother), Brendan McGuigan and other unidentified persons to travel to Lithuania for the purposes of acquiring firearms and explosives, including automatic rifles, sniper guns, projectors, detonators, timers and trotyl [TNT]".

RUSSIA

January 24, 2011: *Reuters* reported on January 20, 2021 that Russian forces in Katyr-Yurt killed six terrorists, including Chechen separatist commander Aslan Byutukayev, believed to have been involved in the bombing of the arrivals hall of Moscow's Domodedovo airport on January 24, 2011 that killed 37 and injured 173 others, including 86 who were hospitalized. He was also accused of taking part in other attacks, including on Grozny. The U.S. named him a Specially Designated Global Terrorist in 2016.

SPAIN

August 16-18, 2017: On May 27, 2021, *AP, BBC,* and *AFP* reported that Spain's National Court in San Fernando de Henares on the outskirts of Madrid sentenced Mohamed Houli Chemlal, Driss Oukabir, and Said Ben Iazza to between eight and 53 years in prison for two ISIS attacks in Barcelona on August 16-18, 2017 that killed 16 people and injured 140. The trio were accused of forming part of the cell or aiding it, but not of carrying out the attacks. Two cell members, including a Muslim cleric, 44, believed to have been the ringleader, died in an apparently accidental blast at an Alcanar country house while preparing explosives the day before the attacks. Police shot to death six others who drove vehicles into groups of bystanders in Barcelona on August 17, 2017 and nearby Cambrils.

Spanish citizen Mohamed Houli Chemlal, 24, who survived the explosion, and Driss Oukabir, 32, originally from Morocco, who had been involved in their preparation but opted out of taking part in the end, were convicted of belonging to a terrorist organization and manufacturing explosives. They were also found guilty on 29 counts of mass destruction with terrorist intent. The duo were sentenced to 53 1/2 and 46 years in prison. The court cleared them of 14 counts of terrorist murder and other injury-related charges. The 1,000+-page ruling indicated that they were expected to serve only a maximum of 20 years.

The court sentenced Moroccan-born Said Ben Iazza, 28, who bought materials for the explosives, to eight years for cooperating with a terrorist organization.

TURKEY

January 12, 2016: *Deutsche Welle* reported on April 6, 2021 that a Turkish court sentenced four men to life in prison without possibility of parole for the January 12, 2016 suicide bombing in historic Sultanahmet Square in central Istanbul that killed 12 German tourists and wounded 16 other people. Turkey blamed ISIS, which never claimed credit. The foursome, already in jail, received aggravated life sentences. *DHA* reported that the court called the attack "an attempt to violently overthrow the constitutional order". *Anadolu* added that each defendant also received 328 years for aiding deliberate murder with terrorist intent, among other charges. Another suspect was sentenced to over six years in jail for membership in a terrorist organization. An appeals court overturned a 2018 verdict against 26 suspects. *Anadolu* reported that a trial in absentia would continue against three fugitives.

In 2018, Turkey sentenced three Syrians to life for involvement in the bombing. An appeals court overturned the verdict, deeming the sentences too lenient.

December 19, 2016: *Al-Jazeera* reported on March 9, 2021 that a Turkish court sentenced five people to life in prison for the December 19, 2016 murder by off-duty policeman Mevlut Mert Altintas, 22, of Russian Ambassador to Turkey Andrei Karlov at a photo exhibition opening at an art gallery in Ankara. State broadcaster *TRT Haber* reported that three defendants were given two life sentences without parole; the other two received one life sentence each, also without parole. *NTV* reported that six suspects were acquitted; seven others were convicted of membership in an armed terrorist group.

UNITED KINGDOM

December 21, 1988: *Reuters* and *AFP* reported on January 15, 2021 that five judges at the Court of Criminal Appeal in Scotland rejected an appeal of the conviction of now-deceased Libyan intelligence officer Abdel Basset Ali Mohmed al-Megrahi, found guilty of the 1988 Lockerbie Pan Am 103 bombing which killed 270 people.

Attorney Aamer Anwar said Megrahi's son Ali told him the family planned to appeal to the UK Supreme Court.

February 2015: On February 26, 2021, *Reuters, AFP,* and *CNN* reported that Britain's five-judge Supreme Court unanimously ruled that Shamima Begum, 21, a UK-born woman who went to Syria as a schoolgirl to join ISIS, should not be allowed to return to the UK to challenge the government taking away her citizenship, because she posed a security risk. She left London at age 15 in February 2015 to go to Syria via Turkey with two school friends. While there, she married a Dutch convert ISIS fighter. She gave birth to three children, all of whom died as infants. She lived in Raqqa for four years. The then-Home Secretary Sajid Javid revoked her British citizenship on February 19, 2019 on national security grounds, after she was discovered nine months pregnant in a Syrian refugee camp. She was being held in the Kurdish-run Roj detention camp in Syria. The Supreme Court overturned a 2020 Court of Appeal decision, saying it had made four errors. Lord Robert Reed, the President of the Supreme Court, said, "The right to a fair hearing does not trump all other considerations, such as the safety of the public... If a vital public interest makes it impossible for a case to be fairly heard, then the courts cannot ordinarily hear it." In 2019, she told *The Times* that she did not regret travelling to Syria and was not "fazed" by seeing a severed head dumped in a bin. Her husband is reportedly in jail in Syria. She is of Bangladeshi heritage, but the Bangladesh Foreign Minister refused to grant her citizenship.

AP and *ITV* reported on September 15, 2021, that Shamima Begum, now 22, asked for forgiveness and appealed to Prime Minister Boris Johnson to let her come home.

June 16, 2016: *AFP* reported on May 24, 2021 that the opposition Labour Party announced that Kim Leadbeater, 44, the sister of murdered British lawmaker Jo Cox, was selected to stand in an upcoming by-election for Batley and Spen in northern England, the Yorkshire constituency Jo Cox represented at the time of her death on June 16, 2016. A right-wing gunman shot and stabbed Cox several times while she was on her way to meet constituents in Birstall.

May 22, 2017: *Reuters* and *CNN* reported on October 22, 2021 that Greater Manchester Police investigating the 2017 Manchester Arena suicide bombing arrested a man, 24, from the Fallowfield area of Manchester "shortly after arriving back in the UK" on suspicion of a terror offence. The attack on the Ariana Grande concert killed 23, including the attacker, and wounded 1,017.

April 18, 2019: *Reuters* and *UPI* reported on September 15, 2021 that Northern Irish police arrested four men, aged 19, 20, 21 and 33, under the Terrorism Act in relation to the April 18, 2019 killing of journalist Lyra McKee, 29, in Londonderry. The New IRA said one of its members accidentally shot her dead when they opened fire in the direction of police during a riot McKee was watching. In 2020, police charged Paul McIntyre, 52, from Derry, with her murder, but the shooter remained at large. *AFP, CNN,* and *AP* reported on September 16, 2021 that Gearoid Cavanagh, 33, and Jordan Devine, 21, were charged with murder, possession of a firearm and ammunition with intent to endanger life, possession of petrol bombs, throwing petrol bombs, arson, and rioting. Cavanagh was also charged with robbery. Prosecutors argued that the duo were with the gunman who fired the fatal shot. Joe Campbell, 20, was charged with rioting, possession of petrol bombs, and throwing petrol bombs. A judge on September 17 granted bail and scheduled their next hearing for October 7. The fourth, aged 19, was released pending further inquiries. *AP, Reuters,* and *AFP* added on September 22 that the Police Service Northern Ireland (PSNI) in Londonderry arrested two more male suspects, aged 24 and 29, under the Terrorism Act for McKee's death. *AP* reported on October 1, 2021 that the Police Service of Northern Ireland arrested two more men, aged 44 and 53, in Londonderry under the Terrorism Act regarding McKee's death.

November 29, 2019: The *Evening Standard* reported on June 11, 2021 that a jury in a two-week inquest at the City of London's Guildhall ruled that firearms officers "lawfully killed" terrorist Usman Khan, 28, on London Bridge outside Fishmongers' Hall on November 29, 2019 after he stabbed two Cambridge university graduates because they believed he was trying to set off a suicide belt, which was later determined to be fake. Khan had fatally stabbed Jack Merritt and Saskia Jones. He also stabbed Stephanie Szczotko and Isobel Rowbotham, plus Fishmongers' Hall porter Lukasz Koczocik.

September 6, 2020: *AFP* reported Zephaniah McLeod stabbed to death university worker Jacob Billington, 23, who was on a night out with friends in Birmingham. On November 18, 2021, Judge Edward Pepperall of Birmingham Crown Court sentenced McLeod, 28, who has paranoid schizophrenia, to life in prison, with a minimum of 21 years, for the random knife rampage. The Judge ordered that the term be served initially at a high-security psychiatric hospital. McLeod pleaded guilty to four counts of attempted murder and three counts of wounding with intent to cause grievous bodily harm. McLeod stabbed in the neck a friend of Billington, leaving him partially paralyzed. Authorities arrested McLeod on September 7, 2020. He complained of hearing voices. He initially reported symptoms of paranoid schizophrenia in 2012 and had been released unsupervised from prison in April 2020. McLeod told a psychiatrist that he had been a heavy user of crack cocaine, cannabis, and alcohol from August 2020 and had no memory of the attack.

LATIN AMERICA

CHILE

April 1, 1991: The Manuel Rodriguez Patriotic Front was suspected of murdering Chilean Senator Jaime Guzman at a campus of Catholic University in Santiago, Chile, on April 1, 1991. He had supported dictator Augusto Pinochet, who had left office a year earlier. *AP* reported on September 23, 2021 that Mexico's Attorney General's Office announced it had handed former Chilean guerrilla Raúl Julio Escobar Poblete, alias Comandante Emilio, to Chilean authorities to be put on a flight to Chile, where he would

face trial. *AP* reported that while in Mexico, he led a ring that kidnapped people, including former Mexican presidential candidate Diego Fernández de Cevallos. Escobar Poblete was arrested in Mexico in 2017, convicted of kidnapping, and sentenced to 60 years in prison.

HONDURAS

March 3, 2016: *AFP* reported on April 7, 2021 that the trial in Tegucigalpa began of businessman David Castillo Mejía, accused of being the "intellectual author" of the March 3, 2016 murder of high-profile Honduran prize-winning environmental and indigenous rights defender Berta Cáceres, a member of the Lenca indigenous group. David Castillo was president of electric group Desarrollos Energeticos (DESA), the company behind the Agua Zarca hydroelectric dam against which Caceres was organizing opposition. Gunmen killed her in her house in La Esperanza. Castillo, a former military officer who trained at West Point, was arrested in March 2018 and accused of masterminding her murder, in connection with other DESA employees who were convicted. In 2019 a top DESA official, Sergio Rodriguez, was jailed for 30 years for orchestrating the killing with Douglas Bustillo, DESA's former chief of security, and soldier Mariano Diaz. The court determined that they paid four gunmen $4,000 for the murder.

AP reported on July 5, 2021 that following a three-month trial, a court unanimously found Roberto David Castillo Mejía guilty of participating in killing Berta Cáceres. Cáceres was a co-founder of the National Council of Popular and Indigenous Organizations of Honduras. Sentencing was scheduled for August 2. He faced between 24 and 30 years. Castillo Mejía was arrested in 2018. Prosecutors believed he paid the hitmen, gave logistical support, and helped those already convicted.

In December 2019, four men received 34 years for the murder and 16 years for attempted murder. Three others were sentenced to 30 years.

MIDDLE EAST

AFGHANISTAN

2008: *Bloomberg, The Hill,* and *AP* reported on May 19, 2021 that the U.S. Department of State's Rewards for Justice program offered a $5 million reward for information about American woman Cydney Mizell, a humanitarian aid worker, who was kidnapped with her driver, Mohammad Hadi, in southern Kandahar Province in 2008. She was teaching English at Kandahar University and embroidery at a local girl's school. State suggested that the kidnappers probably killed them and buried her in Kandahar. She had lived in the province for three years and was fluent in Pashto.

2012: *AP* reported on October 11, 2021 that Qatar released from custody Afghan army deserter Hekmatullah, who murdered three Australian soldiers and wounded two others on a base in 2012. He was sentenced to death in 2013. He was transferred from Afghanistan to Qatar in September 2020 in a deal brokered by the U.S. before peace talks between the Afghan government and the Taliban. His whereabouts were unknown.

January 31, 2020: *AP* reported on January 30, 2021 that a year after his kidnapping, apparently by the Taliban, U.S. Navy veteran and engineer Mark Frerichs of Lombard, Illinois remained a hostage, probably held by the Haqqani Network. His family asked the Biden administration to not withdraw additional troops without his release. The State Department offers $5 million for information leading to his return.

ALGERIA

September 30, 1956: The *Washington Post* reported on July 9, 2021 that Zohra Drif, then 21, a member of the Algerian resistance, set off a bomb hidden in her beach bag in the Milk Bar in Algiers, killing three people and injuring dozens. After escaping from the scene, she worked for the armed wing of the National Liberation Front (FLN), which became the country's ruling party after independence. She was arrested at a hideout in the casbah in September 1957, but freed in 1962 at independence. Drif married Rabah Bitat, one of the masterminds of the independence movement and later interim president of Algeria. She worked as a lawyer and became the vice president of Algeria's senate. The couple raised three children before Bitat died in 2000. Drif wrote a memoir entitled *Inside the Battle of Algiers: Memoir of a Woman Freedom Fighter.* She gave an interview to the *Post* at age 86, noting that her bombing established that Europeans were also a target of the war.

Three Algerian woman had planted bombs in Algiers that day. Drif's close friend Samia Lakhdari and her mother posed as Frenchwomen and set off a bomb in a popular cafe. Djamila Bouhired planted a third bomb in an Air France office, but it failed to detonate.

The bombings were depicted in *The Battle of Algiers,* the 1966 film directed by Gillo Pontecorvo.

September 24, 2014: *AFP* reported on February 18, 2021 that the trial in an Algiers court began of Abdelmalek Hamzaoui, accused in the September 24, 2014 kidnapping and beheading of French mountain guide instructor Herve Gourdel, 55, claimed by the Jund al-Khilafa (Soldiers of the Caliphate), an ISIS affiliate. The trial was attended by Gourdel's partner, Francoise Grandclaude. Another seven defendants were at large. Hamzaoui faced the death penalty. Six other defendants in court were accused of failing to inform authorities promptly of Gourdel's abduction; five were Gourdel's climbing companions and spent 14 hours in captivity with him. A sixth was accused of failing to promptly report the theft of his car by the kidnappers to transport the captive Frenchman. The six faced five years in prison. The kidnappers had demanded an end to air strikes against ISIS in Iraq and Syria by a US-led coalition that included France. Three days after kidnapping him, the terrorists released a video of his beheading. Gourdel's body was recovered in January 2015.

IRAN

November 4, 1979: The *Washington Post* reported on April 16, 2021 that Penelope Laingen, 89, had died on April 3, 2021, in Marshall, Virginia. She was the wife of L. Bruce Laingen, who was chargé d'affaires when the U.S. Embassy in Tehran was overrun on November 4, 1979 and 52 Americans were held in captivity for 444 days. Bruce was one of three hostages detained, separately from their embassy colleagues, at the Iranian Foreign Ministry. She led family efforts to obtain the freedom of the hostages. She helped found the Family Liaison Action Group (FLAG), and was best known for the yellow ribbon she tied around the oak tree outside her home in Bethesda, Maryland, sparking a hit song and a popular nationwide sign of solidarity with deployed troops. Bruce, a former U.S. ambassador to Malta, died in 2019 at age 96.

November 2020: The *Jewish Chronicle, Reuters,* and *Wana News Agency* reported on February 10, 2021 that prominent Iranian scientist Mohsen Fakhrizadeh, 59, was killed by one-ton automated gun smuggled into Iran in pieces in an attack outside Tehran solely attributable to Mossad. The news services found no evidence of American involvement. Some 20 agents were involved. The remotely-operated gun was on a Nissan pickup which was also carrying a bomb.

IRAQ

2006: *AP* reported on July 15, 2021 that U.S. Magistrate Judge Michael Morrissey held a hearing in Arizona regarding the strength of the evidence supporting Iraq's request to extradite Phoenix driving school owner Ali Yousif Ahmed al-Nouri, who was arrested by the Maricopa County Sheriff's Office in January 2020 on charges that he participated in the 2006 killings by masked men on the streets of Fallujah of two Iraqi police officers as the leader of an al-Qaeda in Iraq group. Al-Nouri entered the U.S. as a refugee in 2009 and obtained U.S. citizenship in 2015. He was represented by attorney Jami Johnson.

In the first shooting, an attacker held a gun to a witness's head, but another attacker's gun misfired when he tried to shoot police officer Lt. Issam Ahmed Hussein. A third attacker killed Hussein. A witness said al-Nouri, who did not wear a mask, was the group's leader.

Four months later, Iraqi authorities claimed that al-Nouri and other men fatally shot police officer Khalid Ibrahim Mohammad, who was sitting outside a store. Ahmed's mask had fallen off.

His attorneys said al-Nouri fled the violence in Iraq and lived in a Syrian refugee camp and a Syrian prison for three years before moving to the U.S.

July 3, 2016: *AP* reported on October 18, 2021 that two Iraqi intelligence officials announced the arrest of Ghazwan al-Zobai, alias Abu Obaida, the Iraqi mastermind behind a deadly July 3, 2016 suicide car bombing in a Baghdad shopping center in the central Karradah district, which killed 292 people and wounded 250. They said that al-Zobai was detained in an unidentified foreign country and transported to Iraq on October 16, 2021. Al-Zobai, 29, was an al-Qaeda terrorist when the Americans held him at Cropper prison until 2008. He then escaped from Abu Ghraib prison in 2013 and joined ISIS.

January 10, 2020: *AP* reported on November 1, 2021 that Iraq's supreme court sentenced a man to death by hanging for killing two prominent Iraqi journalists, Ahmed Abdul Samad, a *Dijlah TV* reporter, and Safaa Ghali, his cameraman, who were found shot and killed in a car parked near a police station on January 10, 2020. The duo had covered anti-government protests in Basra. Mohammed Samad, the brother of the slain reporter, identified the convicted killer as Hamza Kadhim al-Aidani, "a police officer who had worked at the same court that sentenced him today". Samad claimed that four people were responsible for the murders.

July 2020: *AP* and *Iraqiya* state TV reported on July 16, 2021 that Iraqi police two weeks earlier had arrested the shooter in the July 2020 drive-by murder by two attackers on a motorcycle of prominent public commentator and well-connected security analyst Hisham al-Hashimi, 47, outside his Baghdad home. Ahmed Hamdawi al-Kinani, who confessed, was connected to a militia group. He said he was a police officer with the rank of first lieutenant in the Interior Ministry. Officials said they were searching for six others, some of them believed to be abroad. Al-Kinani said he had worked with four other accomplices.

LEBANON

February 14, 2005: *AFP* reported on April 6, 2021 that the Special Tribunal for Lebanon in the Netherlands ruled that Hizballah fugitive Salim Ayyash, 57, who was convicted for the February 14, 2015 assassination of former Lebanese Prime Minister Rafic Hariri, cannot appeal against the verdict until he turns himself in. The Tribunal found Ayyash guilty in absentia and sentenced him to life imprisonment in 2020. Hizballah chief Hassan Nasrallah refused to hand Ayyash over and rejected the court's authority. Ayyash's defense team had appealed the decision in January 2021. Ayyash faced a separate case at the tribunal for three attacks on politicians in Lebanon that was due to open in June 2021. The U.S. Department of State's Rewards for Justice Program in March 2021 offered a reward of $10 million for "information leading to the location or identification" of Ayyash or "information leading to preventing him from engaging in an act of international terrorism against a US person or US property".

August 4, 2020: *AP* and the state-run *National News Agency* reported on April 15, 2021 that Judge Tarek Bitar, who was leading the investigation into the August 4, 2020 explosion at Beirut's port, ordered the release of six people, including Major Joseph Naddaf of the State Security department, Major Charbel Fawaz of the General Security Directorate, and four customs and port employees, who had been detained for months. The six were not to leave the country. Another 19 people were still being held, including the head of the customs department and his predecessor, plus the port's director general. Naddaf had written a detailed warning to top officials prior to the

explosion about the dangers of the nearly 3,000 tons of ammonium nitrates, a highly explosive material used in fertilizers, which had been improperly stored in the port. The explosion killed 216 people and wounded more than 6,000.

AP and Lebanon's *National News Agency* reported on June 23, 2021 that Lebanese prosecutor Ghassan Khoury ordered the release of six men and one woman, most of them junior port employees, who were detained following the explosion at Beirut's port. On June 22, 2021, Judge Bitar requested the release of 13 people who were detained. Khoury rejected the request to release senior employees, among them the head of the customs department, his predecessor, and the port's director general at the time.

AP and Lebanon's state-run *National News Agency* reported on August 26, 2021 that Judge Bitar issued a subpoena for caretaker prime minister Hassan Diab after he failed to appear for questioning.

On September 16, 2021, *AP* and the state-run *National News Agency* reported that Judge Bitar issued an arrest warrant for Youssef Fenianos, the former public works minister who failed to appear for questioning. Bitar had charged Fenianos and three other former senior government officials with intentional killing and negligence. Bitar summoned the former and current security chiefs. The former prime minister also refused to appear.

AP and the state-run *National News Agency* reported on October 12, 2021, that Judge Bitar issued an arrest warrant for Ali Hassan Khalil, Lebanon's former finance minister and current member of parliament, after he did not show up for questioning. The former minister and another former government member formally asked a court to replace Bitar, who suspended the investigation until a ruling on him was issued. Hours earlier, the head of Lebanese Hizballah called on authorities to fire Bitar.

AP reported on December 10, 2021 that Judge Tarek Bitar demanded the arrest of former Finance Minister Ali Hassan Khalil, who had been implicated in the explosion.

SYRIA

July 2012: *AP* and *Radio.com* reported on January 18, 2021 that German prosecutors charged two Syrians with alleged links to the Nusra Front—al-Qaeda's Syrian affiliate—on suspicion they were involved in the killing of a captured Syrian Army Lieutenant Colonel in Syria in July 2012. Khedr A.K. was charged with membership in a terrorist organization; Sami A.S. was charged with supporting a terrorist organization. The duo were arrested in the summer of 2020 in Naumburg, in eastern Germany, and in the western city of Essen. Prosecutors claimed that Khedr A.K. guarded the officer as he was brought to the execution site. Sami A.S. was suspected of filming the officer's shooting and preparing the footage for use as propaganda.

August 18, 2015: During its rule in Syria in 2015, ISIS beheaded Syrian citizen Khaled al-Assaad, 82, chief archaeologist of Palmyra. The *SANA* news agency reported in February 2021 that authorities had uncovered three corpses in Kahloul, six miles east of Palmyra where Assaad was killed, but two months later, DNA results showed that his body was not among those remains. *AFP* reported that his remains had not been recovered as of April 15, 2021. Assaad was director of antiquities in Palmyra for 40 years until 2003. He orchestrated the discovery of several ancient cemeteries and oversaw the excavation of 1,000 columns as well as the site's necropolis of 500 tombs.

YEMEN

December 30, 2020: *AP* reported on March 30, 2021 that U.N. experts said it was likely that the missile attack on the airport in Aden as Yemen's new government was arriving was conducted by Houthi rebels. Yemeni Prime Minister Maeen Abdulmalik Saeed said 25 people were killed and 110 were wounded. The U.N. panel concluded "with very high confidence" that "at least two missiles were launched from Taiz airport towards Aden on Dec. 30, 2020, and that it is likely that two additional missiles were launched from the police training center in Dhamar City… The

panel has been able to confirm that both locations were under the control of the Houthi forces at the time of the launches."

NORTH AMERICA

CANADA

October 5, 1970: The *Washington Post* reported on January 21, 2021 that James "Jasper" Richard Cross, 99, British trade commissioner who was kidnapped on October 5, 1970 by the Front de Libération du Québec (FLQ), died on January 6 at his home in Seaford, East Sussex, England, of COVID-19. He had been held hostage for 59 days during the October Crisis, losing 22 pounds. Cross was born September 29, 1921, in Nenagh, County Tipperary, Ireland. The *Montreal Gazette* reported that Cross survived a Zionist attack on the King David Hotel in Jerusalem in 1946 that killed more than 90 people. His wife, Barbara nee Dagg, died in 2018 after 73 years of marriage.

April 23, 2018: On March 3, 2021, *Reuters* and *AP* reported that Judge Anne Molloy convicted incel Alek Minassian, 28, on all 26 counts (10 of first degree murder, 16 of attempted murder) for crashing his rented van into dozens of people in Toronto on April 23, 2018, killing ten. Judge Malloy rejected the defense claim that his autism spectrum disorder deprived him of the capacity to know his actions were wrong. She referred to him as John Doe to prevent his obtaining further publicity, adding, "Mr. Doe thought about committing these crimes over a considerable period of time and made a considered decision to proceed. His attack on these 26 victims that day was an act of a reasoning mind notwithstanding its horrific nature and notwithstanding that he has no remorse for it, and no empathy for his victims." He faced an automatic life sentence; he would become eligible for parole in 25 years. Sentencing was scheduled for January 11, 2022.

UPI reported on November 11, 2021 that Amaresh Tesfamariam, 65, died from her injuries on October 28, 2021. She was injured in the attack. Tesfamariam, a nurse, was paralyzed from the neck down.

UNITED STATES

June 5, 1968: Palestinian Sirhan Bishara Sirhan, born on March 19, 1944, assassinated United States Senator Robert F. Kennedy (D-N.Y.) in the kitchen of the Ambassador Hotel in Los Angeles, California, on June 5, 1968. Kennedy died the following day at Good Samaritan Hospital. Sirhan was sentenced to death in 1969, but his sentence was commuted in 1972 to life in prison with the possibility of parole after the California State Supreme Court declared the death penalty unconstitutional. He was incarcerated at Richard J. Donovan Correctional Facility in San Diego County, California. His 16th parole hearing was scheduled for August 27, 2021. Los Angeles County District Attorney George Gascón said his team would not object to release. Sirhan was represented by attorney Angela Berry. The *Washington Post* reported on August 27 that a two-person California parole board panel voted in favor of Sirhan's request for release from prison on parole, finding that he was no longer a threat to society. The decision will be reviewed by the full parole board for 90 days before it is final. Then the California governor, currently Gavin Newsom (D), will have 30 days to uphold the decision, reverse it, or send it back to the board.

September 11, 2001: The *New York Times* reported in May that the Pentagon had reversed its decision to give early COVID-19 vaccinations to the 40 Guantánamo Bay detainees.

The Guardian and *AP* reported on June 24, 2021 that lawyers for the victim families questioned in court depositions former Saudi officials Omar al-Bayoumi, Fahad al-Thumairy, and Musaed al-Jarrah about their alleged links to two 9/11 hijackers, Khalid al-Mihdhar and Nawaf al-Hazmi, in southern California in the months leading up to the 9/11 attacks.

- Former civil servant al-Bayoumi worked in civil aviation and was officially a student in California. The lawsuit alleges he was acting as a Saudi agent in 2000 and 2001, receiving large stipends from the Saudi government. Soon after 9/11, he moved to the UK. He claimed he had only a passing acquaintance with Mihdhar and Hazmi, who were part of the team that crashed American Airlines Flight 77 into the Pentagon. The U.S. revoked his visa after the 9/11 attacks, on grounds of "quasi-terrorist activities". Al-Bayoumi was questioned on June 9-11.

- Al-Thumairy was a Saudi consular official in Los Angeles and the imam of the King Fahad mosque there. Bayoumi is said to have visited him before meeting Mihdhar and Hazmi. Thumairy said he never met the hijackers but witnesses told the FBI that they had seen him with them. After the 9/11 attacks, his diplomatic visa was withdrawn on suspicion he could be linked to terrorist activity. He was to be deposed in late June.

- Jarrah was a mid-level diplomat at the Saudi embassy in 1999 and 2000, overseeing Islamic affairs ministry employees at mosques and cultural centers around the U.S. He was deposed in mid-June.

All depositions were performed via Zoom by the families' legal team, who were not allowed to share the results with their clients.

On August 25, 2021, Taliban spokesman Zabihullah Mujahid told *NBC News* that there was "no proof" that Osama bin Laden was involved in the 9/11 terrorist attacks. The Taliban pledged to not permit al-Qaeda to establish a base in Afghanistan. "When Osama bin Laden became an issue for the Americans, he was in Afghanistan. Although there was no proof he was involved... Now, we have given promises that Afghan soil won't be used against anyone."

AFP reported on September 7, 2021 that the prosecution of alleged 9/11 mastermind Khalid Sheikh Mohammed, Ammar al-Baluchi, Walid bin Attash, Ramzi bin al-Shibh, and Mustafa al-Hawsawi restarted for the first time since early 2019. Air Force Colonel Matthew McCall became the trial's eighth military judge.

CNN, AP, and the *Washington Post* reported on September 12, 2021 that following an executive order by President Joe Biden, the FBI released the first of what was expected to be several documents related to its investigation of the 9/11 attacks and suspected Saudi government support for the hijackers. The 2016 document included details of the FBI investigation of former Saudi consular official Fahad al-Thumairy and Saudi student Omar al-Bayoumi who was a suspected Saudi intelligence agent in Los Angeles who provided "translation, travel assistance, lodging and financing" to hijackers Nawaf al-Hazmi and Khalid al-Mihdhar.

April 15, 2013: On March 22, 2021, *AP* reported that the U.S. Supreme Court announced that it will consider whether to reinstate the death penalty for Dzhokhar Tsarnaev, who was convicted in the April 15, 2013 Boston Marathon bombing that killed three and injured hundreds. A three-judge panel of the U.S. Court of Appeals for the 1st Circuit had held that the judge in his trial did not adequately vet potential jurors for bias. Judge O. Rogeriee Thompson wrote, "Make no mistake: Dzhokhar will spend his remaining days locked up in prison, with the only matter remaining being whether he will die by execution." *AP* reported on October 10, 2021 that the U.S. Department of Justice planned to argue for reinstatement of the death penalty.

June 17, 2015: On August 25, 2021, the 4th U.S. Circuit Court of Appeals in Richmond unanimously upheld the conviction and death sentence of Dylann Roof for the June 17, 2015 racist murder of nine members of the historic Black Mother Emanuel AME Church in Charleston, South Carolina.

On October 28, 2021, the *Washington Post* reported that the Department of Justice agreed to pay $88 million to victims of Roof's murder of nine parishioners, a symbolic figure meant to compensate for a background-check failure that allowed Roof to buy a weapon. A lawyer for the victims, Bakari Sellers, said the number 88 is significant among white supremacists who use it as code for "Heil Hitler"; "H" is the eighth letter of the alphabet. Roof earlier wore a shirt with the number 88. He also brought 88 bullets with him to the attack. Roof wrote in a jailhouse journal: "I would like to make it crystal clear, I do not regret what I did. ... I am not sorry. I have not shed a tear for the innocent people I killed."

December 11, 2017: *CNN* and *AP* reported on April 22, 2021 that Judge Richard J. Sullivan in a court in the Southern District of New York sen-

tenced Bangladeshi man Akayed Ullah, 31, to life in prison for the December 11, 2017 morning rush hour bombing in an underground tunnel walkway that connects two subway lines beneath the Port Authority Bus Terminal in New York City. The explosion injured six people. Ullah sustained wounds to his hands and stomach. Ullah was convicted on six counts after a one-week trial in 2018. Two of the charges, including using a weapon of mass destruction, carried a life sentence. Ullah had posted an ISIS slogan on *Facebook*. The bomb contained a battery, wires, metal screws, and a Christmas tree light bulb.

February 14, 2018: On October 15, 2021, David Wheeler, attorney for defendant Nikolas Cruz, 23, told Circuit Judge Elizabeth Scherer that on October 20 his client would plead guilty to 17 counts of first-degree murder in the February 14, 2018 shooting at Marjory Stoneman Douglas High School in Parkland outside Fort Lauderdale, Florida. Cruz later entered the Broward County courtroom to plead guilty to attempted aggravated battery on a law enforcement officer, battery on a law enforcement officer, depriving an officer of means of protection, and use of a self-defense weapon against a law enforcement officer regarding an attack on a jail guard in November 2018. He faced a minimum sentence of 14½ months. *CNN* reported on October 20, 2021 that Cruz pleaded guilty in a Florida courtroom to 17 counts of murder and 17 counts of attempted murder. A *South Florida Sun Sentinel* op-ed called for a life sentence.

April 26, 2019: *UPI* reported on November 2, 2021, that the U.S. Department of Justice announced that Army veteran Mark Steven Domingo, 28, of Reseda was sentenced to 25 years in federal prison for plotting to bomb an April 2019 rally in Long Beach, California. He was convicted in August of providing material support to terrorism and attempting to use a weapon of mass destruction by plotting to bomb a California White nationalist rally in 2019. He had been deployed to Afghanistan. He was arrested on April 26, 2019 after receiving what he thought were two live bombs. In March 2019, he had posted calls for retribution for Brenton Tarrant's attacks on two mosques in Christchurch,

New Zealand that killed 51 people. He had discussed such targets as Jewish people, churches, and police officers. He asked an undercover FBI agent to invite a bombmaker (another FBI undercover agent) to use 3½-inch nails he provided in a bomb.

April 27, 2019: The *Washington Post* reported on July 12, 2021 that San Diego County Superior Court Judge Kenneth J. Medel ruled on July 7, 2021 that survivors and families of victims of the April 27, 2017 shooting at San Diego, California's Chabad of Poway synagogue may proceed with a lawsuit filed against Smith & Wesson, the manufacturer of the weapon used in the attack, as well as San Diego Guns, which sold it. John T. Earnest allegedly fired a Smith & Wesson M&P 15 rifle, killing Poway resident Lori Gilbert Kaye, 60, and injuring three, including a rabbi and an 8-year-old, on the last day of Passover. Earnest faced state and federal charges of murder and hate crimes and for alleged civil rights violations.

CNN reported on December 28, 2021 that a federal court sentenced John T. Earnest, who admitted to the shooting at the synagogue, to a second life sentence of life plus 30 years in prison. He earlier pleaded guilty to a 113-count indictment that included hate crime and weapons violations. He was previously sentenced to life in prison without the possibility of parole following a plea agreement in state court.

December 6, 2019: *Navy Times* reported on February 22, 2021 that victims and the families of the December 6, 2019 shooting at Naval Air Station Pensacola filed suit in the Northern District of Florida against Saudi Arabia, claiming the kingdom knew gunman Mohammed Saeed Alshamrani had been radicalized and that it could have prevented the killings. The plaintiffs added that Saudi trainees knew in advance about his plans for the shooting but did nothing to stop it. Alshamrani had communicated with AQAP about the attack. The lawsuit noted, "Al-Shamrani was a Trojan Horse sent by his country, the Kingdom of Saudi Arabia, and its proxy, al Qaeda in the Arabian Peninsula, for flight training at Naval Air Station Pensacola, Florida, under the auspices of a program tied to billions of dollars in military arms sales from the United States to

the Kingdom... Little did the American people know that such an arrangement would soon devolve into a horrific, Faustian bargain."

January 2020: *Military Times* reported on October 25, 2021 that U.S. District Judge Theodore Chuang decided to apply a "terrorism enhancement" in sentencing two neo-Nazi The Base members—Canadian Armed Forces reservist Patrik Jordan Mathews and U.S. Army veteran Brian Mark Lemley, Jr. Prosecutors recommended 25-year sentences. Judge Chuang said that the duo planned to engage in terrorist activity before FBI agents arrested them ahead of a pro-gun rally in Richmond, Virginia. He was to sentence them at separate hearings on October 28 at the federal courthouse in Greenbelt, Maryland. The duo pleaded guilty in June 2021 to illegally transporting a firearm and obstruction of justice, by destroying cellphones when FBI agents raided their apartment. Defense attorney Ned Smock said Lemley was diagnosed with PTSD after he returned home from Iraq. Mathews was represented by attorney Joseph Balter. Co-defendant William Garfield Bilbrough, IV, was sentenced to five years in prison after pleading guilty in December 2020 to helping Mathews illegally enter the U.S. from Canada in 2019.

February 9, 2020: *WJCT* and the *Florida Times-Union* reported that at 2:45 p.m., Gregory Williams Loel Timm, 27, crashed his GMC Safari minivan into a red tent in the Walmart Supercenter in the Kernan Village shopping complex in the 11900 Atlantic Boulevard area in the Sandalwood neighborhood of Jacksonville, Florida where Republican volunteers were registering people to vote. He fled, but was captured 4½ hours later a mile away at his home in the 2000 block of Brighton Bay Trail by the Jacksonville Sheriff's Office, who held him on two counts of aggravated assault on a person older than 65 and one count each of criminal mischief and driving with a suspended license. No one was hurt. Circuit Judge Mark Borello ordered Timm held in lieu of $500,000 bail ($250,000 on the two aggravated assault charges; $5,003 on the criminal mischief count; and $2,503 on the suspended license count). Timm did not qualify for a public defender. Timm was not a registered voter.

He told police he was a stage hand, and was a member of the local branch of the International Alliance of Theatrical Stage Employees. He had lived in Jacksonville for two years. He was born in Des Moines, Iowa.

The *Florida Times-Union* reported on February 12 that Timm said that someone "had to take a stand" against President Trump.

The *Florida Times-Union* reported that on April 22, 2021, a jury acquitted Timm on two counts of aggravated assault on a person 65 years old or older. The jurors spent less than an hour of deliberation. He was convicted of criminal mischief. *First Coast News* reported that Judge Meredith Charbula sentenced him to 60 days, with credit for time served, and ordered him to pay multiple fees and court costs.

May 29, 2020: *Military Times* and *AP* reported on September 24, 2021 that four members of a California Grizzly Scouts boogaloo militia pleaded guilty to conspiring to obstruct justice in the case of a federal guard who was fatally shot in Oakland on May 29, 2020. His partner was wounded as the duo were guarding the Donald V. Dellums Federal Building in Oakland during a demonstration over the police killing of George Floyd. In April, a federal grand jury indicted Jessie Alexander Rush, 29, of Turlock; Robert Jesus Blancas, 33, of Castro Valley; Simon Sage Ybarra, 23, of Los Gatos; and Kenny Matthew Miksch, 21, of San Lorenzo, of conspiring to destroy communications and other records about the killing of federal security officer David Patrick Underwood and attempted murder of his partner by one of their members. All four faced 20 years in prison and a fine of $250,000. Sentencing was scheduled for December.

Blancas also pleaded guilty to a child enticement charge after federal prosecutors said they discovered dozens of pornographic photos and videos of a 15-year-old during the investigation.

Prosecutors said Air Force Staff Sgt. Steven Carrillo, 32, fatally shot Underwood and wounded his partner. He was arrested after the June 6, 2020 killing of Santa Cruz Sheriff Sgt. Damon Gutzwiller in an ambush in the community of Ben Lomond. He pleaded not guilty to both murders.

Miksch handled training and firearms instruction. Rush, who had military experience, deemed himself the group's "commanding officer". Ybarra handled recruitment. Blancas oversaw security and intelligence.

Prosecutors said that the militia group had about 25 members and had formed a "Quick Reaction Force" that was supposed to carry out attacks during mass demonstrations.

August 25, 2020: Kyle Rittenhouse, 17, from Antioch, Illinois, shot a Smith & Wesson M&P15 rifle and killed Joseph Rosenbaum and Anthony Huber and wounded Gaige Grosskreutz, 26, during multiple confrontations at two locations in Kenosha, Wisconsin. On July 1, 2021, prosecutors asked the Kenosha County Circuit Court to permit evidence showing Rittenhouse's association with the Proud Boys.

The Guardian reported on October 31, 2021, that Kenosha county circuit judge Bruce Schroeder, who was presiding over the trial of Rittenhouse, now 18, said that the individuals Rittenhouse shot and killed cannot be called "victims" but did not forbid them being called "looters" and "arsonists". The *New York Times* reported on October 31, 2021 that jury selection was to begin on November 1, 2021. Rittenhouse was charged with first-degree reckless homicide, first-degree intentional homicide, attempted first-degree intentional homicide, and unlawful possession of a firearm by a minor.

October 7, 2020: *CNN* reported on January 27, 2021 that Ty Garbin, 25, one of six men federally charged on suspicion of being involved in a plot to kidnap Michigan Governor Gretchen Whitmer in 2020, signed an agreement pleading guilty in federal court in Michigan to the sole charge of kidnapping conspiracy. He agreed to continue to cooperate with prosecutors against the five other defendants, whose trial was scheduled to begin on March 23. Prosecutors agreed to recommend a sentence less than the maximum carried by the charge, which would have been life in prison. Chief Judge Robert J. Jonker set sentencing for July 8, 2021. *CNN* and the *Detroit News* reported on August 25, 2021 that Chief District Judge Robert Jonker sentenced Ty Garbin to more than six years in federal prison.

On April 28, 2021, *CNN* reported that federal prosecutors in the U.S. Attorney's Office for the Western District of Michigan released new charges in a superseding indictment against Adam Fox, 40; Barry Croft, 45; and Daniel Joseph Harris, 23; who earlier were accused in an alleged plot to kidnap Michigan Governor Gretchen Whitmer. They added charges of knowingly conspiring to use weapons of mass destruction. The new indictment also charged Croft and Harris with possessing an unregistered destructive device.

December 25, 2020: *Al-Jazeera, Reuters, USA Today*, and the *Nashville Tennessean* reported on March 16, 2021 that the FBI determined that Anthony Quinn Warner, 63, acted alone when he set off a bomb-laden recreational vehicle outside an AT&T office tower in Nashville at 6:30 a.m. on Christmas Day 2020, and had wanted to end his own life. The bomb injured three people, damaged dozens of buildings, and knocked telecommunications systems offline after a recorded messaged played from the RV warning that "a bomb would detonate in 15 minutes". The FBI said he experienced "paranoia, long-held individualized beliefs adopted from several eccentric conspiracy theories, and the loss of stabilizing anchors and deteriorating interpersonal relationships". The Bureau found no "indications of a specific personal grievance focused on individuals or entities in and around the location of the explosion".

December 31, 2020: *CNN* and *WTMJ* reported on January 4, 2021 that Wisconsin pharmacist Steven Brandenburg, 46, who was arrested on December 31, 2020 after allegedly removing 57 vials of the Moderna COVID-19 vaccine from cold storage at the Aurora Medical Center in Grafton on December 24 and 25, is a conspiracy theorist who believes the vaccine could harm people by changing their DNA.

The Ozaukee County District Attorney's Office charged Brandenburg on January 4, 2021 with two felonies, second-degree recklessly endangering safety, and criminal damage to property. Ozaukee County Circuit Court Judge Paul Malloy scheduled a court date for January 19. Grafton Police Sgt. Patrick Brock said that

Brandenburg was released on signature bond that requires him to pay $10,000 if he fails to show up for court. Brandenburg was represented by defense attorney Jason Baltz.

BIBLIOGRAPHY

GENERAL

Colin P. Clarke "Trends in Terrorism: What's on the Horizon in 2022?" *Foreign Policy Research Institute* December 8, 2021.

Daniel Dory "L'Analyse de L'acte Terroriste: Un Chantier Indispensable" 26 *Sécurité Globale* 2021, pp. 113-127.

Daniel Dory "Livre – Edward Mickolus. Une source importante pour la recherche sur le terrorisme" *Conflits* November 20, 2021.

Daniel Dory "Les Terrorisme Studies a L'Heure du Bilan" 22 *Sécurité Globale* 2020, pp. 123-142.

Alex Lubin *Never-Ending War on Terror*, volume 13 University of California Press, 2021.

Keith W. Ludwick *The Legend of the Lone Wolf: Categorizing Singular and Small Group Terrorism* dissertation submitted to the graduate faculty of George Mason University in partial fulfillment of the requirements for the degree of Doctor of Philosophy Biodefense, 2016, 195 pp.

AFRICA

Edith Blais *The Weight of Sand: My 450 Days Held Hostage in the Sahara* Greystone Books, 2021, 296 pp.

EUROPE

Samanta Randazzo Childress and Carol "Rollie" Flynn "Terror in Athens: Remembering Station Chief Dick Welch" 26, 2 *The Intelligencer: Journal of U.S. Intelligence Studies* (Winter-Spring 2021), pp. 37-45.

Aaron Edwards *Agents of Influence: Britain's Secret Intelligence War Against the IRA* Merrion Press, 2021

Julie Kavanagh *The Irish Assassins: Conspiracy, Revenge and the Phoenix Park Murders That Stunned Victorian England* Atlantic Monthly Press, 2021, 473 pp.

LATIN AMERICA

Daniel Dory "The Shining Path: An Important Resource for Terrorism Studies" 7, 2 *International Journal on Criminology* 2020, pp. 55-77

Hervé Théry and Daniel Dory "Le Terrorisme au Brésil: Réalités, Évolutions et Incertitudes" 26 *Sécurité Globale* 2021, pp. 17-35.

MIDDLE EAST

Peter Bergen *The Rise and Fall of Osama Bin Laden* New York: Simon and Schuster, 2021, 416 pp.

Margaret Coker *The Spymaster of Baghdad: A True Story of Bravery, Family, and Patriotism in the Battle Against ISIS* Dey Street, 2021.

David B. Edwards *Caravan of Martyrs: Sacrifice and Suicide Bombing in Afghanistan* University of California Press, 2019, 296 pp.

Carter Malkasian *The American War in Afghanistan: A History* London: Oxford University, 2021.

Andrew Mumford *The West's War Against Islamic State: Operation Inherent Resolve in Syria and Iraq* I.B. Tauris, 2021.

Theo Padnos *Blindfold: A Memoir of Capture, Torture, and Enlightenment* NY: Scribner, 2021, 375 pp.

Paul Pillar "Afghanistan Isn't Good Terrorist Real Estate" *Foreign Policy* October 3, 2021.

Hervé Théry and Daniel Dory "Solhan: cartographier le terrorisme et la dynamique territoriale d'une insurrection" 131 *Mappe Monde* 2021.

Hervé Théry and Daniel Dory "Terrorisme et insurrection en Afghanistan: quelques données de base" *Conflits* 23 Aout 2021.

NORTH AMERICA

Spencer Ackerman *Reign of Terror: How the 9/11 Era Destabilized America and Produced Trump* NY: Viking, 2021, 448 pp.

Dick Lehr *White Hot Hate: A True Story of Domestic Terrorism in America's Heartland* Mariner, 2021, 416 pp.

Mark Oppenheimer *Squirrel Hill: The Tree of Life Synagogue Shooting and the Soul of a Neighborhood* NY: Knopf, 2021, 320 pp.

Joseph Pfeifer *Ordinary Heroes: A Memoir of 9/11* Portfolio, 2021, 256 pp.

RESPONSES

Mansoor Adayfi with Antonio Aiello *Don't Forget Us Here: Lost and Found at Guantanamo* NY: Hachette, 2021, 366 pp.

Doug Irving "Pathways to Deradicalization; Strategies to Mitigate Homegrown Terrorism and Ideologically Inspired Violence" *Rand Review*, September-October 2021, pp. 12-15.

Aki J. Peritz *Disruption: Inside the Largest Counterterrorism Investigation in History* Lincoln, Nebraska: Potomac Books, 2021, 400 pp.

Ric Prado *Black Ops: The Life of a CIA Shadow Warrior* New York: St. Martin's Press, 2022.

FICTION

Flynn Berry *Northern Spy* NY: Viking, 2021.

Hillary Clinton and Louise Penny *State of Terror* NY: Simon and Schuster/St. Martin's, 2021.

Charlie Donlea *Twenty Years Later* Kensington, 2021, 357 pp.

Dan Fesperman *The Cover Wife* Alfred A. Knopf, 2021, 321 pp.

Sebastian Fitzek *Seat 7A* Head of Zeus Press, 2021, 416 pp.

Cheryl Head *Warn Me When It's Time* Bywater, 2021, 285 pp.

Clare Mackintosh *Hostage* Sourcebooks Landmark, 2021, 368 pp.

John Monaghan *The Guns of Antwerp: NYPD Takes Boston* sp, 2021, 334 pp.

T.J. Newman *Falling* Avid Reader Press, 2021, 304 pp.

Bill Yancey *Exploded View: Nightmare Cruise* self-published, 2021, 276 pp.

www.ingramcontent.com/pod-product-compliance
Lightning Source LLC
Chambersburg PA
CBHW052111020426
42335CB00021B/2718